GREEK-ENGLISH LEXICON

TO THE

NEW TESTAMENT

BY

W. J. HICKIE, M.A.

BAKER BOOK HOUSE
Grand Rapids, Michigan

Reprinted 1977 by
Baker Book House

ISBN: 0-8010-4164-3

First printing, September 1977
Second printing, November 1979

PHOTOLITHOPRINTED BY CUSHING - MALLOY, INC.
ANN ARBOR, MICHIGAN, UNITED STATES OF AMERICA
1979

GREEK-ENGLISH LEXICON

TO THE NEW TESTAMENT

Α, α, Ἄλφα, τὸ, indecl., the first letter of the Greek alphabet. As a numeral α = 1, but ͵α = 1000. Hence τὸ Ἄλφα = *the first*, Rev. i. 8. xxi. 6. xxii. 13. Its force, in composition, is (1) *privative*, as if from ἄνευ; as ἄτιμος, *without honour*; (2) *copulative*, as if from ἅμα; as ἄλοχος, *a spouse*; (3) *intensive*, as if from ἄγαν; as ἀτενὴς, *closely-clinging*. This last sense is denied by some scholars.

Ἀαρὼν, indecl., *Aaron*, the brother of Moses, and the first high-priest of the Israelites, Luke, i. 5. Acts, vii. 40. Hebr. v. 4. vii. 11. ix. 4.

Ἀβαδδὼν, indecl., *the Destroyer*. Also called Apollyon, Rev. ix. 11.

ἀβαρὴς, from βάρος, *without weight, not burdensome*, 2 Cor. xi. 9.

Ἀββᾶ, indecl., *father*, Mrk. xiv. 36. Rom. viii. 15. Gal. iv. 6. [Chaldee.]

Ἀβιὰ, indecl., *Abia* or *Abijah*, son of Rehoboam, Matt. i. 7. Also a priest, the head of a sacerdotal family, from whom the class *Abia*, the eighth in order, took its name, after David divided the priests into 24 classes, Luke, i. 5.

Ἀβιληνή, ἡ, *Abilene*, a district lying between Lebanon and Hermon, 18 miles from Damascus and 37 from Heliopolis, Luke, iii. 1.

Ἀβραὰμ, indecl., *Abraham*, the founder of the Jewish nation, Matt. i. 1. xxii. 32. Luke, xix. 9 etc. etc.

ἄβυσσος, ἡ, *the abode of demons, the abyss*, Luke, viii. 31. Rev. ix. 1, 11. xvii. 8. xx. 3. Also = *Hades*, Rom. x. 7. (In classical authors always an Adjective = *bottomless*.)

ἀγαθοεργέω, *to do good*, 1 Tim. vi. 18. (For ἀγαθουργέω, Acts, xiv. 17.)

ἀγαθοποιέω, *to do good, to benefit*, Mrk. iii. 4. Luke, vi. 9; *to act right*, 1 Pet. ii. 15, 20.

ἀγαθοποιΐα, ἡ, *well-doing*, 1 Pet. iv. 19.

ἀγαθοποιὸς, *acting rightly*, 1 Pet. ii. 14.

ἀγαθὸς, *good in its kind*, Matt. vii. 18, 19. James, i. 17; *fertile*, Luke, viii. 15; ἀγαθά, **good things, Luke, i. 53,** xvi. 25.

ἀγαθωσύνη, ἡ, *benevolence, goodness*, Gal. v. 22. 2 Thess. i. 11. Rom. xv. 14. Ephes. v. 9.

ἀγαλλίασις, ἡ, from ἀγαλλιάω, *gladness, joy*, Luke, i. 14, 44. Acts, ii. 46. Hebr. i. 9. Jude, 24.

ἀγαλλιάω, *to exult, to rejoice*, Luke, i. 47. Rev. xix. 7. 1 Pet. i. 8. Also ἀγαλλιάομαι = id., Matt. v. 12. Luke, x. 21. Acts, ii. 26. Joh. viii. 56.

ἄγαμος, *unmarried*, 1 Cor. vii. 8, 11, 32, 34.

ἀγανακτέω, *to be indignant, to be moved with indignation*, Matt. xx. 24. xxi. 15. Mrk. x. 41. Luke, xiii. 14.

ἀγανάκτησις, ἡ, *indignation*, 2 Cor. vii. 11.

ἀγαπάω, *to love*, Luke, vii. 47. 1 Joh. iv. 7; *to wish well to*, Matt. v. 43. xix. 19; *to take pleasure in*, Hebr. i. 9. Joh. iii. 19. 1 Joh. ii. 15; *to long for*, 2 Tim. iv. 8.

ἀγάπη, ἡ, *love, benevolence, charity*, Joh. xv. 13. Rom. xiii. 10. Luke, xi. 42. Rom. v. 8. 1 Cor. xiii. 1; ἀγάπαι, *love-feasts*, Jude, 12 (purely biblical word)

ἀγαπητὸς, *beloved*, Matt. iii. 17 etc

ἀγγαρεύω, *to employ a courier*, from ἄγγαρος, *a courier employed by the kings of Persia to convey messages, who was authorised to press others into the service*. Hence ἀγγαρεύειν τινὰ = *to compel one to go a journey, to bear a burden, or to perform any other service*, Matt. **v. 41.** xxvii. 32. Mrk. xv. 21.

ἀγγεῖον, τὸ, *a vessel, a receptacle*, Matt. xxv. 4.

ἀγγελία, ἡ, *a message*, or *announcement*, 1 Joh. i. 5.

ἄγγελος, ὁ, *a messenger*, Matt. xi. 10; *an angel*, Matt. iv. 6 etc.; perhaps *bishop*, Rev. i. 20 etc.

ἀγγέλλω, *to announce*, Joh. xx. 18.

ἄγγος, τὸ, *a vessel*, Matt. xiii. 48.

ἄγε, interj., *come!* James, iv. 13. v. 1. (In both AV and RV rendered *go to!* It is properly Imperat. of ἄγω.)

ἀγέλη, ἡ, *a herd*, Matt. viii. 30. Mrk. v. 11. Luke, viii. 32.

ἀγενεαλόγητος, *of whose descent there is no account*, Hebr. vii. 3. (In AV, *without descent*; in RV, *without genealogy*.)

ἀγενὴς, *of low birth, ignoble, base*, 1 Cor. i. 28.

ἁγιάζω, *to make holy, to hallow*, Matt. vi. 9. Luke, xi. 2; *to sanctify*, 1 Pet. iii. 15. Matt. xxiii. 17. Hebr. ix. 13.

ἁγιασμὸς, *sanctification*, 1 Cor. i. 30. 1 Thess. iv. 3.

ἅγιος, *holy*, Rev. iv. 8. Luke, ii. 23; τὸ ἅγιον and τὰ ἅγια, *the sanctuary*, Hebr. ix. 1, 2, 24; οἱ ἅγιοι, *the saints*, Rom. i. 7. viii. 27. 1 Thess. iii. 13.

ἁγιότης, ἡ, *sanctity, holiness*, 2 Cor. i. 12. Hebr. xii. 10.

ἁγιωσύνη, ἡ, *holiness*, Rom. i. 4; *purity*, 2 Cor. vii. 1. (It is a purely biblical word.)

ἀγκάλη, ἡ, *the arm*, Luke, ii. 28.

ἄγκιστρον, τὸ, *a fish-hook*, Matt. xvii. 27.

ἄγκυρα, ἡ, *an anchor*, Acts, xxvii. 29. Hebr. vi. 19.

ἄγναφος, *unfulled, undressed*, Matt. ix. 16. Mrk. ii. 21.

ἀγνία, and ἀγνεία, ἡ, *purity*, 1 Tim. iv. 12.

ἁγνίζω, *to purify*, Joh. xi. 55. James, iv. 8; the Passive, in a *reflexive* sense, *to take upon one's self a purification*, Acts, xxi. 24; ἡγνισμένον, *purified*, Acts, xxiv. 18.

ἁγνισμὸς, ὁ, *purification*, Acts, xxi. 26.

ἀγνοέω, *to be ignorant, not to know*, Acts, xiii. 27; *not to understand*, Mrk. ix. 32. Luke, ix. 45; ἀγνοεῖται, *he is disregarded*, 1 Cor. xiv. 38.

ἀγνόημα, τὸ, *sin of ignorance, error*, Hebr. ix. 7.

ἄγνοια, ἡ, *ignorance*, Acts, xvii. 30.

ἁγνὸς, *pure*, 2 Cor. vii. 11; *chaste*, Tit. ii. 5.

ἁγνότης, ἡ, *pureness*, 2 Cor. vi. 6.

ἁγνῶς, *sincerely*, Philipp. i. 17.

ἀγνωσία, ἡ, *ignorance*, 1 Pet. ii. 15. 1 Cor. xv. 34.

ἄγνωστος, *unknown*, Acts, xvii. 23.

ἀγορὰ, ἡ, *forum, marketplace*, Acts, xvi. 19. xvii. 17. Mrk. vii. 4. Matt. xxiii. 7.

ἀγοράζω, *to buy*, Matt. xiii. 44, 46. 1 Cor. vi. 20. Rev. v. 9.

ἀγοραῖος, *lounging in the market-place, vile;* οἱ ἀγοραῖοι, *the rabble*, Acts, xvii. 5; of affairs usually transacted in the marketplace; hence ἀγοραῖοι (sc. ἡμέραι), *court days*, Acts, xix. 38. (The supposed distinction between ἀγόραιος and ἀγοραῖος is without foundation.)

ἄγρα, ἡ, *a catching*, Luke, v. 4; also *what is taken, a draught*, Luke, v. 9.

ἀγράμματος, *illiterate*, Acts, iv. 13

ἀγραυλέω, *to live in the fields, to be in the open air*, Luke, ii. 8.

ἀγρεύω, *to catch, to entrap*, Mrk. xii. 13. Cf. Luke, xx. 20.

ἀγριέλαιος, ἡ, *the wild olive*, Rom. xi. 17, 24.

ἄγριος, *wild*, Matt. iii. 4. Mrk. i. 6; *fierce*, Jude, 13.

ἀγρὸς, ὁ, *a field*, Matt. vi. 28. xiii. 24; *an estate, a farm*, Acts, iv. 37; οἱ ἀγροὶ, as oppos. to ἡ πόλις, *the country*, Mrk. v. 14. Luke, ix. 12.

ἀγρυπνέω, *to be sleepless, to watch;* hence, *to be watchful, to be circumspect*, 1 Pet. v. 8. Luke, xxi. 36. Hebr. xiii. 17.

ἀγρυπνία, ἡ, *sleeplessness, watching*, 2 Cor. vi. 5. xi. 27.

ἄγω, *to lead*, Rom. ii. 4. Luke, iv. 1; *to bring*, Joh. vii. 45. Acts, xxi. 16; *to spend, to keep*, of festivals and days, Luke, xxiv. 21. Acts, xix. 38; and intrans., *to go, to depart*, Joh. xiv. 31. Matt. xxvi. 46. Mrk. xiv. 42.

ἀγωγὴ, ἡ, *a leading; a way or course of life*, 2 Tim. iii. 10. (RV, *conduct*.)

ἀγών, ὁ, *a contest, a fight*, Philipp. 1. 30. 1 Tim. vi. 12. 2 Tim. iv. 7; *a race*, Hebr. xii. 1; *anxiety, solicitude*, Coloss. ii. 1.

ἀγωνία, ἡ, *mental emotion, agony*, Luke, xxii. 44.

ἀγωνίζομαι, *to enter into a contest*, 1 Cor. ix. 25; *to contend in*, 1 Tim. vi. 12; *to strive*, Luke, xiii. 24. Joh. xviii. 26. Coloss. i. 29. 1 Tim. iv. 10.

'Αδάμ, indecl., *Adam, the first man, and the parent of the human race*, Rom. v. 14 etc. In 1 Cor. xv. 45 Christ is called ὁ ἔσχατος 'Αδάμ, and contrasted with ὁ πρῶτος ἄνθρωπος.

ἀδάπανος, *without expense*, 1 Cor. ix. 18.

ἀδελφή, ἡ, *a sister*, Luke, x. 39. Rom. xvi. 15; *a Christian woman especially dear to one*, Rom. xvi. 1. Philem. 2.

ἀδελφός, ὁ, *a brother*, Joh. i. 40; *a near relation*, Luke, viii. 19. Joh. ii. 12; *a fellow-countryman*, Acts, xiii. 26; *a fellow-believer*, Matt. xxiii. 8. Acts, vi. 3; οἱ ἀδελφοί, *the Apostles*, Joh. xxi. 23.

ἀδελφότης, ἡ, *brotherhood; Christian brethren*, 1 Pet. ii. 17. v. 9.

ἄδηλος, *not manifest, out of sight*, Luke, xi. 44; *indistinct, uncertain*, 1 Cor. xiv. 8.

ἀδηλότης, ἡ, *uncertainty*, 1 Tim. vi. 17.

ἀδήλως, *uncertainly*, 1 Cor. ix. 26.

ἀδημονέω, *to be troubled, to be distressed*, Matt. xxvi. 37. Mrk. xiv. 33. Philipp. ii. 26.

"Αιδης, ὁ, *Hades; the place of departed spirits*, Acts, ii. 27, 31; *hell*, Luke, xvi. 23. Matt. xvi. 18. Rev. i. 18; *the lowest condition*, Matt. xi. 23. Luke, x. 15.

ἀδιάκριτος, *without uncertainty, unambiguous*, James, iii. 17.

ἀδιάλειπτος, *unceasing*, Rom. ix. 2. 2 Tim. i. 3.

ἀδιαλείπτως, *without ceasing, unceasingly*, Rom. i. 9. 1 Thess. i. 2. ii. 13. v. 17.

ἀδιαφθορία, ἡ, *uncorruptness, soundness*, Tit. ii. 7.

ἀδικέω, *to be unjust*, Rev. xxii. 11. Coloss. iii. 25; *to do wrong*, Acts, xxv. 11. 1 Cor. vi. 8; *to do hurt*, Rev. ix. 19; *to wrong, to injure*, Acts, vii. 26. Matt. xx. 13; ἀδικεῖσθαι, *to suffer wrong*, 2 Pet. ii. 13.

ἀδίκημα, τὸ, *a wrong committed, a misdeed*, Acts, xxiv. 20. Rev. xviii. 5.

ἀδικία, ἡ, *injustice*, Rom. ix. 14. Luke, xviii. 6; *unrighteousness*, 1 Joh. v. 17; αἱ ἀδικίαι *iniquities*, Hebr. viii. 12.

ἄδικος, *unjust*, Rom. iii. 5. Hebr. vi. 10; *sinful*, 1 Pet. iii. 18. Matt. v. 45.

ἀδίκως, *unjustly, wrongfully*, 1 Pet. ii. 19.

ἀδόκιμος, *that has not stood the test, disapproved*, Hebr. vi. 8; *reprobate*, 2 Cor. xiii. 5. Rom. i. 28. 2 Tim. iii. 8; *worthless*, Tit. i. 16.

ἄδολος, *without guile, pure*, 1 Pet. ii. 2.

ἁδρότης, ἡ, *liberality, bounty*, 2 Cor. viii. 20.

ἀδυνατέω, to be without power, Luke, i. 37 ; to be impossible, Matt. xvii. 20.

ἀδύνατος, without strength, weak, Acts, xiv. 8. Rom. xv. 1 ; impossible, Matt. xix. 26. Luke, xviii. 27.

ᾄδω, to sing, Rev. v. 9. Ephes. v. 19. Coloss. iii. 16.

ἀεί, always, at all times, 1 Pet. iii. 15. Hebr. iii. 10.

ἀετὸς, ὁ, an eagle, Rev. iv. 7. viii. 13.

ἄζυμος, unleavened, unfermented; hence devoid of iniquity, 1 Cor. v. 7 ; τὰ ἄζυμα, the feast of unleavened bread, Luke, xxii. 1.

ἀὴρ, ὁ, the air, the atmosphere, Acts xxii. 23. 1 Cor. ix. 26.

ἀθανασία, ἡ, immortality, 1 Cor. xv. 53. 1 Tim. vi. 16.

ἀθέμιτος, unlawful, criminal, 1 Pet. iv. 3. Acts, x. 28.

ἄθεος, without God, Ephes. ii. 12.

ἄθεσμος, lawless, licentious, 2 Pet. ii. 7.

ἀθετέω, to do away with, make void, reject, Mrk. vii. 9. Luke, vii. 30. x. 16. Gal. iii. 15.

ἀθέτησις, ἡ, a disannulling, a rejection, a putting away, Hebr. vii. 18. ix. 26.

ἀθλέω, to contend as in the public games, 2 Tim. ii. 5.

ἄθλησις, ἡ, a contest, a conflict, Hebr. x. 32.

ἀθροίζω, to collect together; pass., to be assembled, Luke, xxiv. 33.

ἀθυμέω, to be dispirited, to be disheartened, Coloss. iii. 21.

ἀθῶος, unpunished ; innocent, Matt. xxvii. 24.

αἴγειος, of a goat, Hebr. xi. 37.

αἰγιαλὸς, ὁ, the shore of a sea or lake, the beach, Matt. xiii. 2. Joh. xxi. 4. Acts, xxi. 5.

ἀΐδιος, eternal, everlasting, Rom. i. 20. Jude, 6.

αἰδὼς, ἡ, modesty, 1 Tim. ii. 9.

αἷμα, τὸ, blood, Acts, xv. 20 ; death, Hebr. xii. 4 ; murder, Rev. xviii. 24.

αἱματεκχυσία, ἡ, a shedding of blood, Hebr. ix. 22.

αἱμορροέω, to suffer from an issue of blood, Matt. ix. 20.

αἴνεσις, ἡ, praise, Hebr. xiii. 15.

αἰνέω, to praise, Acts, ii. 47 ; with dative, to give praise to, Rev. xix. 5.

αἴνιγμα, τὸ, a dark saying ; ἐν αἰνίγματι, darkly, 1 Cor. xiii. 12.

αἶνος, ὁ, praise, Luke, xviii. 43.

αἵρεσις, ἡ, a tenet, a heresy, 2 Pet. ii. 1 ; a sect, Acts, v. 17. xv. 5. xxiv. 5 ; dissension, Gal. v. 20. 1 Cor. xi. 19. [lit. a choice.]

αἱρετίζω, to choose, Matt. xii. 18.

αἱρετικὸς, schismatic, factious, Tit. iii. 10.

αἱροῦμαι, to choose, 2 Thess. ii. 13. Philipp. i. 22. Hebr. xi. 25. (αἱρέω is not used in the NT.)

αἴρω, to raise, to draw up, Acts, xxvii. 17. Matt. xvii. 27 ; to take up, Joh. viii. 59. Matt. xvi. 18 ; to lift up, Luke, xvii. 13. Acts, iv. 24 ; to carry, Matt. iv. 6. Luke, iv. 11 ; to take away, Matt. xiii. 12 ; to excite, to keep in suspense, Joh. x. 24.

αἰσθάνομαι, to perceive, to understand, Luke, ix. 45.

αἴσθησις, ἡ, *perception, discernment,* Philipp. i. 9.

αἰσθητήριον, τὸ, *perceptive faculty, sense,* Hebr. v. 14.

αἰσχροκερδής, *eager for base gain,* 1 Tim. iii. 8.

αἰσχροκερδῶς, *from eagerness for base gain,* 1 Pet. v. 2.

αἰσχρολογία, ἡ, *filthy language,* Coloss. iii. 8.

αἰσχρὸς, *shameful,* 1 Cor. xiv. 35. Ephes. v. 12.

αἰσχρότης, *base conduct,* Ephes. v. 4.

αἰσχύνη, ἡ, *shame,* Luke, xiv. 9. 2 Cor. iv. 2; *ignominy,* Hebr. xii. 2; αἰ αἰσχῦναι. *shameful deeds,* Jude, 13.

αἰσχύνομαι, *to be ashamed,* 1 Pet. iv. 16.

αἰτέω, *to ask,* Matt. v. 42, xx. 20; αἰτέομαι, *to ask for,* Joh. xvi. 26.

αἴτημα, τὸ, *a request,* Philipp. iv. 6. 1 Joh. v. 15.

αἰτία, ἡ, *a cause, a reason,* Luke, viii. 47. Matt. xix. 3; *a crime,* Matt. xxvii. 37; *an accusation,* Acts, xxv. 18, 27; *a case* (cf. *res*), Matt. xix. 10.

αἴτιος, *causative;* ὁ αἴτιος, *the author,* Hebr. v. 9; τὸ αἴτιον, *the cause,* Acts, xix. 40; *a fault,* Luke, xxiii. 4, 14.

αἰτίωμα, τὸ, *a charge, an accusation,* Acts, xxv. 7.

αἰφνίδιος, *sudden,* Luke, xxi. 34. 1 Thess. v. 3.

αἰχμαλωσία, ἡ, *captivity,* Rev. xiii. 10. Ephes. iv. 8.

αἰχμαλωτεύω, *to take captive, to lead captive,* Ephes. iv. 8.

αἰχμαλωτίζω, *to lead away captive,* Luke, xxi. 24; *to captivate,* 2 Tim. iii. 6; *to subjugate,* 2 Cor. x. 5.

αἰχμάλωτος, *captive,* Luke, iv. 18.

αἰών, ὁ, *an indefinitely long period of time, an age;* hence εἰς τὸν αἰῶνα, *for ever,* Joh. vi. 51; and εἰς τὸν αἰῶνα τοῦ αἰῶνος, or εἰς τοὺς αἰῶνας τῶν αἰώνων, *for ever and ever,* Hebr. i. 8. Gal. i. 5. 1 Tim. i. 17; ἀπὸ τῶν αἰώνων, *from all eternity,* Coloss. i. 26. Ephes. iii. 9; πρὸ τῶν αἰώνων, *before time was, before the foundation of the world,* 1 Cor. ii. 7; πρόθεσις τῶν αἰώνων, *eternal purpose,* Ephes. iii. 11; ἀπὸ τοῦ αἰῶνος, *from of old,* Luke, i. 70; ὁ νῦν αἰών, and ὁ ἐνεστὼς αἰών, *the present age,* 1 Tim. vi. 17. Gal. i. 4; ὁ αἰὼν ἐκεῖνος, *the time to come, life eternal,* Luke, xx. 35; οἱ αἰῶνες, *the universe,* Hebr. xi. 3.

αἰώνιος, *without beginning or end, eternal,* Rom. xvi. 26. Hebr. ix. 14; *without end, everlasting,* 2 Cor. iv. 18. 2 Pet. i. 11. Hebr. ix. 15.

ἀκαθαρσία, ἡ, *uncleanness,* Matt. xxiii. 27. Rom. i. 24 etc.

ἀκάθαρτος, *unclean,* Ephes. v. 5. Rev. xvii. 4. Acts, x. 28.

ἀκαιρέομαι, *to lack opportunity,* Philipp. iv. 10.

ἀκαίρως, *unseasonably, out of season,* 2 Tim. iv. 2.

ἄκακος, *guileless,* Hebr. vii. 26; *simple-minded,* Rom. xvi. 18.

ἄκανθα, ἡ, *a thorn*, Matt. vii. 16. xxvii. 29.

ἀκάνθινος, *made of thorns*, Mrk. xv. 17. Joh. xix. 5.

ἄκαρπος, *without fruit*, Jude, 12; *barren, unfruitful*, Matt. xiii. 22. Tit. iii. 14; *pernicious*, Ephes. v. 11.

ἀκατάγνωστος, *that cannot be condemned*, Tit. ii. 8.

ἀκατακάλυπτος, *uncovered, unveiled*, 1 Cor. xi. 5, 13.

ἀκατάκριτος, *uncondemned*, Acts xvi. 37. xxii. 25.

ἀκατάλυτος, *not subject to dissolution, endless*, Hebr. vii. 16.

ἀκατάπαυστος, *that is not satiated*, 2 Pet. ii. 14. (Some MSS. read ἀκαταπαύστους in this passage = *that never cease*.)

ἀκαταστασία, ἡ, *confusion*, 1 Cor. xiv. 33. James, iii. 16; in plur., *dissensions*, 2 Cor. xii. 20; *tumults*, Luke, xxi. 9. 2 Cor. vi. 5.

ἀκατάστατος, *unstable*, James, i. 8. iii. 8.

ἀκατάσχετος, *that cannot be restrained*, a var. lect. ad James, iii. 8.

ἀκέραιος, *pure, innocent*, Matt. x. 16. Rom. xvi. 19. Philipp. ii. 15.

ἀκλινής, *firm, unwavering*, Hebr. x. 23.

ἀκμάζω, *to be ripe*, Rev. xiv. 18.

ἀκμή, ἡ, *a point of time, a crisis;* ἀκμήν, adverbially, *even yet,* Matt. xv. 16.

ἀκοή, ἡ, *hearing*, 1 Cor. xii. 17. Acts, xxviii. 26; *the ear*, Mrk. vii. 35. Luke, vii. 1; *a report*, Joh. xii. 38. Rom. x. 16.

ἀκολουθέω, *to follow*, Matt. iv. 25. ix. 19.

ἀκούω, *to hear*, Matt. xi. 15; *to hearken to*, Joh. v. 25. Matt. ii. 9; *to understand*, 1 Cor. xiv. 2. Mrk. iv. 33.

ἀκρασία, ἡ, *intemperance*, Matt. xxiii. 25; *incontinence*, 1 Cor. vii. 5.

ἀκράτης, *without control*, 2 Tim. iii. 3.

ἄκρατος, *unmixed*, Rev. xiv. 10.

ἀκρίβεια, *exactness*, Acts, xxii. 3.

ἀκριβὴς, *exact, strict*, Acts, xxvi. 5.

ἀκριβόω, *to ascertain exactly*, Matt. ii. 7, 16.

ἀκριβῶς, *accurately*, Luke, 1. 3; *circumspectly*, Ephes. v. 15.

ἀκρὶς, ἡ, *a locust*, Matt. iii. 4.

ἀκροατήριον, τὸ, *the place of audience*, Acts, xxv. 23.

ἀκροατὴς, ὁ, *a hearer*, James, i. 22, 25.

ἀκροβυστία, ἡ, *the foreskin*, Acts, xi. 3; *uncircumcision*, Rom. iv. 10; met., *an uncircumcised person*, Rom. ii. 26. (It is a purely biblical word.)

ἀκρογωνιαῖος, *placed at the extreme corner;* λίθος ἀκρογ., *a corner-stone*, 1 Pet. ii. 6. (It is a purely biblical word.)

ἀκροθίνιον, τὸ, usually in the plur., *the first-fruits*, Hebr. vii. 4. (In RV *the chief spoils*.)

ἄκρος, *extreme;* τὸ ἄκρον, *the topmost point*, Hebr. xi. 21; *the tip*, Luke, xvi. 24; *the extremity*, Mrk. xiii. 27.

ἀκυρόω, *to invalidate, to make void*, Matt. xv. 6. Gal. iii. 17.

ἀκωλύτως, *without hindrance*, Acts, xxviii. 31.

ἄκων, *unwilling*, 1 Cor. ix. 17.

ἀλάβαστρον, τό, *a box made of alabaster*, Mrk. xiv. 3 (fem. form), Luke, vii. 37. Matt. xxvi. 7.

ἀλαζονία, ἡ, *vaunting*, James, iv. 16; *vain display*, 1 Joh. ii. 16.

ἀλαζών, ὁ, *a boaster*, 2 Tim. iii. 2. Rom. i. 30.

ἀλαλάζω, *to wail, to lament*, Mrk. v. 38; *to ring loudly, to clang*, 1 Cor. xiii. 1.

ἄλαλος, *dumb*, Mrk. vii. 37. ix. 17.

ἅλας, τό, *salt*, Matt. v. 13; met., *wisdom*, Coloss. iv. 6. (a NT form for ἅλς.)

ἁλεεύς, ὁ, for ἁλιεύς, *a fisherman*, Luke, v. 2. Matt. iv. 18. (This form is not recognized in Pape's Lexicon.)

ἀλείφω, *to anoint*, Luke, vii. 46.

ἀλεκτροφωνία, ἡ, *cock-crowing*, used of the third watch of the night, Mrk. xiii. 35.

ἀλέκτωρ, ὁ, *a cock*, Matt. xxvi. 74. etc.

ἄλευρον, τό, *wheaten flour*, Matt. xiii. 33.

ἀλήθεια, ἡ, *truth*, Joh. v. 33. Rom. i. 25.

ἀληθεύω, *to speak the truth*, Gal. iv. 16. Ephes. iv. 15.

ἀληθής, *true*, Joh. x. 41; *truthful*, Joh. vii. 18. Matt. xxii. 16.

ἀληθινός, *true*, Joh. xix. 35; *real*, Luke, xvi. 11; *sincere*, Hebr. x. 22.

ἀλήθω, *to grind*, Matt. xxiv. 41. Luke, xvii. 35.

ἀληθῶς, *of a truth, really*, Joh. vi. 14.

ἁλιεύς: see ἁλεεύς.

ἁλιεύω, *to fish*, Joh. xxi. 3.

ἁλίζω, *to season with salt, to salt*, Matt. v. 13. Mrk. ix. 49.

ἀλίσγημα, τό, *pollution*, Acts, xv. 20. (It is a purely NT form.)

ἀλλά, *but, however*.

ἀλλάσσω, *to change*, Acts, vi. 14; *to transform*, 1 Cor. xv 51.

ἀλλαχόθεν, *from another place*, Joh. x. 1.

ἀλλαχοῦ, *elsewhere*, Mrk. i. 38.

ἀλληγορέω, *to speak allegorically*, Gal. iv. 24.

ἀλληλουιά, *hallelujah = praise ye the Lord!* Rev. xix. 1, 3, 6.

ἀλλήλων, ἀλλήλους, *one another*, Acts, xxviii. 25.

ἀλλογενής, *of another race or nation, a foreigner*, Luke, xvii. 18.

ἄλλομαι, *to leap*, Acts, iii. 8; *to spring up*, Joh. iv. 14.

ἄλλος, *another, other*, Matt. xxvii. 42. Mrk. vi. 15; ὁ ἄλλος, *the other*, Matt. v. 39; οἱ ἄλλοι, *the rest*, 1 Cor. xiv. 29.

ἀλλοτριοεπίσκοπος, ὁ, *a meddler in other men's matters*, 1 Pet. iv. 15.

ἀλλότριος, *belonging to another, not one's own*, Rom. xiv. 4. Hebr. ix. 25; *foreign, strange*, Acts, vii. 6; *a stranger, an alien*, Matt. xvii. 25; *an enemy*, Hebr. xi. 34.

ἀλλόφυλος, *of another nation*, Acts, x. 28.

ἄλλως, *otherwise*, 1 Tim. v. 25.

ἀλο] *TO THE NEW TESTAMENT* [ἀμ

ἀλοάω, *to thresh*, 1 Cor. ix. 10.
ἄλογος, *without reason*, Jude, 10; *unreasonable, absurd*, Acts, xxv. 27.
ἀλόη, ἡ, *the aloe*, Joh. xix. 39.
ἅλς, ὁ: see ἅλας. ἁλὶ and ἅλα occur.
ἁλυκὸς, *brackish, salt*, James, iii. 12.
ἄλυπος, *free from grief*, Philipp. ii. 28.
ἅλυσις, ἡ, *a chain*, Mrk. v. 3. Acts, xxi. 33. 2 Tim. i. 16.
ἀλυσιτελὴς, *unprofitable*, Hebr. xiii. 17.
ἄλφα, τό : see A.
ἅλων, η, *the threshing-floor*, Matt. iii. 12. Luke, iii. 17.
ἀλώπηξ, ἡ, *a fox*, Matt. viii. 20; met., *a crafty man*, Luke, xiii. 32.
ἅλωσις, ἡ, *a catching, a capture*, 2 Pet. ii. 12.
ἅμα, *together*, Rom. iii. 12; *at the same time*, Acts, xxvii. 40; ἅμα πρωὶ, *early in the morning*, Matt. xx. 1.
ἀμαθὴς, *ignorant*, 2 Pet. iii. 16.
ἀμαράντινος, *composed of amaranth*, i.e. *everlasting*, 1 Pet. v. 4.
ἁμαρτάνω, *to sin*, Matt. xxvii. 4. Joh. v. 14; ἁμαρτάνειν ἁμαρτίαν, *to commit a sin*, 1 Joh. v. 16.
ἁμάρτημα, τὸ, *an evil deed, a sin*, Mrk. iii. 28.
ἁμαρτία, ἡ, *the principle of sinfulness, a sinning, a sin*, 1 Joh. iii. 4. (Nouns in -μα denote the dead result of the action of the Verb, while those in -ία and -ις denote the active principle. Cf. σόφισμα and σοφία.)

ἁμάρτυρος, *without witness*, Acts, xiv. 17.
ἁμαρτωλός, *sinful, a sinner*, Luke, v. 8, 32. Matt. ix. 10. Mrk. ii. 15.
ἄμαχος, *without fighting ;* met., *not contentious*, 1 Tim. iii. 3. Tit. iii. 2.
ἀμάω, *to mow down*, James, v. 4.
ἀμέθυστος, ἡ, *amethyst*, Rev. xxi. 20.
ἀμελέω, *to be careless of, to neglect*, Hebr. ii. 3. Matt. xxii. 5.
ἄμεμπτος, *blameless*, Luke, i. 6. Philipp. ii. 15. iii. 6.
ἀμέμπτως, *blamelessly*, 1 Thess. ii. 10.
ἀμέριμνος, *free from care*, 1 Cor. vii. 32. Matt. xxviii. 14.
ἀμετάθετος, *immutable*, Hebr. vi. 18; τὸ ἀμετάθετον, *the immutability*, Hebr. vi. 17.
ἀμετακίνητος, *immovable*, 1 Cor. xv. 58.
ἀμεταμέλητος, *not to be repented of*, 2 Cor. vii. 10 ; *without repentance*, Rom. xi. 29.
ἀμετανόητος, *impenitent*, Rom. ii. 5.
ἄμετρος, *without measure, beyond measure*, 2 Cor. x. 13.
ἀμὴν, a Hebrew word, *amen! of a truth, verily*, Matt. v. 18. Joh. iii. 3 ; *so be it*, Ephes. iii. 21. Gal. i. 5 ; *so it is*, Rom. ix. 5. 1 Pet. iv. 11 ; ὁ Ἀμὴν, *the true One*, Rev. iii. 14 ; τὸ Ἀμὴν, *certainty*, 2 Cor. i. 20.
ἀμήτωρ, *without mother*, Hebr. vii. 3.
ἀμίαντος, *undefiled*, Hebr. vii. 26. xiii. 4. James, i. 27.

ἄμμος, ἡ, *sand*, Rom. ix. 27. Matt. vii. 26.

ἀμνὸς, ὁ, *a lamb*, Joh. i. 29, 36. Acts, viii. 32.

ἀμοιβὴ, ἡ, *a requital, a recompense*, 1 Tim. v. 4.

ἄμπελος, ἡ, *a vine*, Joh. xv. 1. Matt. xxvi. 29.

ἀμπελουργὸς, ὁ, *a vine-dresser*, Luke, xiii. 7.

ἀμπελὼν, ὁ, *a vineyard*, Matt. xx. 1.

ἀμύνομαι, *to avenge*, Acts, vii. 24.

ἀμφιάζω, *to clothe*, Luke, xii. 28.

ἀμφιβάλλω, *to cast*, Mrk. i. 16.

ἀμφίβληστρον, *a net*, Matt. iv. 18.

ἀμφιέζω, *to clothe*, a var. lect. ad Luke, xii. 28.

ἀμφιέννυμι, *to clothe*, Matt. vi. 30. xi. 8. Luke, vii. 25.

ἄμφοδον, τὸ, *a street*, Mrk.xi.4.

ἀμφότεροι, *both*, Matt. ix. 17 etc.

ἀμώμητος, *blameless*, 2 Pet. iii. 14.

ἄμωμον, τὸ, *amomum*, a plant from which a fragrant ointment was made, Rev. xviii. 13.

ἄμωμος, *without blemish*, 1 Pet. i. 19. Hebr. ix. 14; *unblamable*, Ephes. i. 4. v. 27. Coloss. i. 22.

ἂν, a particle modifying certain forms. The reader is referred to his Greek Grammar. When it stands at the *beginning* of a sentence, it is but another form of ἐάν. See Joh. xx. 23.

ἀνὰ, a preposition, *upwards*. In the NT it forms a variety of phrases; ἀνὰ δύο, *two and two*, Luke, x. 1; ἀνὰ δηνάριον, *at the rate of a denarius apiece*, Matt. xx. 9; ἀνὰ μέσον, *in the midst*, Matt. xiii. 25; ἀνὰ μέρος, *in turn*, 1 Cor. xiv. 27 etc. etc.

ἀναβαθμὸς, ὁ, *a flight of steps, a stair*, Acts, xxi. 35, 40.

ἀναβαίνω, *to go up, to ascend*, Matt. v. 1. xx. 17; *to climb*, Luke, xix. 4; *to come up, to rise up*, Matt. xvii. 27. Rev. viii. 4; met. 1 Cor. ii. 9; *to grow up*, Matt. xiii. 7. Mrk. iv. 7, 32.

ἀναβάλλομαι, *to put off, to defer*, Acts, xxiv. 22.

ἀναβιβάζω, *to draw up*, Matt. xiii. 48.

ἀναβλέπω, *to look up*, Matt. xiv. 19. Mrk. viii. 24; *to recover one's sight*, Luke, xviii. 41. Matt. xi. 5.

ἀνάβλεψις, ἡ, *recovery of sight*, Luke, iv. 18.

ἀναβοάω, *to cry out*, a var. lect. ad Luke, ix. 38. Matt. xxvii. 46.

ἀναβολὴ, ἡ, *a delay*, Acts, xxv. 17.

ἀνάγαιον, τὸ, *an upper room*, Mrk. xiv. 15. Luke, xxii. 12.

ἀναγγέλλω, *to declare, to make known*, Acts, xiv. 27. xix. 18; *to report*, 2 Cor. vii. 7.

ἀναγεννάω, *to beget again*, 1 Pet. i. 3, 23.

ἀναγιγνώσκω, *to read*, Acts, viii. 28, 30. Matt. xxii. 31; *to read to others, to read aloud*, 1 Thess. v. 27. Coloss. iv. 16. 2 Cor. iii. 15. Acts, xv. 21.

ἀνα] TO THE NEW TESTAMENT [ἀνα

ἀναγκάζω, to compel, to constrain, Matt. xiv. 22. Luke, xiv. 23.

ἀναγκαῖος, necessary, 1 Cor. xii. 22. 2 Cor. ix. 5; needful, Philipp. i. 24; closely connected, intimate, Acts, x. 24.

ἀναγκαστῶς, of constraint, 1 Pet. v. 2.

ἀνάγκη, ἡ, necessity, 1 Cor. ix. 16. Philem. 14; calamity, distress, Luke, xxi. 23. 1 Cor. vii. 26.

ἀναγνωρίζω, to make known, a var. lect. ad Acts, vii. 13.

ἀνάγνωσις, ἡ, reading, 1 Tim. iv. 13. 2 Cor. iii. 14. Acts, xiii. 15. (Nowhere used for studying.)

ἀνάγω, to lead up, Luke, ii. 22. iv. 5; to raise, to bring up, Hebr. xiii. 20. Rom. x. 7; to bring out, Acts, xii. 4; ἀνάγομαι, to set sail, Acts, xxvii. 2, 4, 12, etc.

ἀναδείκνυμι, to show clearly, Acts, i. 24; to appoint, Luke, x. 1.

ἀνάδειξις, ἡ, manifestation, Luke, i. 80.

ἀναδέχομαι, to receive, Hebr. xi. 17; entertain, Acts, xxviii. 7.

ἀναδίδωμι, to deliver, to hand in, Acts, xxiii. 33.

ἀναζάω, to live again, Luke, xv. 24, a var. lect. ad Rom. xiv. 9; to revive, Rom. vii. 9.

ἀναζητέω, to seek for, Luke, ii. 44. Acts, xi. 25.

ἀναζώννυμι, to gird up, 1 Pet. i. 13.

ἀναζωπυρέω, to rekindle, 2 Tim. i. 6.

ἀναθάλλω, to revive, Philipp. iv. 10.

ἀνάθεμα, τὸ, a thing devoted; a person accursed, Gal. i. 8. 1 Cor. xii. 3. xvi. 22; a curse, Acts, xxiii. 14.

ἀναθεματίζω, to bind oneself by a curse, Acts, xxiii. 12, 21; to curse, Mrk. xiv. 71.

ἀναθεωρέω, to consider, Hebr. xiii. 7. Acts, xvii. 23.

ἀνάθημα, τὸ, a votive offering, Luke, xxi. 5.

ἀναίδεια, ἡ, shamelessness, importunity, Luke, xi. 8.

ἀναιδία, ἡ, a var. lect. ad Luke, xi. 8.

ἀναίρεσις, ἡ, death, slaying, Acts, viii. 1.

ἀναιρέω, to take away, to abolish, Hebr. x. 9; to slay, Acts, x. 39. xxii. 20. Matt. ii. 16; ἀναιρεῖσθαι, to take up, to adopt, Acts, vii. 21.

ἀναίτιος, guiltless, innocent, Matt. xii. 5, 7.

ἀνακαθίζω, to sit up, Luke, vii. 15. Acts, ix. 40.

ἀνακαινίζω, to renew, Hebr. vi. 6.

ἀνακαινόω, to make new; pass., to be renewed, 2 Cor. iv. 16. Coloss. iii. 10.

ἀνακαίνωσις, ἡ, a renewal, Rom. xii. 2. Tit. iii. 5.

ἀνακαλύπτω, to unveil; pass., to be unveiled, 2 Cor. iii. 18; to be unlifted, 2 Cor. iii. 14.

ἀνακάμπτω, to return, Matt. ii. 12. Luke, x. 6. Acts, xviii. 21. Hebr. xi. 15.

ἀνάκειμαι, to recline at meals, Matt. ix. 10. xxvi. 7, 20. Joh. vi. 11.

ἀνα] GREEK-ENGLISH LEXICON [ἀνα

ἀνακεφαλαιόω, *to sum up*, Rom. xiii. 9; *to bring together, to combine*, Ephes. i. 10.

ἀνακλίνω, *to lay*, Luke, ii. 7; *to make to recline*, Luke, xii. 37; pass., *to recline*, Mrk. vi. 39. Matt. xiv. 19. Luke, xiii. 29.

ἀνακόπτω, *to hinder*, a var. lect. ad Gal. v. 7.

ἀνακράζω, *to cry out*, Mrk. i. 23. Luke, iv. 33. viii. 28.

ἀνακρίνω, *to search, to examine*, Acts, xvii. 11. Luke, xxiii. 14; *to judge, to determine*, 1 Cor. ii. 15. iv. 3. xiv. 24; *to ask questions*, 1 Cor. x. 25, 27.

ἀνάκρισις, ἡ, *examination*, Acts, xxv. 26.

ἀνακυλίω, *to roll back*, Mrk. xvi. 4. Cf. ἀποκυλίω.

ἀνακύπτω, *to raise oneself up*, Luke, xiii. 11. Joh. viii. 7, 10; *to be elated*, Luke, xxi. 28.

ἀναλαμβάνω, *to take up, to raise*, Mrk. xvi. 19. Acts, i. 11. x. 16; *to take in*, Acts, xx. 13.

ἀνάλημψις, ἡ, and ἀνάληψις, ἡ, *a taking up*, Luke, ix. 51.

ἀναλίσκω, *to consume, to destroy*, Luke, ix. 54. Gal. v. 15.

ἀναλογία, ἡ, *proportion*, Rom. xii. 6.

ἀναλογίζομαι, *to consider*, Hebr. xii. 3.

ἄναλος, *without salt, saltless*, Mrk. ix. 50.

ἀνάλυσις, ἡ, *a departure*, 2 Tim. iv. 6.

ἀναλύω, *to unloose; to depart*, Philipp. i. 23; *to return*, Luke, xii. 36.

ἀναμάρτητος, *without sin, sinless*, Joh. viii. 7.

ἀναμένω, *to wait for*, 1 Thess. i. 10.

ἀναμιμνήσκω, *to remind*, 1 Cor. iv. 17; *to admonish*, 2 Tim. i. 6; ἀναμιμνήσκομαι, *to remember*, Mrk. xi. 21. xiv. 72. Hebr. x. 32.

ἀνάμνησις, ἡ, *a remembrance*, Hebr. x. 3.

ἀνανεόω, *to renew*; pass., *to be renewed*, Ephes. iv. 23.

ἀνανήφω, *to return to soberness*, 2 Tim. ii. 26.

ἀναντίρητος, *not to be gainsaid*, Acts, xix. 36. (Here the common texts give ἀναντίρρητος.)

ἀναντιρήτως, *without gainsaying*, Acts, x. 29. (See the preceding article.)

ἀνάξιος, *unworthy*, 1 Cor. vi. 2.

ἀναξίως, *unworthily*, 1 Cor. xi. 27.

ἀνάπαυσις, ἡ, *intermission*, Rev. iv. 8; *rest*, Matt. xi. 29. xii. 43. Rev. xiv. 11.

ἀναπαύω, *to cause to rest, to give rest tò*, Matt. xi. 28; *to refresh*, 1 Cor. xvi. 18. Philem. 20; mid., *to rest*, Rev. xiv. 13. Mrk. vi. 31. xiv. 41.

ἀναπείθω, *to persuade*, Acts, xviii. 13.

ἀνάπειρος, *maimed*, Luke, xiv. 13, 21. (But see ἀνάπηρος.)

ἀναπέμπω, *to send back*, Philem. 12. Luke, xxiii. 11; *to send*, Acts, xxv. 21. Luke, xxiii. 7.

ἀναπηδάω, *to spring up*, Mrk. x. 50.

ἀνάπηρος, *maimed;* see ἀνάπειρος.

ἀναπίπτω, to sit down, Joh. vi. 10. Matt. xv. 35. Luke, xiv. 10; to lean back, Joh. xiii. 25.

ἀναπληρόω, to fill up, to complete, 1 Thess. ii. 16. Matt. xxiii. 32; to fulfil, Gal. vi. 2. Matt. xiii. 14; to supply, Philipp. ii. 30. 1 Cor. xvi. 17.

ἀναπολόγητος, without excuse, Rom. i. 20. ii. 1.

ἀναπτύσσω, to unfold, to open, a var. lect. ad Luke, iv. 7.

ἀνάπτω, to kindle, Luke, xii. 49. James, iii. 5.

ἀναρίθμητος, innumerable, Hebr. xi. 12.

ἀνασείω, to stir up, to excite, Luke, xxiii. 5. Mrk. xv. 11.

ἀνασκευάζω, to unsettle, to subvert, Acts, xv. 24.

ἀνασπάω, to draw up, Luke, xiv. 5. Acts, xi. 10.

ἀνάστασις, ἡ, a rising up, Luke, ii. 34; the resurrection, Matt. xxii. 23, 28. Acts, ii. 31. iv. 33. Rom. vi. 5.

ἀναστατόω, to disturb, to stir up, Acts, xvii. 6. xxi. 38; to unsettle, Gal. v. 12. (It is a purely biblical word.)

ἀνασταυρόω, to crucify afresh, Hebr. vi. 6.

ἀναστενάζω, to sigh deeply, Mrk. viii. 12.

ἀναστρέφω, to overturn, Joh. ii. 15; intrans., to return, Acts, v. 22. xv. 16; to conduct oneself, to live, 2 Cor. i. 12. 1 Tim. iii. 15.

ἀναστροφὴ, ἡ, manner of life, conduct, Gal. i. 13. Ephes. iv. 22; life, Hebr. xiii. 7.

ἀνατάσσομαι, to arrange in order, to compare, Luke, i. 1.

ἀνατέλλω, to make to rise, Matt. v. 45; intrans., to rise, Matt. xiii. 6. Mrk. iv. 6. Luke, xii. 54; to be descended from, Hebr. vii. 14.

ἀνατίθεμαι, to set forth, to declare, Acts, xxv. 14. Gal. ii. 2.

ἀνατολὴ, ἡ, sunrise, Luke, i. 78; the East, Matt. ii. 2, 9. Rev. xxi. 13.

ἀνατρέπω, to overturn, to subvert, 1 Tit. i. 11. 2 Tim. ii. 18.

ἀνατρέφομαι, to be nourished, to be brought up, Acts, vii. 20. xxii. 3.

ἀναφαίνω, to get a sight of, to come in sight of, Acts, xxi. 3; pass., to appear, Luke, xix. 11.

ἀναφέρω, to lead up, Matt. xvii. 1. Mrk. ix. 2; to carry up, 1 Pet. ii. 24; to offer, Hebr. vii. 27. xiii. 15; to take upon oneself, Hebr. ix. 28.

ἀναφωνέω, to cry aloud, Luke, i. 42.

ἀνάχυσις, ἡ, excess, 1 Pet. iv. 4 [lit. a flood].

ἀναχωρέω, to return, Matt. ii. 12; to withdraw, to retire, Matt. ii. 14, 22. ix. 24. Acts xxvi. 31.

ἀνάψυξις, ἡ, a refreshing, Acts iii. 20.

ἀναψύχω, to refresh, 2 Tim. i. 16.

ἀνδραποδιστὴς, ὁ, a manstealer, a slavedealer, 1 Tim. i. 10.

ἀνδρίζομαι, to shew oneself brave, to be brave, 1 Cor. xvi. 13.

ἀνδροφόνος, ὁ, a manslayer, a homicide, 1 Tim. i. 9.

ἀνέγκλητος, *that cannot be accused, irreproachable, blameless,* Coloss. i. 22. 1 Cor. i. 8. 1 Tim. iii. 10. 1 Tit. i. 6, 7.

ἀνεκδιήγητος, *unspeakable, indescribable,* 2 Cor. ix. 15. (It is a purely eccles. word.)

ἀνεκλάλητος, *unspeakable,* 1 Pet. i. 8.

ἀνέκλειπτος, *unfailing,* Luke, xii. 33.

ἀνεκτὸς, *bearable, tolerable,* Matt. x. 15. xi. 22, 24. Luke, x. 12.

ἀνελεήμων, *merciless,* Rom. i. 31.

ἀνέλεος, *without mercy,* James, ii. 13.

ἀνεμίζομαι, *to be driven by the winds,* James, i. 6.

ἄνεμος, ὁ, *the wind,* Matt. xi. 7; οἱ τέσσαρες ἄνεμοι = the four cardinal winds, Rev. vii. 1; also = the four quarters of the heavens, Matt. xxiv. 31. Mrk. xiii. 27; met. *variableness, change,* Ephes. iv. 14.

ἀνέκδεκτος, *inadmissible, impossible,* Luke, xvii. 1.

ἀνεξεραύνητος, and **ἀνεξερεύνητος,** *that cannot be searched out, unsearchable,* Rom. xi. 33.

ἀνεξίκακος, *patient of wrongs,* 2 Tim. ii. 24. (RV *forbearing.*)

ἀνεξιχνίαστος, *that cannot be traced out, unsearchable,* Rom. xi. 33. Ephes. iii. 8.

ἀνεπαίσχυντος, *having no cause to be ashamed,* 2 Tim. ii. 15.

ἀνεπίλημπτος, *that cannot be censured, without reproach,* 1 Tim. iii. 2. v. 7. vi. 14. (Commonly written ἀνεπίληπτος.)

ἀνέρχομαι, *to go up,* Joh. vi. 3. Gal. i. 17.

ἄνεσις, η, *relaxation from restraint, indulgence,* Acts, xxiv. 23; *relief, rest,* 2 Thes. i. 7. 2 Cor. ii. 13. vii. 5. viii. 13.

ἀνετάζω, *to examine,* Acts, xxii. 24, 29. (It is a purely biblical word.)

ἄνευ, prepos., *without;* ἄνευ τοῦ πατρὸς ὑμῶν, *without your Father's permission,* Matt. x. 29.

ἀνεύθετος, *incommodious,* Acts, xxvii. 12.

ἀνευρίσκω, *to find,* Acts, xxi. 4. Luke, ii. 16.

ἀνέχομαι, *to bear, to endure, bear with,* 2 Tim. iv. 3. Hebr. xiii. 22. Matt. xvii. 17. Acts, xviii. 14. (The form ἀνέχω does not appear in the NT.)

ἀνεψιὸς, ὁ, *a cousin,* Coloss. iv. 10.

ἄνηθον, τὸ, *anise,* Matt. xxiii. 23.

ἀνήκω, *to pertain to;* ὡς ἀνῆκεν, *as was fitting,* Coloss. iii. 18; ἃ οὐκ ἀνῆκεν, *which are not befitting,* Ephes. v. 4; τὸ ἀνῆκον, *what is fitting,* Philem. 8.

ἀνήμερος, *fierce, savage,* 2 Tim. iii. 3.

ἀνήρ, ὁ, *a man,* Acts, viii. 12. xvii. 12; *a husband,* Matt. i. 16. Joh. iv. 17; with apellative nouns, ἀνὴρ προφήτης, *a prophet,* Luke, xxiv. 19; ἀνὴρ φονεὺς, *a murderer,* Acts, iii. 14.

ἀνθίστημι, *to set against;* ἀνθίσταμαι, *to withstand, to oppose,* Acts, vi. 10. xiii. 8.

ἀνθομολογέομαι, *to confess; to give thanks to*, Luke, ii. 38.

ἄνθος, τὸ, *a flower*, James, i. 10. 1 Pet. i. 24.

ἀνθρακιά, ἡ, *a fire of charcoal*, Joh. xviii. 18. xxi. 9,

ἄνθραξ, ὁ, *charcoal;* ἄνθρακες, *burning coals*, Rom. xii. 20.

ἀνθρωπάρεσκος, *studying to please men*, Coloss. iii. 22. Ephes. vi. 6.

ἀνθρώπινος, *human*, Acts, xvii. 25. 1 Cor. ii. 13; *within man's power to bear*, 1 Cor. x. 13.

ἀνθρωποκτόνος, *murderous*, Joh. viii. 44. 1 Joh. iii. 15.

ἄνθρωπος, ὁ, *a man*, Acts, x. 26; ἄνθρωπος Χριστὸς Ἰησοῦς, i.e. *Christ Jesus in His humanity*, 1 Tim. ii. 5. S. Paul seems to have had no other mode of expressing this idea; for the proper word for *humanity* (ἀνθρωπότης) did not come into use till more than 130 years after the time of S. Paul, while the use of the word ἀνθρωπισμὸς, if known to him at all, which is very doubtful, would certainly have been rejected by him, just as in his own writings he has carefully avoided the use of the word βωμός.

ἀνθυπατεύω, *to be proconsul*, var. lect. ad Acts, xviii. 12.

ἀνθύπατος, ὁ, *a proconsul*, Acts, xiii. 7, 8, 12. xviii. 12.

ἀνίημι, *to loosen*, Acts, xvi. 26. xxvii. 40; *to give up, to forbear*, Ephes. vi. 9; *to leave, to forsake*, Hebr. xiii. 5.

ἀνίλεως, *without mercy*, James, ii. 13. (See ἀνέλεος.)

ἄνιπτος, *unwashed*, Matt. xv. 20. Mrk. vii. 2.

ἀνίστημι, *to cause to rise, to raise up*, Acts, ix. 41. xiii. 34. Joh. vi. 39. Matt. xxii. 24; ἀναστῆναι, *to stand up, to rise*, Luke, viii. 55. xxii. 45; ἀνίστασθαι, *to arise, to appear*, Rom. xv. 12. Hebr. vii. 11.

ἀνόητος, *senseless, foolish*, Rom. i. 14. Luke, xxiv. 25.

ἄνοια, ἡ, *senselessness, folly*, 2 Tim. iii. 9; *madness*, Luke, vi. 11.

ἀνοίγω, *to open*, Acts, v. 19. xii. 14; ἀνέῳγα, *to be open*, 2 Cor. vi. 11. 1 Cor. xvi. 9.

ἀνοικοδομέω, *to build again*, Acts, xv. 16.

ἄνοιξις, ἡ, *an opening*, Ephes. vi. 19.

ἀνομία, ἡ, *lawlessness, iniquity*, Matt. xxiii. 28. xxiv. 12; αἱ ἀνομίαι, *iniquities*, Rom. iv. 7.

ἄνομος, *without law*, 1 Cor. ix. 21; *lawless, unjust, wicked*, 1 Tim. i. 9. Luke, xxii. 37. Acts, ii. 23.

ἀνόμως, *illegally; without the law*, Rom. ii. 12 (i.e. in ignorance of it).

ἀνορθόω, *to raise up, to make straight*, Luke, xiii. 13. Hebr. xii. 12; *to raise again, to rebuild*, Acts, xv. 16.

ἀνόσιος, *unholy*, 1 Tim. i. 9. 2 Tim. iii. 2.

ἀνοχή, ἡ, *forbearance*, Rom. ii. 4. iii. 25.

ἀνταγωνίζομαι, *to strive against*, Hebr. xii. 4.

ἀντάλλαγμα, τὸ, *what is given in exchange, an equivalent*, Matt. xvi. 26. Mrk. viii. 37.

ἀνταναπληρόω, *to fill up in turn*, Coloss. i. 24.

ἀνταποδίδωμι, *to repay*, Rom. xi. 35. Luke, xiv. 14; *to render, to return*, 1 Thess. iii. 9; *to recompense, to requite*, Rom. xii. 19. Hebr. x. 30.

ἀνταπόδομα, τὸ, *a recompense*, Luke, xiv. 12. Rom. xi. 9.

ἀνταπόδοσις, ἡ, *a recompense*, Coloss. iii. 24.

ἀνταποκρίνομαι, *to make a reply*, Luke, xiv. 6; *to reply against*, Rom. ix. 20.

ἀντειπεῖν, *to gainsay*, Luke, xxi. 15. Acts, iv. 14.

ἀντέχομαι, *to hold to, to cleave to*, Matt. vi. 24. Luke, xvi. 13. Tit. i. 9; *to aid, to support*, 1 Thess. v. 14. (The form ἀντέχω does not appear in the NT.)

ἀντὶ, prepos., *instead of, in place of*, Luke, xi. 11; ἀνθ' ὧν, *wherefore*, Luke, xii. 3; ἀντὶ τούτου, *for this cause*, Ephes. v. 31; *because*, Luke, i. 20. xix. 44.

ἀντιβάλλω, *to exchange; to converse about*, Luke, xxiv. 17.

ἀντιδιατίθεμαι, *to oppose*, 2 Tim. ii. 25.

ἀντίδικος, ὁ, *an adversary*, Matt. v. 25. Luke, xii. 58. 1 Pet. v. 8.

ἀντίθεσις, ἡ, *opposition*, 1 Tim. vi. 20.

ἀντικαθίστημι, (in 2nd aor.), *to resist*, Hebr. xii. 4.

ἀντικαλέω, *to invite in turn*, Luke, xiv. 12.

ἀντίκειμαι, *to oppose, to withstand*, Luke, xxi. 15; *to be contrary to*, Gal. v. 17. 1 Tim. i. 10; ὁ ἀντικείμενος, *the adversary*, Luke, xiii. 17. Philipp. i. 28.

ἀντικρὺ, *over against, opposite*, Acts, xx. 15.

ἀντιλαμβάνω, *to help, to succour*, Luke, i. 54. Acts, xx. 35; *to partake of*, 1 Tim. vi. 2.

ἀντιλέγω, *to speak against, to gainsay*, Acts, xiii. 45. xxviii. 19; *to oppose*, Joh. xix. 12.

ἀντίλημψις, ἡ, *help, ministration*, 1 Cor. xii. 28.

ἀντιλογία, ἡ, *gainsaying, dispute*, Hebr. vi. 16. vii. 7; *rebellion*, Jude, 11.

ἀντιλοιδορέω, *to revile in turn*, 1 Pet. ii. 23.

ἀντίλυτρον, τὸ, *a ransom*, 1 Tim. ii. 6.

ἀντιμετρέω, *to measure in return*, Luke, vi. 38.

ἀντιμισθία, ἡ, *a recompense*, 2 Cor. vi. 13. Rom. i. 27.

ἀντιπαρέρχομαι, *to pass by on the other side*, Luke, x. 31.

ἀντίπερα, adv., *over against*, Luke, viii. 26.

ἀντιπίπτω, *to oppose, to resist*, Acts, vii. 51.

ἀντιστρατεύομαι, *to war against, to oppose*, Rom. vii. 23.

ἀντιτάσσομαι, *to oppose, to resist*, Rom. xiii. 2. James, iv. 6. 1 Pet. v. 5.

ἀντίτυπος, *like in pattern*, Hebr. ix. 24; τὸ ἀντίτυπον, *an antitype*, 1 Pet. iii. 21.

ἀντίχριστος, ὁ, *the Antichrist*, 1 Joh. iv. 3. (This word appears only in S. John and in the ecclesiastical writers.)

ἀντλέω, *to pump out; to draw water*, Joh. ii. 8. iv. 15.

ἄντλημα, τό, *a vessel to draw with*, Joh. iv. 11.

ἀντοφθαλμέω, *to stand up against, to withstand to the face*, Acts, xxvii. 15.

ἄνυδρος, *waterless, without water*, 2 Pet. ii. 17. Jude, 12. Matt. xii. 43. Luke, xi. 24.

ἀνυπόκριτος, *without hypocrisy, unfeigned*, Rom. xii. 9. 2 Cor. vi. 6.

ἀνυπότακτος, *unsubjected*, Hebr. ii. 8; *that cannot be subjected, disobedient, unruly*, 1 Tim. i. 9. Tit. i. 6, 10.

ἄνω, adv., *upwards, up*, Joh. xi. 41. Hebr. xii. 15; ἕως ἄνω, *up to the brim*, Joh. ii. 7; ἡ ἄνω Ἰερουσαλήμ, *the heavenly Jerusalem*, Gal. iv. 26; ἡ ἄνω κλῆσις, *the heavenly calling*, Philipp. iii. 14. (Cf. Hebr. iii. 1); τὰ ἄνω, *heavenly things*, Coloss. iii. 1; ἐκ τῶν ἄνω, *from Heaven*, Joh. viii. 23.

ἀνώγεον, τό: see ἀνάγαιον.

ἄνωθεν, adv., *from above, from Heaven*, Joh. iii. 31. xix. 11; *from the first*, Luke, i. 3. Acts, xxvi. 5; *afresh, anew*, Joh. iii. 3, 7; ἀπ' ἄνωθεν, and ἐκ τῶν ἄνωθεν, *from the top*, Mrk. xv. 38. Joh. xix. 23; πάλιν ἄνωθεν, *over again*, Gal. iv. 9.

ἀνωτερικὸς, *upper, inland*, Acts, xix. 1.

ἀνώτερος, *higher;* ἀνώτερον as adv., *higher*, Luke, xiv. 10; *in a preceding passage*, Hebr. x. 8.

ἀνωφελὴς, *unprofitable*, Tit. iii. 9; τὸ ἀνωφελὲς, *unprofitableness*, Hebr. vii. 18.

ἀξίνη, ἡ, *an axe*, Matt. iii. 10. Luke, iii. 9.

ἄξιος, *worthy*, Hebr. xi. 38. Matt. x. 10; *deserving of*, Luke, xii. 48. xxiii. 15; *meet, befitting*, Matt. iii. 8. Acts, xxvi. 20. 2 Thess. i. 3.

ἀξιόω, *to deem worthy*, Luke, vii. 7. 2 Thess. i. 11; *to think it right*, Acts, xv. 38. xxviii. 22.

ἀξίως, *worthily*, Coloss. i. 10. Ephes. iv. 1.

ἀόρατος, *unseen; invisible*, Coloss. i. 15. 1 Tim. i. 17.

ἀπαγγέλλω, *to bring word, to report*, Acts, iv. 23. Matt. ii. 8; *to declare*, 1 Joh. i. 2. Acts, xxvi. 20.

ἀπάγχομαι, *to hang himself*, Matt. xxvii. 5.

ἀπάγω, *to lead away*, Luke, xiii. 15. Matt. xxvi. 57; *to lead*, Matt. vii. 13; *to lead astray*, 1 Cor. xii. 2.

ἀπαίδευτος, *uninstructed; ignorant*, 2 Tim. ii. 23.

ἀπαίρω, *to take away*, Matt. ix. 15. Luke, v. 35.

ἀπαιτέω, *to demand back*, Luke, vi. 30. xii. 20.

ἀπαλγέω, *to be past feeling*, Ephes. iv. 19.

ἀπαλλάσσω, *to remove; to deliver*, Hebr. ii. 15; ἀπαλλάσσομαι, *to depart*, Acts, xix. 12; *to be released*, Luke, xii. 58.

ἀπαλλοτριόω, *to estrange, to alienate*, Ephes. ii. 12. iv. 18. Coloss. i. 21.

ἀπαλὸς, *tender*, Mrk. xiii. 28. Matt. xxiv. 32.

ἀπαντάω, *to meet*, Mrk. xiv. 13. Luke, xvii. 12.

ἀπάντησις, ἡ, *a meeting*, Acts, xxviii. 15. 1 Thess. iv. 17.

ἅπαξ, adv., *once*, 1 Thess. ii. 8; *once for all*, 1 Pet. iii. 18.

ἀπαράβατος, *inviolable; unchangeable*, Hebr. vii. 24.

ἀπαρασκεύαστος, *unprepared*, 2 Cor. ix. 4.

ἀπαρνέομαι, *to deny*, Matt. xxvi. 34, 75. Mrk. xiv. 30, 72; *to lose sight of, to disregard*, Matt. xvi. 24. Mrk. viii. 34.

ἀπάρτι, for ἀπ' ἄρτι, *henceforth*, Matt. xxiii. 39. xxvi. 29. (Contra, ἀπαρτὶ, *exactly*: see Pape's Lex. in voc. ἀπαρτί.)

ἀπαρτισμὸς, ὁ, *completion*, Luke, xiv. 28.

ἀπαρχὴ, ἡ, *the first fruits*, Rom. xi. 16. 1 Cor. xvi. 5. James, i. 18.

ἅπας, *all*, Luke, iv. 6. Mrk. xvi. 15.

ἀπασπάζομαι, *to take leave of*, Acts, xxi. 6.

ἀπατάω, *to deceive*, James, i. 26. Ephes. v. 6.

ἀπάτη, ἡ, *deceit*, Coloss. ii. 8; *deceitfulness*, Matt. xiii. 22. Mrk. iv. 19.

ἀπάτωρ, *without father*, Hebr. vii. 3.

ἀπαύγασμα, τὸ, *the effulgence*, Hebr. i. 3.

ἀπείδον, *to look at, to perceive*, a var. lect. for ἀφεῖδον, ad Philipp. ii. 23.

ἀπείθεια, ἡ, and **ἀπειθία**, ἡ, *disobedience*, Rom. xi. 30, 32. Hebr. iv. 6, 11. Ephes. ii. 2. v. 6.

ἀπειθέω, *to be disobedient*, 1 Pet. ii. 8. iii. 1; *to disbelieve*, Joh. iii. 36. Rom. ii. 8. 1 Pet. iv. 17.

ἀπειθής, *disobedient*, Luke, i. 17. Tit. i. 16. iii. 3.

ἀπειλέω, *to threaten*, 1 Pet. ii. 23; and ἀπειλέομαι=ἀπειλέω, Acts, iv. 17.

ἀπειλὴ, ἡ, *a threat*, Acts, iv. 29. ix. 1. Ephes. vi. 9.

ἄπειμι, (from εἰμί), *to be absent*, 1 Cor. v. 3. 2 Cor. x. 1, 11. Coloss. ii. 5.

ἄπειμι, (from εἶμι), *to go away, to depart*, Acts, xvii. 10.

ἀπεῖπον, and **ἀπειπάμην**, *to renounce*, 2 Cor. iv. 2.

ἀπείραστος, *that cannot be tempted*, James, i. 13.

ἄπειρος, *without experience*, Hebr. v. 13.

ἀπεκδέχομαι, *to wait for*, Rom. viii. 19, 23, 25. Philipp. iii. 20.

ἀπεκδύομαι, *to put off*, Coloss. iii. 9; *to despoil*, Coloss. ii. 15. (RV *having put off from himself*.)

ἀπέκδυσις, ἡ, *a putting off*, Coloss. ii. 11. (Found in no other writer, but only in this passage.)

ἀπελαύνω, *to drive away*, Acts, xviii. 16.

ἀπελεγμὸς, ὁ, *disesteem, disrepute*, Acts, xix. 27. (Found nowhere else.)

ἀπελεύθερος, ὁ, ἡ, *a freedman*, 1 Cor. vii. 22.

ἀπελπίζω, *to despair*, Luke, vi. 35.
ἀπέναντι, adv., *over against, opposite*, Matt. xxvii. 6; *in sight of, before*, Acts, iii. 16. Rom. iii. 18; *contrary to, against*, Acts, xvii. 7.
ἀπέραντος, *endless*, 1 Tim. i. 4.
ἀπερισπάστως, adv., *without distraction*, 1 Cor. vii. 35.
ἀπερίτμητος, *uncircumcised*, Acts, vii. 51.
ἀπέρχομαι, *to go away, to depart*, Matt. xiii. 25. xix. 22. Joh. xvi. 7; *to go forth, to spread abroad*, Matt. iv. 24; ἀπέρχεσθαι ὀπίσω τινὸς, *to go after, to follow*, Mrk. i. 20. Joh. xii. 19; ἀπέρχεσθαι εἰς τὰ ὀπίσω, *to go back, to forsake*, Joh. vi. 66; *to draw back, to retire*, Joh. xviii. 6.
ἀπέχω, *to receive*, Matt. vi. 2, 5, 16. Luke, vi. 24; intrans., *to be away, to be distant*, Luke, xv. 20. xxiv. 13; ἀπέχεσθαι, *to abstain*, Acts, xv. 20, 28. 1 Thess. iv. 3. v. 22; ἀπέχει, impers., *it sufficeth, it is enough*, Mrk. xiv. 41.
ἀπιστέω, *to be unfaithful, to be without faith*, Rom. iii. 3. 2 Tim. ii. 13; *to disbelieve*, Luke, xxiv. 41. Mrk. xvi. 11, 16.
ἀπιστία, ἡ, *want of faith, unbelief*, Rom. iv. 20. Hebr. iii. 19; *unfaithfulness*, Rom. iii. 3.
ἄπιστος, *faithless, unfaithful*, Matt. xvii. 17. Mrk. ix. 19. Luke, xii. 46; *unbelieving*, 1 Cor. vii. 12. Joh. xx. 27. Rev. xxi. 8; *incredible*, Acts, xxvi. 8.

ἁπλότης, ἡ, *singleness, simplicity, sincerity*, 2 Cor. xi. 3. Coloss. iii. 22. Ephes. vi. 5; *liberality*, 2 Cor. viii. 2. ix. 11. Rom. xii. 8.
ἁπλοῦς, *single, sound*, Matt. vi. 22. Luke, xi. 34.
ἁπλῶς, *frankly, liberally*, James, i. 5.
ἀπὸ, prepos., *from; out of, of*, Luke, i. 52. Matt. xv. 27; ἀπὸ τοῦ νῦν, *henceforth*, Luke, i. 48. v. 10; ἀπὸ τότε, *from that time*, Matt. iv. 17. xvi. 21; ἀπὸ πρωὶ, *from early morn*, Acts, xxviii. 23; ἀπὸ πέρυσι, *since last year*, 2 Cor. viii. 10. ix. 2; ἀπ᾽ ἐμαυτοῦ, *of my own will, of myself*, Joh. vii 17, 28; ἀπὸ μέρους, *in part*, 2 Cor. i. 14. ii. 5; ἀπὸ μιᾶς, (sc. γνώμης,) *with one consent*, Luke, xiv. 18; *by reason of*, Luke, xix. 3. Joh. xxi. 6. Acts, xxii. 11.
ἀποβαίνω, *to go out, to disembark*, Luke, v. 2. Joh. xxi. 9; *to turn out, to result*, Luke, xxi. 13. Philipp. i. 19.
ἀποβάλλω, *to throw off, to cast away*, Mrk. x. 50. Hebr. x. 35.
ἀποβλέπω, *to look attentively*, Hebr. xi. 26.
ἀπόβλητος, *to be thrown away, to be rejected*, 1 Tim. iv. 4.
ἀποβολὴ, ἡ, *a throwing away, a rejection*, Rom. xi. 15; *loss*, Acts, xxvii. 22.
ἀπογίγνομαι, *to die;* with dat., *to die unto, to be separated from*, 1 Pet. ii. 24.
ἀπογραφὴ, ἡ, *a registration, a census*, Acts, v. 37. Luke, ii. 2.

ἀπο] *GREEK-ENGLISH LEXICON* [ἀπο

ἀπογράφω, to enrol, to register, Luke, ii. 1, 3, 5; οἱ ἐν οὐρανοῖς ἀπογεγραμμένοι, those who are registered in Heaven, Hebr. xii. 23.

ἀποδείκνυμι, to shew forth, to exhibit, 1 Cor. iv. 9. 2 Thess. ii. 4; to prove, Acts, xxv. 7; to approve, Acts, ii. 22.

ἀπόδειξις, ἡ, a proof, a demonstration, 1 Cor. ii. 4.

ἀποδεκατεύω, to pay tithes of, Luke, xviii. 12.

ἀποδεκατόω, to exact tithes, to tithe, Hebr. vii. 5: to pay tithes, Matt. xxiii. 23. Luke, xi. 42.

ἀπόδεκτος, agreeable, acceptable, 1 Tim. ii. 3. v. 4.

ἀποδέχομαι, to accept, Acts, ii. 41. xxiv. 3; to receive, Acts, xviii. 27; to welcome, Luke, viii. 40. ix. 11.

ἀποδημέω, to go into foreign parts, to go abroad, Matt. xxi. 33. xxv. 14. Luke, xv. 13.

ἀπόδημος, away abroad, Mrk. xiii. 34.

ἀποδίδωμι, to pay, Luke, vii. 42. x. 35. Matt. v. 26; to deliver up, Matt. xxvii. 58; to render, to give, Matt. xii. 36. Luke, xvi. 2; to give back, to restore, Luke, iv. 20; to recompense, Matt. vi. 4, 6, 18; ἀποδίδομαι, to sell, Acts, v. 8. vii. 9. Hebr. xii. 16.

ἀποδιορίζω, to separate, to cause separations, Jude, 19.

ἀποδοκιμάζω, to disapprove, to reject, Matt. xxi. 42. Mrk. viii. 31. Luke, xvii. 25. 1 Pet. ii. 4, 7.

ἀποδοχὴ, acceptance, 1 Tim. i. 15. iv. 9.

ἀπόθεσις, ἡ, a putting off, 1 Pet. iii. 21. 2 Pet. i. 14.

ἀποθήκη, ἡ, a granary, a barn, Matt. iii. 12. vi. 26. xiii. 30.

ἀποθησαυρίζω, to store up, 1 Tim. vi. 19.

ἀποθλίβω, to squeeze, to press hard, Luke, viii. 45.

ἀποθνήσκω, to die, Matt. xxvi. 35. Acts, xxi. 13. Rom. vi. 8.

ἀποκαθίστημι, to restore to its former state; 2nd aor. and pass., to be restored, Mrk. viii. 25. Matt. xii. 13. Luke, vi. 10. Mrk. iii. 5. Acts, i. 6.

ἀποκαλύπτω, to uncover, to disclose, to reveal, Matt. x. 26. Luke, xii. 2; pass., to become manifest, to appear, Joh. xii. 38. Rom. i. 18. viii. 18.

ἀποκάλυψις, ἡ, a revelation, a manifestation, Luke, ii. 32. 2 Thess. i. 7. 2 Cor. xii. 1.

ἀποκαραδοκία, ἡ, expectation, Rom. viii. 19. Philipp. i. 20.

ἀποκαταλλάσσω, to reconcile, Ephes. ii. 16. Coloss. i. 20, 22. (It is a purely NT word.)

ἀποκατάστασις, ἡ, a restoration, Acts, iii. 21.

ἀπόκειμαι, to be laid up, to be reserved, Luke, xix. 20. Coloss. i. 5. 2 Tim. iv. 8; to be appointed, Hebr. ix. 27.

ἀποκεφαλίζω, to behead, Luke, ix. 9. Matt. xiv. 10. Mrk. vi. 16, 27.

ἀποκλείω, to shut, Luke, xiii. 25.

ἀποκόπτω, to cut off, Mrk. ix. 43. Joh. xviii. 10, 26. Gal. v. 12. Acts, xxvii. 32.

ἀπό] TO THE NEW TESTAMENT [ἀπό

ἀπόκριμα, τό, *an answer*, 2 Cor. i. 9.

ἀποκρίνω, *to separate;* 1 aor. pass., *to answer*, Mrk. xii. 28, 34. Luke, x. 28. Matt. xxvii. 14; the classical form, ἀπεκρίνατο, is much less frequent in the NT, Matt. xxvii. 12. Mrk. xiv. 61 etc.

ἀπόκρισις, ἡ, *an answer*, Joh. i. 22. xix. 9. Luke, ii. 47.

ἀποκρύπτω, *to hide*, Luke, x. 21. 1 Cor. ii. 7. Coloss. i. 26.

ἀπόκρυφος, *hidden, concealed*, Mrk. iv. 22. Luke, viii. 17; *stored up*, Coloss. ii. 3.

ἀποκτείνω, *to kill, to slay*, Matt. xvi. 21. xxii. 6; *to do away with, to abolish*, Ephes. ii. 16.

ἀποκυέω, *to be pregnant; to bring forth*, James, i. 15, 18.

ἀποκυλίω, *to roll away*, Matt. xxviii. 2. Mrk. xvi. 3. Luke, xxiv. 2. (See ἀνακυλίω.)

ἀπολαμβάνω, *to receive*, Luke, xvi. 25. xxiii. 41. Gal. iv. 5; *to receive back, to recover*, Luke, xv. 27; ἀπολαμβάνομαι, *to take* a person *aside*, Mrk. vii. 33.

ἀπόλαυσις, ἡ, *enjoyment*, 1 Tim. vi. 17. Hebr. xi. 25.

ἀπόλλυμι, and **ἀπολλύω**, *to destroy*, Luke, iv. 34. xvii. 27, 29. Jude, 5; *to kill*, Matt. ii. 13. xii. 14. Mrk. xi. 18; *to lose*, Matt. x. 42. Joh. vi. 39. xii. 25; ἀπόλλυμαι, *to perish*, Matt. viii. 25. Luke, xiii. 3, 5, 33. xv. 17. xxi. 18.

Ἀπολλύων, ὁ, *Apollyon*, i.e. *The Destroyer*, Rev. ix. 11. (See Ἀβάδδων.)

ἀπολογέομαι, *to make a defence*, Luke, xxi. 14. Acts, xix. 33. xxvi. 1, 24; *to defend, to excuse*, Rom. ii. 15.

ἀπολογία, ἡ, *a verbal defence, a speech in defence*, Acts, xxii. 1. xxv. 16. 1 Cor. ix. 3.

ἀπολούομαι, *to wash away*, Acts, xxii. 16. 1 Cor. vi. 11.

ἀπολύτρωσις, ἡ, *redemption*, Ephes. i. 7. Coloss. i. 14. Rom. iii. 24; *deliverance*, Hebr. xi. 35. Luke, xxi. 28.

ἀπολύω, *to set free, to release*, Luke, xiii. 12. xxiii. 22. Joh. xix. 10; *to send away, to dismiss*, Matt. xiv. 15, 22. xv. 23. Luke, ii. 29; *to put away, to divorce*, Matt. i. 19. v. 31. xix. 3; ἀπολύομαι, *to depart*, Acts, xxviii. 25.

ἀπομάσσομαι, *to wipe off*, Luke, x. 11.

ἀπονέμω, *to distribute, to assign*, 1 Pet. iii. 7.

ἀπονίπτομαι, *to wash*, Matt. xxvii. 24.

ἀποπίπτω, *to fall off*, Acts, ix. 18.

ἀποπλανάω, *to lead astray*, Mrk. xiii. 22; pass., *to go astray*, 1 Tim. vi. 10.

ἀποπλέω, *to sail away, to set sail*, Acts, xiii. 4. xiv. 26.

ἀποπλύνω, *to wash*, a var. lect. ad Luke, v. 2.

ἀποπνίγω, *to suffocate, to choke*, Matt. xiii. 7. Luke, viii. 7; pass., *to be drowned*, Luke, viii. 33.

ἀπορέομαι, *to be in doubt, to be perplexed*, 2 Cor. iv. 8. Gal. iv. 20. Luke, xxiv. 4. Acts, xxv. 20. [Act. ἀπορέω, Mrk. vi. 20.]

ἀπο] *GREEK-ENGLISH LEXICON* [ἀπο

ἀπορία, ἡ, *perplexity*, Luke, xxi. 25.

ἀπορρίπτω, *to throw themselves overboard*, Acts, xxvii. 43.

ἀπορφανίζομαι, *to be bereaved*, 1 Thess. ii. 17.

ἀποσκευάζομαι, *to collect the baggage*, a var. lect. ad Acts, xxi. 15. (See ἐπισκευαζόμαι.)

ἀποσκίασμα, τὸ, *a shadow*, James, i. 17.

ἀποσπάω, *to draw away*, Acts, xx. 30; *to draw*, Matt. xxvi. 51; pass., *to be separated, to part*, Luke, xxii. 41. Acts, xxi. 1.

ἀποστασία, ἡ, *a falling away, an apostasy*, 2 Thess. ii. 3. Acts, xxi. 21.

ἀποστάσιον, τὸ, *a divorce, a bill of divorcement*, Matt. v. 31. xix. 7. Mrk. x. 4.

ἀποστεγάζω, *to uncover, to strip off*, Mrk. ii. 4.

ἀποστέλλω, *to send*, Joh. iii. 17. x. 36. xvii. 18; *to send away*, Mrk. v. 10. viii. 26. xii. 3.

ἀποστερέω, *to defraud*, Mrk. x. 19. 1 Cor. vi. 8. vii. 5; ἀποστερέομαι, *to allow one'self to be defraucled*, 1 Cor. vi. 7; ἀπεστερημένος, *deprived, bereft*, 1 Tim. vi. 5; in James, v. 4. a var. lect. for ἀφυστερημένος, *withheld, kept back*. (See ἀφυστερέω.)

ἀποστολὴ, ἡ, *a sending away; the office of an apostle, the apostleship*, Acts, i. 25. Rom. i. 5. 1 Cor. ix. 2. Gal. ii. 8.

ἀπόστολος, ὁ, *a messenger, a delegate*, Joh. xiii. 16; *an apostle*, Hebr. iii. 1. Matt. x. 2. Acts, i. 26. Gal. i. 1.

ἀποστοματίζω, *to urge to speak offhand*, Luke, xi. 53.

ἀποστρέφω, *to turn away*, 2 Tim. iv. 4. Acts, iii. 26; *to remove*, Rom. xi. 26; *to put back, to return*, Matt. xxvi. 52; *to pervert*, Luke, xxiii. 14; ἀποστρέφομαι, with accus., *to turn away from*, Matt. v. 42. Hebr. xii. 25. Tit. i. 14. 2 Tim. i. 15.

ἀποστυγέω, *to hate, to abhor*, Rom. xii. 9.

ἀποσυνάγωγος, *put out of the synagogue*, Joh. ix. 22. xii. 42. xvi. 2. (It is a purely biblical word.)

ἀποτάσσομαι, with dat., *to take leave of*, Acts, xviii. 18, 21. 2 Cor. ii. 13. Luke, ix. 61; *to renounce*, Luke, xiv. 33.

ἀποτελέω, *to accomplish, to perform*, Luke, xiii. 32; pass., *to be matured*, James, i. 15.

ἀποτίθεμαι, *to put off*, Acts, vii. 58; *to put away, to renounce*, Rom. xiii. 12. Ephes. iv. 22. Coloss. iii. 8. James, i. 21; *to put*, Matt. xiv. 3.

ἀποτινάσσω, *to shake off*, Luke, ix. 5. Acts, xxviii. 5.

ἀποτίνω, *to repay*, Philem. 19.

ἀποτολμάω, *to assume boldness*, Rom. x. 20.

ἀποτομία, ἡ, *severity*, Rom. xi. 22.

ἀποτόμως, *sharply, severely*, Tit. i. 13. 2 Cor. xiii. 10.

ἀποτρέπομαι, *to turn away from, to avoid*, 2 Tim. iii. 5.

ἀπουσία, ἡ, *absence*, Philipp. ii. 12.

ἀποφέρω, *to carry away*, Mrk. xv. 1. Rev. xvii. 3. xxi. 10; pass., *to be carried away*, Acts, xix. 12. Luke, xvi. 22.

ἀποφεύγω, with accus., *to fly from, to escape from*, 2 Pet. ii. 18; also with genit., 2 Pet. i. 4.

ἀποφθέγγομαι, *to speak out, to declare*, Acts, ii. 14. xxvi. 25.

ἀποφορτίζομαι, *to unlade, to discharge*, Acts, xxi. 3.

ἀπόχρησις, ἡ, *abuse*, Coloss. ii. 22. (RV *with the using*.)

ἀποχωρέω, *to go away, to depart*, Acts, xiii. 13 etc.

ἀποχωρίζω, *to sever*, Rev. vi. 14; mid. *to separate*, Acts, xv. 39.

ἀποψύχω, *to breathe out life, to faint*, Luke, xxi. 26.

ἀπρόσιτος, *unapproachable*, 1 Tim. vi. 16.

ἀπρόσκοπος, actively, *not causing to stumble*, 1 Cor. x. 32; passively, *not led into sin, without offence, blameless*, Philipp. i. 10. Acts, xxiv. 16.

ἀπροσωπολήμπτως, *without respect of persons, impartially*, 1 Pet. i. 17. (It is a purely ecclesiastical word.)

ἄπταιστος, *without stumbling*, Jude, 24.

ἅπτω, *to kindle, to light*, Luke, viii. 16. Acts, xxviii. 2; ἅπτομαι, *to touch*, Matt. viii. 3. Joh. xx. 17; *to handle*, Coloss. ii. 21; *to assail*, 1 Joh. v. 18.

ἀπωθέομαι, *to thrust away, to reject*, Acts, vii. 27, 39. xiii. 46. Rom. xi. 1. 1 Tim. i. 19.

ἀπώλεια, ἡ, *destruction*, Rom. ix. 22. Acts, viii. 20; αἱρέσεις ἀπωλείας, *destructive heresies*, 2 Pet. ii. 1; *perdition*, Rev. xvii. 8, 11. 2 Thess. ii. 3. Philipp. iii. 19; *waste*, Mrk. xiv. 4. Matt. xxvi. 8.

ἄρα, an *illative particle, consequently, then;* in good Greek writers always *subjoined*, but in the NT sometimes placed *first* (Luke, xi. 48. Rom. x. 17. 1 Cor. xv. 18).

ἆρα, an *interrogative* particle, corresponding to the Latin *-ne*.

ἀρά, ἡ, *imprecation, cursing*, Rom. iii. 14.

ἀραβὼν, ὁ. See ἀρραβών.

ἄραφος, *not sewn together, without seam*, Joh. xix. 23.

ἀργέω, *to be idle; to linger*, 2 Pet. ii. 3.

ἀργὸς, *idle*, Matt. xx. 3, 6. 1 Tim. v. 13; *shunning labour, lazy*, 2 Pet. i. 8; γαστέρες ἀργαί, *idle gluttons*, Tit. i. 12; *unprofitable*, James, ii. 20. Matt. xii. 36.

ἀργύρεος, -ους, Acts, xix. 24; *of silver*, 2 Tim. ii. 20. Rev. ix. 20.

ἀργύριον, τὸ, *silver*, Acts, iii. 6. xx. 33; *money*, Matt. xxv. 18, 27. Luke, ix. 3; *a piece of silver;* ἀργυρίου μυριάδες πέντε, *fifty thousand pieces of silver*, Acts, xix. 19. Cf. Matt. xxvi. 15.

ἀργυροκόπος, ὁ, *a silversmith*, Acts, xix. 24.

ἄργυρος, ὁ, *silver*, Acts, xvii. 29. James, v. 3. Rev. xviii. 12.

Ἄρειος, *of or belonging to Mars;* Ἄρειος πάγος, *Mars' Hill, The Areopagus*, Acts, xvii. 19, 22.

Ἀρειοπαγίτης, ὁ, *a member of the court of Areopagus, an Areopagite*, Acts. xvii. 34.

ἀρεσκία, ἡ, *a pleasing*, Coloss. i. 10.

ἀρέσκω, *to please*, Matt. xiv. 6. 1 Thess. ii. 4.

ἀρεστὸς, *pleasing*, Joh. viii. 29. Acts, xii. 3; *fitting*, Acts, vi. 2.

ἀρετὴ, ἡ, *excellence, perfection*, 1 Pet. ii. 9; *virtue*, Philipp. iv. 8. 2 Pet. i. 5.

ἀρὴν, ὁ, ἀρνὸς, ἀρνὶ, ἄρνα, ἄρνες, ἀρνῶν, ἀρνάσι, ἄρνας, *a lamb*, Luke, x. 3. (The nom. sing. is not in use, and in Attic writers is supplied by ὁ ἀμνός.)

ἀριθμέω, *to number*, Rev. vii. 9. Matt. x. 30.

ἀριθμὸς, ὁ, *a number*, Joh. vi. 10. Rev. xiii. 18.

ἀριστάω, *to breakfast*, Joh. xxi. 12, 15; *to dine*, Luke, xi. 37.

ἀριστερός, *left*; ἡ ἀριστερά (sc. χείρ), *the left hand*, Matt. vi. 3. Luke, xxiii. 33; ὅπλα ἀριστερά, *armour on the left hand*, 2 Cor. vi. 7.

ἄριστον, τὸ, *breakfast; dinner*, Matt. xxii. 4. Luke, xi. 38. xiv. 12.

ἀρκετὸς, *sufficient*, Matt. vi. 34. x. 25. 1 Pet. iv. 3.

ἀρκέω, *to be enough, to be sufficient*, Matt. xxv. 9. Joh. vi. 7. 2 Cor. xii. 9; impersonally, ἀρκεῖ ἡμῖν, *it sufficeth us*, Joh. xiv. 8; pass., *to be satisfied, to be content*, Luke, iii. 14. 1 Tim. vi. 8. Hebr. xiii. 5.

ἄρκος, ὁ, ἡ, *a bear*, Rev. xiii. 2. (It is a late form for ἄρκτος.)

ἅρμα, τὸ, *a chariot*, Acts, viii. 28, 38. Rev. ix. 9.

Ἁρμαγεδὼν, indecl., *Harmagedon*, the name of a place where the kings opposed to Christ are to be destroyed, Rev. xvi. 16. (RV *Har-Magedon*.)

ἁρμόζομαι, *to join in marriage, to espouse*, 2 Cor. xi. 2.

ἁρμὸς, ὁ, *a joint*, Hebr. iv. 12.

ἀρνέομαι, *to deny*, Matt. xxvi. 70. Joh. i. 20; *to renounce*, Tit. ii. 12; *to reject*, Acts, iii. 14. vii. 35.

ἀρνίον, τὸ, *a little lamb, a lamb*, Joh. xxi. 15. Rev. v. 6, 8, 12, 13.

ἀροτριάω, *to plough*, Luke, xvii. 7. 1 Cor. ix. 9.

ἄροτρον, τὸ, *a plough*, Luke, ix. 62.

ἁρπαγὴ, ἡ, *the plundering, the despoiling*, Hebr. x. 34; *extortion*, Matt. xxiii. 25. Luke, xi. 39.

ἁρπαγμὸς, ὁ, *a thing to be seized; an accidental acquisition*, Philipp. ii. 6. ("Quod quis non jure sed casu accipit= ἑρμαῖον, S. Paul. Philipp. ii. 6," Toup ad Long. *Subl.* iv. 5.)

ἁρπάζω, *to seize*, Joh. x. 12; *to take by force*, Matt. xi. 12. Joh. vi. 15. Acts, xxiii. 10. *to snatch away*, Matt. xiii. 19. Joh. x. 28. Acts, viii. 39; *to snatch out, to rescue*, Jude, 23.

ἅρπαξ, *ravenous,* Matt. vii. 15; *an extortioner,* Luke, xviii. 11. 1 Cor. v. 10. vi. 10.

ἀρραβών, ὁ, *an earnest, a pledge,* Ephes. i. 14. 2 Cor. i. 22. v. 5.

ἄρραφος: see ἄραφος.

ἄρρητος, *unspeakable,* 2 Cor. xii. 4.

ἄρρωστος, *without strength, sick,* Mrk. vi. 5, 13. xvi. 18.

ἀρσενοκοίτης, ὁ, *an abuser of himself with men,* 1 Cor. vi. 9. 1 Tim. i. 10.

ἄρσην, and ἄρρην, *male,* Matt. xix. 4. Gal. iii. 28.

ἀρτέμων, ὁ, *the foresail,* Acts, xxvii. 40.

ἄρτι, *just now,* Matt. ix. 18. 1 Thess. iii. 6; *at this time, now,* Joh. ix. 19, 25. xvi. 12, 31; ἄχρι τῆς ἄρτι ὥρας, *up to the present hour,* 1 Cor. iv. 11; ἕως ἄρτι, *until now,* Matt. xi. 12. Joh. ii. 10. ἀπ' ἄρτι: see ἀπάρτι.

ἀρτιγέννητος, *newly born,* 1 Pet. ii. 2.

ἄρτιος, *complete, perfect,* 2 Tim. iii. 17.

ἄρτος, ὁ, *a loaf, bread,* Matt. iv. 3. vii. 9.

ἀρτύω, *to season,* Mrk. ix. 50. Luke, xiv. 34. Coloss. iv. 6.

ἀρχάγγελος, ὁ, *an archangel,* 1 Thess. iv. 16. Jude, 9.

ἀρχαῖος, *ancient, old,* Luke, ix. 8, 19; οἱ ἀρχαῖοι, *the ancients, the early Israelites,* Matt. v. 21, 33.

ἀρχή, ἡ, *the beginning,* Joh. i. 1. Matt. xxiv. 21; *the first principles,* Hebr. v. 12. vi. 1; *the author,* Rev. iii. 18; *an extremity, a corner,* Acts, x. 11. xi. 5; *a magistrate, an authority,* Luke, xii. 11. xx. 20. Tit. iii. 1.

ἀρχηγός, ὁ, *a leader, a prince,* Acts, v. 31; *an author,* Acts, iii. 15. Hebr. ii. 10. xii. 2.

ἀρχιερατικὸς, *of the high-priest, high-priestly,* Acts, iv. 6.

ἀρχιερεύς, ὁ, *chief-priest,* Matt. xxvi. 3; *high priest,* Acts, iv. 6. Hebr. ii. 17.

ἀρχιποίμην, ὁ, *the chief shepherd,* 1 Pet. v. 4.

ἀρχισυνάγωγος, ὁ, *a ruler of the synagogue,* Luke, viii. 49. xiii. 14.

ἀρχιτέκτων, ὁ, *a master-builder,* 1 Cor. iii. 10.

ἀρχιτελώνης, ὁ, *a chief publican,* Luke, xix. 2.

ἀρχιτρίκλινος, ὁ, *the superintendent of a dining room,* Joh. ii. 8, 9. (RV *the ruler of the feast.*)

ἄρχω, *to rule over,* Rom. xv. 12. Mrk. x. 42; ἄρχομαι, *to begin,* Matt. xii. 1. Luke, xv. 14. 1 Pet. iv. 17.

ἄρχων, *a ruler, a chief,* Matt. xx. 25. Acts, vii. 27, 35. xxiii. 5.

ἄρωμα, τὸ, *spice,* Luke, xxiii. 56. xxiv. 1. Joh. xix. 40.

ἀσάλευτος, *unshaken, unmoved,* Acts, xxvii. 41; *firm, immovable,* Hebr. xii. 28.

ἄσβεστος, *unquenchable,* Matt. iii. 12. Luke, iii. 17. Mrk. ix. 43.

ἀσέβεια, ἡ, *ungodliness,* Rom. i. 18. xi. 26.

ἀσεβέω, *to be ungodly,* 2 Pet. ii. 6. Jude, 15.

ἀσεβής, *ungodly*, Rom. iv. 5.
v. 6. Jude, 4, 15.

ἀσέλγεια, ἡ, *wantonness, lasciviousness*, 2 Cor. xii. 21. Gal.
v. 19. Ephes. iv. 19.

ἄσημος, *of no mark, insignificant*, Acts, xxi. 39.

ἀσθένεια, ἡ, *weakness, infirmity*,
1 Cor. xv. 43. 2 Cor. xiii. 4;
sickness, Joh. xi. 4.

ἀσθενέω, *to be weak*, Rom. viii.
3. 2 Cor. xii. 10. xiii. 4; *to
be sick*, Matt. x. 8. Joh. vi. 2.
Mrk. vi. 56.

ἀσθένημα, τὸ, *infirmity*, Rom.
xv. 1.

ἀσθενής, *weak*, Mrk. xiv. 38.
Rom. v. 6; *sick*, Matt. xi. 39. Luke, x. 9. Acts, v. 15.

Ἀσιάρχης, ὁ, *an Asiarch, a
president of Asia*, a title
given under the Roman government
to the citizen annually
selected to preside
over the games to be exhibited
that year, Acts, xix.
31.

ἀσιτία, ἡ, *abstinence from food*,
Acts, xxvii. 21.

ἄσιτος, *without having eaten,
fasting*, Acts, xxvii. 33.

ἀσκέω, *to exercise oneself*, Acts,
xxiv. 16.

ἀσκὸς, ὁ, *a leather bottle, a wineskin*,
Matt. ix. 17. Luke, v.
37. Mrk. ii. 22.

ἀσμένως, *gladly*, Acts, xxi.
17.

ἄσοφος, *unwise, foolish*, Ephes.
v. 15.

ἀσπάζομαι, *to greet, to salute*,
Acts, xxi. 19. Matt. x. 12.
Luke, i. 40; *to welcome*,
Hebr. xi. 13.

ἀσπασμὸς, ὁ, *a salutation*, Luke,
i. 29, 41, 44. 1 Cor. xvi. 21.
2 Thess. iii. 17. Coloss. iv.
18.

ἄσπιλος, *without spot, spotless*,
1 Pet. i. 19. 1 Tim. vi. 14.
2 Pet. iii. 14; *unsullied*,
James, i. 27.

ἀσπὶς, ἡ, *an asp*, a species of
venomous serpent, Rom. iii.
13.

ἄσπονδος, *implacable*, 2 Tim.
iii. 3.

ἀσσάριον, τὸ, a dimin. of the
Roman *as*, and equal to the
tenth part of a drachma,
Matt. x. 29. Luke, xii. 6.
(The AV and RV render it
a farthing.)

ἆσσον, adv., *nearer*, a doubtful
reading ad Acts, xxvii. 13.
(RV *sailed along Crete, close
in shore*.)

ἀστατέω, *to be without a settled
abode*, 1 Cor. iv. 11. (RV
have no certain dwellingplace.)

ἀστεῖος, *comely, fair*, Hebr. xi.
23. Acts, vii. 20.

ἀστὴρ, ὁ, *a star*, Matt. ii. 2, 7,
9, 10. Rev. i. 16; ἀστέρες
πλανῆται, *wandering stars*,
Jude, 13. ("These are not
planets, but far more probably
comets, which Jude
regards as stars which have
left the course prescribed
them by God, and wander
about at will," Thayer.)

ἀστήρικτος, *unstable, unstedfast*,
2 Pet. ii. 14. iii. 16.

ἄστοργος, *without natural affection*,
Rom. i. 31. 2 Tim.
iii. 3.

ἀστοχέω, to deviate from, to miss, 1 Tim. i. 6; to err, 1 Tim. vi. 21. 2 Tim. ii. 18.

ἀστραπή, ἡ, lightning, Matt. xxiv. 27. Rev. iv. 5; brightness, Luke, xi. 36.

ἀστράπτω, to lighten, Luke, xvii. 24; to shine, Luke, xxiv. 4. (RV in dazzling apparel.)

ἄστρον, τό, a star, Luke, xxi. 25. Hebr. xi. 12.

ἀσύμφωνος, at variance, Acts, xxviii. 25.

ἀσύνετος, without understanding, Matt. xv. 16. Mrk. vii. 18; unintelligent, foolish, Rom. i. 21. x. 19.

ἀσύνθετος, not keeping their covenant, faithless, Rom. i. 31.

ἀσφάλεια, ἡ, safety, security, Acts, v. 23. 1 Thess. v. 3; certainty, Luke, i. 4.

ἀσφαλής, safe, Philipp. iii. 1; secure, firm, Hebr. vi. 19; certain, Acts, xxv. 26; τὸ ἀσφαλὲς, the certainty, Acts, xxi. 34. xxii. 30.

ἀσφαλίζομαι, to be made secure, Matt. xxvii. 64; mid., to make secure, to make fast, Acts, xvi. 24. Matt. xxvii. 65.

ἀσφαλῶς, adv., safely, Acts, xvi. 23. Mrk. xiv. 44; for a certainty, assuredly, Acts, ii. 36.

ἀσχημονέω, to act unbecomingly, 1 Cor. vii. 36. xiii. 5.

ἀσχημοσύνη, ἡ, unseemliness, Rom. i. 27; shame, nakedness, Rev. xvi. 15.

ἀσχήμων, uncomely, 1 Cor. xii. 23.

ἀσωτία, ἡ, profligacy, 1 Pet. iv. 4. Tit. i. 6. Ephes. v. 18.

ἀσώτως, adv., dissolutely, prodigally, Luke, xv. 13.

ἀτακτέω, to lead a disorderly life, 2 Thess. iii. 7.

ἄτακτος, disorderly, 1 Thess. v. 14.

ἀτάκτως, adv., in a disorderly manner, 2 Thess. iii. 6, 11.

ἄτεκνος, childless, Luke, xx. 28, 29.

ἀτενίζω, to fix the eyes upon, Luke, iv. 20. xxii. 56; to look stedfastly, Acts, i. 10. vii. 55.

ἄτερ, prepos., without, Luke, xxii. 6, 35.

ἀτιμάζω, to dishonour, Joh. viii. 49. Rom. ii. 23. Mrk. xii. 4.

ἀτιμάω, a var. lect. ad Mrk. xii. 4.

ἀτιμία, ἡ, dishonour, 1 Cor. xi. 14. xv. 43; κατ' ἀτιμίαν, with contempt, 2 Cor. xi. 21; εἰς ἀτιμίαν, for dishonourable use, Rom. ix. 21. 2 Tim. ii. 20; πάθη ἀτιμίας, vile passions, Rom. i. 26.

ἄτιμος, without honour, Matt. xiii. 57. Mrk. vi. 4; ἀτιμότερος, of less esteem, 1 Cor. xii. 23.

ἀτιμόω, a var. lect. ad Mrk. xii. 4. (See ἀτιμάζω and ἀτιμάω.)

ἀτμίς, ἡ, vapour, James, iv. 14. Acts, ii. 19.

ἄτομος, that cannot be cut, indivisible; ἐν ἀτόμῳ, in a moment, 1 Cor. xv. 52.

ἄτοπος, out of place; wrong, wicked, Acts, xxv. 5. Luke, xxiii. 41; unrighteous, 2

αὐγ] *GREEK-ENGLISH LEXICON* [ἀφα

Thess. iii. 2. (RV *unreasonable*) ; μηδὲν ἄτοπον, *no harm*, Acts, xxviii. 6.

αὐγάζω, *to shine forth*, 2 Cor. iv. 4.

αὐγὴ, ἡ, *brightness;* ἄχρι αὐγῆς, *till daylight*, Acts, xx. 11.

αὐθάδης, *self-willed*, Tit. i. 7. 2 Pet. ii. 10.

αὐθαίρετος, *voluntary; of one's own accord*, 2 Cor. viii. 3, 17.

αὐθεντέω, *to have dominion over, to govern*, 1 Tim. ii. 12.

αὐλέω, *to play on the flute, to pipe*, Matt. xi. 17. Luke, vii. 32. 1 Cor. xiv. 7.

αὐλή, ἡ, *a sheepfold*, Joh. x. 1, 16 ; *a court*, Rev. xi. 2. Matt. xxvi. 69. Luke, xxii. 55.

αὐλητὴς, ὁ, *a flute-player*, Matt. ix. 23. Rev. xviii. 22.

αὐλίζομαι, *to pass the night, to lodge*, Matt. xxi. 17. Luke, xxi. 37.

αὐλὸς, ὁ, *a flute, a pipe*, 1 Cor. xiv. 7.

αὐξάνω, *to cause to grow, to augment*, 1 Cor. iii. 6. 2 Cor. ix. 10 ; intrans., *to grow, to increase*, Acts, vi. 7. vii. 17. Matt. vi. 28. Joh. iii. 30 ; pass., *to grow, to increase, to become greater*, Matt. xiii. 32. Mrk. iv. 8. 2 Cor. x. 15. Coloss. i. 6, 10.

αὔξησις, ἡ, *increase*, Ephes. iv. 16. Coloss. ii. 19.

αὔριον, adv., *to-morrow*, Matt. vi. 30. Luke, xiii. 32 ; ἡ αὔριον (sc. ἡμέρα), *the morrow*, Matt. vi. 34 ; τῆς αὔριον, *on the morrow*, James, iv. 14.

αὐστηρὸς, *rigid, austere*, Luke, xix. 21, 22.

αὐτάρκεια, ἡ, *sufficiency*, 2 Cor. ix. 8 ; *contentment*, 1 Tim. vi. 6.

αὐτάρκης, *contented*, Philipp. iv. 11.

αὐτοκατάκριτος, *self-condemned*, Tit. iii. 11.

αὐτόματος, *spontaneous, of its own accord*, Acts, xii. 10. Mrk. iv. 28.

αὐτόπτης, ὁ, *an eye-witness*, Luke, i. 2.

αὐτὸς, *himself*, Joh. ii. 24. iv. 2 ; τὰ ἔργα αὐτά, or αὐτὰ τὰ ἔργα, *the works themselves*, Joh. v. 36. xiv. 11. (But τὰ αὐτὰ ἔργα, *the same works*. Cf. Matt. xxvii. 44) ; κατὰ τὸ αὐτὸ, or ἐπὶ τὸ αὐτὸ, *together*, Luke, xvii. 35. Acts, xiv. 1. 1 Cor. xi. 20 ; εἰς αὐτὸ τοῦτο, *for this very purpose*, Rom. ix. 17 ; αὐτοῦ, *there*, Acts, xviii. 19 ; *here*, Matt. xxvi. 36. (For αὑτοῦ, αὑτὸν etc., see ἑαυτοῦ, ἑαυτὸν etc.)

αὐτόφωρος, *caught in the act of theft;* hence ἐπ' αὐτοφώρῳ, *in the very act*, Joh. viii. 4.

αὐτόχειρ, *with his own hand*, Acts, xxvii. 19.

αὐχέω, *to boast*, James, iii. 5.

αὐχμηρὸς, *dirty ; dark*, 2 Pet. i. 19.

ἀφαιρέω, *to take away*, Luke, i. 25. x. 42. Rev. xxii. 19 ; *to cut off*, Matt. xxvi. 51. Luke, xxii. 50. Mrk. xiv. 47 ; ἀφαιρέομαι, *to take away*, Luke, xvi. 3. Rom. xi. 27.

ἀφανὴς, *not manifest, hidden* Hebr. iv. 13.

ἀφα] TO THE NEW TESTAMENT **[ἀφο**

ἀφανίζω, *to put out of sight; to destroy, to consume,* Matt. vi. 19; *to disfigure,* Matt. vi. 16; pass., *to perish,* Acts, xiii. 41; *to disappear, to vanish away,* James, iv. 14.

ἀφανισμὸς, ὁ, *destruction,* Hebr. viii. 13.

ἄφαντος, *out of sight, invisible;* ἄφαντος γενέσθαι, *to vanish,* Luke, xxiv. 31.

ἀφεδρῶν, ὁ, *a privy,* Matt. xv. 17. Mrk. vii. 19.

ἀφειδία, ἡ, *severity, unsparing treatment,* Coloss. ii. 23.

ἀφελότης, ἡ, *simplicity, singleness,* Acts, ii. 46. (Cf. Pape's Lex. in voc.)

ἄφεσις, ἡ, *release, deliverance,* Luke, iv. 18; *remission, forgiveness,* Matt. xxvi. 28. Acts, ii. 38. Ephes. i. 7.

ἀφὴ, ἡ, *a joint,* Coloss. ii. 19. Ephes. iv. 16.

ἀφθαρσία, ἡ, *incorruption,* 1 Cor. xv. 42, 53. Rom. ii. 7; *immortality,* 2 Tim. i. 10; *incorruptness,* a var. lect. ad Tit. ii. 7.

ἄφθαρτος, *incorruptible,* 1 Cor. ix. 25. xv. 52. 1 Pet. i. 4, 23. iii. 4; *immortal,* 1 Tim. i. 17. Rom. i. 23.

ἀφθορία, ἡ, *incorruptness,* Tit. ii. 7. (See ἀφθαρσία.)

ἀφίημι, *to give up, to yield up,* Matt. xxvii. 50; *to utter,* Mrk. xv. 37; *to pass over, to neglect,* Hebr. vi. 1; *to remit, to forgive,* Matt. ix. 2, 5. xviii. 27, 32; *to retain no longer, to desert,* Rev. ii. 4; *to give up, to surrender,* Matt. v. 40; *to leave,* Matt. xxii. 22. xxvi. 44. Joh. iv. 3. xvi. 28; *to leave behind, to leave* on dying, Matt. xxii. 25. Mrk. xii. 20; *to permit, to suffer,* Matt. iii. 15. xiii. 30. Mrk. x. 14.

ἀφικνέομαι, *to arrive at, to come to* the knowledge of, Rom. xvi. 19.

ἀφιλάγαθος, *not loving goodness,* 2 Tim. iii. 3. (Found only in this passage.)

ἀφιλάργυρος, *free from avarice,* Hebr. xiii. 5. 1 Tim. iii. 3. (It is a purely NT form.)

ἄφιξις, ἡ, *a departure,* Acts, xx. 29.

ἀφίστημι, *to cause to revolt, to draw away,* Acts, v. 37; intrans., *to depart,* Luke, xiii. 27. Acts, xii. 10. xix. 9; *to refrain,* Acts, v. 38. 2 Tim. ii. 19; mid., *to depart,* Luke, ii. 37; *to fall away,* Luke, viii. 13. 1 Tim. iv. 1.

ἄφνω, adv., *suddenly,* Acts, ii. 2. xvi. 26. xxviii. 6.

ἀφόβως, adv., *without fear, boldly,* Luke, i. 74. Jude, 12. 1 Cor. xvi. 10.

ἀφομοιόω, *to make like;* pass., *to be made like,* Hebr. vii. 3.

ἀφοράω, *to see in the distance; to see clearly,* Philipp. ii. 23; *to look towards,* Hebr. xii. 2.

ἀφορίζω, *to limit; to separate,* Gal. ii. 12. Acts, xix. 9. Matt. xxv. 32; *to set apart,* Acts, xiii. 2. Gal. i. 15; *to excommunicate,* Luke, vi. 22: pass., *to be separated,* 2 Cor. vi. 17; *to be set apart,* Rom. i. 1.

ἀφορμή, ἡ, *an occasion*, Rom. vii. 8, 11. Gal. v. 13. 2 Cor. v. 12. 1 Tim. v. 14.

ἀφρίζω, *to foam*, Mrk. ix. 18, 20.

ἀφρός, ὁ, *foam*, Luke, ix. 39.

ἀφροσύνη, ἡ, *foolishness*, 2 Cor. xi. 1, 17, 21. Mrk. vii. 22.

ἄφρων, *senseless, foolish*, Luke, xi. 40. xii. 20.

ἀφυπνόω, *to fall asleep*, Luke, viii. 23.

ἀφυστερέω, *to keep back by fraud*, James, v. 4.

ἄφωνος, *dumb*, Acts, viii. 32. 2 Pet. ii. 16. 1 Cor. xii. 2; *unmeaning*, 1 Cor. xiv. 10.

ἀχάριστος, *unthankful*, Luke, vi. 35. 2 Tim. iii. 2.

ἀχειροποίητος, *not made with hands*, 2 Cor. v. 1. Coloss. ii. 11.

ἀχλύς, ἡ, *a mist*, Acts, xiii. 11.

ἀχρεῖος, *unprofitable*, Luke, xvii. 10. Matt. xxv. 30.

ἀχρειόω, *to make unprofitable*, Rom. iii. 12.

ἄχρηστος, *unprofitable*, Philem. 11.

ἄχρι, and ἄχρις, *even to, up to, until*; ἄχρι ἧς ἡμέρας, *up to the day that*, Matt. xxiv. 38. Luke, i. 20 ; ἄχρις οὗ, *until*, Acts, vii. 18 ; ἄχρι καιροῦ, *for a season*, Acts, xiii. 11. Luke, iv. 13.

ἄχυρον, τὸ, *chaff*, Matt. iii. 12. Luke, iii. 17.

ἀψευδής, *truthful*, Tit. i. 2.

ἄψινθος, ὁ and ἡ, *wormwood*, Rev. viii. 11.

ἄψυχος, *without life*, 1 Cor. xiv. 7.

B.

Βαάλ, indecl., *Baal*, the name of the pagan deity worshipped by the Canaanites, Phoenicians, Babylonians and others, and generally identified with the *Sun God*, Rom. xi. 4. (See also Βεελζεβούβ and Βεελζεβούλ.)

βαθέως, adv., *deeply*; ὄρθρου βαθέως, *at early dawn*, Luke, xxiv. 1. (But this form is not recognized at all in Pape's Lexicon, and βαθέως here is generally taken as the genitive of βαθύς.)

βαθμός, ὁ, *a step; position, rank*, 1 Tim. iii. 13.

βάθος, τὸ, *depth*, Matt. xiii. 5. Rom. viii. 39 ; ἡ κατὰ βάθους πτωχεία αὐτῶν, *their deep poverty*, 2 Cor. viii. 2 ; τὰ βάθη τοῦ θεοῦ, *the deep things of God*, 1 Cor. ii. 10.

βαθύνω, *to make deep*; ἔσκαψε καὶ ἐβάθυνε, *digged deep*, Luke, vi. 48. (RV *digged and went deep*.)

βαθύς, *deep*, Joh. iv. 11 ; met., βαθὺς ὕπνος, *a deep sleep*, Acts, xx. 9 ; ὄρθρος βαθύς, *early dawn*: see βαθέως.

βαΐον, τὸ, *a palm branch*, Joh. xii. 13. (Hence ἡ κυριακὴ τῶν βαΐων, *Palm Sunday*.)

βαλλάντιον, and βαλάντιον, τὸ, *a purse*, Luke, x. 4. xii. 33. xxii. 35.

βάλλω, *to cast*, Joh. viii. 7, 59. Matt. iv. 18 ; *to send*, Matt. x. 34 ; *to put, to insert*, Joh. xx. 25, 27. Mrk. vii. 33 ; *to thrust in*, Rev. xiv. 19 ; *to pour,* Joh. xiii. 5. Matt. ix. 17; intrans., *to rush,* Acts, xxvii. 6; pass., *to lie,* Matt. viii. 6. ix. 2. Mrk. vii. 30; *to be cast down,* Rev. xii. 10.

βαπτίζω, *to wash; to cleanse; to baptize,* Mrk. i. 4. Joh. i. 25, 28; pass., *to wash,* Luke, xi. 38; mid., *to receive baptism,* Acts, xxii. 16.

βάπτισμα, τὸ, *baptism,* Matt. iii. 7. xxi 25. Ephes. iv. 5.

βαπτισμὸς, ὁ, *a washing,* Mrk. vii. 4. Hebr. vi. 2. ix. 10.

βαπτιστὴς, ὁ, *one who baptizes; the Baptist,* Matt. iii. 1. xi. 11. Mrk. vi. 25. viii. 28.

βάπτω, *to dip,* Luke, xvi. 24. Joh. xiii. 26; *to dye,* a var. lect. ad Rev. xix. 13.

βάρβαρος, *a foreigner,* 1 Cor. xiv. 11; *a barbarian,* Coloss. iii. 11. Rom. i. 14. Acts, xxviii. 2, 4.

βαρέω, *to weigh down;* in the NT used only in the pass.; βεβαρημένος, *weighed down,* Matt. xxvi. 43. Luke, ix. 32. 2 Cor. l. 8; βαρεῖσθαι, *to be burdened,* 1 Tim. v. 16. 2 Cor. v. 4; βαρηθῶσιν, *be overpowered,* Luke, xxi. 34. (RV *overcharged.*)

βαρέως, *heavily, with difficulty,* Matt. xiii. 15. Acts, xxviii. 27.

βάρος, τὸ, *a weight,* 2 Cor. iv. 17; ἐν βάρει, *in authority,* 1 Thess. ii. 6. (RV *might have been burdensome*); *a burden,* Matt. xx. 12. Gal. vi. 2. Acts, xv. 28. Rev. ii. 24. ("The meaning of the last passage is, *I put upon you no other injunction which it might be difficult to observe,*" Thayer.,

βαρύνω, *to weigh down,* a var. lect. ad Luke, xxi. 34.

βαρὺς, *heavy,* Matt. xxiii. 4; *burdensome,* 1 Joh. v. 3; *grievous,* Acts, xx. 29. xxv. 7; *weighty,* 2 Cor. x. 10. Matt. xxiii. 23.

βαρύτιμος, *very costly,* Matt. xxvi. 7.

βασανίζω, *to test; to vex, to torment,* Matt. viii. 29. Luke, viii. 28. 2 Pet. ii. 8; pass., *to be tormented,* Matt. viii. 6. Rev. ix. 5; *to be distressed,* Matt. xiv. 24. Mrk. vi. 48.

βασανισμὸς, ὁ, *a testing; torment,* Rev. ix. 5. xiv. 11. xviii. 7, 10.

βασανιστὴς, ὁ, *a torturer, a tormentor,* Matt. xviii. 34. (Thayer, *a jailer.*)

βάσανος, ἡ, *the touchstone; grievous pain,* Matt. iv. 24; *torment,* Luke, xvi. 23, 28.

βασιλεία, ἡ, *a kingdom,* Matt. iv. 23. xii. 25; *kingship,* Luke, i. 33.

βασίλειος, *royal,* 1 Pet. ii. 9; τὰ βασίλεια, *palaces,* Luke, vii. 25.

βασιλεὺς, ὁ, *a king,* Matt. xvii. 25. Luke, xxii. 25.

βασιλεύω, *to be king; to reign over,* Matt. ii. 22; *to reign,* Rom. v. 14, 17, 21.

βασιλικὸς, *kingly, royal,* Acts, xii. 21. James, ii. 8; *belonging to the king,* Acts, xii. 20; *a courtier,* Joh. iv. 46. (RV *a nobleman.*)

βασίλισσα, ἡ, *a queen,* Matt. xii. 42. Acts, viii. 27.

βάσις, ἡ, *the foot*, Acts, iii. 7.
βασκαίνω, *to bewitch; to deceive*, Gal. iii. 1.
βαστάζω, *to take up*, Joh. x. 31; *to carry, to bear*, Mrk. xiv. 13. Luke, xiv. 27; *to carry off*, Matt. viii. 17; *to endure*, Joh. xvi. 12. Gal. vi. 5. Acts, xv. 10; *to support, to sustain*, Rom. xi. 18; *to spread abroad* by preaching, Acts, ix. 15.
βάτος, ὁ and ἡ, *a bramble, a thorn*, Luke, vi. 44; *a thorn-bush*, Acts, vii. 30, 35. (at the episode) *of the bush*, Luke, xx. 37. Mrk. xii. 26.
βάτος, ὁ, *a bath*, a Jewish liquid measure, Luke, xvi. 6. (About 8 or 9 gallons.)
βάτραχος, ὁ, *a frog*, Rev. xvi. 13.
βατρολογέω, and **βατταλογέω**, *to use vain repetitions*, Matt. vi. 7. ("Of kindred origin with βατταρίζω," Pape.)
βδέλυγμα, τὸ, *an abominable thing, an abomination*, Luke, xvi. 15. Matt. xxiv. 15. Rev. xvii. 4, 5. xxi. 27.
βδελυκτὸς, *abominable*, Tit. i. 16.
βδελύσσω, *to defile*; βδελύσσομαι, *to detest, to abhor*, Rom. ii. 22; ἐβδελυγμένος, *abominable*, Rev. xxi. 8. ("The Active only in ecclesiastical writers," Pape.)
βέβαιος, *firm, stedfast*, Hebr. iii. 14. vi. 19. 2 Cor. i. 7; *sure, trustworthy*, Rom. iv. 16. 2 Pet. i. 19. Hebr. ii. 2; *in force, valid*, Hebr. ix. 17.
βεβαιόω, *to make stedfast*, 1 Cor. i. 8. 2 Cor. i. 21. Hebr. xiii. 9; *to confirm*, Mrk. xvi. 20. Rom. xv. 8. 1 Cor. i. 6.
βεβαίωσις, ἡ, *confirmation*, Philipp. i. 7. Hebr. vi. 16.
βέβηλος, *profane*, 1 Tim. iv. 7. vi. 20. 2 Tim. ii. 16; *ungodly*, 1 Tim. i. 9. Hebr. xii. 16.
βεβηλόω, *to profane*, Matt. xii. 5. Acts. xxiv. 6.
Βεελζεβοὺβ, and **Βεελζεβοὺλ**, ὁ, indecl., *Beelzebub*, or *Beelzebul*, a name of Satan, the prince of evil spirits, Matt. x. 25. xii. 24, 27. The form Βεελζεβοὺβ = *lord of flies*, but the Israelites, to shew their detestation of him, are said to have turned the name into βεελζεβοὺλ = *lord of excrement*.
βελόνη, ἡ, *a needle*, Luke, xviii. 25.
βέλος, τὸ, *a missile, a dart*, Ephes. vi. 16.
βελτίων, *better*; βέλτιον, adverbially, 2 Tim. i. 18. (AV and RV *very well*.)
βῆμα, τὸ, *a step*; βῆμα ποδὸς, *a foot-breadth*, Acts, vii. 5; *the judgment-seat*, Joh. xix. 13. Rom. xiv. 10. 2 Cor. v. 10; *the rostrum*, Acts, xii. 21. (AV and RV *throne*.)
βήρυλλος, ἡ, *the beryl*, a precious stone of a pale green colour, Rev. xxi. 20.
βία, ἡ, *force, violence*, Acts, v. 26. xxvii. 41.
βιάζω, *to use force;* pass., *to be taken by storm*, Matt. xi. 12; mid., *to force their way*, Luke, xvi. 16.
βίαιος, *violent*, Acts, ii. 2.
βιαστὴς, ὁ, *a violent man*, Matt. xi. 12.

βιβλαρίδιον, τό, *a little book*, Rev. x. 2, 9, 10.

βιβλιδάριον, τό, *a little book*, a var. lect. ad Rev. x. 8.

βιβλίον, τό, *a scroll, a small book*, Luke, iv. 17, 20. Joh. xx. 30. Gal. iii. 10 ; *a written document*; βιβλίον ἀποστασίου, *a bill of divorcement*, Matt. xix. 7. Mrk. x. 4 ; τὸ βιβλίον ζωῆς, *the book of life*, Rev. xiii. 8. xvii. 8.

βίβλος, ἡ, *a book*, Luke, iii. 4. Mrk. xii. 26. Acts, i. 20; ἡ βίβλος τῆς ζωῆς, *the book of life*, Rev. iii. 5. Philipp. iv. 3.

βιβρώσκω, *to eat*, Joh. vi. 13.

βίος, ὁ, *life*, Luke, viii. 14 ; *substance, living*, Mrk. xii. 44. Luke, xv. 12, 30; *goods*, 1 Joh. iii. 17.

βιόω, *to live*; βιῶσαι χρόνον, *to spend the time*, 1 Pet. iv. 2.

βίωσις, ἡ, *manner of living*, Acts, xxvi. 4. (It is a purely ecclesiastical word.)

βιωτικὸς, *pertaining to this life*, Luke, xxi. 34. 1 Cor. vi. 3.

βλαβερὸς, *hurtful*, 1 Tim. vi. 9.

βλάπτω, *to hurt, to injure*, Matt. xvi. 18. Luke, iv. 35.

βλαστάνω, *to spring up*, Matt. xiii. 26. Mrk. iv. 27 ; *to sprout, to bud*, Hebr. ix. 4.

βλασφημέω, *to speak blasphemy, to blaspheme*, Acts, xxvi. 11. 1 Tim. i. 20 ; *to revile*, Matt. xxvii. 39. Luke, xxii. 65; pass., *to be evil spoken of*, Rom. xiv. 16. 1 Cor. x. 30. 2 Pet. ii. 2.

βλασφημία, ἡ, *blasphemy*, Matt. xii. 31. xxvi. 65. Mrk. iii. 28 ; *railing, reviling*, Matt. xv. 19. Mrk. vii. 22.

βλάσφημος, *slanderous, blasphemous*, Acts, vi. 11. 2 Pet. ii. 11; as subst., *a blasphemer*, 1 Tim. i. 13. 2 Tim. iii. 2.

βλέμμα, τό, *sight ;* βλέμματι καὶ ἀκοῇ, *in seeing and hearing*, 2 Pet. ii. 8.

βλέπω, *to be possessed of sight, to see*, Matt. xiii. 16. xv. 31 ; *to look upon*, Matt. v. 28 ; *to take care*, 1 Cor. viii. 9. xvi. 10. Matt. xxiv. 4 ; βλέπειν ἀπὸ, *to beware of*, Mrk. viii. 15. xii. 38; of places, *to look towards, to face*, Acts, xxvii. 12.

βλητέος, *to be put*, Luke, v. 38.

βοάω, *to cry aloud*, Matt. iii. 3. Gal. iv. 27 ; *to cry for help*, Luke, xviii. 7.

βοή, ἡ, *a cry*, James, v. 4.

βοήθεια, ἡ, *help*, Hebr. iv. 16. Acts, xxvii. 17.

βοηθέω, *to help, to succour*, Matt. xv. 25. Mrk. ix. 22, 24.

βοηθὸς, *helping ;* as subst., *a helper*, Hebr. xiii. 6.

βόθυνος, ὁ, *a ditch, a pit*, Matt. xii. 11. xv. 14.

βολή, ἡ, *a cast, a throw ;* ὡσεὶ λίθου βολήν, *about a stone's throw*, Luke, xxii. 41.

βολίζω, *to take soundings*, Acts, xxvii. 28.

βολὶς, ἡ, *a dart*, a var. lect. ad Hebr. xii. 20.

βόρβορος, ὁ, *dung, mire*, 2 Pet. ii. 22.

βορρᾶς, ὁ, *the north-west wind ; the north*, Luke, xiii. 29. Rev. xxi. 13.

βόσκω, *to feed*, Luke, xv. 15. Joh. xxi. 15, 17; ὁ βόσκων, *the herdsman*, Matt. viii. 33. Luke, viii. 34; βόσκομαι, *to graze, to feed*, Mrk. v. 11. Matt. xii. 30.

βοτάνη, ἡ, *a plant, an herb*, Hebr. vi. 7.

βότρυς, ὁ, *a cluster* of grapes, Rev. xiv. 18.

βουλευτής, ὁ, *a senator, a councillor*, Mrk. xv. 43. Luke, xxiii. 50.

βουλεύομαι, *to deliberate, to consider*, Luke, xiv. 31; *to take counsel*, Joh. xi. 53. Acts, xxvii. 39; *to purpose*, Acts, v. 33. xv. 37.

βουλή, ἡ, *counsel*, Luke, xxiii. 51. Acts, v. 38; *purpose*, Acts, xx. 27.

βούλημα, τό, *counsel, purpose*, Acts, xxvii. 43; *will*, Rom. ix. 19.

βούλομαι, *to will*, James, i. 18. 1 Cor. ii. 11; *to purpose, to be minded*, Matt. i. 19. Acts, v. 33. xviii. 27. xix. 30; *to desire*, 1 Tim. vi. 9. Acts, xvii. 20.

βουνός, ὁ, *a hill*, Luke, iii. 5. xxiii. 30.

βοῦς, ὁ and ἡ, *an ox, a cow*, Joh. ii. 14. Luke, xiii. 15.

βραβεῖον, τό, *the prize*, 1 Cor. ix. 24. Philipp. iii. 14.

βραβεύω, *to be an umpire; to rule*, Coloss. iii. 15.

βραδύνω, *to retard;* intrans., *to be slow, to linger*, 1 Tim. iii. 15; οὐ βραδύνει τῆς ἐπαγγελίας, *is not slack as regards his promise*, 2 Pet. iii. 9.

βραδυπλοέω, *to sail slowly*, Acts, xxvii. 7.

βραδύς, *slow*, James, i. 19; *dull*, Luke, xxiv. 25.

βραδυτής, ἡ, *slowness, slackness*, 2 Pet. iii. 9.

βραχίων, ὁ, *the arm*, Luke, i. 51. Acts, xiii. 17; *power, might*, Joh. xii. 38.

βραχύς, *short, little;* βραχὺ, *a little*, Joh. vi. 7; διὰ βραχέων, *briefly*, Hebr. xiii. 22; βραχὺ, *a short distance*, Acts, xxvii. 28; βραχύ τι, *for a short while*, Hebr. ii. 7, 9. Cf. Acts, v. 34; μετὰ βραχὺ, *shortly after*, Luke, xxii. 58.

βρέφος, τό, *an unborn child*, Luke, i. 41, 44; *a newborn child, an infant*, Luke, ii. 12, 16. Acts, vii. 19; ἀπὸ βρέφους, *from childhood*, 2 Tim. iii. 15.

βρέχω, *to wet*, Luke, vii. 38; *to send rain*, Matt. v. 45; impers., *to rain*, James, v. 17. Luke, xvii. 29; with subject (ὑετὸς) added, Rev. xi. 6.

βροντή, ἡ, *thunder*, Mrk. iii. 17. Joh. xii. 29. Rev. iv. 5.

βροχή, ἡ, *rain*, Matt. vii. 25, 27.

βρόχος, ὁ, *a noose, a constraint*, 1 Cor. vii. 35.

βρυγμός, ὁ, *a gnashing* of teeth, Luke, xiii. 28. Matt. viii. 12. xiii. 42, 50.

βρύχω, *to gnash* the teeth, Acts, vii. 54.

βρύω, *to gush forth;* trans., *to send forth*, James, iii. 11.

βρῶμα, τό, *food, meat*, 1 Cor. viii. 8, 13. x. 3. Joh. iv. 34.

Rom. xiv. 15, 20; βρώματα καὶ πόματα, *meats and drinks*, Hebr. ix. 10.

βρώσιμος, *eatable*, Luke. xxiv. 41.

βρῶσις, ἡ, *eating*, Rom. xiv. 17; *food*, Joh. iv. 32. vi. 27. 2 Cor. ix. 10. Coloss. ii. 16; *rust*, Matt. vi. 19.

βυθίζω, *to cause to sink, to plunge*, 1 Tim. vi. 9; pass., ὥστε βυθίζεσθαι αὐτά, *so that they began to sink*, Luke, v. 7.

βυθός, ὁ, *the deep; the deep sea*, 2 Cor. xi. 25.

βυρσεὺς, ὁ, *a tanner*, Acts, ix. 43. x. 6, 32.

βύσσινος, *made of fine linen*; βύσσινον (sc. ἱμάτιον), *fine linen*, Rev. xviii. 12, 16. xix. 8, 14.

βύσσος, ἡ, *byssus*, a species of Egyptian flax; *fine linen*, Luke, xvi. 19.

βωμὸς, ὁ, *an altar*, Acts, xvii. 23. (Found no where else in the NT. The ecclesiastical word is θυσιαστήριον.)

Γ

γάγγραινα, ἡ, *a gangrene*, 2 Tim. ii. 17.

γάζα, ἡ, *a treasure*, Acts, viii. 27. ("A Persian word," Pape.)

γαζοφυλάκιον, τὸ, *the treasury*, Mrk. xii. 41, 43. Luke, xxi. 1. Joh. viii. 20.

γάλα, τὸ, *milk*, 1 Cor. ix. 7; met., of *the more elementary doctrines* of Christianity, 1 Cor. iii. 2. Hebr. v. 12. 1 Pet. ii. 2. (Cf. βρῶμα.)

γαλήνη, ἡ, *a calm*, Matt. viii. 26. Luke, viii. 24.

γαμέω, *to take to wife, to marry*, Matt. v. 32. xix. 9; γαμέομαι, of the woman, *to give herself in marriage, to marry*, 1 Cor. vii. 39; γαμέω, for γαμέομαι, of the woman, 1 Tim. v. 11. 1 Cor. vii. 28, 34.

γαμίζω, *to give in marriage*, 1 Cor. vii. 38; γαμίζομαι, *to be given in marriage*, Luke, xvii. 27. xx. 35.

γαμίσκω=γαμίζω, a var. lect. ad Matt. xxiv. 38; γαμίσκομαι=γαμίζομαι, Luke, xx. 34.

γάμος, ὁ, *marriage, matrimony*, Hebr. xiii. 4; *a marriage-feast*, kept on the third day after the marriage, the Lat. *Repotia*, Joh. ii. 1. (See Toup ad Longin. *Subl.* iv. 5.)

γὰρ, a postpositive conjunction, *for*. (The reader is referred to his Greek Grammar.)

γαστὴρ, ἡ, *the belly; the womb*, Matt. i. 18, 23. Luke, xxi. 23; *a glutton*, Tit. i. 12.

γὲ, an enclitic, throwing an emphasis on the word to which it is subjoined; when used in the *second* clause of a sentence = *at least*. (For further information the reader is referred to his Greek Grammar.)

γέεννα, ἡ, *gehenna*, the valley of Hinnom, south of Jerusalem, formerly the scene of the worship of Moloch; in later times the name was transferred to *the place of* *punishment* in Hades, Matt. v. 22, 29. x. 28. Luke, xii. 5. Mrk. ix. 43, 45.

γείτων, ὁ and ἡ, *a neighbour*, Luke, xv. 6, 9. Joh. ix. 8.

γελάω, *to laugh*, Luke, vi. 21, 25.

γέλως, ὁ, *laughter*, James, iv. 9.

γεμίζω, *to fill*, Joh. ii. 7. vi. 13. Mrk. xv. 36.

γέμω, *to be full*, Matt. xxiii. 25, 27. Luke, xi. 39. Rom. iii. 14.

γενεά, ἡ, *a generation*, Matt. i. 17. xvii. 17. Luke, vii. 31; *an age*, Ephes. iii. 5. Acts, xiv. 16. xv. 21.

γενεαλογέω, *to trace the descent;* pass., *to derive one's genealogy*, Hebr. vii. 6.

γενεαλογία, ἡ, *a genealogy*, 1 Tim. i. 4. Tit. iii. 9.

γενέσια, τὰ, *a birthday celebration*, Matt. xiv. 6. Mrk. vi. 21.

γένεσις, ἡ, *lineage, descent*, Matt. i. 1; *nativity, birth*, Matt. i. 18. Luke, i. 14; met., τὸ πρόσωπον τῆς γενέσεως αὐτοῦ, *his natural face*, James, i. 23; *existence, life;* ὁ τροχὸς τῆς γενέσεως, *the course of life*, James, iii. 6.

γενετή, ἡ, *birth*, Joh. ix. 1.

γένημα, τὸ, the NT form of γέννημα, *offspring*, Matt. iii. 7. xii. 34; (Westcott reads γεννήματα in both passages); *fruit*, Matt. xxvi. 29. Mrk. xiv. 25. Luke, xxii. 18; met., *fruit, profit*, 2 Cor. ix. 10. (The form γένημα is not recognized in Pape's Lexicon. See γέννημα.)

γεννάω, *to beget*, Matt. i. 16. Acts, vii. 8, 29; *to cause, to excite*, 2 Tim. ii. 23; of the woman, *to bear, to bring forth*, Luke, i. 13, 57. xxiii. 29; pass., *to be begotten*, Matt. i. 20; *to be born*, Matt. ii. 1, 4. Joh. ix. 2, 19, 32.

γέννημα, τὸ, see γένημα.

γέννησις, ἡ, a var. lect. ad Matt. i. 18. Luke, i. 14. (See γένεσις.)

γεννητός, *born*, Matt. xi. 11. Luke, vii. 28.

γένος, τὸ, *offspring*, Acts, xvii. 28. Rev. xxii. 16; *family, kindred*, Acts, iv. 6; *race, stock*, 1 Pet. ii. 9. Acts, vii. 13. xiii. 26. Philipp. iii. 5; *nation*, 2 Cor. xi. 26. Gal. i. 14; *nationality*, Mrk. vii. 26. Acts, iv. 36. xviii. 2, 24; *sort, kind*, 1 Cor. xii. 10, 28. xiv. 10. Matt. xiii. 47. Mrk. ix. 29.

γερουσία, ἡ, *the Senate, the Sanhedrim* of the Jews, Acts, v. 21.

γέρων, ὁ, *an old man*, Joh. iii. 4.

γεύω, *to cause to taste;* in the NT only in the mid., *to taste*, Joh. ii. 9. Matt. xxvii. 34; *to take food, to eat*, Acts, x. 10. xx. 11. xxiii. 14; met., *to experience, to feel*, Matt. xvi. 28. Luke, ix. 27. Mrk. ix. 1.

γεωργέω, *to till* the ground, Hebr. vi. 7.

γεώργιον, τὸ, *a field*, 1 Cor. iii. 9. (RV *husbandry*.)

γεωργός, ὁ, *a husbandman*, 2 Tim. ii. 6. James, v. 7.

γῆ, ἡ, *earth, ground*, Mrk. iv.
8, 20, 26, 28, 31. Matt. xii.
5, 8, 23; *the earth*, Ephes. i.
10. Matt. v. 18, 35; *the
land*, Mrk. iv. 1. vi. 47, Luke,
v. 3; *country*, Acts, vii. 3.
γῆρας, τὸ, *old age*, Luke, i. 36.
γηράσκω, and γηράω, *to grow
old*, Joh. xxi. 18. Hebr. viii.
13.
γίνομαι, a later form for γίγ-
νομαι, *to become, to be, to
exist*, Joh. i. 15, 30. viii. 58.
1 Cor. xv. 37; *to be born*,
Rom. i. 3. Gal. iv. 4; *to
arise, to ensue*, Matt. viii. 26.
Rev. viii. 5. xvi. 18; *to take
place, to happen*, Matt. i. 22.
xxi. 4. xxvi. 56; μὴ γένοιτο,
far be it! God forbid! Rom.
iii. 4, 6, 31; *to come forth,
to appear*, Mrk. i. 4. 2 Pet.
ii. 1. 1 Joh. ii. 18; *to be
done, to be wrought*, Acts, ii.
43. iv. 30; γίνεσθαι ἐν ἑαυτῷ,
to come to himself, Acts, xii.
11.
γινώσκω, a later form for γιγ-
νώσκω, *to know*, Luke, xii.
47. xvi. 15; *to understand*,
Acts, viii. 30. Luke, xviii.
34; *to perceive*, Mrk. v. 29.
Luke, viii. 46; *to resolve*,
Luke, xvi. 4; *to know* car-
nally, Matt. i. 25. Luke, i.
34.
γλεῦκος, τὸ, *must, new wine*,
Acts, ii. 13.
γλυκὺς, *sweet*, James, iii. 11.
Rev. x. 9, 10.
γλῶσσα, ἡ, *the tongue*, James,
i. 26. iii. 5, 6, 8. 1 Cor. xiv.
9; *a language*, Acts, ii. 11.
1 Cor. xii. 10, 28.

γλωσσόκομον, τὸ, *a money-box,
a purse*, Joh. xii. 6. xiii. 29.
γναφεὺς, ὁ, *a fuller*, Mrk. ix.
3.
γνήσιος, *sincere;* τὸ τῆς ἀγάπης
γνήσιον, *the sincerity of your
love*, 2 Cor. viii. 8; *true*,
Philipp. iv. 3. 1 Tim. i. 2.
Tit. i. 4.
γνησίως, *sincerely, faithfully*,
Philipp. ii. 20.
γνόφος, ὁ, *gloom, blackness*,
Hebr. xii. 18.
γνώμη, ἡ, *opinion*, 1 Cor. vii.
25, 40. 2 Cor. viii. 10; *judgment*, 1 Cor. i. 10; *mind*,
Rev. xvii. 17; *consent*, Philem.
14; *determination*, Acts, xx.
3.
γνωρίζω, *to make known*, 1 Cor.
xv. 1. Ephes. i. 9. Joh. xv.
15; *to know*, Philipp. i. 22;
pass., *to be made known*,
Acts, vii. 13. Rom. xvi. 26.
Philipp. iv. 6.
γνῶσις, ἡ, *knowledge*, Luke, i.
77. 2 Cor. ii. 14. iv. 6.
γνώστης, ὁ, *one who thoroughly
understands, an expert*, Acts,
xxvi. 3.
γνωστὸς, *known*, Acts, i. 19. ix.
42. Joh. xviii. 15; *notable*,
Acts, iv. 16; τὸ γνωστὸν,
what is cognizable, Rom. i.
19; οἱ γνωστοὶ, *acquaintance*,
Luke, ii. 44. xxiii. 49.
γογγύζω, *to murmur*, 1 Cor. x.
10. Matt. xx. 11. Joh. vi. 41,
43, 61; *to privately discuss*,
Joh. vii. 32.
γογγυσμὸς, ὁ, *a murmuring*,
Philipp. ii. 14. 1 Pet. iv. 9.
Act. vi. 1; *private discussion*,
Joh. vii. 12.

γογγυστὴς, ὁ, *a murmurer*, Jude, 16.

γόης, ὁ, *an impostor*, 2 Tim. iii. 13.

γόμος, ὁ, *the cargo* of a ship, Acts, xxi. 3; *merchandise*, Rev. xviii. 11.

γονεύς, ὁ, *a parent*, Luke, ii. 41, 43. Joh. ix. 2, 3, 20, 22.

γόνυ, τὸ, *the knee*, Luke, v. 8. Hebr. xii. 12; τιθέναι τὰ γόνατα, *to kneel down*, Luke, xxii. 41. Acts, vii. 60; κάμπτειν γόνυ, *to bow the knee*, Rom. xi. 4. Philipp. ii. 10.

γονυπετέω, *to fall on the knees, to kneel before one*, Matt. xvii. 14. xxvii. 29. Mrk. x. 17.

γράμμα, τὸ, *a letter*, Gal. vi. 11; *a bill* or *bond*, Luke, xvi. 6; *an epistle*, Acts, xxviii. 21; τὰ ἱερὰ γράμματα=*the Scriptures*, 2 Tim. iii. 15 (Westcott omits τά); *the létter*, i.e. *the written law*, Rom. ii. 27, 29. vii. 6. 2 Cor. iii. 6; γράμματα, *learning*, Acts, xxvi. 24. Joh. vii. 15.

γραμματεύς, ὁ, *a clerk*, Acts, xix. 35, (RV *town-clerk*); *one learned in the Mosaic law, a scribe*, Matt. xxiii. 34. 1 Cor. i. 20. Cf. Matt. ii. 4. xiii. 52.

γραπτὸς, *written*, Rom. ii. 15.

γραφή, ἡ, *a writing*; πᾶσα γραφὴ *every Scripture*, 2 Tim. iii. 16; plur., γραφαὶ ἅγιαι, *the Holy Scriptures*, Rom. i. 2. Cf. Rom. xvi. 26. Matt. xxvi. 56; so also ἡ γραφὴ, *the Scripture*, Rom. ix. 17. Gal. iv. 30.

γράφω, *to write*, Joh. viii. 8. Gal. vi. 11; *to commit to writing, to record*, Rev. i. 11, 19. xvii. 8.

γραώδης, *old-womanish*, 1 Tim. iv. 7.

γρηγορέω, *to watch*, Matt. xxiv. 43. xxvi. 38, 40; *to be cautious, to be watchful*, 1 Pet. v. 8. Rev. iii. 2. 1 Thess. v. 6. 1 Cor. xvi. 13; *to be alive, to live*, 1 Thess. v. 10.

γυμνάζω, *to exercise*, 1 Tim. iv. 7; γεγυμνασμένος, *exercised*, Hebr. v. 14. xii. 11; καρδίαν γεγυμνασμένην πλεονεξίας, *a heart trained in covetousness*, 2 Pet. ii. 14.

γυμνασία, ἡ, *exercise*, 1 Tim. iv. 8.

γυμνητεύω, *to be poorly clad*, 1 Cor. iv. 11.

γυμνὸς, *naked*, Mrk. xiv. 52. Rev. xvi. 15; τὸ γυμνὸν, *the naked body*, Mrk. xiv. 51; *poorly clad*, Matt. xxv. 38, 43, 44. James, ii. 15; *without the outer garment*, Joh. xxi. 7; of the soul, *without a body*, 2 Cor. v. 3; *uncovered*, Hebr. iv. 13; *mere, bare*, 1 Cor. xv. 37.

γυμνότης, ἡ, *nakedness*, Rev. iii. 18; *want of clothing*, Rom. viii. 35. 2 Cor. xi. 27.

γυναικάριον, *a silly woman*, 2 Tim. iii. 6.

γυναικεῖος, *belonging to a woman, female*, 1 Pet. iii. 7.

γυνή, ἡ, *a woman*, Matt. ix. 20. xiii. 33; *a wife*, 1 Cor. vii. 3, 10. Ephes. v. 22.

γωνία, ἡ, *a corner*, Matt. vi. 5. xxi. 42. Luke, xx. 17; *an*

δαι]   TO THE NEW TESTAMENT   [δει

extreme limit, Rev. vii. 1. xx. 8; *a secret place*, Acts, xxvi. 26.

Δ.

δαιμονίζομαι, *to be possessed by an evil spirit*, Matt. iv. 24. viii. 16, 28, 33. Mrk. i. 32.

δαιμόνιον, τὸ, *a deity*, Acts, xvii. 18; *a demon, a devil*, Luke, iv. 33, 35. viii. 31, 33. 1 Cor. x. 20. Rev. xvi. 14 ("Ethnici non credebant diabolum esse; Socratis daemonium vel deum vel genium esse credebant," Scaliger's *Table-Talk*).

δαιμονιώδης, *demon-like, devilish*, James, iii. 15.

δαίμων, ὁ, = δαιμόνιον (in all the passages cited by Thayer, Westcott gives δαιμόνιον).

δάκνω, *to bite*; met., *to offend, to distress*, Gal. v. 15.

δάκρυ, τὸ, and **δάκρυον**, τὸ, *a tear*, Luke, vii. 38, 44. Rev. vii. 17. Hebr. v. 7.

δακρύω, *to weep*, Joh. xi. 25.

δακτύλιος, ὁ, *a ring*, Luke, xv. 22. Cf. James, ii. 2.

δάκτυλος, ὁ, *a finger*, Joh. viii. 6. Matt. xxiii. 4. Luke, xvi. 24; ἐν δακτύλῳ θεοῦ = *by the Holy Ghost*,—which words are explained in Matt. xii. 28 by ἐν πνεύματι θεοῦ.

δαμάζω, *to tame*, Mrk. v. 4. James, iii. 7; *to curb, to restrain*, James, iii. 8.

δάμαλις, ἡ, *a heifer*, Hebr. ix. 13.

δανείζω, *to lend*, Luke, vi. 34, 35; mid., *to borrow*, Matt. v. 42.

δάνειον, τὸ, and **δάνιον**, τὸ, *a loan, a debt*, Matt. xviii. 27.

δανειστὴς, ὁ, *a moneylender, a creditor*, Luke, vii. 41.

δαπανάω, *to spend*, Mrk. v. 26. 2 Cor. xii. 15; *to lay out money, to be at expense*, Acts, xxi. 24; *to waste, to consume*, James, iv. 3. Luke, xv. 14.

δαπάνη, ἡ, *expense, cost*, Luke, xiv. 28.

δὲ, *a disjunctive particle, but, on the other hand, and, now*, etc. (The reader is referred to his Greek Grammar.)

δέησις, ἡ, *supplication, prayer*, James, v. 16. 1 Pet. iii. 12. Philipp. i. 4.

δεῖ, impers., *it is necessary, it must be that, it behoves*, Matt. xxvi. 35. Joh. ii. 4. Acts, xxvii. 21 etc., etc.

δεῖγμα, τὸ, *an example*, Jude, 7.

δειγματίζω, *to make an example of*, Matt. i. 19. Coloss. ii. 15. (It is a purely biblical word.)

δεικνύω, and **δείκνυμι**, *to shew*, Luke, iv. 5. Joh. ii. 18; *to demonstrate*, James, ii. 18. iii. 13; *to make known*, Acts, x. 28. Matt. xvi. 21.

δειλία, ἡ, *timidity, fear*, 2 Tim. i. 7.

δειλιάω, *to be timid, to be fearful*, Joh. xiv. 27.

δειλὸς, *timid, fearful*, Matt. viii. 26. Rev. xxi. 8. Mrk. iv. 40.

δεῖνα, ὁ, ἡ, τὸ, *a certain person, such a one*, Matt. xxvi. 18 (found nowhere else in the NT).

δεινῶς, adv., *terribly, grievously*, Matt. viii. 6; *urgently, vehemently*, Luke, xi. 53.

δειπνέω, *to sup*, Luke, xvii. 8. 1 Cor. xi. 25. Rev. iii. 20.

δεῖπνον, τὸ, *supper*, Joh. xiii. 2, 4. xxi. 20. Luke, xiv. 17, 24. (See ἄριστον.)

δεισιδαιμονία, ἡ, *superstition; religion*, Acts, xxv. 19.

δεισιδαίμων, *superstitious, religious*, Acts, xvii. 22.

δέκα, *ten*, Matt. xx. 24; θλίψιν ἡμερῶν δέκα, i.e. *to last only a short time*, Rev. ii. 10.

δεκαδύο, *twelve*, a var. lect. for δώδεκα ad Acts, xix. 7. xxiv. 11.

δεκαπέντε, *fifteen*, Joh. xi. 18. Acts, xxvii. 28. Gal. i. 18.

δεκατέσσαρες, *fourteen*, Matt. i. 17. Gal. ii. 1. 2 Cor. xii. 2.

δεκάτη, ἡ, *the tenth part* of anything, *a tithe*, Hebr. vii. 2, 4, 8.

δέκατος, *the tenth*, Joh. i. 39. Rev. xxi. 20; τὸ δέκατον, *the tenth part*, Rev. xi. 13.

δεκατόω, *to receive tithes*, Hebr. vii. 6; pass., *to pay tithes*, Hebr. vii. 9.

δεκτὸς, *acceptable*, Luke, iv. 19, 24. 2 Cor. vi. 2. Acts, x. 35.

δελεάζω, *to ensnare, to beguile*, 2 Pet. ii. 14, 18. James, i. 14.

δένδρον, τὸ, *a tree*, Matt. vii. 17, 18. Luke, xiii. 19.

δεξιοβόλος, ὁ, *a slinger*, a var. lect. ad Acts, xxiii. 23.

δεξιολάβος, ὁ, *a spearman*, Acts, xxiii. 23. (In Pape rendered "*a slinger* or *archer*".)

δεξιὸς, *right*, as opposed to left, Matt. v. 29, 39; ἡ δεξιὰ (sc. χείρ), *the right hand*, Matt. vi. 3; ἐν τοῖς δεξιοῖς, *on the right side*, Mrk. xvi. 5; ἐκ δεξιῶν καθῆσθαι, καθίζειν, ἑστάναι, *to sit* or *stand on one's right hand*, Matt. xxvi. 64. Acts, vii. 55; τὰ ὅπλα τὰ δεξιὰ, *armour on the right hand*, 2 Cor. vi. 7; εἶναι ἐκ δεξιῶν τινος, *to be on one's right hand*, Acts, ii. 25.

δέομαι, *to pray, to beseech*, Acts, viii. 34; *to pray to*, Acts, x. 2.

δέον, τὸ, *what is needful, what is proper;* δέον ἐστί, *it is necessary*, Acts, xix. 36; τὰ μὴ δέοντα, *what is improper*, 1 Tim. v. 13.

δέος, τὸ, *fear*, Hebr. xii. 28.

δέρμα, τὸ, *a skin*, Hebr. xi. 37.

δερμάτινος, *leathern*, Mrk. i. 6. Matt. iii. 4.

δέρω, *to beat, to smite*, Matt. xxi. 35. Luke, xxii. 63. 2 Cor. xi. 20; δαρήσεται πολλὰς (sc. πληγὰς), *shall be beaten with many stripes*, Luke, xii. 47.

δεσμεύω, *to bind*, Luke, viii. 29; *to put in chains*, Acts, xxii. 4.

δεσμέω, *to bind*, a var. lect. ad Luke, viii. 29.

δεσμὴ, ἡ, *a bundle*, Matt. xiii. 30.

δέσμιος, ὁ, *a prisoner*, Matt. xxvii. 15. Acts, xvi. 25, 27. Ephes. iii. 1.

δεσμὸς, ὁ, *a bond* or *band*, Matt. vii. 35. Luke, xiii. 16; τὰ δεσμὰ, *fetters, chains*, Luke, viii. 29. Acts, xvi. 26.

δεσμοφύλαξ, ὁ, *a jailer*, Acts, xvi. 23, 27, 36.

δεσμωτήριον, τό, *a prison,* Matt. xi. 2. Acts, v. 21, 23.

δεσμώτης, ὁ, *a prisoner,* Acts, xxvii. 1, 42.

δεσπότης, ὁ, *a master,* 1 Tim. vi. 1. 2 Tim. ii. 21. Tit. ii. 9; *Lord,* Luke, ii. 29. 2 Pet. ii. 1; Jude, 4, perhaps *God.*

δεῦρο, adv. *hither; come!* Joh. xi. 43. Mrk. x. 21 Acts, vii. 3; ἄχρι δεῦρο, *up to this time,* Rom. i. 13.

δεῦτε, interj., *come!* Matt. xi. 28. xxii. 4; often followed by an imperative, Joh. iv. 29. Matt. xxv. 34. xxviii. 6; sometimes by the subjunct. hortativus, Matt. xxi. 38. Mrk. xii. 7.

δευτεραῖος, *on the second day,* Acts, xxviii. 13.

δευτερόπρωτος, *the second-first,* i.e. *the second after the feast of the Passover,* a doubtful reading ad Luke, vi. 1. (It is omitted by Westcott, the RV, and most editors, and does not appear at all in Pape's Lexicon.)

δεύτερος, *second,* Matt. xxii. 26. Joh. iv. 54; δεύτερον, as adv., *secondly,* 1 Cor. xii. 28; *a second time,* Joh. iii. 4. Rev. xix. 3; πάλιν δεύτερον, *again a second time,* Joh. xxi. 16; also τὸ δεύτερον, *the second time,* 2 Cor. xiii. 2. Jude, 5. (RV *afterward*); and, frequently, ἐκ δευτέρου, *the second time,* Matt. xiv. 72. Joh. ix. 24. etc.; ἐν τῷ δευτέρῳ, *at the second time,* Acts, vii. 13.

δέχομαι, *to receive,* Acts, iii. 21. viii. 14; *to take,* Ephes. vi. 17. Luke, xvi. 6. xxii. 17; *to bear with, to endure,* 2 Cor. xi. 16.

δέω, *to bind, to tie,* Matt. xiii. 30. Luke, xix. 30; *to prohibit,* Matt. xvi. 19. xviii. 18.

δή, adv., *indeed, therefore, then, now;* δή που, *doubtless,* Hebr. ii. 16.

δηλαυγῶς, *clearly,* a var. lect. ad Mrk. viii. 25.

δῆλος, *manifest, evident,* Gal. iii. 11. Matt. xxvi. 73.

δηλόω, *to make manifest,* 1 Cor. iii. 13; *to make known, to declare,* Coloss. i. 8. 1 Cor. i. 11; *to signify,* Hebr. xii. 27. 2 Pet. i. 14; *to point unto,* 1 Pet. i. 11.

δημηγορέω, *to make a speech,* Acts, xii. 21.

δημιουργὸς, ὁ, *an artisan, a builder,* Hebr. xi. 10.

δῆμος, ὁ, *the people,* Acts, xii. 22. xix. 33.

δημόσιος, *belonging to the people, public,* Acts, v. 18; δημοσίᾳ, *publicly,* Acts, xvi. 37. xx. 20.

δηνάριον, τὸ, *a denarius,* a Roman coin, about 8½d., Matt. xviii. 28. xx. 2, 9, 13; τὸ ἀνὰ δηνάριον, *the pay of a denarius apiece,* Matt. xx. 10 (Westcott omits the τό).

δή που; see δή.

διὰ, prepos., taking genit. and accus.; δι' ἄλλης ὁδοῦ, *by another way,* Matt. ii. 12; διὰ πυρὸς, *by fire,* 1 Cor. iii. 15; δι' ὅλου, *throughout,* Joh. xix. 23; διὰ πολλῶν δακρύων, *with many tears,* 2 Cor. ii. 4; διὰ προσκόμματος, *with offence,*

Rom. xiv. 20; διὰ ὅλης νυκτὸς, *all night long*, Luke, v. 5; διὰ παντὸς, *continually, always*, Matt. xviii. 10; δι' ἐτῶν πλειόνων, *after many years*, Acts, xxiv. 17; διὰ στόματος τῶν ἁγίων προφητῶν αὐτοῦ, *by the mouth of his holy prophets*, Luke, i. 70; δι' οὗ ἐποίησεν τοὺς αἰῶνας, *by whose agency he made the worlds*, Hebr. i. 2. Cf. Joh. i. 3. διὰ τοῦτο, *on account of this, for this cause*, Joh. vi. 65. Matt. xiii. 13; διὰ ταῦτα, *because of these things*, Ephes. v. 6; διὰ φθόνον, *for envy*, Matt. xxvii. 18; διὰ τὸν ἄνθρωπον ἐγένετο, *was made for man*, Mrk. ii. 27; διὰ Χριστὸν, *for Christ's sake*, 1 Cor. iv. 10; διὰ τὸ, *because that, for that*, Luke, ix. 7. Hebr. vii. 23.

διαβαίνω, *to pass through*, Hebr. xi. 29; *to cross over*, Luke, xvi. 26. Acts, xvi. 9.

διαβάλλω, *to calumniate; to accuse*, Luke, xvi. 1.

διαβεβαιόομαι, *to assert confidently*, 1 Tim. i. 7. Tit. iii. 8.

διαβλέπω, *to look stedfastly*, Mrk. viii. 25; *to see clearly*, Matt. vii. 5. Luke, vi. 42.

διάβολος, as adj., *prone to slander, slanderous*, 1 Tim. iii. 11. 2 Tim. iii. 3. Tit. ii. 3; as subst., ὁ διάβολος = Σαταναˆς, Matt. iv. 1, 5. Joh. xiii. 2.

διαγγέλλω, *to publish abroad*, Rom. ix. 17. Luke, ix. 60; *to notify, to declare*, Acts, xxi. 26.

διαγίνομαι, *to intervene, to elapse*, Acts, xxv. 13. xxvii. 9. Mrk. xvi. 1.

διαγινώσκω, *to distinguish; to inquire into*, Acts, xxiii. 15; *to decide, to determine*, Acts, xxiv. 22.

διαγνωρίζω, *to make known*, Luke, ii. 17. [Westcott reads γνωρίζω.]

διάγνωσις, ἡ, *decision*, Acts, xxv. 21.

διαγογγύζω, *to murmur*, Luke, xv. 2. xix. 7.

διαγρηγορέω, *to watch through, to remain awake*, Luke, ix. 32.

διάγω, *to spend* time, *to live*, 1 Tim. ii. 2. Tit. iii. 3.

διαδέχομαι, *to receive by transmission, to succeed to*, Acts, vii. 45.

διάδημα, τὸ, *a diadem*, Rev. xii. 3. xiii. 1. xix. 12.

διαδίδωμι, *to distribute*, Luke, xviii. 22. Joh. vi. 11; *to divide*, Luke, xi. 22.

διάδοχος, ὁ, *a successor*, Acts, xxiv. 27.

διαζώννυμι, and **διαζωννύω**, *to gird*, Joh. xiii. 4; pass., *to be girded*, Joh. xiii. 5; mid., *to gird about oneself*, Joh. xxi. 7.

διαθήκη, ἡ, *a will, a testament*, Hebr. ix. 16, 17; and, especially, ἡ καινὴ διαθήκη, *the New Testament*, 1 Cor. xi. 25. 2 Cor. iii. 6; *a covenant*, Hebr. viii. 8, 10. x. 16. Acts, vii. 8.

διαίρεσις, ἡ, *a difference, a diversity*, 1 Cor. xii. 4, 5, 6.

διαιρέω, *to divide, to distribute*, Luke, xv. 12. 1 Cor. xii. 11.

διακαθαίρω, *to thoroughly cleanse*, Luke, iii. 17.

δια] TO THE NEW TESTAMENT [δια

διακαθαρίζω, *to cleanse thoroughly*, Matt. iii. 12.

διακατελέγχομαι, *to confute thoroughly*, Acts, xviii. 28. (It is thus rendered also in Pape's Lexicon. RV *powerfully confuted*. The word is found in no other passage or author.)

διακονέω, *to serve, to minister unto*, Joh. xii. 26. Acts, xix. 22. Matt. xx. 28. xxv. 44; *to attend to*, Acts, vi. 2; *to serve as a deacon*, 1 Tim. iii. 10, 13; *to supply, to furnish*, 1 Pet. i. 12; pass., *to be ministered unto*, Mrk. x. 45. Matt. xx. 28.

διακονία, ἡ, *service, ministration*, Hebr. i. 14. 2 Cor. iii. 7, 8; *a serving*, Luke, x. 40; *relief*, Acts, xi. 29; *the office of a deacon*, Rom. xii. 7.

διάκονος, ὁ, *a servant, a minister*, Joh. ii. 5, 9. Matt. xxii. 13. xxiii. 11. 2 Cor. xi. 23; *a deacon*, 1 Tim. iii. 8, 12. Philipp. i. 1; ἡ διάκονος, *a deaconess*, Rom. xvi. 1.

διακόσιοι, *two hundred*, Joh. vi. 7. Mrk. vi. 37.

διακούω, *to hear fully*, Acts, xxiii. 35.

διακρίνω, *to make a distinction*, Acts, xi. 12. xv. 9; *to decide*, 1 Cor. vi. 5; *to examine*, 1 Cor. xi. 31; *to scrutinise*, 1 Cor. xiv. 29; *to discern, to recognise the presence of*, 1 Cor. xi. 29; *to dispute, to contend*, Acts, xi. 2. Jude, 9; *to doubt*, Mrk. xi. 23. Matt. xxi. 21. James, i. 6; *to hesitate*, Rom. iv. 20.

διάκρισις, ἡ, *a discerning*, 1 Cor. xii. 10. Hebr. v. 14; *a decision*, Rom. xiv. 1.

διακωλύω, *to hinder*, Matt. iii. 14.

διαλαλέω, *to talk with, to commune*, Luke, vi. 11; pass., *to be talked of*, Luke, i. 65.

διαλέγομαι, *to reason with*, Hebr. xii. 5; *to argue*, Acts, xvii. 2, 17. xix. 8; *to contend, to dispute*, Mrk. ix. 34. Jude, 9.

διαλείπω, *to leave off, to cease*, Luke, vii. 45.

διάλεκτος, ἡ, *a language*, Acts, i. 19. ii. 6, 8. xxi. 40.

διαλλάσσω, *to reconcile;* pass., *to be reconciled*, Matt. v. 24.

διαλογίζομαι, *to reason, to deliberate*, Matt. xvi. 7, 8. Mrk. ii. 6, 8. Luke. i. 29.

διαλογισμὸς, ὁ, *a reasoning*, 1 Cor. iii. 20. Rom. i. 21; *a thought*, Matt. xv. 19. Luke, ii. 35. v. 22. vi. 8. James, ii. 4; *a doubt*, Rom. xiv. 1. Luke, xxiv. 38; *a disputing*, Philipp. ii. 14. 1 Tim. ii. 8.

διαλύω, *to break up, to disperse*, Acts, v. 36.

διαμαρτύρομαι, *to solemnly charge*, 1 Tim. v. 21. 2 Tim. ii. 14. iv. 1; *to testify*, Luke, xvi. 28. Acts, x. 42. xx. 21, 23. Hebr. ii. 6.

διαμάχομαι, *to fight it out; to strenuously contend*, Acts, xxiii. 9.

διαμένω, *to continue*, 2 Pet. iii. 4. Luke, i. 22. Hebr. i. 11. Gal. ii. 5.

διαμερίζω, *to distribute*, Acts, ii. 45; *to divide, to share*, Luke, xxii. 17; pass., *to be*

at variance, Luke, xi. 17.
xii. 52, 53; mid., *to share
among themselves*, Luke, xxiii.
34. Matt. xxvii. 35. Mrk. xv.
24.

διαμερισμὸς, ὁ, *distribution; dis-
union, dissension*, Luke, xii.
51.

διανέμω, *to distribute;* pass., *to
be disseminated, to spread
abroad*, Acts, iv. 17.

διανεύω, *to make signs*, Luke,
i. 22.

διανόημα, τὸ, *a thought*, Luke,
xi. 17.

διάνοια, ἡ, *the understanding*,
1 Joh. v. 20. Ephes. iv. 18;
the mind, Luke, x. 27. Matt.
xxii. 37. Ephes. ii. 3. Coloss.
i. 21. 2 Pet. iii. 1; *a thought*,
Luke, i. 51.

διανοίγω, *to open*, Luke, ii. 23.
Mrk. vii. 34, 35. Acts, vii.
56; *to explain, to expound*,
Luke, xxiv. 32. Acts, xvii.
3; *to open*, i.e. *to enlighten*,
Luke, xxiv. 45. Acts, xvi. 14.

διανυκτερεύω, *to pass the whole
night*, Luke, vi. 12.

διανύω, *to finish*, Acts, xxi. 7.

διαπαρατριβὴ, ἡ, *contention,
wrangling*, 1 Tim. vi. 5.

διαπεράω, *to cross over*, Matt.
ix. 1. xiv. 34. Luke, xvi. 26.
Acts, xxi. 2.

διαπλέω, *to sail across*, Acts,
xxvii. 5.

διαπονέω, *to complete;* pass.,
to be vexed, Acts, iv. 2. xvi.
18.

διαπορεύομαι, *to pass* or *go
through*, Luke, vi. 1. Mrk.
ii. 23. Acts, xvi. 4; *to pass
by*, Luke, xviii. 36.

διαπορέω, *to be thoroughly perplexed*, Acts, ii. 12. v. 24. x.
17. Luke, ix. 7.

διαπραγματεύομαι, *to gain by
trading*, Luke, xix. 15. (Cf.
πραγματεύομαι.)

διαπρίω, *to saw through;* mid.,
to be vehemently enraged,
Acts, v. 33. vii. 54. (See
Pape's Lex. in voc.)

διαρπάζω, *to plunder*, Mrk. iii.
27.

διαρρήγνυμι, and **διαρρήσσω**, *to
break asunder*, Luke, v. 6.
viii. 29; *to rend*, Acts, xiv.
14. Matt. xxvii. 65. Mrk.
xiv. 63.

διασαφέω, *to make clear, to
explain*, Matt. xiii. 36; *to
make known*, Matt. xviii.
31.

διασείω, *to extort from*, Luke,
iii. 14. (RV *do violence to;*
but see Pape's Lex. in voc.)

διασκορπίζω, *to scatter abroad,
to disperse*, Acts, v. 37. Joh.
xi. 52. Luke, i. 51. Matt.
xxvi. 31; *to squander, to
waste*, Luke, xv. 13. xvi. 1;
to scatter as seeds, Matt.
xxv. 24, 26.

διασπάω, *to break asunder*,
Mrk. v. 4; *to tear in pieces*,
Acts, xxiii. 10.

διασπείρω, *to disperse*, Acts,
viii. 1, 4. xi. 19.

διασπορὰ, ἡ, *the dispersion*, i.e.
the Israelites who were dis-
persed, Joh. vii. 35. James,
i. 1. 1 Pet. i. 1.

διαστέλλω, *to order, to charge;*
mid., *to give a command* or
injunction, Acts, xv. 24.
Matt. xvi. 20. Mrk. vii. 36.

viii. 15. ix. 9 ; pass., τὸ διαστελλόμενον, *the injunction*, Hebr. xii. 20.

διάστημα, τὸ, *a space or interval*, Acts, v. 7.

διαστολὴ, ἡ, *a distinction*, Rom. iii. 22. x. 12. 1 Cor. xiv. 7.

διαστρέφω, *to turn aside, to pervert*, Acts, xiii. 8, 10. Luke, xxiii. 2; pass., διεστραμμένος, *perverse, corrupt*, Matt. xvii. 17. Luke, ix. 41. Acts, xx. 30. Philipp. ii. 15.

διασώζω, *to save*, i.e. *to heal*, Luke, vii. 3 ; *to bring safe*, Acts, xxiii. 24 ; pass., *to be saved*, 1 Pet. iii. 20 ; *to be healed*, Matt. xiv. 36 ; *to get safe*, Acts, xxvii. 44 ; *to escape*, Acts, xxviii. 1, 4.

διαταγὴ, ἡ, *a command, an ordinance*, Rom. xiii. 2. Acts, vii. 53 ("*at the ministration of angels*," Thayer).

διάταγμα, τὸ, *an injunction, a mandate*, Hebr. xi. 23.

διαταράσσω, *to greatly trouble*, Luke, i. 29.

διατάσσω, *to give commands, to prescribe*, Luke, viii. 55. 1 Cor. ix. 14. xvi. 1. Matt. xi. 1 ; pass., *to be prescribed, to be ordained*, Gal. iii. 19. Luke, iii. 13. xvii. 9. Acts, xxiii. 31 ; mid., *to order, to prescribe*, Tit. i. 5. 1 Cor. vii. 17. xi. 34. Acts, vii. 44 ; so also, οὕτω ἦν διατεταγμένος, Acts, xx. 13 (RV *so he had appointed*).

διατελέω, *to continue*, Acts, xxvii. 33.

διατηρέω, *to carefully keep*, Luke, ii. 51 ; ἑαυτὸν ἔκ τινος, *to carefully keep himself from*, Acts, xv. 29.

διατίθεμαι, *to assign*, Luke, xxii. 29 ; *to make a will*, Hebr. ix. 16 ; *to conclude, to contract* as a covenant, Acts, iii. 25. Hebr. viii. 10. x. 16.

διατρίβω, *to spend* or *pass* (as χρόνον or ἡμέρας), Acts, xiv. 3, 28. xvi. 12 ; absolutely, *to stay, to tarry*, Joh. iii. 22. Acts, xii. 19. xv. 35.

διατροφὴ, ἡ, *sustenance, food*, 1 Tim. vi. 8.

διαυγάζω, *to shine through, to dawn*, 2 Pet. i. 19.

διαυγὴς, *transparent*, Rev. xxi. 21.

διαφανὴς, *transparent*, a var. lect. ad Rev. xxi. 21.

διαφέρω, *to carry through*, Mrk. xi. 16 ; intrans., *to differ*, 1 Cor. xv. 41. Gal. iv. 1. Rom. ii. 18. Philipp. i. 10 (in these two last passages RV renders by *things that are excellent*); *to excel*, Luke, xii. 7, 24. Matt. vi. 26. x. 31; impers., οὐδὲν διαφέρει, *it makes no difference, it matters nothing*, Gal. ii. 6; pass., *to be carried hither and thither, to be driven to and fro*, Acts, xxvii. 27 ; *to be spread abroad*, Acts, xiii. 49.

διαφεύγω, *to escape*, Acts, xxvii. 42.

διαφημίζω, *to publish, to spread abroad*, Mrk. i. 45. Matt. xxviii. 15 ; διεφήμισαν αὐτὸν, *they spread abroad his fame*, Matt. ix. 31.

διαφθείρω, *to destroy*, Rev. xi. 18. Luke, xii. 33; pass., *to be destroyed*, Rev. viii. 9; *to be corrupted*, 1 Tim. vi. 5; *to waste away*, 2 Cor. iv. 16.

διαφθορά, ἡ, *corruption*, Acts, ii. 27, 31. xiii. 34, 35, 36.

διάφορος, *different, varying*, Rom. xii. 6. Hebr. ix. 10; *excellent*, Hebr. i. 4. viii. 6.

διαφυλάσσω, *to carefully guard*, Luke, iv. 10.

διαχειρίζω, in mid., *to slay*, Acts, v. 30. xxvi. 21.

διαχλευάζω, *to mock, to scoff*, Acts, ii. 13.

διαχωρίζομαι, *to part*, Luke, ix. 33.

διδακτικὸς, *apt to teach*, 1 Tim. iii. 2. 2 Tim. ii. 24.

διδακτὸς, *taught*, Joh. vi. 45. 1 Cor. ii. 13.

διδασκαλία, ἡ, *instruction, teaching*, 1 Tim. iv. 13, 16. v. 17. 2 Tim. iii. 10, 16; *doctrine*, Ephes. iv. 14. 1 Tim. iv. 6.

διδάσκαλος, ὁ, *a teacher*, Matt. xxiii. 8. 1 Tim. ii. 7. Acts, xiii. 1 etc., etc.

διδάσκω, *to teach*, Matt. iv. 23. v. 2. xxi. 23. xxii. 16.

διδαχὴ, ἡ, *doctrine*, Mrk. i. 27. Joh. vii. 16. Acts, xiii. 12.

δίδραχμον, τὸ, *a double drachma*, a silver coin equal to two Attic drachmæ, or half a shekel, Matt. xvii. 24.

δίδυμος, *twin*, Joh. xi. 16. xx. 24. xxi. 2.

δίδωμι, *to give*, Acts, xx. 35. Matt. vi. 11. xix. 21; *to grant*, Luke, i. 74. Acts, iv. 29; *to commit, to entrust*, Joh. v. 22. Matt. xvi. 19; *to set before one*, Rev. iii. 8; ἐργασίαν διδόναι, *to endeavour*, *to do one's best*, Luke, xii. 58; τόπον διδόναι, *to give way to*, Luke, xiv. 9.

διεγείρω, *to awaken*, Luke, viii. 24; *to stir up, to rouse*, 2 Pet. i. 13. iii. 1; intrans., *to rise*, Joh. vi. 18.

διενθυμέομαι, *to reflect, to ponder*, Acts, x. 19.

διεξέρχομαι, *to come forth*, a var. lect. ad Acts, xxviii. 3.

διέξοδος, ἡ, *a way out, an outlet;* τὰς διεξόδους τῶν ὁδῶν, *the outlets of the country highways*, Matt. xxii. 9.

διερμηνεία, ἡ, *interpretation*, a var. lect. ad 1 Cor. xii. 10. (Not recognized in Pape's Lexicon.)

διερμηνευτὴς, ὁ, *an interpreter*, 1 Cor. xiv. 28.

διερμηνεύω, *to expound, to interpret*, Luke, xxiv. 27. 1 Cor. xii. 30. xiv. 5, 13, 27; *to translate*, Acts, ix. 36.

διέρχομαι, *to go or pass through*, Luke, iv. 30. Matt. xii. 43. Rom. v. 12; with accus., *to journey through, to pass through*, Luke, xix. 1. Acts, xii. 10; *to pierce*, Luke, ii. 35; absolutely, with genit., *to pass*, Luke, xix. 4; *to go about*, Acts, xx. 25. Luke, ix. 6; *to cross over*, Mrk. iv. 35. Luke, viii. 22; *to get spread abroad*, Luke, v. 15.

διερωτάω, *to inquire after*, Acts, x. 17.

διετὴs, *two years old*, Matt. ii. 16.

διετία, ἡ, *a space of two years*, Acts, xxiv. 27. xxviii. 30.

διηγέομαι, *to state at length, to declare*, Luke, viii. 39. ix. 10. Mrk. v. 16. Acts, ix. 27. xii. 17; *to divulge, to tell*, Mrk. ix. 9.

διήγησις, ἡ, *a statement*, Luke, i. 1.

διηνεκὴς, *continuous;* εἰς τὸ διηνεκὲς, *continually, for ever*, Hebr. vii. 3. x. 1, 12, 14.

διθάλασσος, *between two seas*, Acts, xxvii. 41.

διικνέομαι, *to go through, to pierce*, Hebr. iv. 12.

διΐστημι, *to place asunder;* intrans., *to proceed*, Acts, xxvii. 28; in mid. and perf. and 2nd aor. act., *to part;* διέστη ἀπ' αὐτῶν, *he parted from them*, Luke, xxiv. 51; διαστάσης ὥρας μιᾶς, *when one hour had intervened*, Luke, xxii. 59.

διισχυρίζομαι, *to assert confidently*, Luke, xxii. 59. Acts, xii. 15.

δικάζω, *to judge*, a var. lect. ad Luke, vi. 37.

δικαιοκρισία, ἡ, *a righteous judgment*, Rom. ii. 5.

δίκαιος, *upright, righteous*, Matt. ix. 13. x. 41. xiii. 43, 49; *just*, Matt. i. 19. v. 45. Acts, xxiv. 15; *right*, Ephes. vi. 1. 2 Pet. i. 13. Philipp. i. 7; *innocent*, Matt. xxiii. 35.

δικαιοσύνη, ἡ, *righteousness*, Rom. iv. 11. Hebr. v. 13. vii. 2 etc.

δικαιόω, *to justify*, Luke, vii. 35. Matt. xi. 19. 1 Tim. iii. 16. 1 Cor. iv. 4; *to pronounce righteous*, Rom. iii. 26. iv. 5. viii. 30.

δικαίωμα, τὸ, *an ordinance*, Luke, i. 6. Rom. i. 32. ii. 26. viii. 4; *a righteous act*, Rom. v. 18. Rev. xv. 4. xix. 8; *justification*, Rom. v. 16.

δικαίως, adv., *justly*, Luke, xxiii. 41. 1 Pet. ii. 23; *as is right*, 1 Cor. xv. 34; *righteously*, 1 Thess. ii. 10. Tit. ii. 12.

δικαίωσις, ἡ, *justification*, Rom. iv. 25. v. 18.

δικαστὴς, ὁ, *a judge*, Luke, xii. 14. Acts, vii. 27, 35.

δίκη, ἡ, *justice*, Acts, xxviii. 4; *punishment*, 2 Thess. i. 9. Jude, 7.

δίκτυον, τὸ, *a net*, Joh. xxi. 6, 8, 11. Luke, v. 2, 4, 6. Matt. iv. 20.

δίλογος, *double-tongued*, 1 Tim. iii. 8.

διὸ, *wherefore, on which account*, Rom. i. 24. ii. 1. Matt. xxvii. 8 etc.

διοδεύω, *to pass through*, Acts, xvii. 1; *to go about*, Luke, viii. 1.

διόπερ, *wherefore*, 1 Cor. viii. 13. x. 14.

διοπετὴς, *which fell down from Jupiter*, Acts, xix. 35.

διόρθωμα, τὸ, *a reform*, Acts, xxiv. 2.

διόρθωσις, ἡ, *reformation*, Hebr. ix. 10.

διορύσσω, *to dig through, to break through*, Matt. vi. 19. xxiv. 43. Luke, xii. 39.

Διόσκουροι, οἱ, *the Dioscuri*, i.e. Castor and Pollux, the twin sons of Jupiter and Leda, and the patrons of sailors, Acts, xxviii. 11.

διότι, properly = διὰ τοῦτο, ὅτι; *because*, Luke, ii. 7. xxi. 28. Philipp. ii. 26 etc.

διπλόος, *twofold, double*, 1 Tim. v. 17. Rev. xviii. 6; διπλότερον ὑμῶν, *twofold more than yourselves*, Matt. xxiii. 15.

διπλόω, *to double; to repay in double measure*, Rev. xviii. 6.

δίς, adv., *twice*, Luke, xviii. 12. Jude, 12. 1 Thess. ii. 18.

δισμυριάς, ἡ, *twenty thousand*, a var. lect. ad Rev. ix. 16.

διστάζω, *to doubt*, Matt. xiv. 31. xxviii. 17.

δίστομος, *double-mouthed; two-edged*, Hebr. iv. 12. Rev. i. 16. ii. 12.

δισχίλιοι, *two thousand*, Mrk. v. 13.

διυλίζω, *to remove by filtering, to strain out*, Matt. xxiii. 24.

διχάζω, *to cut asunder; to set at variance*, Matt. x. 35.

διχοστασία, ἡ, *division, dissension*, Rom. xvi. 17. Gal. v. 20.

διχοτομέω, *to cut asunder*, Matt. xxiv. 51. Luke, xii. 46. ("Here the word is more fitly translated *scourge severely*," Thayer.)

διψάω, *to thirst*, Joh. iv. 13, 14, 15. xix. 28; with accus., *to thirst after*, Matt. v. 6.

δίψος, τὸ, *thirst*, 2 Cor. xi. 27.

δίψυχος, *double-minded*, James, i. 8. iv. 8.

διωγμὸς, ὁ, *persecution*, Matt. xiii. 21. Acts, viii. 1. xiii. 50.

διώκτης, ὁ, *a persecutor*, 1 Tim. i. 13. (It is a purely ecclesiastical word.)

διώκω, *to pursue*, Matt. xxiii. 34. Acts, xxvi. 11; *to persecute*, Rev. xii. 13. Matt. v. 10, 12, 44; *to follow after*, Luke, xvii. 23; *to seek after, to cultivate*, Hebr. xii. 14. Rom. ix. 30. xii. 13. xiv. 19.

δόγμα, τὸ, *an opinion; a decree*, Luke, ii. 1. Acts, xvi. 4. xvii. 7; *an ordinance*, Coloss. ii. 14. Ephes. ii. 15.

δογματίζω, *to impose an ordinance;* pass., *to submit to ordinances*, Coloss. ii. 20. (Pape's Lexicon says "In ecclesiastical writers = *to teach*.")

δοκέω, *to think, to suppose*, Joh. v. 39. xvi. 2. Luke, xxiv. 37; intrans., *to seem*, Acts, xvii. 18. 1 Cor. xii. 22; ἔδοξέ μοι, *it seemed good to me*, Luke, i. 2; κατὰ τὸ δοκοῦν αὐτοῖς, *as seemed good to them*, Hebr. xii. 10; *to be accounted, to be reputed*, Luke, xxii. 24; οἱ δοκοῦντες, *those in repute*, Gal. ii. 2, 6.

δοκιμάζω, *to test, to prove*, 1 Cor. iii. 13. 2 Cor. viii. 8. Gal. vi. 4; *to try*, 1 Joh. iv. 1. Luke, xiv. 19; *to approve, to deem worthy*, 1 Cor. xvi. 3. Rom. xiv. 22. 1 Thess. ii. 4.

δοκιμασία, ἡ, *a proving, a testing*, Hebr. iii. 9.

δοκιμὴ, ἡ, *a trial*, 2 Cor. viii. 2. ix. 13; *a probation*, Rom. v. 4; *tried character, worth*, 2 Cor. ii. 9. Philipp. ii. 22; *a proof*, 2 Cor. xiii. 3.

δοκίμιον, τὸ, *a trial*, James, i. 3. 1 Pet. i. 7.

δόκιμος, *approved*, Rom. xvi. 10. 1 Cor. xi. 19. 2 Tim. ii. 15. James, i. 12; *acceptable*, Rom. xiv. 18.

δοκὸς, ἡ, *a beam*, Luke, vi. 41. Matt. vii. 3, 5.

δόλιος, *deceitful*, 2 Cor. xi. 13.

δολιόω, *to use deceit*, Rom. iii. 13. (It is a purely ecclesiastical word.)

δόλος, ὁ, *deceit, guile*, Rom. i. 29. Acts, xiii. 10. Matt. xxvi. 4. Joh. i. 47; λαλεῖν δόλον, *to speak deceitfully*, 1 Pet. iii. 10.

δολόω, *to ensnare; to corrupt*, 2 Cor. iv. 2.

δόμα, τὸ, *a gift*, Matt. vii. 11. Ephes. iv. 8. Philipp. iv. 17.

δόξα, ἡ, *opinion; glory*, Rev. v. 12. Joh. ix. 24. Luke, ii. 14. 2 Cor. vi. 8; *brightness*, Acts, xxii. 11. Rev. xviii. 1. 2 Cor. iii. 7; *magnificence, pomp*, Matt. iv. 8. vi. 29. Rev. xxi. 24, 26; *majesty*, Jude, 25. 2 Pet. i. 17. Coloss. i. 11; *dignity*, Jude, 8. 2 Pet. ii. 10; *a state of blessedness*, 2 Cor. iv. 17. Rom. viii. 21. Coloss. i. 27.

δοξάζω, *to glorify, to magnify*, Matt. v. 16. Luke. iv. 15. Joh. viii. 54. Acts, xiii. 48; *to honour*, 1 Cor. vi. 20. xii. 26; *to make glorious*, 2 Cor. iii. 10. 1 Pet. i. 8.

δόσις, ἡ, *a giving*, Philipp. iv. 15; *a gift*, James, i. 17.

δότης, ὁ, *a giver*, 2 Cor. ix. 7.

δουλαγωγέω, *to bring into subjection*, 1 Cor. ix. 27.

δουλεία, ἡ, *slavery, bondage*, Rom. viii. 15, 21. Gal. iv. 24.

δουλεύω, *to be a slave*, Joh. viii. 33. Acts, vii. 7; *to serve, to do service*, Ephes. vi. 7. 1 Tim. vi. 2. Matt. vi. 24; *to be in bondage*, Gal. iv. 8, 25; *to yield obedience, to obey*, Rom. vii. 25. Philipp. ii. 22.

δοῦλος, ὁ, *a slave, a servant*, 1 Cor. vii. 21. Philipp. ii. 7. Coloss. iii. 11. Matt. xviii. 23, 26; also δούλη, ἡ, *a female slave, a handmaid*, Luke, i. 38, 48. Acts, ii. 18; as adj., *subservient to*, Rom. vi. 19.

δουλόω, *to enslave, to reduce to bondage*, 1 Cor. ix. 19. Acts, vii. 6. 2 Pet. ii. 19; pass., *to be enslaved to*, Tit. ii. 3; *to be under restraint*, 1 Cor. vii. 15; *to become obedient to*, Rom. vi. 18, 22.

δοχὴ, ἡ, *a feast*, Luke, v. 29. xiv. 13.

δράκων, ὁ, *a serpent, a dragon*, Rev. xii. 3, 4, 9, 17. xx. 2 etc.

δράσσομαι, *to grasp with the hand, to take*, 1 Cor. iii. 19.

δραχμὴ, ἡ, *a drachma*, a silver coin nearly of the same weight as the Roman *denarius*, and in value about 8d., Luke, xv. 8.

δρέπανον, τὸ, *a sickle*, Mrk. iv. 29. Rev. xiv. 14, 15, 16, 18, 19.

δρόμος, ὁ, *a course* of life or office, Acts, xiii. 25. xx. 24. 2 Tim. iv. 7.

δύναμαι, *to have power, to be able*, Matt. vi. 24. ix. 15. xx. 22; with accus., *to be able to do*, Mrk. ix. 22. Luke, xii. 26. 2 Cor. xiii. 8.

δύναμις, ἡ, *strength, power*, Luke, i. 17. 2 Cor. xii. 9. Matt. xxii. 29; *authority*, Luke, iv. 36. ix. 1; *a miracle*, Acts, viii. 13. 2 Cor. xii. 12. Matt. xi. 20, 21; *meaning*, 1 Cor. xiv. 11.

δυναμόω, *to make strong*, Hebr. xi. 34. Coloss. i. 11.

δυνάστης, ὁ, *a potentate*, 1 Tim. vi. 15. Luke, i. 52; *a person of great authority*, Acts, viii. 27.

δυνατέω, *to be powerful*, 2 Cor. xiii. 3; *to have power, to be able*, Rom. xiv. 4. 2 Cor. ix. 8. (It is a purely NT form.)

δυνατὸς, *able*, Rom. iv. 21. Luke, xiv. 31; *mighty*, Luke, xxiv. 19. Acts, vii. 22. xviii. 24. 1 Cor. i. 26; ὁ δυνατὸς, *the Almighty*, Luke, i. 49; οἱ δυνατοί, *the chief men*, Acts, xxv. 5; *strong*, Rom. xv. 1. 2 Cor. xii. 10. xiii. 9; δυνατόν ἐστι, *it is possible*, Matt. xix. 26. xxiv. 24. xxvi. 39; τὸ δυνατὸν αὐτοῦ, *his power*, Rom. ix. 22.

δύνω, *to sink, to go under; to set*, as the sun, Mrk. i. 32. Luke, iv. 40.

δύο, numer., *two*, Matt. xix. 6 etc.

δυσβάστακτος, *grievous to be borne, oppressive*, Luke, xi. 46; also as var. lect. ad Matt. xxiii. 4.

δυσεντερία, ἡ, *dysentery*, Acts, xxviii. 8.

δυσεντέριον, τὸ = δυσεντερία, as given in Westcott's text ad Acts, xxviii. 8.

δυσερμήνευτος, *hard to explain*, Hebr. v. 11.

δύσκολος, *peevish, morose; difficult*, Mrk. x. 24.

δυσκόλως, *with difficulty, hardly, with distaste*, Luke, xviii. 24. Mrk. x. 23. Matt. xix. 23.

δυσμὴ, ἡ, but almost always in the plur., δυσμαὶ, *the West*, Rev. xxi. 13. Matt. viii. 11. xxiv. 27 etc.

δυσνόητος, *hard to understand*, 2 Pet. iii. 16.

δυσφημέω, *to defame*, 1 Cor. iv. 13.

δυσφημία, ἡ, *defamation, evil report*, 2 Cor. vi. 8.

δώδεκα, numer., *twelve*, Matt. ix. 20; οἱ δώδεκα, *the twelve Apostles*, Matt. xxvi. 14, 20 etc.

δωδεκάτος, numer. *twelfth*, Rev. xxi. 20.

δωδεκάφυλον, τὸ, *the twelve tribes*, used collectively of the whole people of Israel, Acts, xxvi. 7.

δῶμα, τὸ, *a building;* in the NT *the roof, the housetop*, Luke, v. 19. xvii. 31. Matt. xxiv. 17 etc.

δωρεὰ, ἡ, *a gift*, Joh. iv. 10. Acts, viii. 20; δωρεὰν, as adv., *gratis, for nothing, freely*, Matt. x. 8. Rom. iii. 24. 2 Cor. xi. 7. 2 Thess. iii. 8; also *without just cause*, Joh. xv. 25. Gal. ii. 21.

δωρέομαι, *to present, to bestow*, Mrk. xv. 45. 2 Pet. i. 3, 4.

δώρημα, τὸ, *a gift*, Rom. v. 16. James, i. 17.

δῶρον, τὸ, *a present, a gift*, Ephes. ii. 8. Rev. xi. 10; *an offering, a sacrifice*, Matt. viii. 4. xxiii. 18.

δωροφορία, ἡ, *the offering of gifts*, a var. lect. ad Rom. xv. 31.

E

ἔα, interj., *ha!* Luke, iv. 34. Mrk. i. 24. (In this last passage it is omitted by Westcott.)

ἐάν, compounded of εἰ and ἄν, *if*, Matt. vi. 22 etc. ἐὰν μή, *unless, except*, Matt. x. 13 etc.; in good writers only with subjunctive. (For further information the reader is referred to his Greek Grammar.)

ἑαυτοῦ, or, with contraction, αὑτοῦ, a reflexive pronoun, *of himself;* ὑψώσει ἑαυτὸν, *shall exalt himself*, Matt. xxiii. 12; δι' ἑαυτοῦ, *of itself*, Rom. xiv. 14; εἰς ἑαυτὸν ἔρχεσθαι, *to come to himself*, i.e. *to come to a better mind*, Luke, xv. 17; καθ' ἑαυτὸν, *by himself*, Acts, xxviii. 16; παρ' ἑαυτῷ, *at home*, 1 Cor. xvi. 2; as a reflexive of the *first* person, ἑαυτοὺς, *ourselves*, 1 Cor. xi. 31; of *second* do., ἑαυτοῖς, *to yourselves*, Matt. xxiii. 31; for corresponding cases of ἀλλήλων, Matt. xxi. 38 etc.

ἐάω, *to allow, to permit*, Matt. xxiv. 43; *to suffer, to let alone*, Luke, xxii. 51; *to let go, (cast off*, RV), Acts, xxvii. 40.

ἑβδομήκοντα, numer., *seventy*, Luke, x. 1, 17.

ἑβδομηκοντάκις, numer., *seventy times*, Matt. xviii. 22.

ἕβδομος, numer., *seventh*, Joh. iv. 52 etc.

Ἑβραΐς, ἡ, *the Hebrew language;* ("not that in which the OT was written, but the *Chaldee*," Thayer); τῇ Ἑβραΐδι διαλέκτῳ, *in the Hebrew dialect*, Acts, xxi. 40. xxii. 2.

Ἑβραϊστί, adv., *in Hebrew*, Joh. xix. 13, 17, 20.

ἐγγίζω, *to approach, to come near*, Matt. xxi. 34. Luke, xviii. 40. xxi. 8; with dat., *to draw nigh to*, James, iv. 8; μέχρι θανάτου ἤγγισε, *he came nigh unto death*, Philipp. ii. 30.

ἐγγράφω, *to write in*, 2 Cor. iii. 2, 3; *to record, to register*, Luke, x. 20.

ἔγγυος, ὁ and ἡ, *a surety*, Hebr. vii. 22.

ἐγγὺς, adv., *near*, Joh. xix. 42; ἐγενήθητε ἐγγὺς, *have been brought nigh*, i.e. *to God*, Ephes. ii. 13; of time, *nigh at hand*, Matt. xxiv. 32; ἐγγὺς κατάρας, *near to being cursed*, Hebr. vi. 8; ἐγγὺς ἀφανισμοῦ, *soon to vanish*, Hebr. viii. 13.

ἐγγύτερον, adv., *nearer*, Rom. xiii. 11.

ἐγείρω, *to raise up*, Matt. iii. 9; pass., *to arise*, Joh. xi. 29. xiii. 4. Matt. ix. 19; ἔγειρε, *arise!* Rev. xi. 1. Ephes. v. 4; *to raise*, as from the dead,

Luke, vii. 22. xx. 37. 1 Cor. xv. 15, 16, 29, 32; *to rouse from sleep, to awaken,* Matt. viii. 25. Acts, xii. 7; *to cause to recover,* James, v. 15; ἐγείρομαι, *to appear,* Matt. xi. 11. xxiv. 11, 24.

ἔγερσις, ἡ, *resurrection* from the dead, Matt. xxvii. 53.

ἐγκάθετος, and ἐνκάθετος, *suborned;* as subst., *a spy,* Luke, xx. 20.

ἐγκαίνια, τὰ, *the feast of dedication,* Joh. x. 22. ("An annual feast, celebrated eight days, beginning on the 25 of Chislev (middle of our December) and instituted by Judas Maccabæus, B.C. 164, in memory of the cleansing of the temple from the pollutions of Antiochus Epiphanes," Thayer.)

ἐγκαινίζω, and ἐνκαινίζω, *to dedicate,* Hebr. ix. 18. x. 20. (It is a purely ecclesiastical word.)

ἐγκακέω, and ἐνκακέω, *to be weary, to faint,* 2 Cor. iv. 1, 16. 2 Thess. iii. 13. Gal. vi. 9. Luke, xviii. 1.

ἐγκαλέω, *to bring a charge,* Rom. viii. 33; *to accuse,* Acts, xix. 38. xxiii. 28; pass., *to be accused,* Acts, xix. 40. xxvi. 2, 7.

ἐγκαταλείπω, *to leave in the lurch; to abandon, to forsake,* 2 Tim. iv. 10, 16. Matt. xxvii. 46. Mrk. xv. 34. Hebr. xiii. 5; *to leave,* Acts, ii. 27, 31. Rom. ix. 29; *to neglect,* Hebr. x. 25; pass., *to be forsaken,* 2 Cor. iv. 9.

ἐγκατοικέω, and ἐνκατοικέω, *to dwell among,* 2 Pet. ii. 8.

ἐγκαυχάομαι, and ἐνκαυχάομαι, *to glory in,* 2 Thess. i. 4.

ἐγκεντρίζω, and ἐνκεντρίζω, *to ingraft, to graft in,* Rom. xi. 17, 19, 23.

ἔγκλημα, τὸ, *an accusation,* Acts, xxv. 16; ἔγκλημα ἔχειν, *to be accused,* Acts, xxiii. 29.

ἐγκομβόομαι, *to gird on,* 1 Pet. v. 5.

ἐγκοπὴ, and ἐνκοπὴ, ἡ, *a hindrance,* 1 Cor. ix. 12.

ἐγκόπτω, and ἐνκόπτω, *to impede, to hinder,* Gal. v. 7. 1 Thess. ii. 18; *to detain,* Acts, xxiv. 4 (RV *to be tedious*); pass., *to be hindered,* 1 Pet. iii. 7. Rom. xv. 22.

ἐγκράτεια, ἡ, *continence,* Gal. v. 23. 2 Pet. i. 6. Acts, xxiv. 25.

ἐγκρατεύομαι, *to have continence,* 1 Cor. vii. 9; *to be temperate,* 1 Cor. ix. 25.

ἐγκρατὴς, *temperate, continent,* Tit. i. 8.

ἐγκρίνω, and ἐνκρίνω, *to reckon amongst,* 2 Cor. x. 12.

ἐγκρύπτω, *to hide in,* Matt. xiii. 33.

ἔγκυος, and ἔνκυος, *pregnant,* Luke, ii. 5.

ἐγχρίω, *to anoint,* Rev. iii. 18.

ἐγὼ, pers. pron., *I;* ἰδοὺ ἐγὼ, *here I am!* Acts, ix. 10; τί ἐμοὶ καὶ σοί; *what have I to do with thee?* Joh. ii. 4. Luke, viii. 28. Matt. viii. 29. Mrk. i. 24; τί γάρ μοι; *for what does it concern me?* 1 Cor. v. 12; also ἔγωγε, *a strengthened* form, from the

Æolic ἔγωνγα (cf. the Lat. *egomet*), which has nothing to do with the *enclitic* γέ; otherwise, the accent would be ἐγώγε; for every enclitic *draws the accent towards itself*; as τοῖος (but τοιόσδε), τόσος (but τοσόσδε) etc. etc. (See Pape's Lex. in voc. ἐγώ.)

ἐδαφίζω, *to cast to the ground*, Luke, xix. 44.

ἔδαφος, τὸ, *the base, the ground*, Acts, xxii. 7.

ἑδραῖος, *firm, stedfast*, 1 Cor. vii. 37. xv. 58. Coloss. i. 23.

ἑδραίωμα, τὸ, *the basis, the support*, 1 Tim. iii. 15. (It is a purely ecclesiastical word.)

ἐθελοθρησκεία, and **ἐθελοθρησκία**, ἡ, *voluntary worship*, Col. ii. 23. (RV *will-worship*; Pape's Lex. renders it, *a self-chosen form of worship*.)

ἐθέλω, see θέλω, which latter is the only form used in the NT.

ἐθίζω, *to accustom*; pass., *to be accustomed*; τὸ εἰθισμένον, *the custom*, Luke, ii. 27.

ἐθνάρχης, ὁ, *an ethnarch*, one set over the people as ruler, but without the authority or name of king, 2 Cor. xi. 32 ("the governor of Damascene Syria, ruling in the name of King Aretas," Thayer.)

ἐθνικὸς, *partaking of the nature of the Gentiles, heathenish*; as subst., ὁ ἐθνικὸς, *the pagan, the Gentile*, Matt. v. 47. vi. 7. xviii. 17. 3 Joh. 7.

ἐθνικῶς, adv., *like the Gentiles* Gal. ii. 14.

ἔθνος, τὸ, *a race, a nation*, Matt. xxi. 43. Acts, x. 35. xvii. 26; τὰ ἔθνη, *the Gentiles*, Matt. iv. 15. vi. 32. Luke, ii. 32; used by S. Paul even of the *Christian Gentiles*, Rom. xi. 13. xv. 27. xvi. 4.

ἔθος, τὸ, *a custom*, Luke, xxii. 39; *a usage prescribed by law, a prescription*, Acts, xv. 1. xxi. 21. xxvi. 3. xxviii. 17.

ἔθω, *to be accustomed*, found only in Homer (Il. ix. 540. xvi. 260); perf., εἴωθα, *to be accustomed*; pluperf., εἰώθει, *he was wont*, Matt. xxvii. 15. Mrk. x. 1; κατὰ τὸ εἰωθὸς, *as his custom was*, Luke, iv. 16. Acts, xvii. 2.

εἰ, conj., *if*, Matt. xix. 10 etc.; as introducing a statement, =*viz.*, Acts, xxvi. 23; *whether*, Acts, viii. 22. 1 Cor. i. 16.

εἰδέα, ἡ, = ἰδέα, ἡ, *appearance, aspect*, Matt. xxviii. 3.

εἶδον and **εἶδα**, 2nd aor. of ὁράω, *to see*, Acts, x. 17. Mrk. ii. 12; ἰδὼν εἶδον, *I have surely seen*, Acts, vii. 34; *to experience*, Acts, ii. 27, 31. xiii. 36, 37.

εἶδος, τὸ, *form, shape*, Luke, iii. 22; Joh. v. 37; *kind*, 1 Thess. v. 22.

εἰδωλεῖον, and **εἰδώλιον**, τὸ, *the temple of an idol*, 1 Cor. viii. 10.

εἰδωλόθυτος, *sacrificed to idols*, Acts, xv. 29. xxi. 25. 1 Cor. viii. 1, 4, 10. ("τὸ εἰδωλόθυτον denotes the flesh left over from the heathen sacrifices," Thayer.)

εἰδωλολατρεία, and **εἰδωλολατρία**, ἡ, *idolatry*, Gal. v. 20. 1 Cor. x. 14. 1 Pet. iv. 3. (It is a purely ecclesiastical word, like the preceding and following.)

εἰδωλολάτρης, ὁ, *an idolater*, 1 Cor. v. 10, 11. vi. 9. x. 7. Ephes. v. 5.

εἴδωλον, τὸ, *an image of a heathen god*, *an idol*, Acts, vii. 41. xv. 20. 1 Cor. viii. 4, 7. x. 19. xii. 2.

εἰκῇ, adv., *at random; without just cause, vainly*, Coloss. ii. 18; *to no purpose, in vain*, Rom. xiii. 4. Gal. iii. 4. iv. 11. 1 Cor. xv. 2.

εἴκοσι, numer., *twenty*, Luke, xiv. 31. Acts, i. 15.

εἴκω, *to yield*, *to give way*, Gal. ii. 5.

εἴκω, not used in the present; perf., ἔοικα, *to be like*, James, i. 6, 23.

εἰκών, ἡ, *a likeness*, *an image*, Matt. xxii. 20. Rom. i. 23. 1 Cor. xi. 7. xv. 49.

εἰλικρίνεια, and **εἰλικρινία**, ἡ, *purity, sincerity*, 1 Cor. v. 8. 2 Cor. i. 12. ii. 17.

εἰλικρινής, *pure, sincere*, 2 Pet. iii. 1. Philipp. i. 10.

εἰλίσσω, *to roll up;* pass., *to be rolled up*, Rev. vi. 14 (here Westcott gives ἑλισσόμενον).

εἰμί, *to be, to exist*, Hebr. xi. 6. Joh. i. 1. viii. 58; *to be alive*, Matt. ii. 18. xxiii. 30; ἔστιν, *it is possible*, Hebr. ix. 5.

εἶμι, *to go*, a var. lect. ad Joh. vii. 34, 36.

εἶπα, and **εἶπον**, 1 aor. act. and 2 aor. act. of λέγω, *to say*, *to speak*, Luke, viii. 4. Matt. xxii. 1; ὡς ἔπος εἰπεῖν, *so to say*, Hebr. vii. 9; τί εἴπω; *what shall I say?* Joh. xii. 27; *to speak of*, Joh. i. 15 (but see Westcott), Luke, vi. 26; *to bid*, *to order*, Luke, xii. 13. Mrk. v. 43; *to style*, *to call*, Joh. x. 35.

εἰρηνεύω, *to live in peace, to be at peace*, 2 Cor. xiii. 11. Rom. xii. 18. Mrk. ix. 50. 1 Thess. v. 13.

εἰρήνη, ἡ, *peace*, Acts, ix. 31. xii. 20; *concord, harmony*, Gal. v. 22. Ephes. iv. 3. 2 Pet. iii. 14; *salvation*, Luke, i. 79. Acts, x. 36. Rom. viii. 6.

εἰρηνικὸς, *tending to peace, peaceful*, Hebr. xii. 11; *peaceable*, James, iii. 17.

εἰρηνοποιέω, *to make peace*, Coloss. i. 20.

εἰρηνοποιὸς, *peaceable, peaceful*, Matt. v. 9. ("=εἰρηνικὸς," Pape's Lex.)

εἰς, prepos., *into, to, towards; unto*, Joh. xiii. 1; *at*, Matt. xii. 41. Acts, viii. 40; γενέσθαι (or εἰμί) εἰς, *to amount to*, *to become*, 1 Cor. iv. 3. Matt. xix. 5; εἰς τί; *for what purpose? wherefore?* Matt. xxvi. 8; μὴ δυναμένη εἰς τὸ παντελὲς, *utterly unable*, Luke, xiii. 11.

εἷς, μία, ἓν, numer., *one; εἷς τις, a certain one*, Luke, xxii. 50; εἷς ἕκαστος, *each one*, Acts, ii. 3. Luke, iv. 40; = τις, or α, εἷς γραμματεὺς, *a scribe*, Matt. viii. 19; μία παιδίσκη, *a servant girl*, Matt. xxvi. 69; = πρῶτος,

first, μία σαββάτων, *the first day of the week*, Matt. xxviii. 1. Mrk. xvi. 2. Luke, xxiv. 1; καθ' ἕν, *one by one*, Joh. xxi. 25. 1 Cor. xiv. 31. Acts, xxi. 19.

εἰσάγω, *to lead in, to bring in*, Hebr. i. 6. Luke, ii. 27. xxii. 54. Acts, xxi. 28, 29, 37.

εἰσακούω, *to hearken unto, to obey*, 1 Cor. xiv. 21; pass., *to be heard favourably, to be accepted*, Luke, i. 13. Acts, x. 31.

εἰσδέχομαι, *to receive with favour*, 2 Cor. vi. 17.

εἴσειμι, *to go into, to enter*, Acts, iii. 3. xxi. 18, 26. Hebr. ix. 6.

εἰσέρχομαι, *to go or come into*, Matt. viii. 5. x. 12. Acts, xxiii. 16. Hebr. x. 5; *to arise, to spring up*, Luke, ix. 46.

εἰσκαλέομαι, *to call in*, Acts, x. 23.

εἴσοδος, ἡ, *an entrance*, 2 Pet. i. 11. Hebr. x. 19; *access*, 1 Thess. i. 9; *a coming*, Acts, xiii. 24. 1 Thess. ii. 1.

εἰσπηδάω, *to spring in*, Acts, xvi. 29.

εἰσπορεύομαι, *to enter*, Mrk. i. 21. v. 40; κατὰ τοὺς οἴκους εἰσπορευόμενος, *entering into every house*, Acts, viii. 3; *to visit*, Acts, xxviii. 30.

εἰστρέχω, *to run in*, Acts, xii. 14.

εἰσφέρω, *to bring in*, Luke, v. 18. 1 Tim. vi. 7. Hebr. xiii. 11; *to lead into*, Matt. vi. 13. Luke, xi. 4.

εἶτα, adv., *then*, Mrk. viii. 25. Joh. xiii. 5; *furthermore*, Hebr. xii. 9.

εἶτεν = εἶτα, Mrk. iv. 28. (An Ionic form of the preceding.)

εἴωθα, see ἔθω.

ἐκ, prepos., *from, out of, of*; ἐκ συμφώνου, *by consent*, 1 Cor. vii. 5; ἐξ ἀνάγκης, *of necessity*, 2 Cor. ix. 7; ἐκ μέρους, *proportionately*, 1 Cor. xii. 27.

ἕκαστος, *each, every*, Luke, vi. 44. Joh. xix. 23; εἷς ἕκαστος, *each one, every one*, Acts, ii. 6. xx. 31. Ephes. iv. 16.

ἑκάστοτε, adv., *at every time, always*, 2 Pet. i. 15.

ἑκατὸν *a hundred*, Matt. xviii. 12. Joh. xix. 39.

ἑκατονταετὴς, *a hundred years old*, Rom. iv. 19.

ἑκατονταπλασίων, *a hundredfold, a hundred times as much*, Mrk. x. 30. Luke, viii. 8.

ἑκατοντάρχης, ὁ, *a centurion*, Acts, x. 1, 22 etc.

ἑκατόνταρχος, ὁ, = ἑκατοντάρχης, Matt. viii. 5, 8.

ἐκβαίνω, *to go out*, Hebr. xi. 15.

ἐκβάλλω, *to cast out*, Mrk. vii. 26. ix. 18. Gal. iv. 30; *to drive out*, Matt. xxi. 12. Joh. ii. 15; *to throw out*, Acts, xxvii. 38; *to send out*, James, ii. 25. Acts, ix. 40. Mrk. i. 43; *to send forth*, Matt. xii. 20; *to tear out*, Mrk. ix. 47; *to take out*, Luke, vi. 42. Matt. vii. 5; *to bring forth*, Matt. xii. 35. xiii. 52; *to leave out, to except*, Rev. xi. 2.

ἔκβασις, ἡ, *egress, a way of escape*, 1 Cor. x. 13; *the end, the issue*, Hebr. xiii. 7.

ἐκβολή, ἡ, *a throwing out;* ἐκβολὴν ποιεῖσθαι, *to throw the cargo overboard,* Acts, xxvii. 18.

ἐκγαμίζω, *to give in marriage,* and pass., *to be given in marriage,* a var. lect. ad 1 Cor. vii. 38. Matt. xxii. 30. (Found only in the NT.)

ἐκγαμίσκω = ἐκγαμίζω, a var. lect. ad Luke, xx. 34.

ἔκγονος, *descended from;* ἔκγονα, *grandchildren,* 1 Tim. v. 4.

ἐκδαπανάω, *to expend wholly;* pass., *to be wholly spent,* 2 Cor. xii. 15.

ἐκδέχομαι, *to expect, to wait for,* James, v. 7. Hebr. xi. 10. Acts, xvii. 16. 1 Cor. xi. 33.

ἔκδηλος, *manifest, evident,* 2 Tim. iii. 9.

ἐκδημέω, *to go abroad; to be absent,* 2 Cor. v. 6, 8, 9.

ἐκδίδομαι, *to let out,* Matt. xxi. 33, 41. Luke, xx. 9. Mrk. xii. 1.

ἐκδιηγέομαι, *to narrate at length; to declare,* Acts, xiii. 41.

ἐκδικέω, *to avenge,* Luke, xviii. 3, 5. Rom. xii. 19; ἐκδικεῖν τὸ αἷμά τινος ἔκ τινος, *to avenge one's blood at the hand of,* Rev. vi. 10. xix. 2; *to punish,* 2 Cor. x. 6.

ἐκδίκησις, ἡ, *vengeance,* Rom. xii. 19. Hebr. x. 30. Luke, xxi. 22; ποιεῖν ἐκδίκησίν τινος, *to avenge a person,* Luke, xviii. 7. Cf. Acts, vii. 24; *punishment,* 1 Pet. ii. 14. 2 Thess. i. 8.

ἔκδικος, *unjust;* ὁ ἔκδικος, *the avenger,* Rom. xiii. 4. 1 Thess. iv. 6.

ἐκδιώκω, *to persecute,* 1 Thess. ii. 15. (RV *to drive out.*)

ἔκδοτος, *delivered up,* Acts, ii. 23.

ἐκδοχή, ἡ, *expectation,* Hebr. x. 27.

ἐκδύω, *to strip* a person of his garments, Luke, x. 30. Mrk. xv. 20. Matt. xxvii. 31; mid., *to unclothe oneself,* 2 Cor. v. 4.

ἐκεῖ, adv., *there,* Matt. ii. 13, 15. v. 24; = ἐκεῖσε, Matt. ii. 22. xvii. 20. Joh. xi. 8; also pleonastically after a relative adverb, Rev. xii. 6.

ἐκεῖθεν, *thence, from that place,* Matt. iv. 21. Luke, ix. 4. Joh. iv. 43.

ἐκεῖνος, demonstr. pron., *that person,* Matt. x. 14. xvii. 27 etc. (The reader is referred to his Greek Grammar.)

ἐκεῖσε, adv., *towards that place, thither,* Acts, xxi. 3; for ἐκεῖ, Acts, xxii. 5. (See Pape's Lex. in voc.)

ἐκζητέω, *to search out; to seek after,* Acts, xv. 17. Rom. iii. 11. Hebr. xi. 6; *to exact, to require,* Luke, xi. 50.

ἐκζήτησις, ἡ, *a subtle inquiry, an investigation,* 1 Tim. i. 4.

ἐκθαμβέω, *to greatly amaze;* pass., *to be greatly amazed,* Mrk. ix. 15. xvi. 5, 6; *to be greatly troubled,* Mrk. xiv. 33.

ἔκθαμβος, *greatly astonished,* Acts, iii. 11.

ἐκθαυμάζω, *to marvel greatly,* Mrk. xii. 17.

ἔκθετος, *cast out, exposed;* ποιεῖν ἔκθετα (τὰ βρέφη), *to expose,* Acts, vii. 19.

ἐκκαθαίρω, to cleanse thoroughly, 2 Tim. ii. 21. 1 Cor. v. 7. (RV purge out.)

ἐκκαίω, to burn out, to burn up; pass., to be inflamed, Rom. i. 27.

ἐκκεντέω, to pierce, Joh. xix. 37. Rev. i. 7.

ἐκκλάω, to break off, Rom. xi. 17, 19.

ἐκκλείω, to shut out, Gal. iv. 17; to exclude, Rom. iii. 27.

ἐκκλησία, ἡ, an assembly, Acts, xix. 32, 39, 41; a congregation, Hebr. ii. 12. Acts, vii. 38; an assembly for worship, a church, 1 Cor. xi. 18. xiv. 19, 35; the whole body of Christian believers, Acts, v. 11. viii. 3. Hebr. xii. 23. Matt. xvi. 18.

ἐκκλίνω, to turn aside from what is right, Rom. iii. 12; to turn away from, to shun, 1 Pet. iii. 11. Rom. xvi. 17.

ἐκκολυμβάω, to swim out to land, Acts, xxvii. 42.

ἐκκομίζω, to carry out for burial, Luke, vii. 12.

ἐκκοπή, ἡ, see ἐγκοπή.

ἐκκόπτω, to cut off or out, Matt. v. 30. xviii. 8. Rom. xi. 22,24; to cut down, Matt. iii. 10. vii. 19. Luke, iii. 9. xiii. 7, 9.

ἐκκρέμαμαι, to hang upon, Luke, xix. 48.

ἐκλαλέω, to utter, to tell, Acts, xxiii. 22.

ἐκλάμπω, to shine forth, Matt. xiii. 43.

ἐκλανθάνομαι, to forget, Hebr. xii. 5.

ἐκλέγομαι, to choose, to select, Joh. vi. 70. xiii. 18. Acts, vi. 5; pass., ἐκλελεγμένος, chosen, Luke, ix. 35.

ἐκλείπω, to leave out; intrans., to fail, Hebr. i. 12. Luke, xvi. 9. xxii. 32. xxiii. 45.

ἐκλεκτὸς, chosen, Luke, xxiii. 35. 1 Pet. ii. 9. Matt. xxii. 14; elect, Matt. xxiv. 31. Mrk. xiii. 27; select, excellent, 2 Joh. 1. 13. 1 Pet. ii. 6.

ἐκλογὴ, ἡ, election, choice, Rom. ix. 11. xi. 28; σκεῦος ἐκλογῆς, a chosen vessel, Acts, ix. 15; ἡ ἐκλογὴ = οἱ ἐκλεκτοὶ, Rom. xi. 7.

ἐκλύω, to unloose; pass., to be tired out, to be wearied, Matt. xv. 32. Mrk. viii. 3. Gal. vi. 9. Hebr. xii. 3, 5.

ἐκμάσσω, to wipe, Luke, vii. 38. Joh. xi. 2.

ἐκμυκτηρίζω, to scoff at, Luke, xvi. 14. xxiii. 35.

ἐκνεύω, to withdraw, Joh. v. 13.

ἐκνέω, to retire, a var. lect. ad Joh. v. 13. (lit. to swim away).

ἐκνήφω, to return to soberness of mind, 1 Cor. xv. 34.

ἑκούσιος, voluntary; κατὰ ἑκούσιον, of free will, Philem. 14.

ἑκουσίως, voluntarily, Hebr. x. 26. 1 Pet. v. 2.

ἔκπαλαι, adv., from of old, 2 Pet. ii. 3. iii. 5.

ἐκπειράζω, to try thoroughly; to tempt, Matt. iv. 7. Luke, iv. 12. x. 25. 1 Cor. x. 9.

ἐκπέμπω, to send forth, to send away, Acts, xiii. 14. xvii. 10.

ἐκπερισσῶς, vehemently, Mrk. xiv. 31. (Not found elsewhere.)

ἐκπετάννυμι, to stretch out, Rom x. 21.

ἐκπηδάω, *to spring forth*, Acts, xiv. 14.

ἐκπίπτω, *to fall from, to fall off*, Acts, xii. 7. xxvii. 32; *to fall away from, to lose*, Gal. v. 4. 2 Pet. iii. 17; *to become fruitless, to be ineffectual*, Rom. ix. 6; *to be cast up*, Acts, xxvii. 26.

ἐκπλέω, *to sail away*, Acts, xv. 39. xviii. 18. xx. 6.

ἐκπληρόω, *to fulfil*, Acts, xiii. 33.

ἐκπλήρωσις, ἡ, *fulfilment*, Acts, xxi. 26.

ἐκπλήσσω, *to astonish, to amaze*, Matt. vii. 28. xiii 54. xix. 25.

ἐκπνέω, *to expire*, Mrk. xv. 37, 39. Luke, xxiii. 46.

ἐκπορεύομαι, *to go forth, to depart*, Mrk. x. 46. xi. 19; *to come forth*, Joh. v. 29; *to proceed out of*, Matt. xv. 11, 18. Rev. iv. 5. ix. 17. xxii. 1; *to spread abroad*, Luke, iv. 37.

ἐκπορνεύω, *to give up to fornication*, Jude, 7. ("A strengthened form of πορνεύω," Pape's Lex.)

ἐκπτύω, *to spurn, to reject*, Gal. iv. 14.

ἐκριζόω, *to root up, to tear up*, Matt. xiii. 29. xv. 13. Luke, xvii. 6. Jude, 12.

ἔκστασις, ἡ, *amazement*, Luke, v. 26. Mrk. v. 42. xvi. 8; *a trance*, Acts, x. 10. xi. 5. xxii. 17.

ἐκστρέφω, *to turn aside, to pervert*, Tit. iii. 11.

ἐκσῴζω, *to bring safe*, Acts, xxvii. 39.

ἐκταράσσω, *to trouble greatly*, Acts, xvi. 20.

ἐκτείνω, *to stretch forth*, Matt. viii. 3. xii. 13. Acts, xxvi. 1; *to cast out*, as anchors, Acts, xxvii. 30.

ἐκτελέω, *to complete, to finish*, Luke, xiv. 29.

ἐκτένεια, ἡ, *intentness;* ἐν ἐκτενείᾳ, *earnestly*, Acts, xxvi. 7.

ἐκτενὴς, *intent, earnest*, 1 Pet. iv. 8; ἐκτενέστερον, as adv., *more earnestly*, Luke, xxii. 44.

ἐκτενῶς, *earnestly, fervently*, 1 Pet. i. 22. Acts, xii. 5.

ἐκτίθημι, *to expose;* pass., *to be exposed*, Acts, vii. 21; mid., *to set forth, to expound*, Acts, xi. 4. xviii. 26. xxviii. 23.

ἐκτινάσσω, *to shake off*, Matt. x. 14. Mrk. vi. 11; mid., *to shake off from himself*, Acts, xiii. 51; *to shake out*, Acts, xviii. 6.

ἕκτος, numer., *the sixth*, Matt. xx. 5 etc.

ἐκτὸς, adv., *outside, beyond;* ἐκτὸς τοῦ σώματος, *without the body*, 1 Cor. vi. 18. 2 Cor. xii. 2; *except*, Acts, xxvi. 22. 1 Cor. xv. 27; τὸ ἐκτὸς, *the outside*, Matt. xxiii. 26.

ἐκτρέπω, *to turn aside;* pass., *to be turned aside*, 1 Tim. i. 6. v. 15. 2 Tim. iv. 4; met., *to be put out of joint, to be dislocated*, Hebr. xii. 13 ("as a medical term, *to be dislocated*," Pape's Lex.); mid., with accus., *to turn away from, to shun*, 1 Tim. vi. 20.

ἐκτρέφω, *to nourish*, Ephes. v. 29; *to bring up*, Ephes. vi. 4.

ἔκτρομος, *exceedingly afraid*, a var. lect. ad Hebr. xii. 21. (It is not recognized in Pape's Lexicon.)

ἔκτρωμα, τὸ, *an abortive birth, an abortion*, 1 Cor. xv. 8. (The word is omitted in the Lexicons of Pape and Liddell, though used by both Hippocrates and Aristotle.)

ἐκφέρω, *to carry out* for burial, Acts, v. 6, 9, 10; *to bring out*, Luke, xv. 22. 1 Tim. vi. 7. Acts, v. 15; *to bring forth, to produce*, Hebr. vi. 8; *to lead out*, Mrk. viii. 23.

ἐκφεύγω, *to flee out*, Acts, xix. 16; *to escape*, 1 Thess. v. 3. Hebr. ii. 3. Luke, xxi. 36.

ἐκφοβέω, *to frighten greatly*, 2 Cor. x. 9.

ἔκφοβος, *exceedingly frightened*, Mrk. ix. 6. Hebr. xii. 21.

ἐκφύω, *to put forth*, Matt. xxiv. 32. Mrk. xiii. 28.

ἐκχέω, *to pour out, to spill*, Rev. xvi. 1, 2, 3, 4. Joh. ii. 15. Matt. ix. 17. Acts, ii. 17, 18, 33; *to shed*, as blood, Matt. xxvi. 28. Mrk. xiv. 24 (form ἐκχύνω); pass., *to gush out*, Acts, i. 18; *to be wholly given up to*, Jude, 11.

ἐκχύνω = ἐκχέω.

ἐκχωρέω, *to go out, to depart*, Luke, xxi. 21.

ἐκψύχω, *to expire*, Acts, v. 5, 10. xii. 23.

ἑκών, *willing*; mostly used adverbially, *of one's own accord, voluntarily*, Rom. viii. 20. 1 Cor. ix. 17.

ἐλαία, ἡ, *an olive tree*, Rom. xi. 17, 24. Rev. xi. 4; the fruit of the olive tree, *an olive*, James, iii. 12.

ἔλαιον, τὸ, *olive oil, oil*, Matt. xxv. 3, 4, 8. James, v. 14.

ἐλαιών, ὁ, *an olive garden*, used for the "Mount of Olives," Acts, i. 12. Luke, xix. 29. xxi. 37 (but see text).

ἐλάσσων, *less; younger*, Rom. ix. 12; *inferior*, Hebr. vii. 7; *worse*, Joh. ii. 10; ἔλαττον, as adv., *less, under*, 1 Tim v. 9.

ἐλαττονέω, *to have less*, 2 Cor. viii. 15.

ἐλαττόω, *to make less*, Hebr. ii. 7; pass., *to be made less*, Hebr. ii. 9; *to decrease*, Joh. iii. 30.

ἐλαύνω, *to drive*, James, iii. 4. 2 Pet. ii. 17; *to row*, Joh. vi. 19. Mrk. vi. 48.

ἐλαφρία, ἡ, *lightness, levity*, 2 Cor. i. 17.

ἐλαφρὸς, *light*, Matt. xi. 30; τὸ ἐλαφρὸν, as subst., *lightness*; τὸ ἐλαφρὸν τῆς θλίψεως, *our light affliction*, 2 Cor. iv. 17.

ἐλάχιστος, *smallest, least*, Matt. ii. 6. v. 19. Luke, xii. 26 etc.

ἐλαχιστότερος, a double comparative, *less than the least, far inferior to*, Ephes. iii. 8.

ἐλεάω, adopted by Westcott (Jude, 23. Rom. ix. 16) for the more common ἐλεέω, which see. (It is not recognized in Pape's Lexicon.)

ἐλεγμός, ὁ, *correction, reproof*, 2 Tim. iii. 16

ἔλεγξις, ἡ, *rebuke*, 2 Pet. ii. 16.

ἔλεγχος, ὁ, *a proof; a conviction, a sure persuasion*, Hebr. xi. 1.

ἐλέγχω, *to refute*, 1 Cor. xiv. 24. Tit. i. 9; *to convict*, James, ii. 9. Joh. viii. 46. xvi. 8. Jude, 15; *to reprove*, 1 Tim. v. 20. Joh. iii. 20.

ἐλεεινὸς, and **ἐλεινὸς**, *wretched, miserable*, 1 Cor. xv. 19. Rev. iii. 17.

ἐλεέω, *to have mercy on*, Matt. ix. 27. xv. 22. Rom. ix. 15, 18. xi. 32; *to shew mercy*, Rom. xii. 8; pass., *to obtain mercy*, Matt. v. 7. Rom. xi. 30, 31. 1 Tim. i. 13, 16. 1 Pet. ii. 10.

ἐλεημοσύνη, ἡ, *alms-giving; alms*, Acts, iii. 2, 3, 10. x. 4, 31; ποιεῖν ἐλεημοσύνην, *to bestow alms*, Matt. vi. 4. Acts, ix. 36. x. 2; also διδόναι ἐλ., in the same sense, Luke, xi. 41. xii. 33.

ἐλεήμων, *merciful*, Matt. v. 7. Hebr. ii. 17.

ἔλεος, ὁ, and, in the NT, more commonly ἔλεος, τὸ, *mercy*, Tit. iii. 5. Hebr. iv. 16. Matt. ix. 13 etc.

ἐλευθερία, ἡ, *freedom, liberty*, Gal. ii. 4. 1 Pet. ii. 16. 1 Cor. x. 29; *license*, 2 Pet. ii. 19.

ἐλεύθερος, *free*, 1 Cor. ix. 1, 19. Rom. vii. 3; *freeborn*, 1 Cor. vii. 22. xii. 13. Joh. viii. 33; *exempt*, Matt. xvii. 26.

ἐλευθερόω, *to set at liberty, to make free*, Joh. viii. 32, 36.

ἔλευσις, ἡ, *a coming*, Acts, vii. 52.

ἐλεφάντινος, *of ivory*, Rev. xviii. 12.

ἔλιγμα, τὸ, *a roll*, Joh. xix. 39 (where other texts give μίγμα).

Ἐλισαῖος, ὁ, *Elisha*, Luke, iv. 27.

ἑλίσσω, *to roll up, to fold together*, Heb. i. 12. Rev. vi. 14.

ἕλκος, τό, *a wound; an ulcer, a sore*, Rev. xvi. 2, 11. Luke xvi. 21.

ἑλκόω, *to wound;* pass. ἡλκωμένος, *full of sores*, Luke, xvi. 20.

ἕλκω, *to draw*, Joh. xviii. 10. xxi. 6; *to drag*, Acts, xvi. 19. xxi. 30; met., *to draw*, i.e. *to attract*, Joh. xii. 32. Cf. Joh. vi. 44.

Ἑλληνὶς, ἡ, *a Greek (or Gentile) woman*, Acts, xvii. 12. Mrk. vii. 26.

Ἑλληνιστὴς, ὁ, *a Hellenist;* "employed in the NT of Jews born in foreign lands and speaking Greek (Acts, xi. 20); the name adhered to them even after they had embraced Christianity (Acts, vi. 1)," Thayer.

Ἑλληνιστὶ, adv., *in Greek*, Joh. xix. 20; Ἑλληνιστὶ γινώσκεις; *dost thou understand Greek?* Acts, xxi. 37. Cf. Ἑβραϊστί, Ῥωμαϊστί.

ἐλλογέω, and **ἐλλογάω**, *to set down to one's account*, Philem. 18; *to impute*, Rom. v. 13.

ἐλπίζω, *to hope*, Rom. viii. 25. 1 Cor. xiii. 7; *to place hope in*, Joh. v. 45. 1 Pet. iii. 5. 2 Cor. i. 10. 1 Tim. iv. 10; *to trust in*, Matt. xii. 21. Rom. xv. 12.

ἐλπίς, ἡ, hope, Acts, xxiii. 6. xxvi. 7. Tit. i. 2 etc. ("In the NT always in a good sense, *expectation of good, hope*," Thayer.)

Ἐλύμας = μάγος, Acts, xiii. 8, an Aramaic word.

Ἐλωΐ, *my God*, Mrk. xv. 34.

ἐμαυτοῦ, reflex. pron., *of myself*, Matt. viii. 9 etc. (The reader is referred to his Greek Grammar.)

ἐμβαίνω, *to enter, to go on board*, Matt. viii. 23. etc.

ἐμβάλλω, *to cast into*, Luke, xii. 5.

ἐμβάπτω, *to dip*, Matt. xxvi. 23. Cf. Mrk. xiv. 20.

ἐμβατεύω, *to enter; to search into, to speculate about*, Coloss. ii. 18 ("*going into curious and subtle speculation about things which he has seen* in visions granted him," Thayer).

ἐμβιβάζω, *to put on board*, Acts, xxvii. 6.

ἐμβλέπω, *to look*, Matt. vi. 26; *to look upon*, Mrk. x. 21, 27. xiv. 67; with accus., *to behold*, Mrk. viii. 25; *to see clearly*, Acts, xxii. 11.

ἐμβριμάομαι, *to snort; to be moved with indignation*, Mrk. xiv. 5; *to groan;* Joh. xi. 33, 38; *to charge strictly*, Mrk. i. 43. Matt. ix. 30 (in this last passage Pape (in Lex.) renders it, *to be angry, to express his indignation*).

ἐμέω, *to vomit forth*, Rev. iii. 16.

ἐμμαίνομαι, *to rage against*, Acts, xxvi. 11.

Ἐμμανουήλ, ὁ, indecl., *Immanuel*, Matt. i. 23. ("According to the orthodox interpretation, the name denotes the same as θεάνθρωπος, and has reference to the union of the human and the divine nature in Christ," Thayer.)

ἐμμένω, *to continue in, to persevere in*, Acts, xiv. 22. Gal. iii. 10. Hebr. viii. 9.

ἐμός, possess. pron., *my* or *mine*, Joh. xviii. 36 etc.

ἐμπαιγμονή, ἡ, *mockery, derision*, 2 Pet. iii. 3. (The word is not found elsewhere.)

ἐμπαιγμός, ὁ, *a mocking, a scoffing*, Hebr. xi. 36. (It is a purely ecclesiastical word.)

ἐμπαίζω, *to mock*, Matt. xx. 19. xxvii. 41. Luke, xxiii. 11; pass., *to be deceived*, Matt. ii. 16.

ἐμπαίκτης, ὁ, *a mocker*, 2 Pet. iii. 3. Jude, 18.

ἐμπεριπατέω, and ἐνπεριπατέω, *to walk in*, 2 Cor. vi. 16.

ἐμπίπλημι, and ἐμπιπλάω, *to fill*, Acts, xiv. 17; *to satisfy*, Luke, i. 53; pass., *to be filled, to be full*, Luke, vi. 25. Joh. vi. 12; with genit., *to be satisfied with*, Rom. xv. 24.

ἐμπίπρημι, and ἐμπρήθω, *to set on fire, to burn*, Matt. xxii. 7.

ἐμπίπτω, *to fall into*, Matt. xii. 11. Luke, vi. 39. xiv. 5; *to fall among*, Luke, x. 36.

ἐμπλέκω, *to entangle in, to involve in;* pass., *to be entangled in*, 2 Tim. ii. 4. 2 Pet. ii. 20.

ἐμπλοκὴ, ἡ, *a braiding, a plaiting*, 1 Pet. iii. 3.

ἐμπνέω, *to inhale, to breathe*, Acts, ix. 1.

ἐμπορεύομαι, *to traffic, to trade; to use a person or thing for gain*, 2 Pet. ii. 3 (RV *make merchandise of you*).

ἐμπορία, ἡ, *merchandise*, Matt. xxii. 5.

ἐμπόριον, τὸ, *an emporium; οἶκον ἐμπορίου, a house of merchandise*, Joh. ii. 16.

ἔμπορος, ὁ, *a merchant*, Matt. xiii. 45. Rev. xviii. 3, 11, 15, 23.

ἐμπρήθω, *to burn up*, Matt. xxii. 7.

ἐμπροσθεν, adv., *before*, Matt. vi. 2. Joh. iii. 28. x. 4; *in the presence of*, Matt. x. 32. xxvi. 70. Luke, xii. 8.

ἐμπτύω, *to spit upon*, Mrk. x. 34. xiv. 65. xv. 19 ; pass., *to be spit upon*, Luke, xviii. 32.

ἐμφανὴς, *manifest*, Acts, x. 40. Rom. x. 20.

ἐμφανίζω, *to manifest*, Joh. xiv. 21, 22. Hebr. xi. 14 ; *to make known, to notify*, Acts, xxiii. 15, 22 ; *to lay an information, to inform*, Acts, xxiv. 1. xxv. 2, 15 ; pass., *to be manifested, to appear*, Matt. xxvii. 53. Hebr. ix. 24.

ἔμφοβος, *terrified, frightened*, Luke, xxiv. 5. Acts, x. 4.

ἐμφυσάω, *to breathe on*, Joh. xx. 22.

ἔμφυτος, *implanted*, James, i. 21.

ἐν, prepos., *in, among, by, during* etc.

ἐναγκαλίζομαι, *to take into the arms*, Mrk. ix. 36. x. 16. Luke, ii. 28.

ἐνάλιος, *marine; τὰ ἐνάλια, marine animals*, James, iii. 7.

ἔναντι, adv., *in the presence of, before*, Luke, i. 8. Acts, viii. 21. (It is a purely biblical word.)

ἐναντίος, *over against, opposite*, Mrk. xv. 39; *contrary*, Acts, xxvii. 4. Matt. xiv. 24. Mrk. vi. 48; *adverse, hostile*, 1 Thess. ii. 15. Tit. ii. 8 ; *ἐναντίον*, used adverbially, *in the presence of*, Acts, vii. 10. Luke, xx. 26.

ἐνάρχομαι, *to make a beginning, to begin*, Gal. iii. 3. Philipp. i. 6.

ἔνατος, see ἔννατος.

ἐνδεὴς, *in want*, Acts, iv. 34.

ἔνδειγμα, τὸ, *a proof, a token*, 2 Thess. i. 5.

ἐνδείκνυμαι, *to exhibit, to shew*, Rom. ii. 15. Tit. iii. 2. 2 Cor. viii. 24. Hebr. vi. 10, 11 ; *to put forth, to manifest*, 2 Tim. iv. 14.

ἔνδειξις, ἡ, *a manifestation*, Rom. iii. 25 ; *a proof*, 2 Cor. viii. 24 ; *a sign, a token*, Philipp. i. 28.

ἔνδεκα, numer., *eleven; οἱ ἕνδεκα, the eleven Apostles* remaining after the death of Judas Iscariot, Matt. xxviii. 16. Luke xxiv. 9, 33. Acts, i. 26.

ἐνδέκατος, numer., *eleventh*, Matt. xx. 6, 9. Rev. xxi. 20.

ἐνδέχομαι, *to admit;* impers., *ἐνδέχεται, it is possible*, Luke, xiii. 33.

ἐνδημέω, *to be at home*, 2 Cor. v. 6, 8, 9.

ἐνδιδύσκω, *to put upon one, to clothe in*, Mrk. xv. 17; mid., *to clothe one'self in, to put on*, Luke. xvi. 19. (It is not a classical word.)

ἔνδικος, *righteous, just.* Rom. iii. 8. Hebr. ii. 2.

ἐνδόμησις, ἡ, and **ἐνδώμησις**, ἡ, *what is built in; the material of a building, a structure*, Rev. xxi. 18.

ἐνδοξάζομαι, *to be glorified in*, 2 Thess. i. 10, 12. (It is a purely NT form, ἐνδοξάζω appearing only in the Septuagint.)

ἔνδοξος, *of high repute, highly esteemed*, 1 Cor. iv. 10; *splendid, glorious*, Luke, vii. 25; τὰ ἔνδοξα, *the glorious things*, Luke, xiii. 17; met., *free from sin*, Ephes. v. 27.

ἔνδυμα, τό, *raiment*, Matt. vi. 25, 28. xxviii. 3; ἔνδυμα γάμου, *a wedding garment*, Matt. xxii. 11; ἐνδύματα προβάτων, *sheep's clothing*, Matt. vii. 15.

ἐνδυναμόω, *to endue with strength, to strengthen*, Philipp. iv. 13. 1 Tim. i. 12. 2 Tim. iv. 17; pass., *to be strengthened, to increase in strength*, 2 Tim. ii. 1. Acts, ix. 22. Rom. iv. 20. Ephes. vi. 10.

ἐνδύνω, and **ἐνδύω**, *to enter*, 2 Tim. iii. 6; *to put on a person, to array in*, Matt. xxvii. 31. Mrk. xv. 20. Luke, xv. 22; pass., *to be clothed in*, Matt. xxii. 11. Mrk. i. 6. Rev. i. 13; mid., *to put on oneself*, Matt. vi. 25. Luke. xii. 22. Mrk. vi. 9. Rom. xiii. 14. Acts, xii. 21 etc.

ἔνδυσις, ἡ, *a putting on*, 1 Pet. iii. 3.

ἐνέδρα, ἡ, *a lying in wait*, Acts, xxiii. 16. xxv. 3.

ἐνεδρεύω, *to lie in wait for*, Acts, xxiii. 21. Luke, xi. 54.

ἔνεδρον, τό = ἐνέδρα, a var. lect. ad Acts, xxiii. 16.

ἐνειλέω, *to wrap up in*, Mrk. xv. 46.

ἔνειμι, *to be within*; τὰ ἐνόντα, *the things within your power*, Luke, xi. 41 [or = τὰ ἔσωθεν of verse 39].

ἕνεκα, and **ἕνεκεν**, prepos., *on account of, for the sake of*, Matt. v. 10. xix. 29. Luke, vi. 22; ἕνεκα τούτου, *for this cause*, Matt. xix. 5; τίνος ἕνεκα, *for what cause*, Acts, xix. 32; οὗ εἵνεκεν, *because*, Luke, iv. 18.

ἐνέργεια, ἡ, *working, efficiency*, Ephes. i. 19. iii. 7. Coloss. ii. 12; κατ' ἐνέργειαν ἐν μέτρῳ ἑνὸς ἑκάστου μέρους, Ephes. iv. 16 ("*according to the working which agrees with the measure of every single part*," Thayer); cf. Philipp. iii. 21. ("In the NT used only of superhuman power," Thayer).

ἐνεργέω, *to be operative, to work*, Matt. xiv. 2. Mrk. vi. 14. Ephes. ii. 2; *to work for*, Gal. ii. 8; *to effect*, 1 Cor. xii. 6, 11. Philipp. ii. 13; mid., *to work*, Rom. vii. 5. 2 Cor. i. 6. iv. 12. Gal. v. 6; πολὺ ἰσχύει ἐνεργουμένη, James, v. 16 (RV *availeth much in its working*).

ἐνέργημα, τό, *operation, working*, 1 Cor. xii. 6, 10.

ἐνεργής, *active, effectual*, Hebr. iv. 12. 1 Cor. xvi. 9.

ἐνευλογέω, *to bless*, Gal. iii. 8. (It is a purely ecclesiastical word, and in the NT found only in the passive.)

ἐνέχω, *to have within*; intrans., *to be enraged with*, Mrk. vi. 19. Luke, xi. 53 (RV *press upon*); pass., *to be entangled*, Gal. v. 1.

ἐνθάδε, adv., *here*, Acts, xvi. 28. Luke, xxiv. 41; *hither*, Joh. iv. 15. Acts, xxv. 17.

ἔνθεν, adv., *hence*, Matt. xvii 20. Luke, xvi. 26.

ἐνθυμέομαι, *to revolve in mind*, *to ponder over*, Matt. i. 20; *to think*, Matt. ix. 4; *to reflect*, a var. lect. ad Acts, x. 19.

ἐνθύμησις, ἡ, *a thought*, Matt. ix. 4. xii. 25; *a device*, Acts, xvii. 29.

ἔνι = ἔνεστι, *there is in, there existeth*, Gal. iii. 28. 1 Cor. vi. 5. Coloss. iii. 11; *is possible*, James, i. 17. (See Pape's Lex. in voc.)

ἐνιαυτός, ὁ, *a year*, Acts, xi. 26. xviii. 11; ποιεῖν ἐνιαυτόν, *to spend a year*, James, iv. 13; κατ' ἐνιαυτόν, *yearly*, Hebr. ix. 25. x. 1, 3; *period*, Luke, iv. 19.

ἐνίστημι, *to place in*; in perf. pluperf. and 2nd aor., *to impend, to be at hand*, 2 Thess. ii. 2; *to be present*, 1 Cor. vii. 26. Hebr. ix. 9. Rom. viii. 38. 2 Tim. iii. 1.

ἐνισχύω, *to strengthen*; intr. pass., *to be strengthened*, Acts, ix. 19.

ἔννατος, and ἔνατος, numer., *ninth*, Matt. xx. 5 etc.

ἐννέα, num., *nine*, Luke, xvii. 17.

ἐννενήκοντα, *ninety*, Matt. xviii. 12.

ἐνεός, *speechless*, Acts, ix. 7.

ἐννεύω, *to make signs*, Luke, i. 62. Cf. διανεύω.

ἔννοια, ἡ, *way of thinking, mind*, 1 Pet. iv. 1; *intention*, Hebr. iv. 12.

ἔννομος, *bound by the law*, 1 Cor. ix. 21; *lawful, regular*, Acts, xix. 39.

ἔννυχος, *nightly*; ἔννυχα, adverbially, *in the night*, Mrk. i. 35.

ἐνοικέω, *to dwell in*, Rom. viii. 11. 2 Tim. i. 14.

ἐνορκίζω, with two accus., *to adjure*, 1 Thess. v. 27.

ἑνότης, ἡ, *unity, unanimity*, Ephes. iv. 3, 13.

ἐνοχλέω, *to trouble*, Luke, vi. 18. Hebr. xii. 15.

ἔνοχος, with dat. or genit., *subject to, liable to*, Hebr. ii. 15. Matt. v. 21, 22; *guilty of*, 1 Cor. xi. 27. James, ii. 10. Mrk. iii. 29.

ἔνταλμα, τό, *a precept*, Matt. xv. 9. Mrk. vii. 7. Coloss. ii. 22.

ἐνταφιάζω, *to prepare a body for burial*, Joh. xix. 40. Matt. xxvi. 12.

ἐνταφιασμός, ὁ, *preparation* of a body *for burial*, Mrk. xiv. 8. Joh. xii. 7.

ἐντέλλομαι, *to give orders, to enjoin, to command*, Hebr. xi. 22. Acts, i. 2. xiii. 47. Matt. xvii. 9. xix. 7 etc.

ἐντεῦθεν, adv., *from this place, hence*, Luke, iv. 9. xiii. 31;

ἐντεῦθεν καὶ ἐντεῦθεν, *on the one side and on the other side*, Joh. xix. 18; *from this source*, James, iv. 1.

ἔντευξις, ἡ, *a meeting with, interview; supplication, prayer*, 1 Tim. iv. 5; *intercession*, 1 Tim. ii. 1.

ἔντιμος, *honourable*, Luke, xiv. 8; ἔντιμον ἔχειν, *to hold in honour*, Philipp. ii. 29; *precious*, 1 Pet. ii. 4, 6; *dear*, Luke, vii. 2.

ἐντολή, ἡ, *a command, an injunction*, Luke, xv. 29. Joh. x. 18. xii. 49 etc.; τηρεῖν τὰς ἐντολὰς, *to keep the commandments*, Matt. xix. 17. Joh. xv. 10. 1 Joh. ii. 3. iii. 22.

ἐντόπιος, *dwelling in a place;* as subst., *a resident*, Acts, xxi. 12.

ἐντὸς, adv., *within*, Luke, xvii. 21 (or, *among*); τὸ ἐντὸς, *the inside*, Matt. xxiii. 26.

ἐντρέπω, *to turn about;* met., *to shame*, 1 Cor. iv. 14; pass., *to be ashamed*, 2 Thess. iii. 14. Tit. ii. 8; *to reverence*, Matt. xxi. 37. Mrk. xii. 6. Luke, xx. 13; *to pay regard to*, Luke, xviii. 2, 4.

ἐντρέφω, *to rear in, to educate in*, 1 Tim. iv. 6.

ἔντρομος, *in fear*, Acts, vii. 32. xvi. 29. Hebr. xii. 21.

ἐντροπὴ, ἡ, *shame*, 1 Cor. vi. 5. xv. 34.

ἐντρυφάω, *to revel in*, 2 Pet. ii. 13.

ἐντυγχάνω, *to meet with; to make a petition to*, Acts, xxv. 24; *to intercede for*, Rom. viii. 27, 34. Hebr. vii. 25; *to plead*, Rom. xi. 2.

ἐντυλίσσω, *to wrap in*, Matt. xxvii. 59. Luke, xxiii. 53; pass., *to be rolled up*, Joh. xx. 7.

ἐντυπόω, *to engrave*, 2 Cor. iii. 7.

ἐνυβρίζω, *to treat with contempt*, Hebr. x. 29.

ἐνυπνιάζομαι, *to dream dreams*, Acts, ii. 17. Jude, 8.

ἐνύπνιον, τὸ, *a vision*, Acts, ii. 17.

ἐνώπιον, adv., *in the presence of, before*, Luke, v. 25 etc.

ἐνωτίζομαι, *to give ear to*, Acts, ii. 14.

ἕξ, numer., *six*, Matt. xvii. 1 etc.

ἐξαγγέλλω, *to make known, to publish*, 1 Pet. ii. 9.

ἐξαγοράζω, *to redeem*, Gal. iv. 5; mid., *to save from being wasted, to make the most of*, Coloss. iv. 5. Ephes. v. 16.

ἐξάγω, *to lead out*, Joh. x. 3. Acts, vii. 36 etc.

ἐξαιρέω, *to take out; to pluck out*, Matt. v. 29. xviii. 9; mid., *to choose out, to select*, Acts, xxvi. 17 (RV *delivering*); *to rescue, to deliver*, Acts, vii. 10, 34. xxiii. 27.

ἐξαίρω, *to lift up; to remove*, 1 Cor. v. 13.

ἐξαιτέω, *to demand of;* mid., *to ask for*, Luke, xxii. 31.

ἐξαίφνης, adv., *suddenly*, Mrk. xiii. 36. Luke, ii. 13. ix. 39.

ἐξακολουθέω, *to follow after*, 2 Pet. i. 16. ii. 15; *to imitate*, 2 Pet. ii. 2.

ἐξακόσιοι, numer., *six hundred*, Rev. xiv. 20.

ἐξαλείφω, *to blot out, to erase,* Coloss. ii. 14. Rev. iii. 5. Acts, iii. 19; *to wipe away,* Rev. vii. 17.

ἐξάλλομαι, *to leap up,* Acts, iii. 8.

ἐξανάστασις, ἡ, *a rising again, a resurrection,* Philipp. iii. 11.

ἐξανατέλλω, *to cause to spring up;* intrans., *to spring up,* Matt. xiii. 5. Mrk. iv. 5.

ἐξανίστημι, *to cause to arise, to raise up,* Mrk. xii. 19. Luke, xx. 28; 2 aor. act., *to rise up,* Acts, xv. 5.

ἐξαπατάω, *to thoroughly deceive,* Rom. vii. 11. xvi. 18. 1 Cor. iii. 18 etc.

ἐξάπινα, adv., a late form for ἐξαπίνης, *suddenly,* Mrk. ix. 8.

ἐξαπορέω, *to be thoroughly perplexed, to be in despair,* 2 Cor. i. 8. iv. 8.

ἐξαποστέλλω, *to send forth,* Acts, vii. 12. xxii. 21. Gal. iv. 4. Luke, xxiv. 49; met., *to impart,* Gal. iv. 6. Acts, xiii. 26; *to send away, to dismiss,* Luke, i. 53. xx. 11.

ἐξαρτίζω, *to completely furnish,* 2 Tim. iii. 17; *to complete,* Acts, xxi. 5.

ἐξαστράπτω, *to shine as lightning,* Luke, ix. 29.

ἐξαυτῆς, adv., *forthwith,* Acts, x. 33. xi. 11. xxi. 32 etc.

ἐξεγείρω, *to raise up,* 1 Cor. vi. 14. Rom. ix. 17.

ἔξειμι, *to go out,* Acts, xiii. 42; *to depart,* Acts, xvii. 15. xx. 7; *to make one's escape,* Acts, xxvii. 43.

ἐξέλκω, *to draw away, to allure,* James, i. 14.

ἐξέραμα, τό, *vomit,* 2 Pet. ii. 22.

ἐξεραυνάω, and ἐξερευνάω, *to search diligently,* 1 Pet. i. 10.

ἐξέρχομαι, *to come forth, to proceed,* Matt. ii. 6. xv. 18. 1 Cor. xiv. 36. Hebr. vii. 5; *to come out,* Matt. v. 26. viii. 34. xv. 22; *to go forth,* 1 Joh. iv. 1. Matt. ix. 31; *to depart,* Luke, v. 8. Acts, xvi. 19; *to escape,* Joh. x. 39.

ἔξεστι, impers. verb, *it is permitted, it is lawful,* Matt. xii. 2, 10. 1 Cor. vi. 12; ἐξὸν, *when it was permitted;* but ἃ οὐκ ἐξὸν λαλῆσαι, *which it is not lawful to utter,* sc. ἐξόν ἐστι, 2 Cor. xii. 4; so δ οὐκ ἐξὸν ἦν (= οὐκ ἐξῆν) αὐτῷ φαγεῖν, *which it was not lawful for him to eat,* Matt. xii. 4.

ἐξετάζω, *to search out,* Matt. ii. 8; *to inquire,* Matt. x. 11; with accus. of pers., *to ask,* Joh. xxi. 12.

ἐξηγέομαι, *to set forth, to recount,* Luke, xxiv. 35. Acts, xv. 12, 14. xxi. 19; *to reveal, to make known,* Joh. i. 18.

ἑξήκοντα, numer., *sixty,* Matt., xiii. 8, 23 etc.

ἑξῆς, adv., *in order, in succession;* τῇ ἑξῆς ἡμέρᾳ, *on the next day,* Luke, ix. 37; so τῇ ἑξῆς (sc. ἡμέρᾳ), *next day,* Acts, xxi. 1. xxv. 17; ἐν τῷ ἑξῆς (sc. χρόνῳ), *soon afterwards,* Luke, vii. 11.

ἐξηχέω, *to sound forth, to resound;* pass., *to be sounded forth, to be promulgated,* 1 Thess. i. 8.

ἕξις, ἡ, *a condition of body or mind; use, practice,* Hebr. v. 14.

ἐξίστημι, and **ἐξιστάνω**, *to astonish, to amaze,* Luke, xxiv. 22. Acts, viii. 9, 11; in the perf. pluperf. 2 aor. and mid., *to be astonished, to be amazed,* Acts, ii. 7, 12. viii. 11, 13. x. 45. xii. 16. Matt. xii. 23. Mrk. v. 42. Luke, ii. 47. viii. 56; *to be insane,* 2 Cor. v. 13. Mrk. iii. 21.

ἐξισχύω, *to have full power,* Ephes. iii. 18.

ἔξοδος, ἡ, *exit, departure,* Hebr. xi. 22; *departure from life, decease,* Luke, ix. 31. 2 Pet. i. 15.

ἐξολεθρεύω, *to utterly destroy,* Acts, iii. 23.

ἐξομολογέω, *to promise, to agree,* Luke, xxii. 6; mid., *to confess,* Matt. iii. 6. Mrk. i. 5. James, v. 16. Acts, xix. 18; *to acknowledge openly,* Philipp. ii. 11; with dat. of pers., *to give praise to,* Rom. xiv. 11. Matt. xi. 25. Luke, x. 21.

ἐξορκίζω, *to adjure;* ἐξορκίζω σε κατὰ τοῦ θεοῦ τοῦ ζῶντος, *I adjure thee by the living God,* Matt. xxvi. 63.

ἐξορκιστής, ὁ, *an exorcist* (one who expels devils by conjuration), Acts, xix. 13.

ἐξορύσσω, *to dig through,* Mrk. ii. 4; *to pluck out,* Gal. iv. 15.

ἐξουδενέω, *to set at naught,* Mrk. ix. 12.

ἐξουδενόω = ἐξουδενέω, a var. lect. ad Mrk. ix. 12.

ἐξουθενέω, *to make of no account, to despise utterly,* Luke, xviii. 9. Rom. xiv. 3, 10. Gal. iv. 14. 1 Thess. v. 20 etc.; *to set at naught,* Luke, xxiii. 11; ἐξουθενημένος, *of no account, contemptible,* 2 Cor. x. 10. Cf. 1 Cor. vi. 4; τὰ ἐξουθενημένα, *things despised,* 1 Cor. i. 28; ἐξουθενηθείς, *set at naught, rejected,* Acts, iv. 11. (All of the three above verbs are purely biblical forms.)

ἐξουσία, ἡ, *power,* Matt. ix. 6, 8. Joh. x. 18. xix. 10; *authority,* Luke, iv. 32. Matt. viii. 9. xxi. 23. xxviii. 18 etc.; *liberty,* 1 Cor. viii. 9. ix. 6; plur., *authorities, potentates,* Luke, xii. 11. Rom. xiii. 1. Tit. iii. 1. Coloss. i. 16.

ἐξουσιάζω, *to have authority over,* Luke, xxii. 25; *to be master of, to have power over,* 1 Cor. vii. 4; pass., *to be brought under the power of,* 1 Cor. vi. 12.

ἐξοχή, ἡ, *eminence,* Acts, xxv. 23.

ἐξυπνίζω, with accus., *to awaken a person out of sleep,* Joh. xi. 11.

ἔξυπνος, *aroused from sleep,* Acts, xvi. 27.

ἔξω, adv., *out,* Matt. v. 13. Joh. vi. 37. ix. 34; *outside, without,* Matt. xii. 46. Luke, xiii. 25. Joh. xviii. 16; *away,* Matt. xiii. 48. Luke, xiv. 35;

οἱ ἔξω, *those that are outside our community*, Mrk. iv. 11. 1 Cor. v. 12, 13. Coloss. iv. 5. 1 Thess. iv. 12; ὁ ἔξω ἄνθρωπος, *the outer man*, i.e. the body, 2 Cor. iv. 16; αἱ ἔξω πόλεις, *foreign cities*, Acts, xxvi. 11.

ἔξωθεν, adv., *from without*, Mrk. vii. 18; *outwardly*, Matt. xxiii. 27; *outside, without*, 2 Cor. vii. 5; *out*, Rev. xi. 2; ὁ ἔξωθεν κόσμος, *the outward adorning*, 1 Pet. iii. 3; τὸ ἔξωθεν, *the outside*, Matt. xxiii. 25. Luke, xi. 39; οἱ ἔξωθεν = οἱ ἔξω, 1 Tim. iii. 7; as prepos. with genit., *outside of*, Matt. vii. 15. Rev. xi. 2. xiv. 20.

ἐξωθέω, *to thrust out, to expel*, Acts, vii. 45; *to propel, to drive*, a var. lect. ad Acts, xxvii. 39 (Westcott reads ἐκσῶσαι).

ἐξώτερος, comparative of ἔξω, *outer*; τὸ σκότος τὸ ἐξώτερον, *the outer darkness*, Matt. viii. 12. xxii. 13. xxv. 30.

ἔοικα, see εἴκω.

ἑορτάζω, *to keep a feast*, 1 Cor. v. 8.

ἑορτή, ἡ, *a festival, a feast*, Coloss. ii. 16. Joh. vii. 37; κατὰ ἑορτὴν, *at every feast*, Matt. xxvii. 15. Mrk. xv. 6; ἡ ἑορτὴ τοῦ πάσχα, *the feast of the Passover*, Luke, ii. 41. Joh. xiii. 1; = ἡ ἑορτὴ τῶν ἀζύμων, Luke, xxii. 1.

ἐπαγγελία, ἡ, *a promise*, Rom. iv. 14. ix. 9. xv. 8. Acts, ii. 33 etc.

ἐπαγγέλλω, *to announce;* pass., *to be promised;* ᾧ ἐπήγγελται, *to whom the promise has been made*, Gal. iii. 19; mid., *to promise*, Hebr. vi. 13. x. 23. xi. 11. Tit. i. 2. James, i. 12 etc.; *to profess*, 1 Tim. ii. 10. vi. 21.

ἐπάγγελμα, τὸ, *a promise*, 2 Pet. i. 4. iii. 13.

ἐπάγω, *to bring upon* a person, 2 Pet. ii. 1, 5. Acts, v. 28.

ἐπαγωνίζομαι, with dat. of object, *to contend for*, Jude, 3.

ἐπαθροίζω, *to gather together*, Luke, xi. 29.

ἐπαινέω, *to praise, to commend*, Luke, xvi. 8. 1 Cor. xi. 2, 17.

ἔπαινος, ὁ, *praise, commendation*, Philipp. iv. 8. Rom. ii. 29. xiii. 3. 1 Cor. iv. 5. 2 Cor. viii. 18. Ephes. i. 12 etc.

ἐπαίρω, *to lift up*, 1 Tim. ii. 8. Luke, xxiv. 50. Matt. xvii. 8; *to raise up, to hoist up*, Acts, xxvii. 40; pass., *to be taken up* into heaven, Acts, i. 9; *to be exalted*, 2 Cor. x. 5; mid., *to exalt himself*, 2 Cor. xi. 20.

ἐπαισχύνομαι, *to be ashamed*, 2 Tim. i. 12; *to be ashamed of*, Hebr. xi. 16. Mrk. viii. 38. Luke, ix. 26.

ἐπαιτέω, *to beg, to ask alms*, Luke, xvi. 3.

ἐπακολουθέω, *to follow*, Mrk. xvi. 20; *to follow closely, to imitate*, 1 Pet. ii. 21; *to follow after*, i.e. to be revealed at the day of Judgment, 1 Tim. v. 24; *to pursue, to practise*, 1 Tim. v. 10.

ἐπακούω, *to hearken to*, 2 Cor. vi. 2.

ἐπακροάομαι, *to listen to*, Acts, xvi. 25.

ἐπὰν, conj., *when*, Luke, xi. 31 etc. (The reader is referred to his Greek Grammar.)

ἐπάναγκες, adv., *of necessity, necessarily*; τὰ ἐπάναγκες, *necessary things*, Acts, xv. 28.

ἐπανάγω, *to put out* into deep water, Luke, v. 3, 4; intrans., *to return*, Matt. xxi. 18.

ἐπαναμιμνήσκω, *to remind* one *again*, Rom. xv. 15.

ἐπαναπαύομαι, with dat., *to rest upon, to trust to*, Rom. ii. 17; ἐπί τινα, *to remain upon, to abide with*, Luke, x. 6.

ἐπανέρχομαι, *to come back again*, Luke, x. 35. xix. 15.

ἐπανίσταμαι, *to rise up against*, Matt. x. 21. Mrk. xiii. 12.

ἐπανόρθωσις, ἡ, *restoration to a right state, correction*, 2 Tim. iii. 16.

ἐπάνω, adv., *over*, Luke, xi. 44; *above, more than*, Mrk. xiv. 5. 1 Cor. xv. 6; as prepos. with genit., *above*, Joh. iii. 31; *upon*, Matt. v. 14. xxiii. 18, 20 etc.; *over*, Matt. ii. 9. xxvii. 37. Luke, iv. 39. xix. 17.

ἐπάρατος, *accursed*, Joh. vii. 49.

ἐπαρκέω, *to assist, to relieve*, 1 Tim. v. 10, 16.

ἐπάρχειος, *of or belonging to an* ἔπαρχος; ἡ ἐπάρχειος (sc. ἐξουσία), *a prefecture*, Acts, xxv. 1.

ἐπαρχία, and ἐπαρχεία, ἡ, *a region subject to a prefect, a province*, Acts, xxiii. 34.

ἔπαυλις, ἡ, *a dwelling, a habitation*, Acts, i. 20.

ἐπαύριον, adv., *on the morrow*; τῇ ἐπαύριον (sc. ἡμέρᾳ), *the next day, on the morrow*, Matt. xxvii. 62. Mrk. xi. 12. Joh. i. 29. Acts, x. 9.

ἐπαφρίζω, *to cast out as foam, to foam out*, Jude, 13.

ἐπεγείρω, *to excite against*, Acts, xiii. 50. xiv. 2.

ἐπεὶ, conj., *after*, a var. lect. ad Luke, vii. 1; *since*, Matt. xxvii. 6. 1 Cor. xiv. 12; *seeing that*, Luke, i. 34. 2 Cor. xi. 18. xiii. 3; *because*, Mrk. xv. 42. Matt. xxi. 46; *otherwise*, Rom. xi. 6, 22. Hebr. ix. 26; before a question, *for*, Rom. iii. 6. 1 Cor. xv. 29.

ἐπειδὴ, conj., *after that*, Luke, vii. 1; *forasmuch as*, Acts, xv. 24 etc.

ἐπειδήπερ, conj., *forasmuch as*, Luke, i. 1.

ἐπεῖδον, 2 aor. of ἐφοράω, *to look upon*, Luke, i. 25; (like *animadverto = punish*), Acts, iv. 29.

ἔπειμι, *to come on*; ὁ ἐπιὼν, *the next, the following*, Acts, vii. 26. xvi. 11. xxiii. 11.

ἐπείπερ, conj., *since*, a var. lect. ad Rom. iii. 30 (Westcott reads εἴπερ).

ἐπεισαγωγὴ, ἡ, *a bringing in besides*, Hebr. vii. 19.

ἐπεισέρχομαι, *to come in besides; to come in upon*, Luke, xxi. 35.

ἔπειτα, *then, after that*, Luke, xvi. 7. Gal. i. 21 etc.

ἐπέκεινα, adv., *on that side, beyond*, Acts, vii. 43.

ἐπεκτείνομαι, *to stretch forward to*, Philipp. iii. 13.

ἐπενδύτης, ὁ, *an upper garment*, Joh. xxi. 7.

ἐπενδύω, *to put on besides;* mid., *to put on ourselves in addition*, 2 Cor. v. 2, 4. (RV *to be clothed upon.*)

ἐπέρχομαι, *to arrive*, Acts, xiv. 19; *to come upon*, Acts, i. 8. Luke, i. 35; *to overtake, to come upon suddenly*, Acts, viii. 24. xiii. 40; *to be approaching;* ἐν τοῖς αἰῶσι τοῖς ἐπερχομένοις, *in the ages to come*, Ephes. ii. 7; *to come against, to attack*, Luke, xi. 22.

ἐπερωτάω, *to inquire of, to ask*, Mrk. ix. 32. xiii. 3 etc.; *to inquire after, to desire to know*, Rom. x. 20; *to demand of* a person, Matt. xvi. 1.

ἐπερώτημα, τό, *an inquiry, a question; an earnest desire* (with obj. gen.), 1 Pet. iii. 21.

ἐπέχω, *to hold out, to present*, Philipp. ii. 16; *to tarry, to remain*, Acts, xix. 22; ἐπέχειν (sc. τὸν νοῦν), *to give attention to*, Acts, iii. 5. 1 Tim. iv. 16; *to observe*, Luke, xiv. 7.

ἐπηρεάζω, *to revile, to use despitefully*, Luke, vi. 28.

ἐπί, prepos. with genit. dat. and accus., *upon, in the presence of, over, against, to*, etc.; (of time), *during; towards.* (The reader is referred to his Greek Grammar.)

ἐπιβαίνω, *to mount upon, to ride upon*, Matt. xxi. 5; *to go on board, to embark in*, Acts, xxvii. 2; *to go up*, Acts, xxi. 4; *to set foot in*, Acts, xx. 18; *to enter upon*, Acts, xxv. 1.

ἐπιβάλλω, *to cast upon*, 1 Cor. vii. 35. Mrk. xi. 7; *to lay upon*, Matt. xxvi. 50. Luke, xxi. 12. Acts, v. 18; *to put upon*, Matt. ix. 16. Luke, v. 36; *to put to, to apply*, Luke, ix. 62; intrans., *to dash against*, Mrk. iv. 37; *to reflect upon*, Mrk. xiv. 72 (RV *called to mind*); impers., *to fall to one's lot*, Luke, xv. 12.

ἐπιβαρέω, with accus., *to be burdensome to*, 1 Thess. ii. 9. 2 Thess. iii. 8; *to be too hard on, to censure too heavily*, 2 Cor. ii. 5.

ἐπιβιβάζω, *to cause to mount, to place upon*, Luke, x. 34. xix. 35. Acts, xxiii. 24.

ἐπιβλέπω, *to look upon, to shew respect to*, James, ii. 3; *to look upon in pity*, Luke, i. 48. ix. 38.

ἐπίβλημα, τό, *an addition, a patch*, Matt. ix. 16. Mrk. ii. 21. Luke, v. 36.

ἐπιβοάω, *to cry out*, a var. lect. ad Acts, xxv. 24.

ἐπιβουλή, ἡ, *a plot*, Acts, ix. 24. xx. 3, 19. xxiii. 30.

ἐπιγαμβρεύω, *to marry a deceased brother's wife*, Matt. xxii. 24. (Pape's Lexicon *to marry as a relative.*)

ἐπίγειος, on the earth, Philipp. ii. 10; terrestrial, earthly, 1 Cor. xv. 40. 2 Cor. v. 1. James, iii. 15; τὰ ἐπίγεια, earthly things, Philipp. iii. 19. Joh. iii. 12.

ἐπιγίνομαι, to be born after; to arise, to spring up, as a wind, Acts, xxviii. 13.

ἐπιγινώσκω, to know fully, 1 Cor. xiii. 12. Luke, i. 4; to acknowledge, 1 Cor. xiv. 37. xvi. 18. 2 Cor. i. 13; to recognize, Acts, xii. 14. Matt. xiv. 35. Mrk. vi. 54. Luke, xxiv. 16; to be aware, Acts, xxv. 10.

ἐπίγνωσις, ἡ, accurate knowledge, Philipp. i. 9. Rom. x. 2. Ephes. iv. 13.

ἐπιγραφή, ἡ, an inscription, a title, Luke, xxiii. 38. Mrk. xv. 26; an inscription on a coin, Matt. xxii. 20. Luke, xx. 24. Mrk. xii. 16.

ἐπιγράφω, to write upon, Acts, xvii. 23; to write over, Mrk. xv. 26. Rev. xxi. 12; met., to imprint upon, Hebr. viii. 10. x. 16.

ἐπιδείκνυμι, to shew, Matt. xvi. 1. xxii. 19; to demonstrate, to prove, Hebr. vi. 17. Acts, xviii. 28; mid., to display, Acts, ix. 39.

ἐπιδέχομαι, to receive hospitably, to entertain, 3 Joh. 10; to approve of, to accept, 3 Joh. 9.

ἐπιδημέω, to be a sojourner, to be a foreign resident, Acts, ii. 10. xvii. 21.

ἐπιδιατάσσομαι, to ordain besides, to add to a previous ordinance, Gal. iii. 15. (Found nowhere else.)

ἐπιδίδωμι, to give to, Matt. vii. 9. Luke, xi. 11. xxiv. 30, 42; to give up to the power of, to give way to, Acts, xxvii. 15.

ἐπιδιορθόω, to set in order afterwards, Tit. i. 15.

ἐπιδύω, to go down, to set, as the sun, Ephes. iv. 26.

ἐπιείκεια, and ἐπιεικία, ἡ, mildness, clemency, 2 Cor. x. 1. Acts, xxiv. 4.

ἐπιεικής, suitable; mild, Tit. iii. 2. 1 Tim. iii. 3. James, iii. 17. 1 Pet. ii. 18; τὸ ἐπιεικὲς = ἐπιείκεια, mildness, Philipp. iv. 5.

ἐπιζητέω, to seek for, Acts, xii. 19; to desire, to crave for, Matt. vi. 32. Luke, xii. 30. Rom. xi. 7; to make inquiry about, Acts, xix. 39; to demand, Matt. xii. 39. xvi. 4.

ἐπιθανάτιος, condemned to death, 1 Cor. iv. 9.

ἐπίθεσις, ἡ, a laying on, an imposition, Acts, viii. 18. 1 Tim. iv. 14. 2 Tim. i. 6. Hebr. vi. 2.

ἐπιθυμέω, to desire, Matt. xiii. 17. Luke, xv. 16; to lust after, 1 Cor. x. 6. Matt. v. 28; to covet, Rom. vii. 7. xiii. 9; ἐπιθυμίᾳ ἐπεθύμησα, I have greatly desired, Luke, xxii. 15.

ἐπιθυμητής, ὁ, a coveter, 1 Cor. x. 6.

ἐπιθυμία, ἡ, desire, Luke, xxii. 15. Philipp. i. 23. 1 Thess. ii. 17; lust, concupiscence, James, i. 14. 2 Pet. i. 4. 1 Thess. iv. 5. Coloss. iii. 5.

ἐπικαθίζω, *to seat upon, to cause to sit upon;* intr., *to sit upon*, Matt. xxi. 7.

ἐπικαλέω, *to call*, Matt. x. 25; pass., *to be surnamed*, Acts, x. 18. xi. 13. xii. 12; *to be called*, Hebr. xi. 16. Acts, xv. 17; mid., *to appeal to*, Acts, xxv. 11, 25. xxvi. 32. xxviii. 19; *to call upon, to invoke*, Acts, ii. 21. vii. 59. ix. 14; *to worship, to pray to*, 2 Tim. ii. 22. Rom. x. 13.

ἐπικάλυμμα, *a covering, a veil;* met., *a pretext, a cloak*, 1 Pet. ii. 16.

ἐπικαλύπτομαι, *to be covered over,* i.e. *to be pardoned*, Rom. iv. 7.

ἐπικατάρατος, *lying under God's curse, accursed*, Gal. iii. 10.

ἐπίκειμαι, *to lie upon, to be placed upon*, Joh. xi. 38. xxi. 9. 1 Cor. ix. 16; δικαιώματα ἐπικείμενα, *ordinances imposed upon a person*, Hebr. ix. 10; *to press upon, to crowd upon*, Luke, v. 1; *to be urgent*, Luke, xxiii. 23; of a tempest, *to press heavily upon*, Acts, xxvii. 20.

ἐπικέλλω, *to run* a ship *aground*, Acts, xxvii. 41.

ἐπικεφάλαιον, τὸ, *tribute-money*, a var. lect. ad Mrk. xii. 14. (Westcott reads κῆνσον.)

ἐπικουρία, ἡ, *aid, succour*, Acts, xxvi. 22.

ἐπικρίνω, *to decree, to give sentence*, Luke, xxiii. 24.

ἐπιλαμβάνομαι, *to take hold of*, Matt. xiv. 31. Acts, xvii. 19; *to seize*, Luke, xxiii. 26. Acts, xvi. 19; *to lay hold of* a person's words, Luke, xx. 20, 26; *to keep fast hold of*, 1 Tim. vi. 12, 19; met., *to succour*, Hebr. ii. 16.

ἐπιλανθάνομαι, depon., *to forget*, Mrk. viii. 14. Matt. xvi. 5. Hebr. vi. 10. xiii. 2, 16; as a passive, ἐπιλελησμένος, *forgotten, uncared for*, Luke, xii. 6.

ἐπιλέγω, *to call by a second name*, Joh. v. 2; mid., *to choose*, Acts, xv. 40.

ἐπιλείπω, *to fail*, Hebr. xi. 32.

ἐπιλείχω, *to lick*, Luke, xvi. 21.

ἐπιλησμονὴ, ἡ, *forgetfulness;* ἀκροατὴς ἐπιλησμονῆς, *a forgetful hearer*, James, i. 25.

ἐπίλοιπος, *remaining over;* τὸν ἐπίλοιπον χρόνον, *the rest of your time*, 1 Pet. iv. 2.

ἐπίλυσις, ἡ, *an unloosing; interpretation*, 2 Pet. i. 20.

ἐπιλύω, *to unloose, to untie; to explain*, Mrk. iv. 34; *to settle, to decide*, Acts, xix. 39.

ἐπιμαρτυρέω, *to testify*, 1 Pet. v. 12.

ἐπιμέλεια, ἡ, *care, attention*, Acts, xxvii. 3.

ἐπιμελέομαι, *to take care of*, Luke, x. 34, 35.

ἐπιμελῶς, adv., *carefully, diligently*, Luke, xv. 8.

ἐπιμένω, *to tarry, to remain*, 1 Cor. xvi. 8. Philipp. i. 24. Acts, xxviii. 14; *to continue in, to persevere in*, Rom. vi. 1. xi. 23. Coloss. i. 23.

ἐπινεύω, *to nod to; to assent*, Acts, xviii. 20.

ἐπίνοια, ἡ, *a thought*, Acts, viii. 22.

ἐπιορκέω, *to swear falsely*, Matt. v. 33.

ἐπίορκος, *swearing falsely ;* as subst., *a false swearer*, 1 Tim. i. 10.

ἐπιούσιος, a NT word, found only in Matt. vi. 11 and Luke, xi. 3, in the phrase ἄρτος ἐπιούσιος. "*ἐπιούσιος, for the following day*, ἄρτος *sufficient for the following day*, or, *bread* (usually, *daily*) *sufficient for sustenance*(οὐσία)," Pape (in Lex.). (The old *Italic* renders it *panis quotidianus*, and the RV *our daily bread*. The derivation also is uncertain.)

ἐπιπίπτω, *to fall upon*, Luke, xv. 20. Acts, xx. 37. Rom. xv. 3 etc.; met., *to take possession of*, Luke, i. 12. Acts, xix. 17. Rev. xi. 11; *to press upon*, Mrk. iii. 10.

ἐπιπλήσσω, *to chide, to rebuke*, 1 Tim. v. 1.

ἐπιποθέω, *to desire, to long*, Rom. i. 11. 2 Cor. v. 2. 2 Tim. i. 4 etc.; *to long after, to pursue with love*, Philipp. i. 8. ii. 26.

ἐπιπόθησις, ἡ, *longing*, 2 Cor. vii. 7, 11.

ἐπιπόθητος, *longed for*, Philipp. iv. 1.

ἐπιποθία, and ἐπιπόθεια, ἡ, *a longing*, Rom. xv. 23. (It is a purely NT word, and found only in this passage.)

ἐπιπορεύομαι, *to journey towards*, Luke, viii. 4.

ἐπιρράπτω, *to sew on*, Mrk. ii. 21.

ἐπιρρίπτω, *to throw upon, to place upon*, Luke, xix. 35; *to cast upon, to commit to*, 1 Pet. v. 7.

ἐπίσημος, *noted, of note*, Rom. xvi. 7; *notorious*, Matt. xxvii. 16.

ἐπισιτισμὸς, ὁ, *provisions, food*, Luke, ix. 12.

ἐπισκέπτομαι, *to inspect; to visit*, Acts, vii. 23. xv. 36. Matt. xxv. 36. James, i. 27 ; *to look upon, to have a care for*, Acts, xv. 14. Luke. i. 68, 78 ; *to look out, to select*, Acts, vi. 3.

ἐπισκευάζομαι, *to get ready one's baggage*, Acts, xxi. 15.

ἐπισκηνόω, *to fix a habitation upon;* met., *to rest upon*, 2 Cor. xii. 9.

ἐπισκιάζω, *to overshadow*, Luke, i. 35. ix. 34. Matt. xvii. 5.

ἐπισκοπέω, *to oversee ; to look carefully, to take heed*, Hebr. xii. 15.

ἐπισκοπὴ, ἡ, *inspection, visitation*, Luke, xix. 44. 1 Pet. ii. 12; *superintendence, oversight*, Acts, i. 20; *the office of a bishop*, 1 Tim. iii. 1.

ἐπίσκοπος, ὁ, *an overseer, a superintendent ; a guardian*, 1 Pet. ii. 25; *a bishop*, Philipp. i. 1. 1 Tim. iii. 2. Tit. i. 7. Acts, xx. 25.

ἐπισπάω, *to draw forwards the foreskin ;* μὴ ἐπισπάσθω, 1 Cor. vii. 18 (RV *let him not become uncircumcised*).

ἐπισπείρω, *to sow in addition*, Matt. xiii. 25.

ἐπίσταμαι, *to understand*, Mrk. xiv. 68. Jude, 10 ; *to know*, Hebr. xi. 8. Acts, xv. 7 etc.;

to be acquainted with, Acts, xviii. 25. xix. 15.

ἐπίστασις, ἡ, *oversight,* 2 Cor. xi. 28 (or, *the coming upon*); *a stirring up,* Acts, xxiv. 12.

ἐπιστάτης, ὁ, *a superintendent; a master,* Luke, xvii. 13. (Found only in Luke.)

ἐπιστήμων, *intelligent, experienced,* James, iii. 13.

ἐπιστηρίζω, *to render more firm, to confirm,* Acts, xiv. 22. xv. 32, 41.

ἐπιστολὴ, ἡ, *a letter, an epistle,* Acts, xv. 30. Rom. xvi. 22. 1 Cor. v. 9 etc.; ἐπιστολαὶ συστατικαὶ, *letters of commendation,* 2 Cor. iii. 1.

ἐπιστομίζω, *to stop the mouth of, to reduce to silence,* Tit. i. 11.

ἐπιστρέφω, *to turn to,* Acts, xxvi. 20. Luke, i. 16, 17; intrans., *to turn to,* Acts, ix. 35. xi. 21. xv. 19 etc.; *to turn round, to turn about,* Acts, xvi. 18. Mrk. v. 30. viii. 33. Joh. xxi. 20; *to return,* Acts, xv. 36. Luke, viii. 55. Matt. xii. 44; *to reform, to be converted,* Matt. xiii. 15. Mrk. iv. 12. Acts, iii. 19.

ἐπιστροφὴ, ἡ, *the conversion,* Acts, xv. 3.

ἐπισυνάγω, *to collect in addition; to gather together,* Matt. xxiii. 37. xxiv. 31. Luke, xiii. 34; pass., *to be gathered together,* Mrk. i. 33. Luke, xii. 1. xvii. 37.

ἐπισυναγωγὴ, ἡ, *a gathering together,* 2 Thess. ii. 1 ; *a meeting,* Heb. x. 25.

ἐπισυντρέχω, *to run together in addition,* Mrk. ix. 25.

ἐπισφαλὴς, *dangerous,* Acts, xxvii. 9.

ἐπισχύω, *to be urgent, to insist,* Luke, xxiii. 5.

ἐπισωρεύω, *to heap up,* 2 Tim. iv. 3.

ἐπιταγὴ, ἡ, *a command,* Rom. xvi. 26. Tit. i. 3 ; *authority,* Tit. ii. 15.

ἐπιτάσσω, *to enjoin, order,* Luke, iv. 36. xiv. 22. Philem. 8.

ἐπιτελέω, *to accomplish,* Rom. xv. 28. Philipp. i. 6. Heb. viii. 5. 1 Pet. v. 9; *to perform,* Heb. ix. 6 ; mid. Gal. iii. 3, *to finish up* (or *to be perfected*).

ἐπιτήδειος, *needful;* τὰ ἐπιτηδ., *necessaries,* James, ii. 16.

ἐπιτίθημι, *to lay upon,* Luke, xv. 5. Matt. ix. 18; *to add to,* Rev. xxii. 18; mid. *to provide,* Acts, xxviii. 10 ; *to assault, to set upon,* Acts, xviii. 10.

ἐπιτιμάω, *to censure, to rebuke,* 2 Tim. iv. 2. Luke, xvii. 3; *to admonish,* Mrk. viii. 30. Luke, ix. 21. Matt. xii. 16.

ἐπιτιμία, ἡ, *punishment,* 2 Cor. ii. 6.

ἐπιτρέπω, *to permit, to allow,* 1 Cor. xvi. 7. Hebr. vi. 3. Joh. xix. 38; pass., ἐπιτρέπεταί σοι, *you are permitted,* Acts, xxvi. 1. Cf. 1 Cor. xiv. 34.

ἐπιτροπὴ, ἡ, *commission,* Acts, xxvi. 12.

ἐπίτροπος, ὁ, *a steward,* Matt. xx. 8; *a guardian,* Gal. iv. 2.

ἐπιτυγχάνω, *to attain to, to obtain,* Rom. xi. 7. Hebr. vi. 15.

ἐπιφαίνω, *to give light to,* Luke, i. 79; pass., *to become visible, to appear,* Acts, xxvii. 20 etc.

ἐπιφάνεια, ἡ, *an appearance;*

"in the NT, the advent of Christ,—past (2 Tim. i. 10), and future (1 Tim. vi. 14); *manifestation*, 2 Thess. ii. 8.

ἐπιφανὴς, *illustrious, glorious*, Acts, ii. 20 (RV *notable*).

ἐπιφαύσκω, *to shine upon, to give light to*, Ephes. v. 14.

ἐπιφέρω, *to bring forward*, Jude, 9; *to lay upon, to inflict*, Rom. iii. 5 (RV *who visiteth with wrath*).

ἐπιφωνέω, *to cry out, to shout*, Luke, xxiii. 21. Acts, xii. 22. xxi. 34. xxii. 24.

ἐπιφώσκω, *to begin to dawn*, Luke, xxiii. 54. Matt. xxviii. 1.

ἐπιχειρέω, *to take in hand, to attempt*, Luke, i. 1. Acts, ix. 29. xix. 13.

ἐπιχέω, *to pour upon*, Luke, x. 34.

ἐπιχορηγέω, *to supply, to furnish*, 2 Cor. ix. 10. Gal. iii. 5; *to add besides*, 2 Pet. i. 5; pass., *to be supplied*, Coloss. ii. 19. (An idea of magnificence attaches to the word.)

ἐπιχορηγία, ἡ, *supply*, Philipp. i. 19. Ephes. iv. 16. (It is a purely ecclesiastical word.)

ἐπιχρίω, *to anoint*, Joh. ix. 11.

ἐποικοδομέω, *to build upon, to build up*, 1 Cor. iii. 10, 12, 14. Jude, 20; pass., *to be built upon*, Ephes. ii. 20. Coloss. ii. 7.

ἐποκέλλω, *to run a ship aground*, a var. lect. ad Acts, xxvii. 41. (See ἐπικέλλω.)

ἐπονομάζω, *to name*; pass., *to be called, to bear the name of*, Rom. ii. 17.

ἐποπτεύω, *to look upon, to behold*, 1 Pet. ii. 12. iii. 2.

ἐπόπτης, ὁ, *an eye-witness*, 2 Pet. i. 16.

ἔπος, τὸ, *a word*; ὡς ἔπος εἰπεῖν, *so to speak*, Hebr. vii. 9.

ἐπουράνιος, *celestial, heavenly*, 1 Cor. xv. 40, 48. Joh. iii. 12. 2 Tim. iv. 18; *in heaven*, Philipp. ii. 10. Hebr. xii. 22; τὰ ἐπουράνια, *heavenly things*, Ephes. i. 3, 20. ii. 6. iii. 10.

ἑπτά, numer., *seven*, Matt. xii. 45 etc.

ἑπτάκις, numer., *seven times*, Matt. xviii. 21. Luke, xvii. 4.

ἑπτακισχίλιοι, numer., *seven thousand*, Rom. xi. 4.

ἐραυνάω, a late form for ἐρευνάω, *to search*, Joh. v. 39. vii. 52. Rom. viii. 27 etc. (It is not recognized in Pape's Lex.)

ἐργάζομαι, *to labour, to work*, 1 Cor. iv. 12. Luke, xiii. 14; *to do business, to trade*, Matt. xxv. 16; *to do, to perform*, Joh. vi. 28. ix. 4. 1 Cor. xvi. 10; *to produce*, 2 Cor. vii. 10. James, i. 20; *to work for, to strive after*, Joh. vi. 27; *to work upon, to be employed upon*, Rev. xviii. 17; as pass., εἰργασμένος, *wrought*, Joh. iii. 21.

ἐργασία, ἡ, *a working, a committing*, Ephes. iv. 19; *occupation, business*, Acts, xix. 25; *gain, profit*, Acts, xvi. 16, 19. xix. 24; ἐργασίαν διδόναι=*operam dare*, Luke, xii. 58.

ἐργάτης, ὁ, *a worker, a perpetrator*, Luke, xiii. 27; *a workman*, Matt. ix. 37. x. 10.

ἔργον, τό, *a work*, Joh. iii. 21. Hebr. i. 10. 2 Cor. ix. 8; *a deed*, Luke, xxiv. 19. Rom. xv. 18. 2 Cor. x. 11.

ἐρεθίζω, *to provoke*, Coloss. iii. 21; *to stir up, to instigate*, 2 Cor. ix. 2.

ἐρείδω, *to stick fast*, Acts, xxvii. 41.

ἐρεύγομαι, *to pour forth words, to utter*, Matt. xiii. 35.

ἐρευνάω, see ἐραυνάω.

ἐρημία, ἡ, *a solitary place, a desert*, Hebr. xi. 38. Matt. xv. 33. Mrk. viii. 4.

ἔρημος, *solitary, lonely*, Matt. xiv. 13, 15. Mrk. i. 35. vi. 32; *deserted*, Gal. iv. 27; as subst., *a desert, a wilderness*, Matt. iii. 1. xxiv. 26.

ἐρημόω, *to make desolate;* in the NT only in the pass., *to be made desolate, to be brought to naught*, Matt. xii. 25. Luke, xi. 17. Rev. xviii. 17.

ἐρήμωσις, ἡ, *desolation*, Matt. xxiv. 15. Mrk. xiii. 14. Luke, xxi. 20. (See βδέλυγμα.)

ἐρίζω, *to strive, to wrangle*, Matt. xii. 19.

ἐριθεία, and **ἐριθία**, ἡ, *a factious spirit, contention*, James, iii. 14. Philipp. i. 17. ii. 3. Rom. ii. 8. 2 Cor. xii. 20. Gal. v. 20.

ἔριον, τό, *wool*, Hebr. ix. 19. Rev. i. 14.

ἔρις, ἡ, *strife*, Rom. i. 29. xiii. 13. 1 Cor. i. 11.

ἐρίφιον, τό, and **ἔριφος**, ὁ, *a kid*, Luke, xv. 29. Matt. xxv. 32.

ἑρμηνεία, and **ἑρμηνία**, ἡ, *interpretation*, 1 Cor. xii. 10. xiv. 26.

ἑρμηνευτὴς, ὁ, *an interpreter*, 1 Cor. xiv. 28.

ἑρμηνεύω, *to interpret*, Joh. ix. 7. Hebr. vii. 2.

ἑρπετὸν, τό, *a creeping thing, a reptile*, Acts, x. 12. xi. 6. Rom. i. 23, James, iii. 7.

ἐρυθρὸς, *red;* in the NT only in phrase ἡ ἐρυθρὰ θάλασσα, *the Red Sea*, Acts, vii. 36. Hebr. xi. 29.

ἔρχομαι, *to go, to come;* ὁ ἐρχόμενος, *He that cometh, the coming one* = the Messiah, Matt. xi. 3. Rev. i. 4. iv. 8 etc.

ἐρωτάω, *to ask, to question*, Joh. ix. 21. Luke, xxii. 68. xxiii. 3; *to beseech, to pray*, Joh. xiv. 16. Luke, iv. 38.

ἐσθὴς, ἡ, *clothing, raiment*, Luke, xxiii. 11. xxiv. 4. Acts, x. 30. xii. 21. James, ii. 2.

ἔσθησις, ἡ, *apparel, clothing*, Acts, i. 10.

ἐσθίω, and **ἔσθω**, *to eat*, Matt. vi. 25. (aor. τί φάγητε), xiv. 20. 1 Cor. xi. 22; *to devour, to consume*, Hebr. x. 27. Rev. xvii. 16. James, v. 3.

ἔσοπτρον, τό, *a mirror*, 1 Cor. xiii. 12. James, i. 23.

ἑσπέρα, ἡ, *evening, eventide*, Luke, xxiv. 29. Acts, iv. 3.

ἔσχατος, *the most remote; the last*, Joh. vi. 39, 44. vii. 37. 1 Cor. xv. 52. Rev. i. 17; *the lowest*, Luke, xiv. 9; τὸ ἔσχατον τῆς γῆς, *the uttermost part of the earth*, Acts. i. 8. xiii. 47; τὰ ἔσχατα, *the last state*, Luke, xi. 26. Matt. xii. 45.

ἐσχάτως, adv., *extremely; ἐσχάτως ἔχειν, to be at the last extremity*, Mrk. v. 23.

ἔσω, adv., *within*, Joh. xx. 26. Acts, v. 23; ὁ ἔσω ἄνθρωπος, *the inner man*, 2 Cor. iv. 16; οἱ ἔσω, *those within the Christian fold*, 1 Cor. v. 12.

ἔσωθεν, adv., *from within*, Mrk. vii. 21, 23. Luke, xi. 7. 2 Cor. vii. 5; *inwardly, within*, Matt. vii. 15. xxiii. 25, 27, 28; τὸ ἔσωθεν, *that which is within, the inside*, Luke, xi. 39, 40.

ἐσώτερος, *inner*, Acts, xvi. 24; τὸ ἐσώτερον τοῦ καταπετάσματος, *the inner space which is behind the veil*, i.e. *the Holy of Holies*, Hebr. vi. 19.

ἑταῖρος, ὁ, *a companion;* used as an address, *friend*, Matt. xx. 13. xxii. 12. xxvi. 50.

ἑτερόγλωσσος, *using a foreign language, one who speaks in an unknown tongue*, 1 Cor. xiv. 21.

ἑτεροδιδασκαλέω, *to teach a different doctrine*, 1 Tim. i. 3. vi. 3.

ἑτεροζυγέω, *to be unequally yoked*, 2 Cor. vi. 14.

ἕτερος, *other*, Ephes. iii. 5; ὁ ἕτερος, *the other*, Rom. ii. 1; τῇ ἑτέρᾳ (sc. ἡμέρᾳ), *next day*, Acts, xxvii. 3; ἕτερος, *different*, Rom. vii. 23. (In the NT it is often improperly used for ἄλλος.)

ἑτέρως, adv., *otherwise, differently*, Philipp. iii. 15.

ἔτι, adv., *yet, still*, Matt. xii. 46. xvii. 5; *further*, Rom. iii. 7; *longer*, Rom. vi. 2; ἔτι ἅπαξ, *yet once more*, Hebr. xii. 26.

ἑτοιμάζω, *to make ready, to prepare*, Acts, xxiii. 23. Luke, xxii. 9, 12. Matt. iii. 3.

ἑτοιμασία, ἡ, *preparedness, alacrity;* ἐν ἑτοιμασίᾳ τοῦ εὐαγγελίου, Ephes. vi. 15 ("*with the promptitude and alacrity which the gospel produces*," Thayer).

ἕτοιμος, *ready*, Matt. xxii. 4, 8. 2 Cor. ix. 5. 1 Pet. i. 5 etc.; *done already by others, ready to hand*, 2 Cor. x. 16; ἐν ἑτοίμῳ ἔχειν = ἑτοίμως ἔχειν, *to be ready*, 2 Cor. x. 6.

ἑτοίμως, adv., *readily;* ἑτοίμως ἔχειν, *to be ready*, Acts, xxi. 13. 2 Cor. xii. 14.

ἔτος, τὸ, *a year*, Luke, iii. 1 etc.; πεντήκοντα ἔτη ἔχειν, *to be fifty years old*, Joh. viii. 57; εἶναι, γεγονέναι ἐτῶν δώδεκα, etc., *to be twelve years old*, Mrk. v. 42. 1 Tim. v. 9; κατ' ἔτος, *yearly*, Luke, ii. 41.

εὖ, adv., *well*, Ephes. vi. 3 etc.; εὖ πράξετε, *it will be well with you*, Acts, xv. 29; in commendations, *well done!* Matt. xxv. 21, 23.

εὐαγγελίζω, *to bring good tidings to, to evangelize*, with accus. of person, Rev. x. 7; also ἐπὶ τοὺς καθημένους, *to proclaim it unto them that sit*, Rev. xiv. 6. (The active is found only in these two passages, and in two passages of very late writers); pass., πτωχοὶ εὐαγγελίζονται, *the* poor have the gospel preached unto them, Matt. xi. 5. Cf. Luke, vii. 22. Hebr. iv. 2, 6; mid., *to preach the gospel*, Luke, iv. 18. 1 Cor. xv. 2; with accus. of thing, *to bring good tidings concerning*, 1 Thess. iii. 6. Acts, x. 36.

εὐαγγέλιον, τό, *good tidings; the gospel*, Rom. i. 16. xi. 28. Acts, xv. 7.

εὐαγγελιστής, ὁ, *a bringer of good tidings, an evangelist*, Acts, xxi. 8. Ephes. iv. 11. 2 Tim. iv. 5. ("In the NT the name given to those heralds of salvation through Christ who are not apostles," Thayer. It is a purely ecclesiastical word.)

εὐαρεστέω, *to be well pleasing to*, Hebr. xi. 5; pass., *to be well pleased with*, Hebr. xiii. 16.

εὐάρεστος, *well pleasing, acceptable to*, Rom. xii. 1, 2. xiv. 18. 2 Cor. v. 9; also with ἐν, Tit. ii. 9. Coloss. iii. 20.

εὐαρέστως, adv., *in a manner well pleasing to, acceptably*, Hebr. xii. 28.

εὖγε, *well done!* Luke, xix. 17.

εὐγενής, *of noble birth*, Luke, xix. 12. 1 Cor. i. 26; *noble-minded*, Acts, xvii. 11.

εὐδία, ἡ, *fair weather*, Matt. xvi. 2. (This passage is bracketed in Westcott.)

εὐδοκέω, *to be satisfied with;* with infin., *to be well pleased to do something*, 1 Cor. i. 21. Gal. i. 15. Luke, xii. 32. 1 Thess. ii. 8. iii. 1; with ἔν τινι, *to be well pleased with*, Matt. iii. 17. xvii. 5. Mrk. i. 11; with accus., *to take pleasure in*, Matt. xii. 18. Hebr. x. 6, 8; also with dat. in the same sense, 2 Thess. ii. 12.

εὐδοκία, ἡ, *good pleasure*, Ephes. i. 5, 9. Philipp. ii. 13; *desire*, 2 Thess. i. 11. Rom. x. 1; *good-will*; ἄνθρωποι εὐδοκίας, *men of good-will, i.e. of honest intentions*, Luke, ii. 14 (Vulgate, *pax hominibus bonae voluntatis*). But see RV.

εὐεργεσία, ἡ, *a good deed*, Acts, iv. 9; *a benefit*, 1 Tim. vi. 2.

εὐεργετέω, *to do good*, Acts, x. 38.

εὐεργέτης, ὁ, *a benefactor*, Luke, xxii. 25. (A title of honour.)

εὔθετος, *well placed; fit*, Luke, ix. 62. xiv. 34; *useful, serviceable*, Hebr. vi. 7.

εὐθέως, adv., *immediately, straightway*, Matt. iv. 20, 22. viii. 3; *shortly, presently*, 3 Joh. 14.

εὐθυδρομέω, *to run a straight course*, Acts, xvi. 11. xxi. 1.

εὐθυμέω, *to be of good cheer*, Acts, xxvii. 22, 25. James, v. 13.

εὔθυμος, *of good cheer*, Acts, xxvii. 36.

εὐθύμως, adv., *cheerfully*, Acts, xxiv. 10.

εὐθύνω, *to make straight*, Joh. i. 23; *to guide straight;* ὁ εὐθύνων, *the steersman*, James, iii. 4.

εὐθύς, *straight*, Luke, iii. 4. Acts, ix. 11; εὐθεῖα ὁδός, *the right way*, 2 Pet. ii. 15. Cf. Acts, xiii. 10; ἔσται εἰς εὐθείας (sc. ὁδοὺς), *shall become straight*, Luke, iii. 5; *upright, sincere*, Acts, viii. 21.

εὐθύς, adv., *immediately, straightway*, Matt. iii. 16. xiii. 20. Joh. xiii. 32.

εὐθύτης, ἡ, *uprightness*, Hebr. i. 8.

εὐκαιρέω, *to have opportunity*, 1 Cor. xvi. 12; *to have leisure* to do something, Mrk. vi. 31; *to give one's time to a thing*, Acts, xvii. 21.

εὐκαιρία, ἡ, *seasonable time, opportunity*, Matt. xxvi. 16. Luke, xxii. 6.

εὔκαιρος, *timely, opportune*, Hebr. iv. 16; *convenient*, Mrk. vi. 21.

εὐκαίρως, adv., *conveniently, when the opportunity occurred*, Mrk. xiv. 11; *in season*, 2 Tim. iv. 2.

εὔκοπος, *without trouble, easy to do;* in the NT only in the phrase εὐκοπώτερόν ἐστι, *it is easier*, Matt. ix. 5. xix. 24. Luke, xvi. 17 etc.

εὐλάβεια, ἡ, *caution; godly fear, reverence*, Hebr. v. 7. xii. 28.

εὐλαβέομαι, *to use forethought*, Hebr. xi. 7 (RV *moved with godly fear*).

εὐλαβής, *cautious; reverential, devout*, Acts, ii. 5. viii. 2.

εὐλογέω, *to praise*, Luke, i. 64. ii. 28 (RV *blessed* in both passages); *to bless*, Luke, vi. 28. xxiv. 51. Rom. xii. 14. 1 Cor. iv. 12 etc.; pass., εὐλογημένος, *blessed*, Luke, i. 42. Matt. xxi. 9. xxiii. 39. (See Pape's Lex. in voc.)

εὐλογητός, *blessed*, Luke, i. 68. Rom. i. 25. ix. 5.

εὐλογία, ἡ, *laudation, flattery*, Rom. xvi. 18; *benediction, blessing*, Hebr. xii. 17, James, iii. 10; *consecration;* τὸ ποτήριον τῆς εὐλογίας, *the consecrated cup*, 1 Cor. x. 16; *bounty*, 2 Cor. ix. 5; ἐπ' εὐλογίαις, *bountifully*, 2 Cor. ix. 6.

εὐμετάδοτος, *ready to give, liberal*, 1 Tim. vi. 18.

εὐνοέω, *to be well-disposed, to be of a peaceable spirit*, Matt. v. 25.

εὔνοια, ἡ, *good will*, Ephes. vi. 7. (In 1 Cor. vii. 3 Westcott gives ὀφειλήν.)

εὐνουχίζω, *to emasculate;* εὐνουχίσθησαν ὑπὸ τῶν ἀνθρώπων, *were made eunuchs by men*, Matt. xix. 12; εὐνουχίζειν ἑαυτὸν, *to make himself a eunuch*, i.e. to abstain from marriage, Matt. xix. 12.

εὐνοῦχος, ὁ, *a eunuch*, Acts, viii. 27, 34, 36, 38. Matt. xix. 12.

εὐοδόω, *to cause to prosper;* pass., *to be successful, to prosper*, 3 Joh. 2; εἴ πως εὐοδωθήσομαι ἐλθεῖν, *if haply I shall be so fortunate as to come*, Rom. i. 10; ὅ τι ἂν εὐοδῶται, *whatever business shall have prospered*, i.e. according to his gains, 1 Cor. xvi. 2.

εὐπάρεδρος, *persistent, assiduous;* τὸ εὐπάρεδρον, *assiduity, constant devotion*, 1 Cor. vii. 35. (A purely ecclesiastical form.)

εὐπειθής, *readily obeying, compliant*, James, iii. 17.

εὐπερίστατος, *easily besetting*, Hebr. xii. 1. (The word is found nowhere else.)

εὐποιΐα, ἡ, *well-doing, beneficence*, Hebr. xiii. 16.

εὐπορέομαι, *to have means;* καθὼς εὐπορεῖτο, *according as he had means*, Acts, xi. 29.

εὐπορία, ἡ, *wealth*, Acts, xix. 25.

εὐπρέπεια, ἡ, *beauty, comeliness*, James, i. 11.

εὐπρόσδεκτος, *acceptable*, 2 Cor. vi. 2. viii. 12. Rom. xv. 16, 31.

εὐπρόσεδρος, a var. lect. ad 1 Cor. vii. 35, for εὐπάρεδρος, which see.

εὐπροσωπέω, *to make a fair shew*, Gal. vi. 12. (It is an ecclesiastical and Byzantine form.)

Εὐρακύλων, ὁ, *The Euraquilo*, a NE wind, Acts, xxvii. 14. (The older texts exhibit εὐροκλύδων.)

εὑρίσκω, *to find*, Acts, xvii. 27. Luke, xxiii. 2, 4, 14; *to meet with*, Matt. xviii. 28. xxvii. 32; *to obtain*, Matt. xi. 29. Luke, ix. 12. Hebr. xii. 17; pass., *to be found*, Rom. x. 20. Philipp. ii. 7. iii. 9 etc.

εὐρύχωρος, *spacious, broad*, Matt. vii. 13.

εὑροκλύδων, see εὐρακύλων.

εὐσέβεια, ἡ, *piety, godliness*, Acts, iii. 12. 1 Tim. ii. 2. iv. 7. vi. 3, 5, 11. 2 Tim. iii. 5. 2 Pet. i. 3, 6. iii. 11. Tit. i. 1 (in all these passages *without the article*, except 1 Tim. vi. 5 and 2 Pet. i. 6); but in 1 Tim. iii. 16 μέγα ἐστὶ τὸ τῆς εὐσεβείας (= τῆς θειότητος) μυστήριον, ὅς (reverting to the *natural* gender, ὁ Χριστὸς, in preference to the *grammatical* gender, εὐσέβεια) ἐφανερώθη ἐν σαρκί, *great is the mystery of the divine nature, which was made visible in flesh*. So Joh. i. 14 ὁ λόγος σάρξ ἐγένετο καὶ ἐσκήνωσεν ἐν ἡμῖν. (Or, *great is the mystery which we reverence.*)

εὐσεβέω, *to shew piety*, 1 Tim. v. 4; *to worship*, Acts, xvii. 23.

εὐσεβής, *pious, godly*, Acts, x. 2, 7. 2 Pet. ii. 9.

εὐσεβῶς, adv., *piously, godly*, 2 Tim. iii. 12. Tit. ii. 12.

εὔσημος, *distinct, intelligible*, 1 Cor. xiv. 9.

εὔσπλαγχνος, *compassionate, tender-hearted*, Ephes. iv. 32. 1 Pet. iii. 8.

εὐσχημόνως, *in a seemly manner, decently*, 1 Cor. xiv. 40. Rom. xiii. 13. 1 Thess. iv. 12.

εὐσχημοσύνη, ἡ, *comeliness*, 1 Cor. xii. 23.

εὐσχήμων, *comely*, 1 Cor. xii. 24; πρὸς τὸ εὔσχημον, *to promote decorum*, 1 Cor. vii. 35; *reputable*, Acts, xiii. 50. xvii. 12. Mrk. xv. 43.

εὐτόνως, adv., *vehemently*, Luke, xxiii. 10; *powerfully*, Acts, xviii. 28.

εὐτραπελία, ἡ, *low jesting, ribaldry*, Ephes. v. 4.

εὐφημία, ἡ, *laudation, good report*, 2 Cor. vi. 8.

εὔφημος, *speaking auspiciously;* εὔφημα, *things of good report,* Philipp. iv. 8. (See RV marg.)

εὐφορέω, *to bear well, to be fruitful,* Luke, xii. 16.

εὐφραίνω, *to gladden,* 2 Cor. ii. 2; pass., *to make merry, to rejoice,* Acts, ii. 26. Rom. xv. 10. Gal. iv. 27. Luke, xii. 19. xv. 23, 29, 32; εὐφραίνου ἐπ' αὐτῇ, *exult over her,* Rev. xviii. 20; εὐφραινόμενος λαμπρῶς, *faring sumptuously,* Luke, xvi. 19; with ἔν τινι, *to be delighted with, to rejoice in,* Acts, ii. 26.

εὐφροσύνη, ἡ, *cheerfulness, gladness,* Acts, ii. 28. xiv. 17.

εὐχαριστέω, *to give thanks,* Luke, xvii. 16. Acts, xxvii. 35. xxviii. 15 etc.; pass., ἵνα τὸ χάρισμα εὐχαριστηθῇ, *that thanks may be given for the gift,* 2 Cor. i. 11.

εὐχαριστία, ἡ, *a giving of thanks, thankfulness,* 1 Cor. xiv. 16. Ephes. v. 4. 1 Tim. iv. 3. Acts, xxiv. 3 etc.; plur., 1 Tim. ii. 1. 2 Cor. ix. 12.

εὐχάριστος, *grateful, thankful,* Coloss. iii. 15.

εὐχή, ἡ, *a prayer,* James, v. 15; *a vow,* Acts, xviii. 18. xxi. 23.

εὔχομαι, *to pray,* 2 Cor. xiii. 7. 9; *to wish,* Acts, xxvii. 29. Rom. ix. 3.

εὔχρηστος, *useful,* 2 Tim. ii. 21. iv. 11; *serviceable,* Philem. 11.

εὐψυχέω, *to be of good courage, to be cheerful,* Philipp. ii. 19.

εὐωδία, ἡ, *a sweet savour, fragrance,* Philipp. iv. 18. Ephes. v. 2. 2 Cor. ii. 15.

εὐώνυμος, *of good omen; left,* Acts, xxi. 3. Matt. xx. 21.

ἐφάλλομαι, *to spring upon,* Acts, xix. 19.

ἐφάπαξ, adv., *once for all,* Hebr. vii. 27. ix. 12. x. 10. Rom. vi. 10; *at once,* 1 Cor. xv. 6.

ἐφευρετής, ὁ, *a contriver, an inventor,* Rom. i. 30.

ἐφημερία, ἡ, *a course of daily priestly service,* Luke, i. 5, 8. (It is a purely ecclesiastical word.)

ἐφήμερος, *daily,* James, ii. 15.

ἐφικνέομαι, *to come to, to reach,* 2 Cor. x. 13, 14.

ἐφίσταμαι, *to stand by,* Acts, xxii. 20. Luke, ii. 9. xxiv. 4; *to come upon suddenly,* Acts, vi. 12; of time, *to approach, to be at hand,* 2 Tim. iv. 6; *to be present,* Acts, xxviii. 2; *to be urgent,* 2 Tim. iv. 2.

ἐφφαθά, *be thou opened,* Mrk. vii. 34. (Aramaic.)

ἔχθρα, ἡ, *enmity,* Luke, xxiii. 12. Ephes. ii. 14, 16. Rom. viii. 7.

ἐχθρός, *hostile, inimical,* Matt. xiii. 28. Coloss. i. 21; as subst., *an enemy,* 1 Cor. xv. 25, 26. 2 Thess. iii. 15.

ἔχιδνα, ἡ, *a viper,* Acts, xxviii. 3. Matt. iii. 7. xii. 34. xxiii. 33. Luke, iii. 7.

ἔχω, *to have,* Rev. i. 16. vi. 5; ἐν γαστρὶ ἔχειν, *to be pregnant,* Matt. i. 18, 23; *to regard, to consider,* Matt. xiv. 5. xxi. 26; οὐ and μὴ ἔχειν, *to have not, to be poor,* Matt. xiii. 12. xxv. 29; ἡλικίαν ἔχειν, *to*

be of age, Joh. ix. 21, 23; ἔτη ἔχειν πεντήκοντα, *to be fifty years old*, Joh. viii. 57; τέσσαρας ἡμέρας ἔχειν ἐν τῷ μνημείῳ, *to have been four days buried*, Joh. xi. 17. Cf. Acts, i. 12; κοίτην ἔκ τινος ἔχειν, *to conceive by*, Rom. ix. 10; *to be able*, Matt. xviii. 25. Acts, iv. 14; intrans., ἑτοίμως ἔχειν, *to be ready*, Acts, xxi. 13. 2 Cor. xii. 14; τὸ νῦν ἔχον, *for the present*, Acts, xxiv. 25; mid., *to be closely connected with*; τὰ ἐχόμενα σωτηρίας, *things that tend to salvation*, Hebr. vi. 9; *to be adjacent*, Mrk. i. 38; ἡ ἐχομένη ἡμέρα, *the following day*, Acts. xx. 15.

ἕως, conj. and adverb, *while, up to, until, even to, unto;* used also as a prep. (The reader is referred to his Greek Grammar.)

Z

ζάω, *to live, to be alive*, Rom. vii. 1, 3. Acts, ix. 41. xvii. 28. Matt. ix. 18; met., ὕδωρ ζῶν, *living water*, Joh. iv. 10. vii. 38. Cf. 1 Pet. i. 3. Hebr. x. 20.

ζεστὸς, *fervent, hot*, Rev. iii. 15, 16.

ζεῦγος, τὸ, *a yoke of draught-cattle*, Luke, xiv. 19; *a couple, a pair*, Luke, ii. 24.

ζευκτηρία, ἡ, *a fastening*, Acts, xxvii. 40. (Found nowhere else.)

ζέω, *to boil, to be hot;* met., *to be fervent*, Rom. xii. 11. Acts, xviii. 25.

ζηλεύω, *to be zealous*, Rev. iii. 19.

ζῆλος, ὁ and τὸ, *zeal*, 2 Cor. vii. 11. ix. 2; *jealousy*, Acts, v. 17. xiii. 45. Rom. xiii. 13; *fierceness*, Hebr. x. 27.

ζηλόω, *to be zealous; to envy*, 1 Cor. xiii. 4. James, iv. 2; *to be moved with jealousy*, Acts, vii. 9. xvii. 5; *to be jealous for*, 2 Cor. xi. 2; *to earnestly desire*, 1 Cor. xii. 31. xiv. 1, 39; *to zealously seek after*, Gal. iv. 17; pass., *to be zealously sought after*, Gal. iv. 18.

ζηλωτὴς, ὁ, *a zealot;* "from the time of the Maccabees there existed among the Jews a class of men, called *Zealots*, who rigorously adhered to the Mosaic law, and endeavoured even by resort to violence to prevent religion from being violated by others. To this class perhaps Simon the apostle had belonged, and hence got the surname ὁ ζηλωτής (Luke, vi. 15. Acts, i. 13)," Thayer; with genit. of thing, *zealous for*, Acts, xxi. 20. 1 Cor. xiv. 12. Tit. ii. 14.

ζημία, ἡ, *loss*, Philipp. iii. 7. Acts, xxvii. 10, 21.

ζημιόω, *to damage;* pass., *to incur damage, to suffer loss*, 1 Cor. iii. 15. 2 Cor. vii. 9; with accus. of thing lost, *to lose, to forfeit*, Philipp. iii. 8. Matt. xvi. 26, Mrk. viii. 36. Luke, ix. 25.

ζητέω, *to seek*, Matt. vii. 7. Luke, xi. 9; *to reason, to* *inquire*, Joh. xvi. 19; *to seek for, to strive after*, Coloss. iii. 1. Matt. vi. 33. 1 Cor. vii. 27; *to desire*, Matt. xii. 46. Luke, v. 18. Mrk. xii. 12; *to require, to demand*, 2 Cor. xiii. 3. Mrk. viii. 12.

ζήτημα, τὸ, *a question*, Acts, xv. 2. xxvi. 3; νόμου, concerning their law, Acts, xxiii. 29; περί τινος, Acts, xviii. 15. xxv. 19.

ζήτησις, ἡ, *an inquiry, an investigation*, Acts, xxv. 20; *debate*, Acts, xv. 2, 7; *controversy*, Joh. iii. 25. 1 Tim. vi. 4. 2 Tim. ii. 23.

ζιζάνιον, τὸ, *tares*, a kind of darnel, resembling wheat, except that the grains are black, Matt. xiii. 25, 26 etc.

ζόφος, ὁ, *darkness, blackness*, Hebr. xii. 18. 2 Pet. ii. 4, 17. Jude, 6, 13.

ζυγὸς, ὁ, *a yoke*, Matt. xi. 29, 30; met., *a heavy burden, bondage*, Acts, xv. 10. 1 Tim. vi. 1. Gal. v. 1; *a balance, a pair of scales*, Rev. vi. 5.

ζύμη, ἡ, *leaven*, Matt. xiii. 33. Luke, xiii. 21. Gal. v. 9; *(morally)*, Matt. xvi. 6, 11, 12. 1 Cor. v. 8.

ζυμόω, *to leaven*, Gal. v. 9. 1 Cor. v. 6; pass., *to be leavened*, Matt. xiii. 33. Luke, xiii. 21.

ζωγρέω, *to take alive; to catch, to capture*, Luke, v. 10. 2 Tim. ii. 26.

ζωή, ἡ, *life*, Acts, xvii. 25. Rev. xi. 11. Hebr. vii. 3; *life in Heaven*, 1 Tim. vi. 19. Matt. vii. 14. Joh. vi. 40; *salvation*, Acts, v. 20. Joh. vi. 35, 48; *the author of life eternal*, Joh. xi. 25. Coloss. iii. 4.

ζώνη, ἡ, *a girdle*, Matt. iii. 4. Mrk. i. 6; *a purse*, Matt. x. 9. Mrk. vi. 8.

ζώννυμι, and ζωννύω, *to gird*, Joh. xxi. 18; mid., *to gird himself*, Acts, xii. 8.

ζωογονέω, with accus., *to give life to, to quicken*, 1 Tim. vi. 13; *to preserve alive*, Luke, xvii. 33; pass., *to be preserved alive*, Acts, vii. 19.

ζῶον, τὸ, *a living creature, an animal*, 2 Pet. ii. 12. Jude, 10. Rev. iv. 6, 7. Hebr. xiii. 11. ("The form ζῶον is more correct than ζῷον," Pape's Lexicon.)

ζωοποιέω, *to bring forth living creatures; to give life, to quicken*, Joh. v. 21. vi. 63. 1 Cor. xv. 45. 2 Cor. iii. 6. Gal. iii. 21; pass., *to be quickened*, 1 Pet. iii. 18. 1 Cor. xv. 22, 36.

H

ἤ, conj., *either, or, than*,

ἦ, an *affirmative* particle, *certainly;* in the NT appearing only in the formula ἦ μήν, *most assuredly*, Hebr. vi. 14. (Westcott reads εἰ μήν.)

ἡγεμονεύω, *to rule, to be a governor of*, Luke, ii. 2. iii. 1.

ἡγεμονία, ἡ, *sovereignty, reign*, Luke, iii. 1.

ἡγεμὼν, ὁ, *a governor*, Matt. xxvii. 2. Luke, xxi. 12. 1 Pet. ii. 14; *a chief town*, Matt. ii. 6.

ἡγέομαι, *to think, to consider, to deem*, Acts, xxvi. 2. 2 Cor.ix. 5. Philipp. ii. 3, 6. iii. 7; *to value, to esteem*, 1 Thess. v. 13; *to have authority over;* in this sense, in the NT, only in the present participle, ἡγούμενος=*a ruler, a governor*, Matt. ii. 6. Acts, vii. 10. Hebr. xiii. 7, 17, 24; *a chief*, Luke, xxii. 26; ἄνδρας ἡγουμένους, *leading men*, Acts, xv. 22; ὁ ἡγούμενος τοῦ λόγου, *the chief speaker*, Acts,xiv.12.

ἡδέως, adv., *gladly*, 2 Cor. xi. 19. Mrk. vi. 20. xii. 37.

ἤδη, adv., *already, now; ἤδη ποτε, now at length*, Rom. i. 10.

ἤδιστα, adv., *most gladly*, 2 Cor. xii. 9, 15.

ἡδονὴ, ἡ. *pleasure*, Luke, viii. 14. 2 Pet. ii. 13; *lust*, James, iv. 1, 3.

ἡδύοσμον, τὸ, *mint*, Luke, xi. 42. Matt. xxiii. 23.

ἦθος, τὸ, *a custom, a habit;* plur., *morals*, 1 Cor. xv. 33.

ἥκω, *to have come, to be present*, Mrk. viii. 3. Luke, xv. 27 etc.; but the imperf. ἧκον has the meaning of a pluperfect.

ἡλικία, ἡ, *adult age; ἡλικίαν ἔχειν, to be of age*, Joh. ix. 21; παρὰ καιρὸν ἡλικίας, *past the age for childbearing*, Hebr. xi. 11; *stature*, Luke, ii. 52. xix. 3. Ephes. iv. 13.

ἡλίκος, *how great*, James, iii. 5. Coloss. ii. 1; *how small*, James, iii. 5.

ἥλιος, ὁ, *the sun*, Matt. xiii. 43. xvii. 2; *the light of the sun*, Acts, xiii. 11.

ἧλος, ὁ, *a nail*, Joh. xx. 25.

ἡμέρα, ἡ, *a day* according to Jewish reckoning, i.e. from sunrise to sunset, Luke, ii. 44. Matt. xii. 40; *the civil day*, i.e. a period of twenty-four hours, Matt. vi. 34. Luke, xiii. 14; ἡ κυριακὴ ἡμέρα, *the Lord's day*, Rev. i. 10; *the day of Judgment*, Acts, ii. 20. Luke, xvii. 30; ἡμέρας, *in the daytime*, Rev. xxi. 25; ἡμέρας μέσης, *at midday*, Acts, xxvi. 13; ἡμέραν ἐξ ἡμέρας, *from day to day*, 2 Pet. ii. 8; καθ' ἡμέραν, *every day, daily*, Acts, xvii. 17. Hebr. iii. 13. Matt. xxvi. 55.

ἡμέτερος, *our*, Acts, ii. 11. xxvi. 5. Rom. xv. 4; οἱ ἡμέτεροι, *our brethren*, Tit. iii. 14.

ἡμιθανὴς, *half dead*, Luke, x. 30.

ἥμισυς, *half;* τὰ ἡμίσια τῶν ὑπαρχόντων, *half of my property*, Luke, xix. 8; ἥμισυ, as subst., *a half;* τρεῖς ἡμέρας καὶ ἥμισυ, *three days and a half*, Rev. xi. 9, 11. Cf. Rev. xii. 14; ἕως ἡμίσους τῆς βασιλείας μου, *unto half of my kingdom*, Mrk. vi. 23.

ἡμιώριον, and **ἡμίωρον**, τὸ, *half an hour*, Rev. viii. 1.

ἡνίκα, adv., *when, as often as, whenever, as soon as*. (The reader is referred to his Greek Grammar.)

ἤπιος, *mild, gentle*, 2 Tim. ii. 24.

ἤρεμος, *quiet, tranquil*, 1 Tim. ii. 2.

Ἡρῳδιανοί, οἱ, *Herodians*, the partisans of Herod, Matt. xxii. 16. Mrk. iii. 6. xii. 13.

ἡσσάομαι, see ἡττάομαι.

ἡσυχάζω, *to rest*, Luke, xxiii. 56; *to lead a quiet life*, 1 Thess. iv. 11; *to be silent, to hold their peace*, Luke, xiv. 4. Acts, xi. 18. xxi. 14.

ἡσυχία, ἡ, *quietness*, 2 Thess. iii. 12; *silence*, Acts, xxii. 2. 1 Tim. ii. 11, 12.

ἡσύχιος, *quiet, peaceful*, 1 Tim. ii. 2. 1 Pet. iii. 4.

ἡττάομαι, and **ἡσσάομαι**, *to be made inferior*, 2 Cor. xii. 13; *to be overcome*, 2 Pet. ii. 19, 20.

ἥττημα, τό, *failure*, Rom. xi. 12 (RV *loss*); *a defect*, 1 Cor. vi. 7.

ἥττων, and **ἥσσων**, *inferior; less*, 2 Cor. xii. 15; ἧττον, and ἧσσον, adverbially, εἰς τὸ ἧσσον, *for the worse*, 1 Cor. xi. 17.

ἠχέω, *to sound*, 1 Cor. xiii. 1.

ἦχος, ὁ and τό, *a sound*, Acts, ii. 2. Hebr. xii. 19; *the roaring* of the sea, Luke, xxi. 25; *a rumour, a report*, Luke, iv. 37.

Θ

θάλασσα, ἡ, *the sea*, Matt. xxiii. 15. Luke, xvii. 2, 6; ἡ ἐρυθρὰ θάλασσα, *the Red Sea*, Acts, vii. 36. Hebr. xi. 29.

θάλπω, *to warm*; met., *to cherish*, Ephes. v. 29. 1 Thess. ii. 7.

θαμβέω, in pass., *to be amazed*, Mrk. i. 27. x. 24, 32.

θάμβος, τό, *amazement*, Luke, iv. 36. v. 9. Acts, iii. 10.

θανάσιμος, *deadly*, Mrk. xvi. 18.

θανατηφόρος, *death-bringing, deadly*, James, iii. 8.

θάνατος, ὁ, *death*, Luke, ii. 26. Matt. x. 21; πληγὴ θανάτου, *a deadly wound*, Rev. xiii. 3, 12; *loss of salvation*, Rom. i. 32. vi. 16. Rev. ii. 11.

θανατόω, *to put to death*, Matt. xxvi. 59. Luke, xxi. 16; *to mortify*, Rom. viii. 13; pass., *to be in the state of persons being put to death*, Rom. viii. 36; with dat. of thing, *to be made dead in relation to*, Rom. vii. 4.

θάπτω, *to bury*, Matt. viii. 21, 22. 1 Cor. xv. 4.

θαρρέω, and **θαρσέω**, *to be of good courage*, Matt. ix. 2. 2 Cor. v. 6; *to be bold*, 2 Cor. x. 1, 2.

θάρσος, τό, *confidence, courage*, Acts, xxviii. 15.

θαῦμα, τό, *a wonder*, 2 Cor. xi. 14; θαυμάζειν θαῦμα μέγα, *to wonder exceedingly*, Rev. xvii. 6.

θαυμάζω, *to wonder, to wonder at*, Matt. viii. 10, 27. xv. 31. Luke, xxiv. 12; *to pay regard to*, Jude, 16; pass., *to be wondered at*, 2 Thess. i. 10; ἐθαυμάσθη ἡ γῆ ὀπίσω τοῦ θηρίου, *followed the beast in astonishment*, Rev. xiii. 3. (Other texts here exhibit ἐθαύμασεν.)

θαυμάσιος, *wonderful, marvellous*, Matt. xxi. 15.

θαυμαστὸς, *marvellous*, 1 Pet. ii. 9. Matt. xxi. 42.

θεὰ, ἡ, *a goddess*, Acts, xix. 27.

θεάομαι, *to view, to behold*, Matt. xxii. 11. Luke, vii. 24. Joh. i. 14 ; *to visit*, Rom. xv. 24.

θεατρίζομαι, *to be set forth as a spectacle, to be made a gazing-stock*, Hebr. x. 33.

θέατρον, τὸ, *a theatre*, Acts, ix. 29, 31 ; *a public shew, a spectacle*, 1 Cor. iv. 9.

θεῖον, τὸ, *brimstone*, Luke, xvii. 29. Rev. ix. 17. xiv. 10.

θεῖος, *divine*, 2 Pet. i. 3 ; τὸ θεῖον, *the deity*, Acts, xvii. 29 (RV *the Godhead*).

θειότης, ἡ, *the divinity, the divine nature*, Rom. i. 20.

θειώδης, *of brimstone*, Rev. ix. 17.

θέλημα, τὸ, *the will*, Joh. i. 13. v. 30. Luke, xii. 47 etc.; plur., *commands*, Acts, xiii. 22. (With the exception of one passage in Aristotle, confined to the ecclesiastical writers.)

θέλησις, ἡ, *the will*, Hebr. ii. 4. (Perhaps a vulgarism.)

θέλω, *to will, to be willing*, Matt. ii. 18. xv. 32. Luke, xv. 28 ; *to desire*, Matt. xii. 38. xx. 21. Joh. xv. 7 ; *to prefer*, 1 Cor. xiv. 19 ; *to like, to love*, Luke, xx. 46. (This form alone appears in the NT ; not ἐθέλω.)

θεμέλιος, ὁ, and **θεμέλιον**, τὸ, *a foundation*, Acts, xvi. 26. Ephes. ii. 20. Luke, vi. 48, 49 etc.; *the beginnings, the first principles*, Hebr. vi. 1. Rom. xv. 20.

θεμελιόω, *to lay the foundation, to found*, Hebr. i. 10. Matt. vii. 25. Luke, vi. 48 ; met., *to establish, to ground*, Ephes. iii. 17. Coloss. i. 23.

θεοδίδακτος, *taught of God*, 1 Thess. iv. 9. (Found only in ecclesiastical writers.)

θεομαχέω, *to fight against God*, a var. lect. ad Acts, xxiii. 9. (Omitted by Westcott.)

θεομάχος, *fighting against God*, Acts, v. 39.

θεόπνευστος, *inspired by God*, 2 Tim. iii. 16.

θεὸς, ὁ, *God*, Matt. iii. 9. Luke, ii. 13. Acts, iii. 13. vii. 2. xiii. 17 etc. ; also applied to Christ, Rom. ix. 5. 1 Joh. v. 20. Tit. ii. 13. Joh. i. 1. Philipp. ii. 6. Coloss. ii. 9. Hebr. i. 8 ; the evil principle or thing that men serve, 2 Cor. iv. 4. Philipp. iii. 19. In Acts, vii. 20. ἀστεῖος τῷ Θεῷ = *in sight of God*, or *divinely*.

θεοσέβεια, ἡ, *reverence towards God, fear of God*, 1 Tim. ii. 10.

θεοσεβὴς, *godfearing*, Joh. ix. 31.

θεοστυγὴς, *hateful to God*, Rom. i. 30.

θεότης, ἡ, *Deity, Godhead*, Coloss. ii. 9.

θεραπεία, ἡ, *service, healing*, Luke, ix. 11. Rev. xxii. 2 ; met. (from the idea of attendance), *a household*, Luke, xii. 42.

θεραπεύω, *to serve*, Acts, xvii. 25 ; *to cure, to heal*, Matt. iv. 24. Mrk. vi. 5. Luke, vi. 7. etc.

θεράπων, ὁ, *an attendant, a servant*, Hebr. iii. 5.

θερίζω, *to reap*, Joh. iv. 36, 37. Matt. xxv. 24, 26. Gal. vi. 7.

θερισμὸς, ὁ, *harvest*, Matt. xiii. 30, 39. Luke, x. 2. Mrk. iv. 29.

θεριστὴς, ὁ, *a reaper*, Matt. xiii. 30, 39.

θερμαίνω, *to warm*; mid., *to warm oneself*, Mrk. xiv. 54, 67. Joh. xviii. 18, 25; pass., *to be warmed*. James, ii. 16.

θέρμη, ἡ, *heat*, Acts, xxviii. 3.

θέρος, τὸ, *summer*, Matt. xxiv. 32. Mrk. xiii. 28. Luke, xxi. 30.

θεωρέω, *to behold, to see*, Matt. xxvii. 55. xxviii. 1; *to experience*, Joh. viii. 51; *to perceive*, Acts, xvii. 22. Mrk. xvi. 4; *to consider*, Hebr. vii. 4; *to come to a knowledge of*, Joh. vi. 40.

θεωρία, ἡ, *a spectacle, a sight*, Luke, xxiii. 48.

θήκη, ἡ, *a receptacle; the sheath* of a sword, Joh. xviii. 11.

θηλάζω, *to give suck, to suckle*, Matt. xxiv. 19. Luke, xxi. 23.

θῆλυς, *of the female sex*; ἡ θήλεια, *the female, the woman*, Rom. i. 26, 27; also τὸ θῆλυ = ἡ θήλεια, Matt. xix. 4. Mrk. x. 6. Gal. iii. 28.

θήρα, ἡ, *a hunting* of wild beasts; met., *a trap*, Rom. xi. 9.

θηρεύω, *to hunt; to catch, to lay hold of*, Luke, xi. 54.

θηριομαχέω, *to fight with wild beasts*, 1 Cor. xv. 32.

θηρίον, τὸ, *a little beast;* and, generally, *a beast*, Acts, xxviii. 4, 5. Hebr. xii. 20. Rev. xi. 7. Tit. i. 12.

θησαυρίζω, *to lay up, to store up*, James, v. 3. Matt. vi. 19. Luke, xii. 21. Rom. ii. 5 etc.

θησαυρὸς, ὁ, *a treasure-chamber*, Luke, vi. 45; *a coffer, a casket*, Matt. ii. 11; *a treasure*, Matt. vi. 19, 21. xix. 21. Luke, xii. 33.

θιγγάνω, *to touch*, Coloss. ii. 21. Hebr. xii. 20; *to injure*, Hebr. xi. 28.

θλίβω, *to press, to crowd upon*, Mrk. iii. 9; ὁδὸς τεθλιμμένη, *a straitened way*, Matt. vii. 14; met., *to afflict, to distress*, 2 Thess. i. 6; pass., *to be afflicted*, Hebr. xi. 37. 2 Cor. i. 6. iv. 8. vii. 5.

θλίψις, ἡ, *affliction, tribulation*, Matt. xiii. 21. xxiv. 21, 29. 2 Thess. i. 4. Philipp. i. 16. ("The ι in θλίβω is long by nature; therefore θλίψις is a false accentuation," Pape's Lexicon.)

θνήσκω, *to die;* in the NT appearing only in the perfect = *to be dead*, 1 Tim. v. 6. Matt. ii. 20. Luke, viii. 49 etc.

θνητὸς, *mortal*, Rom. vi. 12. viii. 11. 2 Cor. iv. 11 etc.

θορυβάζω, *to trouble, to disturb;* pass., *to be troubled*, Luke, x. 41. (Found nowhere else in the NT.)

θορυβέω, *to be turbulent*; trans., *to disturb, to throw into confusion*, Acts, xvii. 5; pass., *to make a disturbance*, Matt. ix. 23. Mrk. v. 39. Acts, xx. 10.

θόρυβος, ὁ, *uproar*, Acts, xx. 1. xxi. 34. Mrk. v. 38; *tumult*, Matt. xxvi. 5. xxvii. 24. Mrk. xiv. 2. Acts, xxiv. 18.

θραύω, *to break;* τεθραυσμένοι, *broken by calamity*, Luke, iv. 18 (RV *bruised*).

θρέμμα, τὸ, *a nurseling;* θρέμματα, *cattle*, Joh. iv. 12.

θρηνέω, *to lament*, Joh. xvi. 20; *to mourn, to wail*, Luke, vii. 32. Matt. xi. 17; *to bewail*, Luke, xxiii. 27.

θρῆνος, ὁ, *lamentation*, a var. lect. ad Matt. ii. 18.

θρησκεία, ἡ, *religious worship, religion*, James, i. 26, 27. Acts, xxvi. 5; *a worshipping*, Coloss. ii. 18.

θρῆσκος, *Godfearing, religious*, James, i. 26.

θριαμβεύω, *to celebrate a triumph; to triumph over*, Coloss. ii. 15 (see Pape's Lexicon in voc.); *to cause one to triumph*, 2 Cor. ii. 14.

θρίξ, ἡ, *the hair* of the head, Matt. x. 30. Joh. xi. 2. xii. 3. Acts, xxvii. 34 etc.; also of camels, Mrk. i. 6. Matt. iii. 4.

θροέω, *to make an outcry;* pass. in the NT *to be frightened*, Mrk. xiii. 7. Matt. xxiv. 6. 2 Thess. ii. 2. (See Pape's Lex. in voc.)

θρόμβος, ὁ, *a large drop*, Luke, xxii. 44.

θρόνος, ὁ, *a throne*, Matt. v. 34. Acts, vii. 49. Rev. iii. 21; *kingly power*, Luke, i. 32, 52.

θυγάτηρ, ἡ, *a daughter*, Matt. ix. 18. x. 35, 37. 2 Cor. vi. 18 etc.; *a female descendant*, Luke, i. 5. xiii. 16.

θυγάτριον, τὸ, *a little daughter*, Mrk. v. 23. vii. 25.

θύελλα, ἡ, *a tempest*, Hebr. xii. 18.

θύϊνος, *thyine*, Rev. xviii. 12. (From θύα, the *citrus*, an odoriferous North African tree.)

θυμίαμα, τὸ, *incense*, Luke, i. 11. Rev. v. 8. viii. 3; ἡ ὥρα τοῦ θυμιάματος, *the time to offer incense*, Luke, i. 10.

θυμιατήριον, τὸ, *a censer*, (AV); or *altar of incense*, Hebr. ix. 4.

θυμιάω, *to burn incense*, Luke, i. 9.

θυμομαχέω, *to be very angry*, Acts, xii. 20.

θυμός, ὁ, *anger, wrath*, Luke, iv. 28. Ephes. iv. 31. etc.; *fierceness*, Rev. xvi. 19. xix. 15; θυμοί, *outbursts of wrath*, 2 Cor. xii. 20. Gal. v. 20.

θυμόω, *to provoke to anger;* pass., *to be wroth*, Matt. ii. 16.

θύρα, ἡ, *a door*, Mrk. i. 33. Matt. vi. 6 etc.; *an entrance*, Matt. xxvii. 60. Mrk. xv. 46. xvi. 3; *an opportunity*, Acts, xiv. 27. 1 Cor. xvi. 8. 2 Cor. ii. 12. Coloss. iv. 3; *access, means of entering*, Rev. iii. 8. iv. 1.

θυρεός, ὁ, *a shield* (Lat. *scutum*), Ephes. vi. 16.

θυρίς, ἡ, *a little door; a window*, Acts, xx. 9. 2 Cor. xi. 33.

θυρωρός, ὁ, and ἡ, *a doorkeeper*, Mrk. xiii. 34. Joh. x. 3. xviii. 16.

θυσία, ἡ, *a sacrifice*, Matt. ix. 13. xii. 7. Ephes. v. 2. Hebr. x. 5; *an offering*, Philipp. iv. 18. Hebr. xiii. 16.

θυσιαστήριον, τὸ, *an altar*, Hebr. xiii. 10. 1 Cor. ix. 13. x. 18. Rom. xi. 3. James, ii. 21. (The pagan word for *altar*, viz. βωμὸς, appears only once in the NT, Acts, xvii. 23, and there its use was unavoidable.)

θύω, *to sacrifice*, Acts, xiv. 13, 18. 1 Cor. x. 20; *to slay, to kill*, Acts, x. 13. xi. 7. Joh. x. 10. Luke, xv. 23, 27, 30.

θώραξ, ὁ, *a breastplate*, Ephes. vi. 14. 1 Thess. v. 8. Rev. ix. 9, 17.

I

ἴαμα, τὸ, *healing*, 1 Cor. xii. 9, 28, 30.

ἰάομαι, *to cure, to heal*, Joh. iv. 47. Acts, ix. 34. x. 38; met., *to restore to a spiritual tone of mind*, Matt. xiii. 15. Joh. xii. 40. James, v. 16 etc.

ἴασις, ἡ, *a healing, a cure*, Luke, xiii. 32. Acts, iv. 22, 30.

ἴασπις, ἡ, *a precious stone, the jasper*, Rev. iv. 3. xxi. 11. 18.

ἰατρός, ὁ, *a physician*, Coloss. iv. 14. Luke, iv. 23. Matt. ix. 12.

ἰδὲ, and **ἴδε**, imperat. of εἶδον, but used as an interjection, *see! lo! behold!* Matt. xxvi. 65. Joh. v. 14. Mrk. ii. 24.

ἰδέα, ἡ, *outward form, appearance*, a var. lect. ad Matt. xxviii. 3. (Westcott reads εἰδέα.)

ἴδιος, *one's own*, Joh. x. 3, 12. Hebr. ix. 12. Acts, xxviii. 30. Rom. x. 3; οἱ ἴδιοι, *his own people*, Joh. i. 11. Acts, iv. 23; *thine own*, Luke, vi. 41. Cf. 1 Cor. iv. 12; εἰς τὰ ἴδια, *to his own land*, i.e. *the world which he himself had made*, Joh. i. 11. Cf. xvi. 32; *appropriate, fitting*, 1 Tim. ii. 6. 1 Cor. iii. 8. Gal. vi. 9 (RV *in due season*); *private*, 2 Pet. i. 20; κατ' ἰδίαν, *privately*. Mrk. iv. 34. Gal. ii. 2; *apart*, Matt. xiv. 13. xvii. 19. xx. 17 etc.; ἰδίᾳ, *privately; separately, severally*, 1 Cor. xii. 11.

ἰδιώτης, ὁ, *a private person; an ignorant* or *illiterate person*, Acts, iv. 13. 1 Cor. xiv. 16, 23, 24. 2 Cor. xi. 6.

ἰδοὺ, adv., *lo! behold!* Matt. i. 23. Acts, viii. 36. Luke, i. 38 etc.

ἱδρὼς, ὁ, *sweat*, Luke, xxii. 44. (The passage is bracketed by Westcott.)

ἱερατεία, and **ἱερατία**, ἡ, *the priesthood, the office of priest*, Hebr. vii. 5.

ἱεράτευμα, τὸ, *the priesthood*, 1 Pet. ii. 5, 9. (It is a purely ecclesiastical word.)

ἱερατεύω, *to discharge the office of priest*, Luke, i. 8.

ἱερεὺς, ὁ, *a priest*, Acts, xiv. 13. Matt. viii. 4; applied to Christ, Hebr. v. 6. vii. 16, 17. x. 21; applied to Christians, Rev. i. 6. v. 10. xx. 6.

ἱερόθυτος, *offered in sacrifice*, 1 Cor. x. 28.

ἱερὸν, τό, *a temple*, Acts, xix. 27. 1 Cor. ix. 13. Luke, iv. 9. Matt. xii. 6.

ἱεροπρεπής, *everent*, Tit. ii. 3.

ἱερὸς, *sacred*, 2 Tim. iii. 15; τὰ ἱερὰ, *the holy things*, 1 Cor. ix. 13.

ἱεροσυλέω, *to commit sacrilege*, Rom. ii. 22.

ἱερόσυλος, ὁ, *a temple-robber*, Acts, xix. 37.

ἱερουργέω, *to minister in sacred things*; τὸε ὑαγγέλιον ἱερουργεῖν, *to minister in the gospel*, Rom. xv. 16.

ἱερωσύνη, ἡ, *the priestly office*, *the priesthood*, Hebr. vii. 24.

Ἰησοῦς, -οῦ, -οῦ, -οῦν, -οῦ, ὁ, *Jesus*, *the Son of God*, *the Saviour of mankind*, Matt. i. 21, 25 etc. (The word has no connexion with the verb ἰάομαι; for all the (non-Ionic) derivatives of that verb keep α throughout; as ἰατρὸς, ἰάσιμος, etc.)

ἱκανὸς, *sufficient*, 2 Cor. ii. 6; φῶς ἱκανὸν, *a great light*, Acts, xxii. 6; ὄχλος ἱκανὸς, *a great multitude*, Mrk. x. 46. Acts, xi. 24; ἀργύρια ἱκανὰ, *a large sum of money*, Matt. xxviii. 12; ἱκανῷ χρόνῳ, *for a long time*, Acts, viii. 11. Cf. Luke, viii. 27. xxiii. 8. Rom. xv. 23; ἐφ' ἱκανὸν, *for a long while*, Acts, xx. 11; ἡμέραι ἱκαναί, *many days*, Acts, ix. 23; ἱκανοὶ, *many people*, Acts, xii. 12; τὸ ἱκανὸν, *security*, Acts, xvii. 9; *able*, 2 Tim. ii. 2; *worthy*, 1 Cor. xv. 9. Matt. viii. 8. Luke, iii. 16.

ἱκανότης, ἡ, *sufficiency*, *ability*, 2 Cor. iii. 5.

ἱκανόω, *to make competent*, *to qualify*, 2 Cor. iii. 6. Coloss. i. 12.

ἱκετηρία, ἡ, *supplication*, Hebr. v. 7. (See Pape's Lexicon in voc. ἱκετήριος.)

ἰκμὰς, ἡ, *moisture*, Luke. viii. 6.

ἱλαρὸς, *cheerful*, 2 Cor. ix. 7.

ἱλαρότης, ἡ, *cheerfulness*, Rom. xii. 8.

ἱλάσκομαι, *to propitiate*; with accus. of thing, *to expiate*, *to make an atonement for*, Hebr. ii. 17; with dat. of person, ἱλάσθητί μοι, *be merciful to me*, Luke, xviii. 13.

ἱλασμὸς, ὁ, *propitiation*, 1 Joh. ii. 2. iv. 10.

ἱλαστήριον, τὸ, *the propitiatory*, *the mercy-seat*, Hebr. ix. 5. Cf. Rom. iii. 25. (It is a purely ecclesiastical word.)

ἵλεως, *merciful*, Hebr. viii. 12; ἵλεώς σοι = *God avert that from thee*, Matt. xvi. 22.

ἱμὰς, ὁ, *a thong*, Acts, xxii. 25; *a shoe-latchet*, Luke, iii. 16. Joh. i. 27. Mrk. i. 7.

ἱματίζω, *to clothe*, Luke, viii. 35. Mrk. v. 15. (Found only in the NT.)

ἱμάτιον, τὸ, *a garment*, Luke, v. 36. vii. 25. Matt. ix. 16; especially *an upper garment*, Mrk. v. 27. Matt. v. 24.

ἱματισμὸς, ὁ, *clothing*, *apparel*, Acts, xx. 33. 1 Tim. ii. 9. Luke, vii. 25.

ἱμείρω, *to long for*, var. lect. ad 1 Thess. ii. 8.

ἵνα, conj., *in order that*, *so that*, *that*; ἵνα μὴ, *lest*. (The reader is referred to his Greek Grammar.)

ἵνα τί; *for what purpose? Wherefore? Why?* Matt. ix. 4. xxvii. 46. Luke, xiii. 7.

ἰός, ὁ, *poison*, James, iii. 8. Rom. iii. 13; *rust*, James, v. 3.

Ἰουδαΐζω, *to imitate the Jews, to Judaize*, Gal. ii. 14.

Ἰουδαϊκός, *Jewish*, Tit. i. 14.

Ἰουδαϊκῶς, *Jewishly, after the manner of the Jews*, Gal. ii. 14.

Ἰουδαῖος, *Jewish*, Acts, xvi. 1; as subst. *a Jew*, in Joh. often *Jewish rulers*, and all most opposed to Christ.

Ἰουδαϊσμός, ὁ, *Judaism, the religion of the Jews*, Gal. i. 13.

ἱππεύς, ὁ, *a horseman*, Acts, xxiii. 23, 32.

ἱππικός, *equestrian;* τὸ ἱππικὸν, *the cavalry*, Rev. ix. 16.

ἵππος, ὁ, *a horse*, James, iii. 3. Rev. ix. 17. xix. 11 etc.

ἶρις, ἡ, *a rainbow*, Rev. iv. 3. x. 1.

ἰσάγγελος, *like to the angels*, Luke, xx. 36. (It is a purely ecclesiastical word.)

ἴστε, from οἶδα; ἴστε γινώσκοντες, *ye know full well*, Ephes. v. 5 ("ye know, understanding," Thayer).

ἴσος, *equal*, Matt. xx. 12. Joh. v. 18; τὰ ἴσα ἀπολαβεῖν, *to receive as much back*, Luke, vi. 34; ἡ ἴση δωρεά, *the same gift*, Acts, xi. 17; ἴσαι αἱ μαρτυρίαι οὐκ ἦσαν, *their testimony agreed not together*, Mrk. xiv. 56, 59; the neuters ἴσον and ἴσα are also used adverbially; ἴσα εἶναι, *to be equal*, Rev. xxi. 16; τὸ εἶναι ἴσα θεῷ, *his being equal with God*, Philipp. ii. 6.

ἰσότης, ἡ, *equality*, 2 Cor. viii. 14; *what is equitable*, Coloss. iv. 1.

ἰσότιμος, *equally precious*, 2 Pet. i. 1.

ἰσόψυχος, *alike in soul, likeminded*, Philipp. ii. 20.

Ἰσραήλ, ὁ, indecl., *Israel*, a name given to the patriarch Jacob, Matt. x. 6; ὁ Ἰσραὴλ κατὰ σάρκα, *Israelites by birth*, i.e. *the Jews*, 1 Cor. x. 18; ὁ Ἰσραὴλ τοῦ θεοῦ, i.e. *Christians*, Gal. vi. 16.

ἵστημι, and ἰστάνω, and ἰστάω, used transitively in the pres., imperf., fut., and 1 aor. act.; *to place, to set, to set up*, Matt. xviii. 2. Joh. viii. 4. Acts, iv. 7. vi. 13; *to establish*, Hebr. x. 9. Rom. iii. 31. x. 3; *to verify, to confirm*, Matt. xviii. 16. 2 Cor. xiii. 1; *to appoint*, Acts, xvii. 31. *to weigh out*, i.e. *to pay*, Matt. xxvi. 15; μὴ στήσῃς αὐτοῖς τὴν ἁμαρτίαν ταύτην, *do not impute this sin unto them*, Acts, vii. 60; but used intransitively in the perfect (ἕστηκα, *I stand*), pluperfect (εἱστήκειν, *I was standing*), 2 aorist (ἔστην, *I stood*), and in the passive (ἵσταμαι, σταθήσομαι, etc.); *to continue, to persevere*, Joh. viii. 44. 1 Cor. xv. 1.

ἱστορέω, *to become acquainted with*, Gal. i. 18.

ἰσχυρός, *strong*, 1 Cor. iv. 10. Luke, xi. 21, 22; *mighty*,

Matt. iii. 11. Mrk. i. 7. Rev. xviii. 8; *powerful*, 2 Cor. x. 10; *loud*, Rev. xviii. 2. Hebr. v. 7.

ἰσχύς, ἡ, *strength*, Mrk. xii. 30, 33. 1 Pet. iv. 11.

ἰσχύω, *to be strong*, Matt. ix. 12. Mrk. ii. 17; *to be able*, Matt. viii. 28. xxvi. 40; *to prevail*, Rev. xii. 8. Acts, xix. 16, 20; *to avail*, Hebr. ix. 17. Gal. v. 6; *to be serviceable*, Matt. v. 13.

ἴσως, adv., *perhaps, it may be*, Luke, xx. 13.

ἰχθύδιον, τό, *a little fish*, Matt. xv. 34. Mrk. viii. 7.

ἰχθύς, ὁ, *a fish*, Matt. vii. 10. Luke, v. 6. 1 Cor. xv. 39.

ἴχνος, τό, *a footstep*, Rom. iv. 12. 1 Pet. ii. 21.

ἰῶτα, τό, *iota*, used as an equivalent for the smallest letter in the Hebrew alphabet; therefore as an expression for *the minutest part, a jot*, Matt. v. 18.

K

καθά, adv., for καθ' ἅ, *according as, just as*, Matt. xxvii. 10.

καθαίρεσις, ἡ, *a pulling down*, 2 Cor. x. 4; *a casting down*, 2 Cor. x. 8. xiii. 10.

καθαιρέω, *to take down*, Matt. xv. 36, 46. Luke, xxiii. 53. Acts, xiii. 29; *to cast down*, Luke, i. 52; *to pull down*, Luke, xii. 18; *to refute*, 2 Cor. x. 4; *to destroy*, Acts, xiii. 19. xix. 27 ("τῆς μεγαλειότητος αὐτῆς must be taken as a partitive genitive, *somewhat of her magnificence*," Thayer).

καθαίρω, *to cleanse; to prune*, Joh. xv. 2.

καθάπερ, adv., *even as, just as, according as*, Rom. ix. 13. x. 15. xi. 8 etc.

καθάπτω, *to fasten on*, Acts, xxviii. 3.

καθαρίζω, *to cleanse*, Matt. xxiii. 25, 26. Mrk. vii. 19; *to heal*, Matt. viii. 2. x. 8. xi. 5; *to purify*, Acts, xv. 9. James, iv. 8. Tit. ii. 14 etc.; with ἀπό, *to cleanse* or *purify from*, 2 Cor. vii. 1. Hebr. ix. 14. 1 Joh. i. 7, 9.

καθαρισμός, ὁ, *a cleansing, a purification*, Luke, ii. 22. v. 14. Joh. iii. 25; κατὰ τὸν καθαρισμὸν τῶν Ἰουδαίων, *in accordance with the Jews' manner of purification*, Joh. ii. 6; *purification from*, i.e. *expiation of*, Hebr. i. 3. 2 Pet. i. 9.

καθαρός, *pure*, Matt. xxiii. 26. Tit. i. 15. Hebr. x. 22; *clean*, Joh. xiii. 10. xv. 3; *blameless*, Acts, xviii. 6; with ἀπό, *guiltless of*, Acts, xx. 26.

καθαρότης, ἡ, *purity, cleanness*, Hebr. ix. 13.

καθέδρα, ἡ, *a chair, a seat*, Matt. xxi. 12. xxiii. 2.

καθέζομαι, *to seat one's self, to sit*, Joh. xi. 20. xx. 12. Matt. xxvi. 55 etc.

καθείς, "i.e. καθ' εἷς; also εἷς καθεῖς, *one after the other, one by one*, NT; an erroneous formation, for καθ' ἕνα," Pape's Lexicon. See Joh. viii. 9.

καθεξῆς, adv., *in order, successively*, Luke, i. 3. Acts, xi.

καθ] TO THE NEW TESTAMENT **[και**

4. xviii. 23; οἱ καθεξῆς, *those that came after*, Acts, iii. 24; ἐν τῷ καθεξῆς (sc. χρόνῳ), *soon afterwards*, Luke, viii. 1.

καθεύδω, *to sleep*, Matt. ix. 24. xxv. 5 etc., met., *to be careless*, *to be indifferent*, Ephes. v. 14. 1 Thess. v. 6; *to be dead*, 1 Thess. v. 10.

καθηγητὴς, ὁ, *a guide, a master*, Matt. xxiii. 10.

καθήκω, *to come down, to reach to;* impers., καθήκει, *it is becoming, it is fitting*, Acts, xxii. 22; τὰ μὴ καθήκοντα, *things that are not fitting*, Rom. i. 28.

κάθημαι, *to sit down*, *to sit*, Rev. xx. 11. Matt. xx. 30. xxii. 44 etc.; *to dwell*, Luke, xxi. 35.

καθημερινὸς, *daily*, Acts, vi. 1.

καθίζω, *to make one sit down, to seat a person*, Acts, ii. 30. Ephes. i. 20. 1 Cor. vi. 4; intrans., *to sit down*, Matt. v. 1. xiii. 48. Joh. xix. 13; *to sit*, Matt. xx. 21, 23. xxiii. 2; *to sojourn, to dwell*, Acts, xviii. 11; *to tarry*, Luke, xxiv. 49.

καθίημι, *to send down; to let down*, Luke, v. 19. Acts, ix. 25; καθιέμενος, *let down*, Acts, x. 11. xi. 5.

καθίστημι, and **καθιστάω**, and **καθιστάνω**, *to set down; to place, to set;* with ἐπὶ, *to set over*, Matt. xxiv. 45. xxv. 21, 23. Luke, xii. 42; *to appoint*, Tit. i. 5. Hebr. v. 1. viii. 3; *to constitute, to make*, Luke, xii. 14. Acts, vii. 10, 27, 35. 2 Pet. i. 8; *to set down as,*

to declare to be, Rom. v. 19; *to conduct*, Acts, xvii. 15; mid., *to shew itself as*, James, iii. 6. iv. 4.

καθὸ, adv., for καθ' ὅ, *according as*, 2 Cor. viii. 12; *as*, Rom. viii. 26. (See καθά.)

καθολικὸς, *universal, catholic;* so ἐπιστολαὶ καθολικαὶ, *the Catholic Epistles*, in the title prefixed to the Epistles of S. James, S. Peter, S. John, and S. Jude, because addressed to the whole Catholic Church and not to one only.

καθόλου, adv., for καθ' ὅλον, *in general, altogether;* with a negative, *not at all*, Acts, iv. 18.

καθοπλίζω, *to arm completely*, Luke, xi. 21.

καθοράω, *to see thoroughly;* pass., *to be clearly perceived*, Rom. i. 20.

καθότι, adv., for καθ' ὅτι, *according as*, Acts, ii. 45. iv. 35; *because*, Acts, ii. 24. Luke, i. 7; *inasmuch as*, Acts, xvii. 31. Luke, xix. 9. ("Better written separately," Pape's Lexicon.)

καθὼς, adv., *even as*, Luke, vi. 31. 1 Joh. ii. 27; *as*, Acts, xv. 15. 1 Thess. ii. 13. Joh. vi. 58; *according as*, 1 Pet. iv. 10. Acts, xi. 29; *how*, Acts, xv. 14. 3 Joh. 3; καθώσπερ, *exactly as*, Heb. v. 4.

καὶ, conj., *and, also, even.* (The reader is referred to his Greek Grammar.)

καινὸς, *new*, Joh. xix. 41. Matt. ix. 17. xiii. 52; *novel, unheard of before*, Mrk. i. 27. Acts, xvii. 19. 2 Joh. 5.

και] GREEK-ENGLISH LEXICON [καλ

καινότης, ἡ, *newness*, Rom. vi. 4. vii. 6.

καίπερ, conj., *although*, 2 Pet. i. 12. Philipp. iii. 4. Hebr. v. 8.

καιρὸς, ὁ, *time, season*, 1 Tim. iv. 1. 2 Tim. iv. 3. 1 Cor. vii. 5. Acts, i. 7 ; *a favourable opportunity*, Gal. vi. 10. Acts, xxiv. 25 ; ἐν καιρῷ, *in due season*, Matt. xxiv. 45. Luke, xii. 42 ; πρὸς καιρὸν ὥρας, *for a short season*, 1 Thess. ii. 17 ; ἄχρι καιροῦ, *for a season*, Luke, iv. 13 ; πρὸς καιρὸν, *for a short while*, Luke, viii. 13.

καίτοι, *and yet, although*, Hebr. iv. 3.

καίω, *to burn*, Luke, xii. 35. Joh. v. 35. xv. 6 ; *to kindle, to light*, Matt. 5. 15.

κακία, ἡ, *malice*, Ephes. iv. 31. Coloss. iii. 8. Tit. iii. 3 ; *wickedness*, Acts, viii. 22. 1 Pet. ii. 16 ; *evil*, Matt. vi. 34.

κακοήθεια, and **κακοηθία**, ἡ, *depravity, malignity*, Rom. i. 29.

κακολογέω, *to speak evil of*, Mrk. ix. 39. Acts, xix. 9 ; *to curse*, Matt. xv. 4.

κακοπάθεια, and **κακοπαθία**, ἡ, *suffering, affliction*, James, v. 10.

κακοπαθέω, *to endure affliction, to be afflicted*, 2 Tim. ii. 9. 2 Tim. iv. 5. James, v. 13.

κακοποιέω, *to do harm*, Luke, vi. 9. Mrk. iii. 4 ; *to do wrong*, 1 Pet. iii. 17. 3 Joh. 11.

κακοποιὸς, *doing evil;* as subst., *an evil-doer*, 1 Pet. ii. 12 Joh. xviii. 30.

κακὸς, *evil, bad*, Matt. xxi. 41. xxiv. 48 ; τὸ κακὸν, *wickedness, evil*, Rom. vii. 21. xiii. 4 ; τὰ κακὰ, *evil things*, Luke, xvi. 25.

κακοῦργος, ὁ, *a malefactor*, 2 Tim. ii. 9. Luke, xxiii. 32.

κακουχέω, *to ill-treat, to oppress;* κακουχούμενος, *maltreated*, Hebr. xi. 37. xiii. 3.

κακόω, *to oppress, to afflict*, Acts, vii. 6, 19. xii. 1. xviii. 10 ; *to embitter, to render evil affected*, Acts, xiv. 2.

κακῶς, adv., *badly;* κακῶς ἔχειν, *to be sick*, Matt. iv. 24. viii. 16 ; *evilly, wrongly*, Joh. xviii. 23. James, iv. 3 ; κακῶς εἰπεῖν τινα, *to speak evil of*, Acts, xxiii. 5.

κάκωσις, ἡ, *ill-treatment, affliction*, Acts, vii. 34.

καλάμη, ἡ, *a stalk of grain, stubble*, 1 Cor. iii. 12.

κάλαμος, ὁ, *a reed*, Luke, vii. 24. Matt. xi. 7. Mrk. xv. 19, 36 ; *a measuring rod*, Rev. xi. 1. xxi. 15 ; *a pen*, 3 Joh. 13.

καλέω, *to call*, Matt. ix. 13. Gal. v. 8 ; *to invite*, Joh. ii. 1, 2. Luke, xiv. 16 ; *to name*, Luke, i. 31. Matt. x. 25 ; *to salute as*, Matt. xxiii. 9.

καλλιέλαιος, ἡ, *a cultivated olive-tree*, Rom. xi. 24.

καλοδιδάσκαλος, ὁ and ἡ, *a teacher of goodness*, Tit. ii. 3. (Found nowhere else.)

καλοὶ λιμένες, *Fair Havens*, a harbour of Crete, Acts, xxvii. 8.

καλοποιέω, *to do well*, 2 Thess. iii. 13.

καλὸς, *beautiful*, Luke, xxi. 5; *good*, Matt. xiii. 24, 27, 37, 48; *noble*, 1 Tim. i. 18. vi. 12; καλόν ἐστιν, *it is good, it is expedient*, 1 Cor. vii. 1.

κάλυμμα, τὸ, *a covering, a veil*, 2 Cor. iii. 13, 14, 15, 16.

καλύπτω, *to cover*, Luke, viii. 16. xxiii. 30; *to hide*, Matt. x. 26. 2 Cor. iv. 3; *to procure pardon for*, James, v. 20. 1 Pet. iv. 8. Cf. Rom. iv. 7.

καλῶς, adv., *well*, Joh. iv. 17. Matt. xv. 7. Luke, xx. 39; *rightly*, Mrk. vii. 6; as a formula of approbation, *well!* Rom. xi. 20; *uprightly, honestly*, Hebr. xiii. 18; met., *in an honourable place*, James, ii. 3; καλῶς ποιεῖν, *to do well, to act rightly*, James, ii. 8, 19. 1 Cor. vii. 37, 38; καλῶς εἰπεῖν τινα, *to speak well of one*, Luke, vi. 26; καλῶς ἐποίησας παραγενόμενος, *thou hast done well in coming*, Acts, x. 33. Cf. Philipp. iv. 14. 2 Pet. i. 19. 3 Joh. 6; met., καλῶς ἔχειν, *to recover health*, Mrk. xvi. 18.

κάμηλος, ὁ, and, more frequently, ἡ, *a camel*, Matt. xix. 24. Luke, xviii. 25. Mrk. x. 25. (See Pape's Lexicon in voc.)

κάμιλος, ὁ, *a cable*; ("the reading of certain Mss. in Matt. xix. 24 and Luke, xviii. 25," Thayer).

κάμινος, ὁ, and ἡ, *a furnace, an oven*, Matt. xiii. 42, 50. Rev. i. 15. ix. 2.

καμμύω, *to close the eyes*, Acts, xxviii. 27. Matt. xiii. 15.

κάμνω, *to grow weary*, Hebr. xii. 3; *to be ill*, James, v. 15.

κάμπτω, *to bend*; trans., οὐκ ἔκαμψαν γόνυ τῷ Βάαλ, *have not bowed the knee to Baal*, Rom. xi. 4. Cf. Ephes. iii. 14; intrans., κάμψει πᾶν γόνυ ἐμοί, *every knee shall bow to me*, Rom. xiv. 11. Cf. Philipp. ii. 10.

κἄν, conj., for καὶ ἐὰν, *and if; even if; if it were but*, etc.

κανὼν, ὁ, *a rule, a standard*, Gal. vi. 16. Cf. Philipp. iii. 16; *a limit*, 2 Cor. x. 13, 15.

καπηλεύω, *to be a petty retailer, to peddle*; with accus. of thing, *to adulterate, to corrupt*, 2 Cor. ii. 17. Cf. 2 Cor. iv. 2. (Thus also in Pape's Lexicon.)

καπνὸς, ὁ, *smoke*, Acts, ii. 19. Rev. viii. 4, etc.

καρδία, ἡ, *the heart*, Acts, viii. 21. Matt. v. 8. vi. 21; *the understanding*, Rom. i. 21. Acts, xxviii. 27.

καρδιογνώστης, ὁ, *the knower of hearts*, Acts, i. 24. xv. 8. (It is a purely ecclesiastical and NT form.)

καρπὸς, ὁ, *fruit*, Matt. xii. 33. xxi. 19. Luke, xii. 17; *work, operation*, Gal. v. 22. Philipp. i. 11. Rom. xv. 28; *result*, Philipp. i. 22. Hebr. xii. 11.

καρποφορέω, *to bear fruit*, Matt. xiii. 23. Mrk. iv. 20. Luke, viii. 15; mid., *to bear fruit of itself*, Coloss. i. 6.

καρποφόρος, *fruitbearing, fruitful*, Acts, xiv. 17.

καρτερέω, *to hold out, to endure*, Hebr. xi. 27.

κάρφος, τὸ, *a dry fragment of straw, a mote*, Matt. vii. 3, 5. Luke, vi. 41. (See Pape's Lexicon.)

κατὰ, prep., taking genit. and accus.; with genit. denoting *motion in a vertical line—down from*; κατὰ τῶν ὀρέων, *down from the mountains*; but with accus. denoting *motion in a horizontal line*; κατὰ τὴν ὁδὸν, *along the road*, Luke, x. 4; also *time—about*; κατὰ τὸ μεσονύκτιον, *about midnight*, Acts, xvi. 25. Cf. Acts, xiv. 1; also *manner—according to*, Rom. xii. 6. Ephes. iv. 7; also serving to the formation of divers *adverbial phrases*; κατ' ἀνάγκην, *of necessity*, etc.

καταβαίνω, *to descend, to go down*, Luke, ii. 51. Rev. xii. 12.

καταβάλλω, *to cast down*, Rev. xii. 10. 2 Cor. iv. 9; *to lay, as a foundation*, Hebr. vi. 1.

καταβαρέω, *to weigh down, to burden*, 2 Cor. xii. 16.

καταβαρύνω, *to weigh down*, pass., *to be weighed down, to be heavy with sleep*, Mrk. xiv. 40.

κατάβασις, ἡ, *the descent, the place of descent*, Luke, xix. 37.

καταβιβάζω, *to cause to go down*; *to cast down*, Luke, x. 15. Cf. Matt. xi. 23. (Westcott reads καταβήσῃ in both passages.)

καταβολὴ, ἡ, *a foundation*, Matt. xiii. 35. xxv. 34; εἰς καταβολὴν σπέρματος, *to found a posterity*, Hebr. xi. 11.

καταβραβεύω, *to decide against as judge*; *to condemn*, Coloss. ii. 18. (See Pape's Lexicon in voc.)

καταγγελεὺς, ὁ, *an announcer*, Acts, xvii. 18. (Only in the NT and ecclesiastical writers.)

καταγγέλλω, *to make known, to proclaim*, Acts, iv. 2. xiii. 5. xvii. 13. 1 Cor. xi. 26 etc.

καταγελάω, *to deride*, Matt. ix. 24. Luke, viii. 53. Mrk. v. 40.

καταγινώσκω, *to condemn*, 1 Joh. iii. 20, 21. Gal. ii. 11

κατάγνυμι, *to break*, Matt. xii. 20. Joh. xix. 31, 32, 33.

καταγράφω, *to draw figures*, Joh. viii. 6.

κατάγω, *to lead down, to bring down*, Acts, ix. 30. xxii. 30. xxiii. 15; *to bring a ship to land, to touch at*, Acts, xxvii. 3. xxviii. 12. Cf. Luke, v. 11.

καταγωνίζομαι, *to conquer, to subdue*, Hebr. xi. 33.

καταδέω, *to bind up as a wound*, Luke, x. 34.

κατάδηλος, *thoroughly evident*, Hebr. vii. 15.

καταδικάζω, *to give judgment against, to condemn*, Matt. xii. 7, 37. Luke, vi. 37. James, v. 6.

καταδίκη, ἡ, *a sentence of condemnation*, Acts, xxv. 15.

καταδιώκω, *to pursue*; in a good sense, *to follow*, Mrk. i. 36.

καταδουλόω, *to enslave completely; to enslave*, Gal. ii. 4. 2 Cor. xi. 20.

καταδυναστεύω, *to oppress*, Acts, x. 38. James, ii. 6.

κατάθεμα, τὸ, *a curse*, Rev. xxii. 3. ("= καταναθεμα, NT," Pape in Lexicon.)

καταθεματίζω, *to curse vehemently*, Matt. xxvi. 74.

καταισχύνω, *to dishonour*, 1 Cor. xi. 4, 5 ; *to put to shame*, 1 Cor. i. 27. xi. 22 ; pass., *to be ashamed*, Luke, xiii. 17. Rom. ix. 33. x. 11.

κατακαίω, *to burn up*, Matt. xiii. 30. xix. 19.

κατακαλύπτω, *to completely cover;* mid., of women, *to cover themselves, to be veiled*, 1 Cor. xi. 6, 7.

κατακαυχάομαι, *to glory over*, Rom. xi. 18. James, iii. 14 ; κατακαυχᾶται ἔλεος κρίσεως, *mercy exulteth over judgment*, James, ii. 13. ("Mercy boasts itself superior to judgment, i.e. full of glad confidence has no fear of judgment," Thayer. But?)

κατάκειμαι, *to lie down; to be sick*, Mrk. i. 30. Acts, xxviii. 8 ; *to recline at meals*, 1 Cor. viii. 10. Luke, vii. 37 etc.

κατακλάω, *to break*, Mrk. vi. 41. Luke, ix. 16.

κατακλείω, *to shut up*, Acts, xxvi. 10. Luke, iii. 20.

κατακληροδοτέω, *to distribute by lot*, a var. lect. ad Acts, xiii. 19. (Westcott reads κατεκληρονόμησεν. The word is confined to ecclesiastical writers.)

κατακληρονομέω, *to distribute by lot*, Acts, xiii. 19. (Confined to ecclesiastical writers.)

κατακλίνω, *to make to recline*, Luke, ix. 14 ; pass., *to recline*, Luke xiv. 8. xxiv. 30.

κατακλύζω, *to overwhelm with water, to submerge*, 2 Pet. iii. 6.

κατακλυσμὸς, ὁ, *the deluge*, Matt. xxiv. 38. Luke, xvii. 27. 2 Pet. ii. 5.

κατακολουθέω, *to follow after*, Luke, xxiii. 55. Acts, xvi. 17.

κατακόπτω, *to cut to pieces; to gash, to cut*, Mrk. v. 5.

κατακρημνίζω, *to cast down headlong*, Luke, iv. 29.

κατάκριμα, τὸ, *condemnation*, Rom. v. 16.

κατακρίνω, *to condemn*, Matt. xx. 18. Rom. viii. 3 ; *by good example to make the sins of others more evident and more censurable*, Hebr. xi. 7. Matt. xii. 41. Luke, xi. 31.

κατάκρισις, ἡ, *condemnation*, 2 Cor. iii. 9. vii. 3. (It is a purely NT form.)

κατακυριεύω, *to overcome, to master*, Acts, xix. 16 ; *to hold in subjection, to exercise lordship over*, Matt. xx. 25. Mrk. x. 42.

καταλαλέω, *to speak against*, James, iv. 11. 1 Pet. ii. 12 ; pass., *to be spoken against*, 1 Pet. iii. 16.

καταλαλιὰ, ἡ, *evil speaking*, 2 Cor. xii. 20. 1 Pet. ii. 1. (It is a purely ecclesiastical word.)

κατάλαλος, ὁ, *an evil speaker, a defamer*, Rom. i. 30. (Found no where else.)

καταλαμβάνω, *to obtain, to attain to*, 1 Cor. ix. 24. Philipp. iii. 12. Rom. ix. 30; *to understand, to comprehend*, Acts, iv. 13. Joh. i. 5; *to overtake*, Joh. xii. 35. 1 Thess. v. 4; *to detect, to catch*, Joh. viii. 3, 4; *to perceive, to find*, Acts, xxv. 25.

καταλέγω, *to register, to enrol*, 1 Tim. v. 9.

κατάλειμμα, τὸ, *a remnant*, var. lect. ad Rom. ix. 27.

καταλείπω, *to leave behind* at death, Mrk. xii. 19; *to relinquish*, Mrk. xiv. 52; *to depart from, to leave*, Matt. iv. 13. xvi. 4; *to forsake*, 2 Pet. ii. 15; *to neglect*, Acts, vi. 2; *to leave alone*, Luke, x. 40; *to reserve*, Rom. xi. 4.

καταλιθάζω, *to overwhelm with stones; to stone*, Luke, xx. 6. (Only in ecclesiastical writers.)

καταλλαγή, ἡ, *reconciliation*, 2 Cor. v. 18, 19. Rom. v. 11. xi. 15.

καταλλάσσω, *to reconcile*; κόσμον καταλλάσσων ἑαυτῷ, *reconciling the world to himself*, 2 Cor. v. 18; pass. with dat. of person, *to be reconciled to*, 2 Cor. v. 20. Rom. v. 10. 1 Cor. vii. 11.

κατάλοιπος, *left remaining*; οἱ κατάλοιποι τῶν ἀνθρώπων, *the residue of men*, Acts, xv. 17.

κατάλυμα, τὸ, *an inn*, Luke, ii. 7; *the guest-chamber*, Luke, xxii. 11. Mrk. xiv. 14.

καταλύω, *to destroy*, Matt. xxvi. 61. xxvii. 40; *to overthrow*, Acts, v. 39. Rom. xiv. 20; *to put up at, to lodge*, Luke, ix. 12. xix. 7; pass., *to be thrown down*, Mrk. xiii. 2. Matt. xxiv. 2. Luke, xxi. 6; *to be overthrown, to be brought to nought*, Acts, v. 38.

καταμανθάνω, *to learn thoroughly; to consider well*, Matt. vi. 28.

καταμαρτυρέω, *to testify against*, Matt. xxvi. 62. xxvii. 13.

καταμένω, *to abide*, Acts, i. 13.

καταμόνας, adv., *privately, alone*, Luke, ix. 18. Mrk. iv. 10 (But better written separately, κατὰ μόνας, as Westcott has done.)

καταναλίσκω, *to consume*, Hebr. xii. 29.

καταναρκάω, *to make numb;* intrans. with genit., *to be burdensome to*, 2 Cor. xi. 9. xii. 13, 14.

κατανεύω, *to make signs to*, Luke, v. 7.

κατανοέω, *to perceive*, Acts, xxvii. 39. Matt. vii. 3. Luke, xx. 23; *to observe, to consider*, Luke, xii. 24, 27. Acts, xi. 6. Rom. iv. 19.

καταντάω, *to arrive, to come*, Acts, xvi. 1. xviii. 19, 24. 1 Cor. xiv. 36; εἰς οὓς τὰ τέλη τῶν αἰώνων κατήντηκεν, 1 Cor. x. 11 (RV *upon whom the ends of the ages are come*); *to reach, to attain*, Acts, xxvi. 7. Ephes. iv. 13. Philipp. iii. 11.

κατάνυξις, ἡ, *stupor;* πνεῦμα κατανύξεως, *a spirit of stupor,* Rom. xi. 8. (Found only in the NT and the Septuagint.)

κατανύσσω, *to prick, to wound,* κατενύγησαν τὴν καρδίαν, Acts, ii. 37 (RV *They were pricked in their heart.*)

καταξιόω, *to account worthy,* 2 Thess. i. 5. Acts, v. 41.

καταπατέω, *to tread under foot, to trample on,* Matt. v. 13. Luke, viii. 5. xii. 1; *to treat with contempt, to spurn,* Hebr. x. 29.

κατάπαυσις, ἡ, *a putting to rest;* met., *rest,* Acts, vii. 49. Hebr. iii. 11, 18. iv. 10.

καταπαύω, *to cause to cease; to give rest,* Hebr. iv. 8; *to restrain,* Acts, xiv. 18; intrans., *to rest,* Hebr. iv. 4. 10.

καταπέτασμα, τό, *a veil spread out, a curtain,* — the name given in the Greek Scriptures to the two curtains in the temple at Jerusalem, one of them at the entrance of the temple, the other veiling the Holy of Holies. This latter, called pre-eminently τὸ καταπέτασμα, is the only one mentioned in the NT. See Hebr. ix. 3. Matt. xxvii. 51. Luke, xxiii. 45. Mrk. xv. 38.

καταπίνω, *to swallow up,* Rev. xii. 16. 2 Cor. v. 4; *to swallow,* Matt. xxiii. 24; met., *to destroy,* 1 Pet. v. 8. 1 Cor. xv. 54; pass., *to be consumed,* 2 Cor. ii. 7.

καταπίπτω, *to fall down,* Acts, xxvi. 14. xxviii. 6. Luke, viii. 6.

καταπλέω, *to sail from the deep sea to the coast; to put in,* Luke, viii. 26.

καταπονέω, *to exhaust with labour; to afflict, to distress,* Acts, vii. 24. 2 Pet. ii. 7.

καταποντίζω, *to cast into the sea, to drown;* pass., *to be submerged, to be drowned,* Matt. xviii. 6; *to sink,* Matt. xiv. 30.

κατάρα, ἡ, *cursing, a curse,* James, iii. 10. Gal. iii. 13; γῆ κατάρας ἐγγὺς, *nigh to being cursed* by God, *i.e.* given up unto barrenness, Hebr. vi. 8; ὑπὸ κατάραν εἶναι, *to be under a curse,* Gal. iii. 10; τέκνα κατάρας, *accursed children,* 2 Pet. ii. 14.

καταράομαι, *to curse,* Rom. xii. 14. Luke, vi. 28. Mrk. xi. 21. James, iii. 9; pass., *to be accursed,* Matt. xxv. 41.

καταργέω, *to make idle, to render inoperative; to bring to nought,* Rom. iii. 3. 1 Cor. i. 28; *to cause to cease, to abolish,* 1 Cor. vi. 13. Rom. iii. 31. vi. 6; pass., *to be brought to nought,* 1 Cor. ii. 6. xv. 26; *to pass away, to be done away,* Gal. v. 4. 1 Cor. xiii. 8, 10. (The word occurs 25 times in S. Paul, but only twice, viz. Luke, xiii. 7 = *make barren,* Hebr. ii. 14, in the rest of the NT.)

καταριθμέω, *to number with;* pass., *to be numbered among,* Acts, i. 17.

καταρτίζω, *to mend, to repair,* Matt. iv. 21. Mrk. i. 19; *to restore,* Gal. vi. 1; *to perfect,* 1 Pet. v. 10. Hebr. xiii. 21;

pass., *to be prepared*, Hebr. xi. 3. Rom. ix. 22; *to be perfected*, Luke, vi. 40. 1 Cor. i. 10. 2 Cor. xiii. 11; mid., *to prepare*, Hebr. x. 5. Matt. xxi. 16.

κατάρτισις, ἡ, *a restoration, a perfecting*, 2 Cor. xiii. 9.

καταρτισμὸς, ὁ, *a perfecting*, Ephes. iv. 12.

κατασείω, *to shake*; κατασείειν τὴν χεῖρα, *to make signs with the hand*, Acts, xix. 33. But in Acts, xii. 17. xiii. 16. xxi. 40, τῇ χειρ., in the same sense.

κατασκάπτω, *to dig down, to destroy*, Rom. xi. 3.

κατασκευάζω, *to make ready, to prepare*, Matt. xi. 10. Luke, vii. 27; *to equip, to build*, Hebr. xi. 7. 1 Pet. iii. 20; pass., *to be prepared*, Luke, i. 17.

κατασκηνόω, *to pitch one's tent, to dwell*, Acts, ii. 26. Matt. xiii. 32. Luke, xiii. 19.

κατασκήνωσις, ἡ, *an abode, a roosting-place*, Matt. viii. 20. Luke, ix. 58.

κατασκιάζω, *to overshadow*, Hebr. ix. 5.

κατασκοπέω, *to spy out*, Gal. ii. 4.

κατάσκοπος, ὁ, *a spy*, Hebr. xi. 31.

κατασοφίζομαι, *to circumvent by fraud, to deal craftily with*, Acts, vii. 19.

καταστέλλω, *to restrain, to quiet*, Acts, xix. 35.

κατάστημα, τὸ, *deportment, demeanour*, Tit. ii. 3.

καταστολὴ, ἡ, *dress, attire*, 1 Tim. ii. 9.

καταστρέφω, *to throw down, to overthrow*, Matt. xxi. 12. Mrk. xi. 15; τὰ κατεστραμμένα αὐτῆς, *its ruins*, Acts, xv. 16.

καταστρηνιάω, *to grow wanton against*, 1 Tim. v. 11.

καταστροφὴ, ἡ, *an overthrow; a subverting*, 2 Tim. ii. 14.

καταστρώννυμι, *to overthrow*, 1 Cor. x. 5.

κατασύρω, *to drag by force*, Luke, xii. 58.

κατασφάζω, *to slay*, Luke, xix. 27.

κατασφραγίζω, *to seal up*, Rev. v. 1.

κατάσχεσις, ἡ, *possession, and a possession*, Acts, vii. 5, 45.

κατατίθημι, *to deposit;* mid. *to lay up, to gain*, Acts, xxiv. 27. xxv. 9.

κατατομὴ, ἡ, *mutilation*, Philipp. iii. 2. (RV concision.) Cf. Gal. v. 12.

κατατοξεύω, *to shoot down, to pierce through*, a var. lect. ad Hebr. xii. 20.

κατατρέχω, *to run down*, Acts, xxi. 32.

καταυγάζω, *to shine upon*, a var. lect. ad 2 Cor. iv. 4.

καταφέρω, *to cast down;* ψῆφον καταφέρειν, *to give one's vote against*, Acts, xxvi. 10; *to bring against*, Acts, xxv. 7; pass., *to be borne down, to be overcome*, Acts, xx. 9.

καταφεύγω, *to flee for refuge*, Acts, xiv. 6. Hebr. vi. 18.

καταφθείρω, *to corrupt, to deprave;* κατεφθαρμένοι τὸν νοῦν, *corrupted in mind*, 2 Tim. iii. 8.

καταφιλέω, *to kiss*, Matt. xxvi. 49. Luke, vii. 38, 45. Acts, xx. 37.

καταφρονέω, *to despise*, Matt. vi. 24. xviii. 10. Luke, xvi. 13 etc.

καταφρονητής, ὁ, *a despiser*, Acts, xiii. 41.

καταχέω, *to pour upon*, Matt. xxvi. 7. Mrk. xiv. 3.

καταχθόνιος, *subterrestrial*, Philipp. ii. 10.

καταχράομαι, *to use to the full*, 1 Cor. vii. 31.

καταψύχω, *to cool*, Luke, xvi. 24.

κατείδωλος, *full of idols*, Acts, xvii. 16. (A purely NT and ecclesiastical word.)

κατέναντι, adv., *over against*, *opposite*, Matt. xxi. 2. Luke, xix. 30 ; *before*, Matt. xxvii. 24. Rom. iv. 17. 2 Cor. ii. 17.

κατενώπιον, adv., *before*, Jude, 24. 2 Cor. xii. 19. Ephes. i. 4. (An altogether unclassical form.)

κατεξουσιάζω, *to exercise authority over*, Matt. xx. 25. Mrk. x. 42. (A purely NT form.)

κατεργάζομαι, *to work, to accomplish*, Rom. iv. 15. vii. 15, 17, 20. 2 Cor. xii. 12 ; *to perpetrate*, Rom. ii. 9. 1 Cor. v. 3.

κατέρχομαι, *to come down*, James, iii. 15. Luke, iv. 31. ix. 37 ; *to arrive at*, Acts, xviii. 22. xxi. 3. xxvii. 5.

κατεσθίω, *to devour, to consume*, Matt. xiii. 4. Luke, viii. 5 ; *to squander*, Luke, xv. 30 ; *to rob, to plunder*, 2 Cor. xi. 20. Gal. v. 15.

κατευθύνω, *to guide, to direct*, Luke, i. 79. 1 Thess. iii. 11. 2. Thess. iii. 5.

κατευλογέω, *to greatly bless*, Mrk. x. 16. (In ancient Greek only in the sense of *praise highly*.)

κατεφίστημι, in 2 aor., *rose up against*, Acts, xviii. 12.

κατέχω, *to hinder, to restrain*, 2 Thess. ii. 6,7. Rom. i. 18; *to guide*, as a ship, Acts, xxvii. 40 ; *to hold fast, to retain*, Luke, viii. 15. 1 Thess. v. 21 ; *to take*, Luke, xiv. 9 ; *to possess*, 1 Cor. vii. 30 ; pass., *to be held bound*, Rom. vii. 6.

κατηγορέω, *to accuse*, Matt. xii. 10. Luke, vi. 7. xxiii. 14 ; pass., *to be accused*, Matt. xxvii. 12. Acts, xxii. 30.

κατηγορία, ἡ, *an accusation*, Joh. xviii. 29. 1 Tim. v. 19.

κατήγορος, ὁ, *an accuser*, Acts, xxiii. 30, 35. xxv. 16, 18.

κατήγωρ, ὁ, *an accuser*, Rev. xii. 10. (An altogether unclassical and un-Greek form. It is not recognized in Pape's Lexicon.)

κατήφεια, ἡ, *dejection, heaviness*, James, iv. 9.

κατηχέω, *to instruct, to teach*, 1 Cor. xiv. 19. Gal. vi. 6 ; pass., *to be instructed*, Rom. ii. 18. Acts, xviii. 25. Gal. vi. 6 ; *to be instructed in*, Luke, i. 4 ; *to be informed* by report, Acts, xxi. 21.

κατιόω, *to cover with rust*, James, v. 3.

κατισχύω, *to have power, to be able*, Luke, xxi. 36 ; *to prevail against*, Matt. xvi. 18 ;

κατοικέω, *to dwell*, Acts, i. 20. vii. 2, 14, 48. Rev. iii. 10; trans. with accusative, *to dwell in, to inhabit*, Acts, i. 19. ii. 9, 14. Rev. xvii. 2 etc. — continued from *to be overpowering, to prevail*, Luke, xxiii. 23.

κατοίκησις, ἡ, *an abode, a dwelling*, Mrk. v. 3.

κατοικητήριον, τό, *a habitation, an abode*, Ephes. ii. 22. Rev. xviii. 2. (A purely NT and ecclesiastical word.)

κατοικία, ἡ, *a habitation*, Acts, xvii. 26.

κατοικίζω, *to cause to dwell*, πνεῦμα ὃ κατῴκισεν ἐν ἡμῖν, *which he caused to dwell within us*, James, iv. 5.

κατοπτρίζω, *to mirror, to reflect;* mid., *to behold in a mirror*, 2 Cor. iii. 18.

κατόρθωμα, τό, *a successful achievement; a righteous measure*, a var. lect. ad Acts, xxiv. 2.

κάτω, adv., *downwards; down*, Acts, xx. 9. Matt. iv. 6. Luke, iv. 9. Joh. viii. 6, 8; *below*, Mrk. xiv. 66; *beneath*, Acts, ii. 19; ἐκ τῶν κάτω, *from beneath*, Joh. viii. 23; ἕως κάτω, *to the bottom*, Matt. xxvii. 51. Mrk. xv. 38; ἀπὸ διετοῦς καὶ κατωτέρω, *from two years old and under*, Matt. ii. 16.

κατ.ὁτερος, comp. of κάτω, *lower*, Ephes. iv. 9.

καῦμα, τό, *heat*, Rev. vii. 16. xvi. 9.

καυματίζω, *to burn with heat, to scorch*, Rev. xvi. 8; pass., *to be scorched, to be burned*, Matt. xiii. 6. Mrk. iv. 6. Rev. xvi. 9.

καῦσις, ἡ, *a burning;* ἧς τὸ τέλος εἰς καῦσιν, *whose end is to be burned*, Hebr. vi. 8.

καυσόω, *to burn up*, 2 Pet. iii. 10.

καυστηριάζω, *to burn with a hot iron, to brand*, 1 Tim. iv. 2. (In the NT not found elsewhere.)

καύσων, ὁ, *burning heat*, Matt. xx. 12. Luke, xii. 55; *a scorching wind*, James, i. 11. (See Pape's Lexicon in voc.)

καυτηριάζω, *to brand*, a var. lect. ad 1 Tim. iv. 2.

καυχάομαι, *to boast, to glory*, 1 Cor. i. 31. iv. 7. xiii. 3; with accus., *to boast of*, 2 Cor. vii. 14. ix. 2. xi. 30; with ἐν and dat., *to glory in*, 1 Cor. i. 31. Philipp. iii. 3. James, i. 9; with ὑπὲρ and genit., *on behalf of*, 2 Cor. xii. 5 etc. (Used 35 times by S. Paul and twice by S. James.)

καύχημα, τό, *matter for glorying*, Philipp. ii. 16. Rom. iv. 2. 1 Cor. ix. 15 etc.

καύχησις, ἡ, *a glorying*, Rom. iii. 27. 2 Cor. i. 12. vii. 4, 14.

κέδρος, ἡ, *cedar*, a var. lect. ad Joh. xviii 1. (Westcott reads πέραν τοῦ Χειμάρρου τῶν Κέδρων. See next word.)

Κεδρών, indecl., *Cedron*, the name of a wintry torrent, rising near Jerusalem, and flowing through a valley of the same name.

κεῖμαι, *to lie*, Luke, ii. 12. Matt. xxviii. 6; *to be laid, to be applied*, Matt. iii. 10. Luke, iii. 9; *to be situated*, Matt. v. 14; *to be laid up*, Luke, xii. 19; *to be enacted*, 1 Tim. i. 9; *to be appointed*, 1 Thess. iii. 3. Luke, ii. 34.

κειρία, ἡ, *a girth, a bandage*, Joh. xi. 44.

κείρω, *to clip, to shear*, Acts, viii. 32; mid., *to get shorn*, Acts, xviii. 18. 1 Cor. xi. 6.

κέλευσμα, τὸ, *a command; a loud cry*, 1 Thess. iv. 16.

κελεύω, *to order*, Matt. xiv. 19, 28. xviii. 25 etc. (It is never found with a dative in the NT.)

κενοδοξία, ἡ, *vainglory*, Philipp. ii. 3.

κενόδοξος, *vainglorious*, Gal. v. 26.

κενὸς, *empty, vain*, Ephes. v. 6. 1 Cor. xv. 14. Coloss. ii. 8; *empty-handed*, Luke, xx. 10. Mrk. xii. 3; *fruitless, ineffectual*, 1 Cor. xv. 10, 58. 1 Thess. ii. 1; εἰς κενὸν, *in vain*, Philipp. ii. 16. 2 Cor. vi. 1. Gal. ii. 2.

κενοφωνία, ἡ, *empty talking; babbling*, 1 Tim. vi. 20. 2 Tim. ii. 16.

κενόω, *to empty*; ἑαυτὸν ἐκένωσεν, *emptied himself*, i.e. divested himself of such and such divine prerogatives, Philipp. ii. 7. (Subsequent theology applied the term ἐκκένωσις to this act); *to make void*, 1 Cor. i. 17. ix. 15. Rom. iv. 14.

κέντρον, τὸ, *a sting*, Rev. ix. 10. 1 Cor. xv. 55, 56; *a goad*, Acts, xxvi. 14.

κεντυρίων, ὁ, *a centurion*, Acts, x. 1 etc.

κενῶς, adv., *in vain*, James, iv. 5.

κεραία, and **κερέα**, ἡ, *a point or tip* (of a letter in Hebrew); *the minutest part, a tittle*, Luke, xvi. 17. Matt. v. 18.

κεραμεὺς, ὁ, *a potter*, Rom. ix. 21. Matt. xxvii. 7, 10.

κεραμικὸς, *of or belonging to a potter, of earthenware*, Rev. ii. 27.

κεράμιον, τὸ, *an earthen vessel, a pitcher*, Luke, xxii. 10. Mrk. xiv. 13.

κέραμος, ὁ, *a tile*, Luke, v. 19.

κεράννυμι, *to mix, to mingle*, Rev. xiv. 10 (RV *prepared*.) xviii. 6.

κέρας, τὸ, *a horn*, Rev. v. 6. xii. 3. xiii. 1, 11 etc.; met., κέρας σωτηρίας, *a horn of salvation*, i.e. a mighty deliverer, Luke, i. 69; *an extremity*, Rev. ix. 13.

κεράτιον, τὸ, *a little horn;* the name of the fruit of the κερατία, or *carob tree*, also called *St. John's Bread*. It was not only used for fattening swine, but also eaten by the poorer classes, Luke, xv. 16.

κερδαίνω, *to gain, to acquire*, Matt. xvi. 26. Luke, ix. 25. Philipp. iii. 8; *to win over, to prevail upon*, 1 Pet. iii. 1. Matt. xviii. 15; met., *to get, to meet with*, Acts, xxvii. 21.

κέρδος, τὸ, *gain, advantage*, Philipp. i. 21. iii. 7. Tit. i. 11.

κερέα, ἡ, see κεραία.

κέρμα, τὸ, *small coin, money*, Joh. ii. 15.

κερματιστὴs, ὁ, *a money-changer*, Joh. ii. 14.

κεφάλαιον, τὸ, *the main point*, Hebr. viii. 1 ; *the capital, as distinguished from the interest ; a sum of money*, Acts, xxii. 28.

κεφαλαιόω, *to sum up ; to wound in the head*, a var. lect. ad Mrk. xii. 4. (Westcott reads ἐκεφαλίωσαν. See κεφαλιόω, and Pape's Lex. in voc. κεφαλαιόω).

κεφαλὴ, ἡ, *the head*, Matt. v. 36. Luke, vii. 38 ; *the chief, the master*, Ephes. iv. 15. v. 23. Coloss. i. 18.

κεφαλιόω, *to wound in the head*, as read by Westcott in Mrk. xii. 4.

κεφαλὶs, ἡ, *a roll, a volume*, Hebr. x. 7.

κημόω, *to muzzle*, 1 Cor. ix. 9. (Westcott reads φιμόω.)

κῆνσοs, ὁ, *a tax* or *tribute*, Matt. xvii. 25. xxii. 17. Mrk. xii. 14; τὸ νόμισμα τοῦ κήνσου, *the tribute money*, Matt. xxii. 19.

κῆποs, ὁ, *a garden*, Luke, xiii. 19. Joh. xviii. 1, 26. xix. 41.

κηπουρὸs, ὁ, *a gardener*, Joh. xx. 15.

κηρίον, τὸ, *a honeycomb*, Luke, xxiv. 42. (It is omitted in Westcott's edition.)

κήρυγμα, τὸ, *a proclamation ; a preaching*, Matt. xii. 41. Luke, xi. 32. 1 Cor. i. 21.

κῆρυξ, ὁ, *a herald ; a preacher*, 2 Pet. ii. 5. 1 Tim. ii. 7. 2 Tim. i. 11.

κηρύσσω, *to proclaim, to publish*, Luke, viii. 39 ; *to preach*, Matt. iv. 23. xi. 1. 1 Cor. ix. 27.

κῆτοs, τὸ, *a whale*, Matt. xii. 40.

κιβωτόs, ἡ, *a chest ; the ark of the covenant*, Hebr. ix. 4. Rev. xi. 19 ; *Noah's ark*, Matt. xxiv. 38. Luke, xvii. 27. Hebr. xi. 7.

κιθάρα, ἡ, *a harp*, 1 Cor. xiv. 7. Rev. v. 8. xv. 2.

κιθαρίζω, *to play upon the harp, to harp ;* κιθαριζόντων ἐν ταῖς κιθάραις αὐτῶν, Rev. xiv. 2 (RV *harping with their harps*); τὸ κιθαριζόμενον, *what is harped*, 1 Cor. xiv. 7.

κινάμωμον, and **κιννάμωμον**, τὸ, *cinnamon*, Rev. xviii. 13.

κινδυνεύω, *to be in danger ;* κινδυνεύει εἰs ἀπελεγμὸν ἐλθεῖν, *is in danger of coming into disrepute*, Acts, xix. 27 ; κινδυνεύομεν ἐγκαλεῖσθαι, *we are in danger of being accused*, Acts, xix. 40.

κίνδυνοs, ὁ, *danger, peril*, Rom. viii. 35. 2 Cor. xi. 26, 27.

κινέω, transit., *to move*, Rev. ii. 5. vi. 14. Matt. xxiii. 4 ; *to excite, to stir up*, Acts, xxiv. 5 ; pass. intransit., *to move*, Acts, xvii. 28.

κίνησιs, ἡ, *a moving, an agitation*, Joh. v. 3. (It is omitted by Westcott.)

κίχρημι, *to lend*, Luke, xi. 5.

κλάδοs, ὁ, *a branch, a bough*, Rom. xi. 16, 17, 18, 19, 21. Matt. xiii. 32 etc.

κλαίω, and **κλάω**, *to weep, to mourn*, Luke, vii. 13, 38. Joh. xi. 31, 33 ; trans., *to weep for, to bewail*, Matt. ii. 18.

κλάσις, ἡ, *a breaking*, Luke, xxiv. 35. Acts, ii. 42.

κλάσμα, τὸ, *a broken piece, a fragment*, Matt. xiv. 20. xv. 37. Luke, ix. 17. Joh. vi. 12.

κλαυθμὸς, ὁ, *a weeping, a lamentation*, Matt. ii. 18. xiii. 42, 50. Acts, xx. 37.

κλάω, *to break*, Matt. xiv. 19. xv. 36. 1 Cor. xi. 24; τοὺς πέντε ἄρτους ἔκλασα εἰς τοὺς πεντακισχιλίους = *I broke and distributed amongst the five thousand*, Mrk. viii. 19.

κλεὶς, ἡ, *a key*, Matt. xvi. 19. Luke, xi. 52. Rev. i. 18.

κλείω, *to shut, to shut up*, Matt. vi. 6. xxv. 10. Rev. iii. 8.

κλέμμα, τὸ, *a theft*, Rev. ix. 21.

κλέος, τὸ, *glory*, 1 Pet. ii. 20.

κλέπτης, ὁ, *a thief*, Joh. x. 1, 10. xii. 6.

κλέπτω, *to steal*, Matt. vi. 19. xix. 18. Rom. ii. 21.

κλῆμα, τὸ, *a tender branch, a shoot*, Joh. xv. 2, 4, 6.

κληρονομέω, *to inherit*, Matt. v. 5. xix. 29. xxv. 34.

κληρονομία, ἡ, *an inheritance*, Matt. xxi. 38. Gal. iii. 18. Coloss. iii. 24.

κληρονόμος, ὁ, *an heir*, Matt. xxi. 38. Gal. iv. 1. Hebr. i. 2. Rom. viii. 17.

κλῆρος, ὁ, *a lot*, Acts, i. 26. Matt. xxvii. 35; *a part allotted*, Acts, i. 17.

κληρόω, *to cast lots; to make into a heritage*, Ephes. i. 11.

κλῆσις, ἡ, *a calling, an invitation*, Hebr. iii. 1. 2 Tim. i. 9. Rom. xi. 29. Ephes. i. 18.

κλητὸς, *called*, Rom. i. 6, 7. viii. 28. 1 Cor. i. 24.

κλίβανος, ὁ, *an earthenware vessel for baking bread; an oven*, Luke, xii. 28; Matt. vi. 30.

κλίμα, τὸ, *a slope, a declivity; a tract of land, a region*, Rom. xv. 23. 2 Cor. xi. 10. Gal. i. 21.

κλινάριον, τὸ, *a small bed, a couch*, Acts, v. 15.

κλίνη, ἡ, *a bed*, Mrk. vii. 30. Luke, xvii. 34.

κλινίδιον, τὸ, *a small bed, a couch*, Luke, v. 19, 24.

κλίνω, *to incline, to bow*, Joh. xix. 30. Luke, xxiv. 5; *to put to flight*, Hebr. xi. 34; *to recline*, Luke, ix. 58. Matt. viii. 20; intrans., *to wear away, to be far spent*, Luke, ix. 12. xxiv. 29.

κλισία, ἡ, *a place where one can recline; a company*, Luke, ix. 14.

κλοπὴ, ἡ, *theft*, Matt. xv. 19. Mrk. vii. 21.

κλύδων, ὁ, *a violent agitation of the sea; a wave, a billow*, Luke, viii. 24. James, i. 6.

κλυδωνίζομαι, *to be agitated* like the waves of the sea, Ephes. iv. 14 (RV tossed to and fro).

κνήθω, *to scratch; mid., to have an itching;* κνηθόμενοι τὴν ἀκοὴν, *having itching ears*, 2 Tim. iv. 3.

κοδράντης, ὁ, the Lat. *quadrans*, i.e. the fourth part of the Roman *as*, and equal to two λεπτὰ, Matt. v. 26. Mrk. xii. 42.

κοιλία, ἡ, *the belly*, Matt. xii. 40. xv. 17. Mrk. vii. 19 etc.; *appetite, gluttony*, Philipp. iii. 19. Rom. xvi. 18; *the womb*, Luke, i. 15, 41, 44. Matt. xix. 12; *the innermost part of a man, the heart*, Joh. vii. 38.

κοιμάω, *to put to sleep;* pass., *to fall asleep, to sleep*, Matt. xxviii. 13. Luke, xxii. 45. Joh. xi. 12; met., *to die*, 1 Cor. vii. 39. Acts, vii. 60. xiii. 36. Matt. xxvii. 52.

κοίμησις, ἡ, *taking rest*, Joh. xi. 13.

κοινός, *common*, Acts, ii. 44. iv. 32. Tit. i. 4; *unhallowed, profane*, Acts, x. 14. Rev. xxi. 27, Rom. xiv. 14. Hebr. x. 29.

κοινόω, *to make common; to render unclean, to profane*, Acts, xxi. 28. Matt. xv. 11, 18, 20; *to count unclean*, Acts, x. 15.

κοινωνέω, *to be partaker, to share*, 1 Pet. iv. 13. Hebr. ii. 14. Rom. xv. 27; *to take part in, to be associated in*, 1 Tim. v. 22. 2 Joh. 11; *to communicate to, to assist*, Rom. xii. 13. Philipp. iv. 15.

κοινωνία, ἡ, *association; participation, share*, Philipp. ii. 1. iii. 10. Philem. 6. 1 Cor. x. 16 etc.; *fellowship*, Gal. ii. 9. 2 Cor. vi. 14; *a contribution*, Rom. xv. 26. 2 Cor. ix. 13. Hebr. xiii. 16.

κοινωνικὸς *sociable; liberal*, 1 Tim. vi. 18.

κοινωνὸς, ὁ, and ἡ, *a partner, an associate*, 2 Cor. viii. 23. Luke, v. 10. Philem. 17; *a partaker, a sharer*, 1 Cor. x. 18, 20. 2 Cor. i. 7.

κοίτη, ἡ, *a bed*, Luke, xi. 7; *the marriage-bed*, Heb. xiii. 4; *sexual intercourse, lewdness*, Rom. xiii. 13; κοίτην ἔχειν ἔκ τινος, *to conceive by*, Rom. ix. 10.

κοιτὼν, ὁ, *a bed-chamber*, Acts, xii. 20.

κόκκινος, *scarlet-coloured*, Rev. xvii. 3. Matt. xxvii. 28. Hebr. ix. 19; as subst., *scarlet clothing*, Rev. xvii. 4. xviii. 12, 16.

κόκκος, ὁ, *a grain*, Matt. xiii. 31. xvii. 20. Mrk. iv. 31 etc.

κολάζω, *to punish*, 2 Pet. ii. 9. Acts, iv. 21.

κολακεία, and **κολακία**, ἡ, *flattery;* λόγος κολακίας, *flattering words*, 1 Thess. ii. 5.

κόλασις, ἡ, *punishment*, Matt. xxv. 46. 1 Joh. iv. 18 ("has connected with it the thought of punishment," Thayer).

κολαφίζω, *to strike with the fist; to buffet*, Matt. xxvi. 67. Mrk. xiv. 65. 2 Cor. xii. 7; *to ill-treat*, 1 Pet. ii. 20. 1 Cor. iv. 11.

κολλάω, *to join* (with glue): pass., *to cleave to*, Luke, x. 11. Rom. xii. 9; ἐκολλήθησαν αὐτῆς αἱ ἁμαρτίαι ἄχρι τοῦ οὐρανοῦ, Rev. xviii. 5 (RV *her sins have reached even unto heaven);* with dat. of thing, *to join himself to*, i.e. *to approach*, Acts, viii. 29; *to be united to*, 1 Cor. vi. 16, 17; *to join another as his associate, to associate with*,

Acts, v. 13. ix. 26. x. 28; *to attach himself to a master,* Luke, xv. 15.
κολλούριον, τό, *eye-salve,* Rev. iii. 18.
κολλυβιστὴs, ὁ, *a money-changer,* Matt. xxi. 12. Mrk. xi. 15. Joh. ii. 15.
κολοβόω, *to cut off; to shorten, to abridge,* Matt. xxiv. 22. Mrk. xiii. 20.
κόλπος, ὁ, *the bosom,* Joh. i. 18. xiii. 23. Luke, xvi. 22, 23; *the lap,* Luke, vi. 38; *a bay,* Acts, xxvii. 39.
κολυμβάω, *to dive; to swim,* Acts, xxvii. 43.
κολυμβήθρα, ἡ, *a reservoir, a pool,* Joh. v. 2, 7. ix. 7.
κολωνία, ἡ, *a colony,* Acts, xvi. 12.
κομάω, *to let the hair grow long; to have long hair,* 1 Cor. xi. 14.
κόμη, ἡ, *the hair* of the head, 1 Cor. xi. 15.
κομίζω, *to bring,* Luke, vii. 37; mid., *to obtain,* Hebr. x. 36. xi. 39. 1 Pet. v. 4 etc.; *to get again, to receive back,* Hebr. xi. 19. Matt. xxv. 27. Coloss. iii. 25. Ephes. vi. 8.
κομψὸς, *neat;* κομψότερον, adverbially, *better;* κομψότερον ἔχειν, *to be better in health,* Joh. iv. 52.
κονιάω, *to whitewash,* Matt. xxiii. 27. Acts, xxiii. 3.
κονιορτὸς, ὁ, *dust,* Matt. x. 14. Luke, ix. 5. Acts, xiii. 51 etc.
κοπάζω, *to grow weary;* met., *to abate, to become still,* Matt. **xiv.** 32. Mrk. iv. 39. vi. 51.

κοπετὸς, ὁ, *lamentation,* Acts, viii. 2.
κοπὴ, ἡ, *slaughter,* Hebr. vii. 1.
κοπιάω, *to be weary,* Joh. iv. 6. Matt. xi. 28; *to toil, to labour,* Matt. vi. 28. Luke, v. 5. Joh. iv. 38 etc.
κόπος, ὁ, *labour, trouble,* Luke, xi. 7. xviii. 5. Matt. xxvi. 10. Gal. vi. 17; *toil,* 2 Cor. vi. 5. xi. 23, 27.
κοπρία, ἡ, *dung, manure,* Luke, xiv. 35.
κόπριον, τό, = κοπρία, Luke, xiii. 8.
κόπτω, *to cut;* τὶ ἀπὸ or ἔκ τινος, *to cut off,* Mrk. xi. 8. Matt. xxi. 8; mid., *to lament,* Matt. xi. 17. xxiv. 30; with accus., *to bewail,* Luke, viii. 52. xxiii. 27.
κόραξ, ὁ, *a raven,* Luke, xii. 24.
κοράσιον, τό, *a damsel, a maiden,* Matt. ix. 24, 25. xiv. 11 etc.
κορβὰν, indecl., *an offering, a gift* (to God), Mrk. vii. 11.
κορβανᾶs, ὁ, *the treasury,* Matt. xxvii. 6.
κορέννυμι, *to satisfy,* Acts, xxvii. 38. 1 Cor. iv. 8.
κόρος, ὁ, *a cor,* a Hebrew dry measure, equal to ten Attic medimni, Luke, xvi. 7. (=86 gall.)
κοσμέω, *to adorn,* Luke, xxi. 5. 1 Pet. iii. 5. Tit. ii. 10; *to decorate, to garnish,* Matt. xii. 44. xxiii. 29. Luke, xi. 25, *to trim* (a lamp), Matt. xxv. 7.
κοσμικὸs, *belonging to the world;* τὸ ἅγιον κοσμικὸν, *its sanctuary of this world,* Hebr. ix. 1. See ἅγιος; *worldly,* Tit. ii. 12.

κόσμιος, *orderly, modest,* 1 Tim. ii. 9. iii. 2.

κοσμίως, *decently,* a var. lect. ad 1 Tim. ii. 9.

κοσμοκράτωρ, ὁ, *the ruler of this world,* 2 Cor. iv. 4. Ephes. vi. 12. (Cf. Joh. xii. 31.)

κόσμος, ὁ, *a harmonious arrangement; decoration, adornment,* 1 Pet. iii. 3; *the world,* Acts, xvii. 24. Rom. iv. 13. 1 Cor. iii. 22; *the people of the world,* 2 Pet. ii. 5. 1 Cor. iv. 9. Matt. xviii. 7; *worldly affairs,* Gal. vi. 14. 1 Joh. ii. 15.

κούμ, a Hebrew imperative, *arise!* Mrk. v. 41. (Other texts exhibit κοῦμι.)

κουστωδία, ἡ, the Lat. *custodia, a guard,* Matt. xxvii. 65, 66. xxviii. 11. (It is merely a Latin word written in Greek letters.)

κουφίζω, *to lighten,* Acts, xxvii. 38.

κόφινος, ὁ, *a basket,* Matt. xiv. 20. Joh. vi. 13 etc.

κράβατος, **κράβαττος**, and **κράββατος**, ὁ, *a bed,* Acts, v. 15. ix. 33.

κράζω, *to cry out,* Matt. xxvii. 50. Acts, vii. 57. Rev. vii. 2.

κραιπάλη, and **κρεπάλη**, ἡ, *sickness, surfeiting,* Luke xxi. 34.

κρανίον, τὸ, *a skull,* Matt. xxvii. 33. Joh. xix. 17.

κράσπεδον, τὸ, *the tassel, the hem,* Matt. ix. 20. xiv. 36. xxiii. 5 (RV *border*).

κραταιόω, *to make strong;* pass., *to be strengthened, to grow strong,* Ephes. iii. 16. Luke, i. 80. ii. 40; *to be firm,* 1 Cor. xvi. 13.

κρατέω, *to get possession of, to obtain,* Acts, xxvii. 13; *to take hold of,* Matt. ix. 25. Mrk. ix. 27 ; *to seize,* Matt. xiv. 3. Acts, xxiv. 6 etc.; *to hold,* Rev. ii. 1; *to hold fast,* Mrk. vii. 3. 2 Thess. ii. 15. Rev. ii. 14; *to retain,* i.e. *not to remit,* Joh. xx. 23; *to hold in check, to restrain,* Luke, xxiv. 16. Rev. vii. 1.

κράτιστος, superl. of κρατύς; in the NT a term of respect, *most excellent,* Acts, xxiii. 26. xxiv. 3. xxvi. 25.

κράτος, τὸ, *power, might,* Ephes. i. 19. vi. 10. Coloss. i. 11: κατὰ κράτος, *mightily,* Acts, xix. 20; *a mighty deed,* Luke, i. 51; *dominion,* Rev. i. 6. v. 13. 1 Pet. iv. 11. v. 11.

κραυγάζω, *to cry out, to cry aloud,* Matt. xii. 19. Joh. xi. 43.

κραυγὴ, ἡ, *a cry,* Matt. xxv. 6. Acts, xxiii. 9. Hebr. v. 7.

κρέας, τὸ, *flesh,* Rom. xiv. 21. 1 Cor. viii. 13.

κρείσσων and **κρείττων**, compar. of κρατύς ; *more excellent,* Hebr. i. 4. viii. 6 etc.; κρεῖττόν ἐστι, *it is more advantageous,* 1 Cor. vii. 9. 2 Pet. ii. 21.

κρεμάννυμι, *to hang up, to suspend,* Matt. xviii. 6. Acts, v. 30. x. 39; mid., *to hang,* Acts, xxviii. 4. Gal. iii. 13; with ἔν τινι, *to depend upon,* Matt. xxii. 40. ("All the Law and the Prophets, i.e. the teaching of the OT on morality, is summed up in these two precepts," Thayer.)

κρημνὸς, ὁ, *a steep place, a precipice*, Matt. viii. 32. Mrk. v. 13. Luke, viii. 33.

κριθή, ἡ, *barley*, Rev. vi. 6.

κρίθινος, *of barley*, Joh. vi. 9, 13.

κρίμα, τὸ, *judgment*, Matt. vii. 1. Rom. ii. 2. xi. 33; *condemnation*, Rom. iii. 8. Luke, xxiv. 20. 1 Cor. xi. 29; *a lawsuit*, 1 Cor. vi. 7. (See Pape's Lexicon in voc.)

κρίνον, τὸ, *a lily*, Matt. vi. 28. Luke, xii. 27.

κρίνω, *to judge*, Luke, vii. 43. 1 Cor. xi. 13. Acts, xv. 19; *to approve, to esteem*, Rom. xiv.5; *to resolve, to determine*, Acts, xx. 16. xxv. 25. 1 Cor. vii. 37. 2 Cor. ii. 1; *to go to law*, Matt. v. 40. 1 Cor. vi. 1.

κρίσις, ἡ, *judgment*, Joh. viii. 16. 1 Tim. v. 24. Hebr. ix. 27; *condemnation*, Matt. xxiii. 33. Joh. iii. 19. xii. 31.

κριτήριον, τὸ, *a tribunal*, James, ii. 6. 1 Cor. vi. 2, 4 (or *suits, cases*).

κριτὴς, ὁ, *a judge*, Hebr. xii. 23. James, iv. 12. Acts, x. 42.

κριτικὸς, *fit for judging, able to judge*, Hebr. iv. 12.

κρούω, *to knock*, Matt. vii. 7. Luke, xi. 9, 10. xii. 36; *to knock at*, Luke, xiii. 25. Acts, xii. 13.

κρύπτη, ἡ, *a vault, a cellar*, Luke, xi. 33. (See Pape's Lex. in voc.)

κρυπτὸς, *hidden, secret*, Matt. x. 26. Luke, viii. 17. xii. 2; ἐν κρυπτῷ, *in secret*, Matt. vi. 4, 6, Joh. vii. 4, 10. xviii. 20.

κρύπτω, *to hide, to conceal*, Luke, xiii. 21. Rev. vi. 15. Joh. xii. 36. Ptcp. κεκρυμμένος, *hidden*, i.e. *stored*, Rev. ii. 17.

κρυσταλλίζω, *to shine like crystal*, Rev. xxi. 11. (Found nowhere else.)

κρύσταλλος, ὁ, *crystal*, Rev. iv. 6. xxii. 1.

κρυφαῖος, *secret*, Matt. vi. 18.

κρυφῇ, adv., *secretly*, Ephes. v. 12.

κτάομαι, *to acquire, to get*, Acts, i. 18. viii. 20. xxii. 28. Luke, xviii. 12; κέκτημαι, *to possess*, does not appear in the NT.

κτῆμα, τὸ, *a possession*, Matt. xix. 22. Mrk. x. 22. Acts, ii. 45. v. 1.

κτῆνος, τὸ, *a beast of burden*, Luke, x. 34. Acts, xxiii. 24. Rev. xviii. 13.

κτήτωρ, ὁ, *a possessor*, Acts, iv. 34.

κτίζω, *to found; to create*, 1 Cor. xi. 9. Coloss. i. 16. Ephes. iii. 9 etc.

κτίσις, ἡ, *creation;* πᾶσα ἡ κτίσις συστενάζει, *the whole creation groaneth together with us*, Rom. viii. 22. Cf. Mrk. x. 6. Rev. iii. 14; *the thing created*, Hebr. iv. 13. Rom. viii. 39; *a creature*, Rom. i. 25. viii. 20. 2 Cor. v. 17; *an ordinance*, 1 Pet. ii. 13; (πρωτότοκος πάσης κτίσεως, Coloss. i. 15. Here the AV gives *the firstborn of every creature*, and the RV *the firstborn of all creation*. But how will these fit in with the next verse (16) which immediately follows—"*for by him were all things created.*" See also Joh. i. 3. Rev. iii. 14. Hebr. i. 2. There is, however, another interpretation, to which there is no theological objection, πρωτοτόκος πάσης κτίσεως, *the primeval creator of every created thing.* The only imaginable objection to this view is, that, while the ancient Greeks used πρωτοτόκος, with paroxytone accent, and in an *active* tense (= *bringing forth for the first time*), the later Greeks and the NT writers seem to have restricted themselves to the proparoxytone form πρωτότοκος, and in a *passive* sense. See Rom. viii. 29. Hebr. xii. 23. Coloss. i. 18).

κτίσμα, τὸ, *the thing created*, Rev. v. 13. viii. 9. 1 Tim. iv. 4.

κτιστὴς, ὁ, *a founder; a creator*, 1 Pet. iv. 19. ("More correctly written κτιστὴς than κτίστης," Pape's Lexicon.)

κυβεία, ἡ, *dicing; artifice*, Ephes. iv. 14. (Westcott reads κυβίᾳ.)

κυβέρνησις, ἡ, *government;* met., *a governor*, 1 Cor. xii. 28.

κυβερνήτης, ὁ, *a steersman; a shipmaster*, Acts, xxvii. 11. Rev. xviii. 17.

κυκλεύω, *to encircle, to surround*, Rev. xx. 9.

κυκλόθεν, adv., *round about, all round*, Rev. iv. 3, 8.

κυκλόω, *to surround, to encompass*, Joh. x. 24. Luke, xxi. 20. Acts, xiv. 20.

κύκλῳ, dat. of κύκλος, used as adverb, *around, round about,* Luke, ix. 12. Mrk. iii. 34.

κύλισμα, τὸ, *a wallowing place,* 2 Pet. ii. 22. ("= κυλίστρα, NT," Pape's Lexicon.)

κυλισμὸς, ὁ, *a wallowing*, a var. lect. ad 2 Pet. ii. 22.

κυλίω, *to roll;* pass., *to be rolled, to wallow*, Mrk. ix. 20.

κυλλὸς, *crooked; maimed*, Matt. xv. 30, 31. xviii. 8. Mrk. ix. 43.

κῦμα, τὸ, *a wave*, Matt. viii. 24. xiv. 24. Jude, 13.

κύμβαλον, τὸ, *a cymbal*, 1 Cor. xiii. 1.

κύμινον, τὸ, *cumin*, Matt. xxiii. 23.

κυνάριον, τὸ, *a little dog*, Matt. xv. 26, 27. Mrk. vii. 27, 28.

κύπτω, *to stoop*, Mrk. i. 7. Joh. viii. 6.

Κυρία, ἡ, a Christian woman, to whom S. John addresses his second Epistle, vss. 1, 5. (Westcott reads κυρία, *lady*, in both places.)

κυριακὸς, *of or belonging to the Lord;* κυριακὸν δεῖπνον, *the supper of the Lord*, 1 Cor. xi. 20 ; ἡ κυριακὴ ἡμέρα, *the Lord's day*, Rev. i. 10.

κυριεύω, *to rule over, to have dominion over*, Rom. vi. 14. 2 Cor. i. 24. Luke, xxii. 25 ; οἱ κυριεύοντες, *those that rule*, 1 Tim. vi. 15.

κύριος, ὁ, *lord, master, owner*, Matt. xii. 8. xx. 8. Mrk. xiii. 35 ; *the Lord Christ*, 1 Cor. iv. 5. viii. 6. Luke, x. 1. Mrk. xvi. 19 ; *a prince, a sovereign*, Acts, xxv. 26 ; (in addresses) *Sir!* Joh. xii. 21.

κυριότης, ή, *dominion* (often of persons), Coloss. i. 16. Jude, 8. Ephes. i. 21.

κυρόω, *to make valid, to confirm*, Gal. iii. 15. 2 Cor. ii. 8.

κύων, ὁ and ἡ, *a dog*, Luke, xvi. 1. 2 Pet. ii. 22; *a reprobate*, Rev. xxii. 15. Philipp. iii. 2.

κῶλον, τὸ, *a limb; a carcase*, Hebr. iii. 17.

κωλύω, *to hinder, to forbid*, Acts, viii. 36. x. 47. Matt. xix. 14. Mrk. ix. 38.

κώμη, ἡ, *a village*, Matt. ix. 35. x. 11. Luke, v. 17.

κωμόπολις, ἡ, *a large village*, Mrk. i. 38.

κῶμος, ὁ, *a band of revellers*; in the plur., *revellings, revelries*, Rom. xiii. 13. 1 Pet. iv. 3. Gal. v. 21.

κώνωψ, ὁ, *a gnat*, Matt. xxiii. 24.

κωφὸς, *dumb*, Matt. ix. 32, 33. xii. 22. xv. 30. Luke, i. 22. xi. 14; *deaf*, Matt. xi. 5. Mrk. vii. 32, 37. Luke, vii. 22.

Λ.

λαγχάνω, *to obtain by lot*, Luke, i. 9. Acts, i. 17. 2 Pet. i. 1; *to cast lots*, Joh. xix. 34.

λάθρᾳ, adv., *secretly*, Matt. i. 19. ii. 7. Joh. xi. 28.

λαῖλαψ, ἡ, *a storm*, Mrk. iv. 37. Luke, viii. 23.

λακτίζω, *to kick*, Acts, xxvi. 14.

λαλέω, *to chatter;* in the NT *to speak, to talk*, Matt. x. 20. xiii. 3 etc.; *to utter, to tell*, 2 Cor. xii. 4; *to speak to, to converse with*, Matt. xii. 46.

λαλιὰ, ἡ, *talkativeness; speaking*, Joh. iv. 42; *manner of speaking, dialect*, Matt. xxvi. 73.

λαμὰ, and λαμμᾶ, *why?* doubtful forms ad Matt. xxvii. 46. Mrk. xv. 34. (Neither form is recognized in Pape's Lexicon.)

λαμβάνω, *to receive*, Matt. vii. 8. Joh. vii. 23; *to take*, Matt. xiii. 31, 33; *to get back*, Hebr. xi. 35.

λαμπὰς, ἡ, *a torch, a lamp*, Matt. xxv. 1, 3, 7. Joh. xviii. 3.

λαμπρὸς, *bright*, Rev. xxii. 16; *clear*, Rev. xxii. 1; *splendid, gorgeous*, Luke, xxiii. 11. Acts, x. 30. James, ii. 2; in neut. plural, *splendid things* (= luxuries), Rev. xviii. 14.

λαμπρότης, ἡ, *brightness*, Acts, xxvi. 13.

λαμπρῶς, *magnificently, sumptuously*, Luke, xvi. 19.

λάμπω, *to shine*, Matt. v. 15. xvii. 2 etc.

λανθάνω, *to be hidden*, Mrk. vii. 24. Luke, viii. 47; with accus. of person, *to be hidden from*, Acts, xxvi. 26. 2 Pet. iii. 5, 8; in construction with a participle, *unawares, without knowing*, Hebr. xiii. 2.

λαξευτὸς, *hewn out of the rock*, Luke, xxiii. 53. (It is a purely ecclesiastical form.)

λαὸς, ὁ, *a people, a nation*, Rom. ix. 26. Rev. v. 9. vii. 9; *a multitude*, Matt. xxvii. 25. Luke, viii. 47; *the people of Israel, the Israelites*, Luke, i. 68. ii. 10. vii. 16.

λάρυγξ, ὁ, *the throat*, Rom. iii. 13.
λάσκω, *to emit a loud sound; to burst asunder*, Acts, i. 18.
λατομέω, *to cut stones, to hew out*, Matt. xxvii. 60. Mrk. xv. 46.
λατρεία, ἡ, *religious service, worship*, Hebr. ix. 1, 6. Rom. ix. 4. xii. 1.
λατρεύω, *to render religious service; to worship, to serve*, Matt. iv. 10. Acts, vii. 7. xxiv. 14.
λάχανον, τὸ, *a potherb*, Matt. xiii. 32. Luke, xi. 42. Rom. xiv. 2.
λεγεών, ἡ, Lat. *legio, a legion*, Matt. xxvi. 53.
λέγω, *to speak*, Acts, xiii. 15. xxiv. 10; *to say*, Matt. ix. 34. xii. 44; *to declare*, Luke, iv. 25. Joh. i. 51. iii. 11; *to assert, to maintain*, Matt. xxii. 23. Luke, xxiii. 2. Mrk xii. 18; *to mean*, 1 Cor. i. 12. x. 29; *to call*, Mrk. x. 18. Luke, xviii. 19.
λεῖμμα, τὸ, *a remnant*, Rom. xi. 5. (Westcott gives λίμμα.)
λεῖος, *smooth, level*, Luke, iii. 5.
λείπω, *to leave*; pass., *to be left behind*, so *to want*, James, i. 4; intr. *to fail*, Luke, xviii. 22. Tit. iii. 13.
λειτουργέω, *to render public service to the state at one's own expense; to do a service, to minister*, Hebr. x. 11. Rom. xv. 27. Acts, xiii. 2.
λειτουργία, ἡ, *a public office undertaken at one's own expense; the service or ministry of the priests to God*, Luke, i. 23. Acts, viii. 6. ix. 21; *charitable ministration*, Philipp. ii. 30. 2 Cor. ix. 12.
λειτουργικὸς, *employed in ministering* (i.e. worshipping), Hebr. i. 14.
λειτουργὸς, ὁ, *a servant of the state; a servant, a minister*, Hebr. i. 7. viii. 2. Rom. xiii. 6. xv. 16.
λέντιον, τὸ, Lat. *linteum, a towel*, Joh. xiii. 4.
λεπὶς, ἡ, *a scale*, Acts, ix. 18.
λέπρα, ἡ, *leprosy*, Matt. viii. 3 etc.
λεπρὸς, *afflicted with leprosy, leprous*; as subst., *a leper*, Matt. viii. 2. x. 8. xi. 5.
λεπτὸς, *thin, small*; τὸ λεπτὸν, *a small brass coin, equivalent to the eighth part of the Roman as*, Mrk. xii. 42. Luke, xii. 59. xxi. 2 (RV *a mite*).
Δευείτης, ὁ, *one of Levi's posterity*; in a narrower sense, those were called Levites, who, though not of the race of Aaron, served as assistants to the priests, Luke, x. 32. Joh. i. 19. Acts, iv. 36.
λευκαίνω, *to whiten*, Mrk. ix. 3. Rev. vii. 14.
λευκὸς, *bright*, Matt. xvii. 2; *white*, Mrk. ix. 3. xvi. 5.
λέων, ὁ, *a lion*, Hebr. xi. 33. 1 Pet. v. 8. Rev. iv. 7 etc.
λήθη, ἡ, *forgetfulness*, 2 Pet. i. 9.
ληνὸς, ἡ, *a winepress*, Rev. xiv. 20. xix. 15; *the lower vat*, Matt. xxi. 33. [=ὑπολήνιον.]
λῆρος, ὁ, *idle talk*, Luke, xxiv. 11.
ληστὴς, ὁ, *a robber*, Joh. x. 1, 8. xviii. 40. Matt. xxi. 13 etc.
λῆψις, ἡ, *a receiving*, Philipp. iv. 15.

λίαν, adv., *greatly, much*, Matt. ii. 16. Mrk. vi. 51 etc.

λίβανος, ὁ, and sometimes ἡ, *frankincense*, Matt. ii. 11. Rev. xviii. 13.

λιβανωτός, ὁ, *a censer*, Rev. viii. 3, 5.

λιβερτῖνος, ὁ, Lat. *libertinus*; λιβερτῖνοι, in the NT were probably Jews who had been taken captive by the Romans under Pompey, but afterwards manumitted, and, though residing in Rome, had built for themselves a synagogue at Jerusalem, Acts, vi. 9.

λιθάζω, *to stone*, Joh. x. 31. Acts, xiv. 19.

λίθινος, *of stone*, Joh. ii. 6. 2 Cor. iii. 3. Rev. ix. 20.

λιθοβολέω, *to stone*, Acts, vii. 58. xiv. 5. Matt. xxi. 35 etc.

λίθος, ὁ, *a stone*, Matt. iv. 6. vii. 9 etc.; λίθος μυλικὸς, *a millstone*, Luke, xvii. 2.

λιθόστρωτος, *paved with stone*; τὸ λιθόστρωτον, *The Pavement*, Joh. xix. 13.

λικμάω, *to clear away the chaff from the grain by winnowing*; *to grind to powder*, Matt. xxi. 44. Luke, xx. 18.

λιμήν, ὁ, *a harbour*, Acts, xxvii. 8, 12.

λίμνη, ἡ, *a lake*, Luke, v. 1, 2. viii. 22, 33. Rev. xix. 20.

λιμός, ὁ, and ἡ, *famine*, Luke, xv. 14. Acts, xi. 28. Mrk. xiii. 8.

λίνον, τὸ, *flax* (=*wick*), Matt. xii. 20.

λιπαρὸς, *fat*; τὰ λιπαρὰ, *what is dainty*, Rev. xviii. 14.

λίτρα, ἡ, Lat. *libra, a pound*, a weight of 12 ounces, Joh. xii. 3. xix. 39.

λίψ, ὁ, *the South-West wind; the quarter of the heavens whence the South-West wind blows*, Acts, xxvii. 12.

λογία, ἡ, *a collection for the relief of the poor*, 1 Cor. xvi. 1, 2. (Only in ecclesiastical writers.)

λογίζομαι, *to reckon*, Rom. iv. 3, 5, 6; *to number among*, Luke, xxii. 37; *to think upon*, Philipp. iv. 8; *to impute*, 1 Cor. xiii. 5. 2 Tim. iv. 16. Rom. iv. 8; *to account*, εἰς οὐδὲν λογισθῆναι, Acts, xix. 27 (RV *to be made of no account*); *to think, to judge*, 1 Cor. xiii. 11. 2 Cor. iii. 5; *to purpose*, 2 Cor. x. 2.

λογικὸς, *rational, reasonable*, Rom. xii. 1; τὸ λογικὸν γάλα, 1 Pet. ii. 2 (RV *the spiritual milk*, AV *the milk of the word*).

λόγιον, τὸ, *an oracle*, Acts, vii. 38. Rom. iii. 2.

λόγιος, *learned*, Acts, xviii. 24 (possibly, *eloquent*).

λογισμὸς, ὁ, *a reasoning*, 2 Cor. x. 15. Rom. ii. 15.

λογομαχέω, *to wrangle about words*, 2 Tim. ii. 14. (Only in the NT and late writers.)

λογομαχία, ἡ, *a dispute about words*, 1 Tim. vi. 4.

λόγος, ὁ, *a word*, Matt. xii. 32, 36, 37; *talk, speech*, Matt. xxii. 15. Luke, xx. 20; *a saying*, Mrk. vii. 29; *an announcement*, 2 Cor. v. 19:

λογ] *GREEK-ENGLISH LEXICON* [λυχ

an account, a reason, 1 Pet. iii. 15; *a report*, Matt. xxviii. 15. Joh. xxi. 23; *a narrative*, Acts, i. 1; *doctrine*, Joh. viii. 31, 37. 2 Tim. ii. 17; *affair, matter*, Acts, xv. 6; *a plea*, Matt. v. 32; ὁ λόγος, *the Divine Word, the second person of the Trinity*, Joh. i. 1, 14; κατὰ λόγον, *in all reason, justly*, Acts, xviii. 14; τίνι λόγῳ, *for what reason*, Acts, x. 29.

λόγχη, ἡ, *a spear*, Joh. xix. 34.

λοιδορέω, *to abuse, to rail at*, Joh. ix. 28. Acts, xxiii. 4. 1 Cor. iv. 12.

λοιδορία, ἡ, *abuse, railing*, 1 Pet. iii. 9. 1 Tim. v. 14.

λοίδορος, ὁ, *a railer, a reviler*, 1 Cor. v. 11. vi. 10. (The word is properly an *adjective* =*abusive*.)

λοιμός, ὁ, *a pestilence*, Luke, xxi. 11; met., *a pestilent fellow*, Acts, xxiv. 5.

λοιπὸς, *remaining*; οἱ λοιποί, *the rest*, Matt. xxii. 6. xxvii. 49; τὰ λοιπὰ, *the things that remain, the rest*, Luke, xii. 26. 1 Cor. xi. 34; λοιπὸν, *for the rest*, 1 Cor. i. 16; *at length*, Acts, xxvii. 20; τὸ λοιπὸν, *henceforward*, 1 Cor. vii. 29. Hebr. x. 13; *finally*, Ephes. vi. 10. Philipp. iii. 1. iv. 8; τοῦ λοιποῦ, *for the future*, Gal. vi. 17.

λουτρὸν, τὸ, *a bath*; in the NT *baptism*, Tit. iii. 5. Ephes. v. 26 (= "*baptism*, NT," Pape's Lexicon).

λούω, *to bathe*, Joh. xiii. 10; *to wash*, Acts, ix. 37. xvi. 33. Hebr. x. 23; *to cleanse*, a var. lect. ad Rev. i. 5.

Λυκαονιστὶ, adv., *in the speech of Lycaonia*, Acts, xiv. 11.

λύκος, ὁ, *a wolf*, Matt. x. 16. Joh. x. 12. Acts, xx. 29 etc.

λυμαίνομαι, *to injure, to devastate*, Acts, viii. 3.

λυπέω, *to grieve, to make sorrowful*, 2 Cor. ii. 2, 4, 5. vii. 8. Rom. xiv. 15; *to offend*, Ephes. iv. 30.

λύπη, ἡ, *grief, sorrow*, Joh. xvi. 6, 20, 21; ἀπὸ τῆς λύπης, *for sorrow*, Luke, xxii. 45; ἐκ λύπης, *with sorrow*, 2 Cor. ix. 7 (RV grudgingly); ἡ κατὰ θεὸν λύπη, *godly sorrow*, 2 Cor. vii. 10; *annoyance, affliction*, 1 Pet. ii. 19.

λύσις, ἡ, *a release, a divorce*, 1 Cor. vii. 27.

λυσιτελέω, *to be profitable*; impers., λυσιτελεῖ αὐτῷ ... ἤ, *it is better for him*, Luke, xvii. 2.

λύτρον, τὸ, *a ransom*, Matt. xx. 28. Mrk. x. 45.

λυτρόω, *to liberate on receipt of ransom*, 1 Pet. i. 18; mid., *to ransom, to redeem*, Luke, xxiv. 21. Tit. ii. 14.

λύτρωσις, ἡ, *redemption, deliverance*, Luke, i. 68. ii. 38. Hebr. ix. 12.

λυτρωτὴς, ὁ, *a redeemer, a deliverer*, Acts; vii. 35. (It is a purely ecclesiastical form.)

λυχνία, ἡ, *a lampstand, a candlestick*, Matt. v. 15. Luke, viii. 16. Hebr. ix. 2.

λύχνος, ὁ, *a lamp*, Mrk. iv. 21. Luke, xii. 35. Rev. xxii. 5.

λύω, *to loose*, Matt. xxi. 2. Luke, xix. 30, 33; *to untie*, Joh. i. 27. Luke, iii. 16. Acts, vii. 33; *to set free, to unbind*, Luke, xiii. 16. Joh. xi. 44; *to break up, dismiss*, Acts, xiii. 43; *to destroy, to break*, Matt. v. 19. Joh. v. 18. Acts, xxvii. 41. 1 Joh. iii. 8; *to allow, make lawful*, Matt. xvi. 19.

M

μαγεία, and **μαγία**, ἡ, *magic, sorcery*, Acts, viii. 11.

μαγεύω, *to practise sorcery*, Acts, viii. 9.

μάγος, ὁ, *one of the Magi; a wise man*, Matt. ii. 1, 7, 16; *a sorcerer*, Acts, xiii. 6, 8.

μαζὸς, ὁ, *the breast*, var. lect. ad Rev. i. 13.

μαθητεύω, with dat., *to be a disciple of*, Joh. xix. 38; trans., *to make one a disciple*, Matt. xxviii. 19. Acts, xiv. 21; pass., *to be made a disciple*, Matt. xiii. 52. xxvii. 57.

μαθητὴς, ὁ, *a disciple*, Matt. x. 24. Luke, vi. 13, 17. vii. 11 etc.

μαθήτρια, ἡ, *a female disciple*, Acts, ix. 36.

μαίνομαι, *to be mad*, Joh. x. 20. Acts, xii. 15. xxvi. 24, 25. 1 Cor. xiv. 23.

μακαρίζω, *to pronounce blessed*, Luke, i. 48. James, v. 11.

μακάριος, *blessed, happy*, James, i. 12. Tit. ii. 13. Acts, xx. 35. xxvi. 2.

μακαρισμὸς, ὁ, *a benediction, a blessing*, Rom. iv. 6, 9. Gal. iv. 15.

μάκελλον, τό, *a flesh-market*, 1 Cor. x. 25.

μακρὰν, sc. ὁδὸν, properly accus. fem. of μακρὸς, used adverbially, *far, far off*, Acts, xvii. 27. Luke, vii. 6. xv. 20. Matt. viii. 30; *far hence*, Acts, xxii. 21; οἱ εἰς μακρὰν, *those that are afar off*, i.e. the Gentiles, Acts, ii. 39. Cf. Ephes. ii. 13.

μακρόθεν, adv., *from afar, afar off*, Mrk. viii. 3. xi. 13. Luke, xviii. 13 etc.

μακροθυμέω, *to be long suffering, to be patient with*, 2 Pet. iii. 9. Luke, xviii. 7. Matt. xviii. 26, 29; *to be patient in enduring*, Hebr. vi. 15. James, v. 8.

μακροθυμία, ἡ, *patience*, James, v. 10. Hebr. vi. 12. Coloss. i. 11. 2 Tim. iii. 10; *long suffering*, 1 Tim. i. 16. Gal. v. 22. Ephes. iv. 2. 2 Cor. vi. 6 etc.

μακροθύμως, adv., *patiently*, Acts, xxvi. 3.

μακρὸς, *long*; μακρὰ προσεύχεσθαι, *to make long prayers*, Mrk. xii. 40. Luke, xx. 47; *distant*, Luke, xv. 13. xix. 12.

μακροχρόνιος, *long-lived*, Ephes. vi. 3.

μαλακία, ἡ, *sickness*, Matt. iv. 23. ix. 35. x. 1.

μαλακὸς, *soft*, Luke, vii. 25; τὰ μαλακὰ, *soft raiment*, Matt. xi. 8; *effeminate*, 1 Cor. vi. 9.

μάλιστα, adv., *especially, most of all*, Gal. vi. 10. Philipp. iv. 22. Tit. i. 10 etc.

μάλλον, adv., *more*, Matt. xviii. 13. Joh. v. 18; *rather*, Matt. xxvii. 24. Ephes. iv. 28; τοσούτῳ μᾶλλον, *by so much the more*, Hebr. x. 25.

μάμμη, ἡ, *a mother; a grandmother*, 2 Tim. i. 5. (This second meaning is found only in late writers.)

μαμωνᾶς, ὁ, *mammon, riches*, Luke, xvi. 9, 11, 13. Matt. vi. 24. (Apparently only in the NT.)

μανθάνω, *to learn*, 1 Tim. ii. 11. 2 Tim. iii. 14; *to hear, to be informed*, Acts, xxiii. 27. Gal. iii. 2.

μανία, ἡ, *madness*, Acts, xxvi. 24.

μάννα, τό, indecl., *manna*, Joh. vi. 31, 49. Hebr. ix. 4. Rev. ii. 17.

μαντεύομαι, *to prophesy, to divine*, Acts, xvi. 16.

μαραίνω, *to waste away, to perish*, James, i. 11.

μαραναθὰ, and **μαρὰν ἀθὰ**, = *our Lord cometh*, 1 Cor. xvi. 22.

μαργαρίτης, ὁ, *a pearl*, Matt. vii. 6. xiii. 45, 46. 1 Tim. ii. 9 etc.

μάρμαρος, ὁ, *marble*, Rev. xviii. 12.

μαρτυρέω, *to testify, to bear witness of*, Joh. i. 7. iii. 11, 32. xviii. 23. xix. 35 etc.; pass., *to be well reported of, to be of good report*, Acts, vi. 3. x. 22. 1 Tim. v. 10.

μαρτυρία, ἡ, *testimony*, Joh. v. 34. viii. 17. Rev. i. 2 etc.; *good report*, 1 Tim. iii. 7.

μαρτύριον, τό, *testimony*, 2 Cor. i. 12. Acts, iv. 33. 2 Thess. i. 10; μαρτύριον Χριστοῦ, *testimony concerning Christ*, 1 Cor. i. 6. So also Hebr. iii. 5. 2 Tim. i. 8.

μαρτύρομαι, *to call to witness; to declare solemnly*, Acts, xx. 26. Gal. v. 3; *to exhort solemnly*, Ephes. iv. 17. Acts, xxvi. 22.

μάρτυς, ὁ, *a witness*, Matt. xviii. 16. xxvi. 65. Acts, vi. 13; *a martyr*, Rev. xvii. 6. Acts, xxii. 20.

μασθὸς, ὁ, *the breast*, a var. lect. ad Rev. i. 13. (See μαστός.)

μασσάομαι, *to gnaw*, Rev. xvi. 10.

μαστιγόω, *to scourge*, Matt. x. 17. xx. 19. xxiii. 34. Hebr. xii. 6.

μαστίζω = μαστιγόω, Acts, xxii. 25.

μάστιξ, ἡ, *a scourge*, Acts, xxii. 25. Hebr. xi. 36; *a plague, an affliction*, Luke, vii. 21. Mrk. iii. 10. v. 29, 34.

μαστὸς, ὁ, *the breast*, Rev. i. 13. Luke, xi. 27. xxiii. 29.

ματαιολογία, ἡ, *vain talking*, 1 Tim. i. 6.

ματαιολόγος, *a vain talker*, Tit. i. 10. (But the word is strictly an *adjective*.)

μάταιος, *vain, idle*, 1 Cor. iii. 20. xv. 17. Tit. iii. 9; τὰ μάταια, *what is vain, vanities*, Acts, xiv. 15.

ματαιότης, ἡ, *vanity*, 2 Pet. ii. 18. Ephes. iv. 17; *weakness, foolishness*, Rom. viii. 20. (See Pape's Lexicon in voc. It is a purely biblical and ecclesiastical word.)

ματαιόω, *to make foolish*, Rom. i. 21. (It is a purely biblical and ecclesiastical word.)

μάτην, adv., *in vain*, Matt. xv. 9. Mrk. vii. 7.

μάχαιρα, ἡ, *a sword*, Matt. xxvi. 47, 51, 52. Joh. xviii. 10 etc.

μάχη, ἡ, *battle, contest, quarrel*, 2 Cor. vii. 5. James, iv. 1; μάχαι νομικαί, *contentions about the law*, Tit. iii. 9.

μάχομαι, *to fight*, James, iv. 2; *to contend*, Acts. vii. 26; *to strive, to dispute*, 2 Tim. ii. 24. Joh. vi. 52.

μεγαλαυχέω, *to utter great boasts*, James, iii. 5. (Here Westcott reads μεγάλα αὐχεῖ.)

μεγαλεῖος, *magnificent, wonderful*; τὰ μεγαλεῖα τοῦ θεοῦ, *the wondrous works of God*, Acts, ii. 11.

μεγαλειότης, ἡ, *splendour, magnificence*, Acts, xix. 27; *majesty*, Luke, ix. 43; *glory*, 2 Pet. i. 16.

μεγαλοπρεπής, *magnificent, majestic*, 2 Pet. i. 17.

μεγαλύνω, *to magnify*, Acts, x. 46. xix. 17. 2 Cor. x. 15 etc.; *to exalt, to extol*, Luke, i. 46; *to enlarge*, Matt. xxiii. 5.

μεγάλως, adv., *greatly*, Philipp. iv. 10.

μεγαλωσύνη, ἡ, *majesty*, Hebr. i. 3. viii. 1. Jude, 25. (It is a purely biblical and ecclesiastical form.)

μέγας, *great*, Matt. xxvii. 60. xxviii. 1. Mrk. v. 11 etc.; *strong*, Joh. vi. 18. Mrk. iv. 37. Rev. xiv. 2; *loud*, Joh. xi. 43. Matt. xxvii. 46, 50.

Luke, xxiii. 23; οἱ μεγάλοι, *the leaders*, Mrk. x. 42. Matt. xx. 25.

μέγεθος, τὸ, *greatness*, Ephes. i. 19.

μεγιστᾶνες, οἱ, *the nobles, the chief men*, Rev. vi. 15. xviii. 23. Mrk. vi. 21. (A very late form, and found only once in the singular.)

μεθερμηνεύω, *to interpret*, Matt. i. 23. Acts, iv. 36 etc.

μέθη, ἡ, *intoxication, drunkenness*, Luke, xxi. 34. Gal. v. 21. Rom. xiii. 13.

μεθίστημι, *to remove*, 1 Cor. xiii. 2. Luke, xvi. 4; *to transfer*, Coloss. i. 13; *to lead astray, to pervert*, Acts, xix. 26.

μεθοδία, ἡ, *wile, deceit*, Ephes. iv. 14. vi. 11. (A very late form.)

μεθόριον, τὸ, in the plur., *the confines, the borders*, a var. lect. ad Mrk. vii. 24.

μεθύσκω, *to make drunk*; pass., *to become intoxicated*, Rev. xvii. 2. Luke, xii. 45. 1 Thess. v. 7. Joh. ii. 10.

μέθυσος, *drunken*, 1 Cor. v. 11. vi. 10.

μεθύω, *to be drunken*, Acts, ii. 15. Matt. xxiv. 49. 1 Cor. xi. 21.

μέλας, *black*, Rev. vi. 5, 12; τὸ μέλαν, *ink*, 2 Cor. iii. 3. 2 Joh. 12. 3 Joh. 13.

μέλει, verb impers., *it is a care*; καὶ οὐ μέλει σοι περὶ οὐδενὸς, *and thou carest not for any one*, Matt. xxii. 16; οὐδὲν τούτων τῷ Γαλλίωνι ἔμελεν, *Gallio cared nought for these things*, Acts, xviii. 17; μὴ τῶν βοῶν μέλει τῷ θεῷ; 1 Cor. ix. 9 (RV *is it for the oxen that God careth*

μελετάω, to practise, to attend to, 1 Tim. iv. 15; to devise, Acts, iv. 25; to premeditate, Mrk. xiii. 11.

μέλι, τὸ, honey, Matt. iii. 4. Mrk. i. 6. Rev. x. 9, 10.

μελίσσιος, of bees, made by bees, a var. lect. ad Luke, xxiv. 42. (Found nowhere else: is not recognized in Pape's Lexicon.)

μέλλω, to be about to do something, Joh. iv. 47. Acts, xvi. 27; ἡ μέλλουσα ὀργή, the wrath to come, Matt. iii. 7. Cf. Coloss. ii. 17. 1 Tim. iv. 8; τὸ μέλλον, the future, Luke, xiii. 9; to intend, to propose, Matt. ii. 13. Acts, v. 35. xvii. 31; to delay, Acts, xxii. 16.

μέλος, τὸ, a member, a limb, Matt. v. 29. Rom. vi. 13, 19. 1 Cor. vi. 15. xii. 12, 22 etc.

μεμβράνα, ἡ, parchment, 2 Tim. iv. 13. (It is a purely biblical form.)

μέμφομαι, to find fault, to blame, Rom. ix. 19. Hebr. viii. 8.

μεμψίμοιρος, discontented, Jude, 16.

μέν, an affirmative particle, indeed, Luke, iii. 16; (followed always by δέ).

μενοῦνγε, nay rather, Rom. ix. 20. x. 18.

μέντοι, however, Joh. iv. 27. 2 Tim. ii. 19. Jude, 8.

μένω, to remain, to abide, Matt. xxvi. 38. Joh. ii. 12. xix. 31; to last, to endure, Joh. vi. 27. 1 Cor. xiii. 13. Hebr. vii. 24; to wait for, to await, Acts, xx. 5, 23.

μερίζω, to divide, to distribute, Mrk. vi. 41. 1 Cor. vii. 17. Rom. xii. 3; pass., to be divided, 1 Cor. i. 13; to be at variance, Matt. xii. 25. Mrk. iii. 24, 26; to differ; μεμέρισται ἡ γυνὴ καὶ ἡ παρθένος, there is a difference between (Westcott puts the word in previous sentence = is divided), 1 Cor. vii. 33; mid., to share, a thing with another, Luke, xii. 13.

μέριμνα, ἡ, (distracting) care, anxiety, Matt. xiii. 22. Mrk. iv. 19. 2 Cor. xi. 28. 1 Pet. v. 7.

μεριμνάω, to be anxious, to be troubled with cares, Matt. vi. 25, 27, 31. Luke, xii. 25; μηδὲν μεριμνᾶτε, be ye anxious for nothing, Philipp. iv. 6; to care for, 1 Cor. vii. 32, 34. xii. 25. Philipp. ii. 20.

μερίς, ἡ, a division, a part, Acts, xvi. 12; a share, a portion, 2 Cor. vi. 15. Acts, viii. 21.

μερισμὸς, ὁ, a distribution, a gift, Hebr. ii. 4; a dividing, a partition, Hebr. iv. 12.

μεριστὴς, ὁ, a divider, Luke, xii. 14.

μέρος, τὸ, a part, a share, Rev. xx. 6. xxii. 19. Joh. xix. 23; lot, portion, Matt. xxiv. 51. Luke, xii. 46; a region, a district, Matt. ii. 22. xv. 21. Acts, xix. 1. xx. 2; a trade, a handicraft, Acts, xix. 27; κατὰ μέρος, severally, in detail, Hebr. ix. 5; μέρος τι, in some measure, partly, 1 Cor. xi. 18; ἀπὸ μέρους, in some degree, 2 Cor. i. 14. ii. 5. Rom. xi. 25; ἐκ μέρους, individually, 1 Cor. xii. 27; in part, im-

perfectly, 1 Cor. xiii. 9, 12. Cf. 2 Cor. i. 14; τὸ ἐκ μέρους, *that which is imperfect*, 1 Cor. xiii. 10; ἐν τῷ μέρει τούτῳ, *in this respect*, 2 Cor. iii. 10.

μεσημβρία, ἡ, *noon*, Acts, xxii. 6; *the South*, Acts, viii. 26.

μεσιτεύω, *to act as mediator*; met., *to pledge one's self, to give surety*, Hebr. vi. 17 (RV *interposed*).

μεσίτης, ὁ, *a mediator*, Hebr. viii. 6. ix. 15. xii. 24. 1 Tim. ii. 5. Gal. iii. 20. (See ἄνθρωπος.)

μεσονύκτιος, *of midnight*; τὸ μεσονύκτιον, *midnight*, Acts, xvi. 25. xx. 7; μεσονυκτίου, *at midnight*, Mrk. xiii. 35 (Here Westcott reads μεσονύκτιον.)

μέσος, *central, in the middle*; μέσης νυκτὸς, *at midnight*, Matt. xxv. 6; μέσης ἡμέρας, *at midday*, Acts, xxvi. 13; μέσος ὑμῶν, *in the midst of you*, Joh. i. 26; ἐσχίσθη μέσον, *was rent in the midst*, Luke, xxiii. 45; διὰ μέσου αὐτῶν, *through the midst of them*, Luke, iv. 30; ἐκ τοῦ μέσου, *out of the way, out of sight*, Coloss. ii. 14; γενέσθαι ἐκ μέσου, *to be taken out of the way*, 2 Thess. ii. 7; ἐκ μέσου τινῶν, *from amongst*, Matt. xiii. 49. Acts, xvii. 33. 1 Cor. v. 2.

μεσότοιχον, τὸ, *a partition-wall*, Ephes. ii. 14 (RV *the middle wall of partition*).

μεσουράνημα, τὸ, *mid-heaven*, Rev. viii. 13.

μεσόω, *to be in the middle*; τῆς ἑορτῆς μεσούσης, *when it was the midst of the feast*, Joh. vii. 14.

μεστὸς, *full*, Joh. xix. 29. xxi. 11. James, iii. 8.

μεστόω, *to fill*, Acts, ii. 13.

μετὰ, prepos., with genit., *with, together with, in confederacy with*; with accus., *after*. (The reader is referred to his Greek Grammar.)

μεταβαίνω, *to pass from one place to another; to depart*, Matt. viii. 34. xi. 1. Acts, xviii. 7 etc.; μετάβα, *be thou removed*, Matt. xvii. 20; μεταβέβηκεν ἐκ τοῦ θανάτου εἰς τὴν ζωὴν, *hath passed from death into life*, Joh. v. 24. 1 Joh. iii. 14.

μεταβάλλω, *to turn round*; mid., *to change one's mind*, Acts, xxviii. 6.

μετάγω, *to turn about, to direct*, James, iii. 3.

μεταδίδωμι, *to give a share to another*; *to impart* of his substance, Rom. xii. 8. Ephes. iv. 28; and, generally, *to impart*, 1 Thess. ii. 8. Rom. i. 11. Luke, iii. 11.

μετάθεσις, ἡ, *a change of place*; *a translation* to heaven, Hebr. xi. 5; *a change*, Hebr. vii. 12; *a removal*, Hebr. xii. 27.

μεταίρω, *to transfer*; in the NT intrans., *to depart*, Matt. xiii. 53. xix. 1.

μετακαλέω, *to call from one place to another*; mid., *to send for*, Acts, vii. 14. xx. 17. xxiv. 25, 26.

μετακινέω, *to move away*; pass., *to be moved away*, Coloss. i. 23.

μεταλαμβάνω, *to partake of*, 2 Tim. ii. 6. Acts, xxvii. 33. Hebr. xii. 10; with accus., *to obtain, to get*, Acts, xxiv. 25.

μετάληψις, ἡ, *a participation, a receiving*; εἰς μετάληψιν, *to be received*, 1 Tim. iv. 3.

μεταλλάσσω, *to exchange*, τί ἔν τινι, *one thing for another*, Rom. i. 25; *to change*, τί εἴς τι, *one thing into another*, Rom. i. 26.

μεταμέλομαι, *to repent*, Matt. xxi. 30, 32. xxvii. 3. 2 Cor. vii. 8. Hebr. vii. 21.

μεταμορφόω, *to transform, to transfigure*, Matt. xvii. 2. Mrk. ix. 2; μεταμορφοῦσθε, *be ye transformed*, Rom. xii. 2; τὴν αὐτὴν εἰκόνα μεταμορφούμεθα, *we are transformed into the same image*, 2 Cor. iii. 18.

μετανοέω, *to change one's mind, to repent*, Mrk. i. 15. Matt. iii. 2. Luke, x. 13; with ἐπί τινι, *on account of* something, 2 Cor. xii. 21; with ἀπό, or ἐκ, *to withdraw from, to depart from*, Acts, viii. 22. Rev. ii. 21. ix. 20. xvi. 11.

μετάνοια, ἡ, *change of mind, repentance*, Matt. iii. 8. Luke, iii. 8. xv. 7 etc.

μεταξὺ, adv., *between*; ἐν τῷ μεταξὺ, *meanwhile, in the meantime*, Joh. iv. 31; with genit., *between*, Matt. xxiii. 35. Luke, xi. 51. xvi. 26; *afterwards*; τὸ μεταξὺ σάββατον, *the following sabbath*, Acts, xiii. 42.

μεταπέμπω, *to send after*; μετα πεμφθείς, *sent for*, Acts, x. 29; mid., *to send for*, Acts, x. 5. xi. 13. xxiv. 24, 26.

μεταστρέφω, *to turn about; to turn;* τί εἴς τι, *to turn one thing into another*, Acts, ii. 20. James, iv. 9; *to pervert*, Gal. i. 7.

μετασχηματίζω, *to transfigure, to change*, Philipp. iii. 21; mid., *to transform*, 2 Cor. xi. 13, 14, 15; *to transfer*, 2 Cor. iv. 6.

μετατίθημι, *to transpose, to transfer*, Acts, vii. 16. Hebr. xi. 5; *to pervert*, Jude, 4; pass., *to be changed*, Hebr. vii. 12; mid., *to apostatize, to fall away*, Gal. i. 6.

μετατρέπω, *to change*, James, iv. 9. (A non-Attic word.)

μετέπειτα, adv., *afterwards, after that*, Hebr. xii. 17.

μετέχω, *to partake*, 1 Cor. ix. 12. x. 21, 30; met., *to belong to*, Hebr. vii. 13.

μετεωρίζω, *to raise on high*; pass., *to be troubled with anxiety, to be in suspense*, Luke, xii. 29.

μετοικεσία, ἡ, *a removal from one abode to another, a migration*, Matt. i. 11, 12, 17.

μετοικίζω, *to remove inhabitants to another land*, Acts, vii. 4, 43.

μετοχή, ἡ, *communion, fellowship*, 2 Cor. vi. 14.

μέτοχος, ὁ, *a partaker*, Hebr. iii. 1, 14. xii. 8; *a partner, an associate*, Luke, v. 7. Hebr. i. 9.

μετρέω, to measure, Rev. xi. 1, 2. xxi. 16, 17; to mete out to others, Luke, vi. 38. Matt. vii. 2. Mrk. iv. 24; to estimate, to judge, 2 Cor. x. 12.

μετρητής, ὁ, a measure for liquids, containing somewhat less than 9 gallons, Joh. ii. 6.

μετριοπαθέω, to be patient with, to bear with, Hebr. v. 2.

μετρίως, adv., moderately; οὐ μετρίως, not a little, exceedingly, Acts, xx. 12.

μέτρον, τό, a measure, Matt. xxiii. 32. Ephes. iv. 13; ἐν μέτρῳ, in due measure, Ephes. iv. 16; ἐκ μέτρου, sparingly, Joh. iii. 34; a measuring rod, Rev. xxi. 15, 17; a definite portion or measure, 2 Cor. x. 13. Rom. xii. 3.

μέτωπον, τό, the forehead, Rev. vii. 3. ix. 3. xvii. 5 etc.

μέχρι, prepos., with genit., until, Luke, xvi. 16; as conj., Ephes. iv. 13; as far as, unto, Hebr. iii. 6, 14. Rom. xv. 19. Philipp ii. 8.

μή, a particle of subjective negation, as distinguished from οὐ, not, lest; μηδαμῶς, by no means; μηδὲ, neither, nor, not even, nor yet; μηδεὶς, no one; μηδέποτε, never at any time; μηδέπω, not yet; μηκέτι, no longer; μήτε, neither, nor. μήτι, whether at all. (The reader is referred to his Greek Grammar.)

μῆκος, τό, length, Rev. xxi. 16. Ephes. iii. 18.

μηκύνω, to lengthen; pass., to grow up, Mrk. iv. 27.

μηλωτή, ἡ, a sheepskin, Hebr. xi. 27.

μήν, ὁ, a month, Luke, i. 24, 26. Acts, vii. 20; new moon, Gal. iv. 10.

μηνύω, to signify, to make known, Joh. xi. 57. Luke, xx. 37.

μηρὸς, ὁ, the thigh, Rev. xix. 16.

μήτηρ, ἡ, a mother, Matt. i. 18. ii. 11. xii. 49 etc.

μήτιγε, much more, 1 Cor. vi. 3.

μήτρα, ἡ, the womb, Luke, ii. 23. Rom. iv. 19.

μητραλῴας, and μητραλοίας, ὁ, a matricide, 1 Tim. i. 9.

μιαίνω, to pollute, to defile, Jude, 8. Tit. i. 15. Joh. xviii. 28.

μίασμα, τό, a defilement, 2 Pet. ii. 20.

μιασμὸς, ὁ, a defiling, a defilement, 2 Pet. ii. 10.

μίγμα, τό, a mixture, a var. lect. ad Joh. xix. 39. (Westcott reads ἕλιγμα.)

μίγνυμι, to mix, to mingle, Rev. viii. 7. xv. 2 ; also μετά τινος, Luke, xiii. 1. Matt. xxvii. 34.

μικρὸς, small, little, Luke, xix. 3. Matt. xiii. 32; μετὰ μικρὸν, after a little while, Matt. xxvi. 73.

μίλιον, τό, Lat. miliarium, a Roman mile, i.e. a thousand paces, Matt. v. 41.

μιμέομαι, to imitate, 2 Thess. iii. 7, 9. Hebr. xiii. 7. 3 Joh. 11.

μιμητὴς, ὁ, an imitator, 1 Cor. iv. 16. xi. 1. 1 Thess. i. 6 etc.

μιμνήσκω, to remind; pass., to remember, Acts, xi. 16. Matt.

xxvi. 75. Luke, xxiv. 8; *to be remembered*, Acts, x. 31.

μισέω, *to hate*, Matt. v. 43. vi. 24. Luke, vi. 22, 27 etc.

μισθαποδοσία, ἡ, *payment of wages, recompense*, Hebr. ii. 2. x. 35. xi. 26.

μισθαποδότης, ὁ, *a recompenser, a rewarder*, Hebr. xi. 6. (This and the preceding are purely ecclesiastical words.)

μίσθιος, *hired*; as subst., *a hired servant*, Luke, xv. 17, 19.

μισθὸς, ὁ, *hire, wages, reward*, Matt. xx. 8. Luke, x. 7. Rom. iv. 4 etc.

μισθόω, *to let out for hire*; mid., *to hire*, Matt. xx. 1, 7.

μίσθωμα, τὸ, *the price for which anything is either let out or hired; a hired dwelling, lodgings*, Acts, xxviii. 30.

μισθωτὸς, *hired*; as subst., *a hired servant, a hireling*, Mrk. i. 20. Joh. x. 12.

μνᾶ, ἡ, *a mina*, a sum of money equal to 100 drachmae, Luke, xix. 13, 16, 18, 20. (According to Pape = 22½ thalers, i.e. £3 7s. 6d.)

μνεία, ἡ, *remembrance*, 2 Tim. i. 3. 1 Thess. iii. 6; ἐπὶ πάσῃ τῇ μνείᾳ ὑμῶν, *in all my remembrance of you*, Philipp. i. 3; *mention*; μνείαν ὑμῶν ποιοῦμαι, *I make mention of you*, Rom. i. 9. Cf. Ephes. i. 16. 1 Thess. i. 2.

μνῆμα, τὸ, *a memorial; a tomb, a sepulchre*, Luke, viii. 27. xxiii. 53. Acts, ii. 29 etc.

μνημεῖον, τὸ, *a monument; a sepulchre, a tomb*, Matt. xxiii. 29. xxviii. 8. Luke, xi. 47.

μνήμη, ἡ, *memory, remembrance*; μνήμην ποιεῖσθαί τινος, *to recollect*, 2 Pet. i. 15.

μνημονεύω, *to remember, to call to mind*, Matt. xvi. 9. Luke, xvii. 32. Acts, xx. 31; *to be mindful of*, Gal. ii. 10. Hebr. xi. 15; *to make mention of*, Hebr. xi. 22; perhaps also Hebr. xi. 15.

μνημόσυνον, τὸ, *a memorial*, Acts, x. 4. Matt. xxvi. 13. Mrk. xiv. 9.

μνηστεύω, *to ask in marriage*; pass., *to be betrothed*, Matt. i. 18.

μογιλάλος, *speaking with difficulty, having an impediment in his speech*, Mrk. vii. 32.

μόγις, adv., *with difficulty, hardly*, Luke, ix. 39. (Here Westcott reads μόλις, which see.)

μόδιος, ὁ, Lat. *modius*, a dry measure, containing 16 *sextarii*, i.e. about a peck, Matt. v. 15. Luke, xi. 33. Mrk. iv. 21.

μοιχαλὶς, ἡ, *an adulteress*, Rom. vii. 3. James, iv. 4; met., *adultery, lustfulness*, 2 Pet. ii. 14; as adj., *faithless, apostate*, Matt. xii. 39. xvi. 4. Mrk. viii. 38.

μοιχάω, *to seduce*; mid., *to commit adultery*, Matt. v. 32. Mrk. x. 11, 12.

μοιχεία, ἡ, *adultery*, Joh. viii. 3. Matt. xv. 19. Mrk. vii. 21.

μοιχεύω, *to commit adultery*, Matt. v. 27, 28. Luke, xvi. 18. xviii. 20 etc.

μοιχὸς, ὁ, *an adulterer*, Luke, xviii. 11. 1 Cor. vi. 9.

μόλις, adv., *with difficulty, hardly, scarcely*, Acts, xiv. 18. xxvii. 7. 16. Rom. v. 7.

μολύνω, *to defile, to pollute*, Rev. iii. 4. xiv. 4. 1 Cor. viii. 7.

μολυσμὸς, ὁ, *defilement*, 2 Cor. vii. 1.

μομφή, ἡ, *blame, complaint*, Coloss. iii. 13.

μονή, ἡ, *a dwelling, an abode*, Joh. xiv. 2, 23.

μονογενὴς, *only begotten*, Joh. iii. 16, 18. Luke, ix. 38. Hebr. xi 17 etc. (In Joh. i. 18 it is hard to see why μονογενὴς υἱὸς, the reading of some editors, must be translated *the only begotten Son*, while μονογενὴς θεὸς, which is given by Westcott and Tregelles after the very oldest MSS, must not be translated *the only begotten God*, but *God only begotten*.)

μόνος, *alone, only*, Joh. v. 44. xvii. 3. Rom. xvi. 27. Jude, 4; *deserted, forsaken*, Joh. xvi. 32.

μονόφθαλμος, *having only one eye, one-eyed*, Matt. xviii. 9. Mrk. ix. 47.

μονόω, *to leave alone*, 1 Tim. v. 5.

μορφή, ἡ, *form*, Philipp. ii. 7. Mrk. xvi. 12; ἐν μορφῇ θεοῦ ὑπάρχων, Philipp. ii. 6. (Here, perhaps, = *essence*, the *forma* of the Schoolmen. See Ast's Lexicon Platonicum in voc. μορφή.)

μορφόω, *to form*, Gal. iv. 19.

μόρφωσις, ἡ, *a semblance*, 2 Tim. iii. 5; *the true form*, Rom. ii. 20.

μοσχοποιέω, *to make an image of a calf*, Acts, vii. 41. (It is a purely ecclesiastical form.)

μόσχος, ὁ, *a calf*, Luke, xv. 23, 27, 30. Hebr. ix. 12, 19.

μουσικὸς, *skilled in music, a minstrel*, Rev. xviii. 22.

μόχθος, ὁ, *toil, travail*, 2 Cor. xi. 27. 1 Thess. ii. 9. 2 Thess. iii. 8.

μυελὸς, ὁ, *marrow*, Hebr. iv. 12.

μυέω, *to initiate, to teach*; pass., *to be instructed, to learn*; μεμύημαι, *I have learned*, Philipp. iv. 12.

μῦθος, ὁ, *a fable*, 2 Pet. i. 16. 1 Tim. i. 4. 2 Tim. iv. 4.

μυκάομαι, *to bellow; to roar*, as a lion, Rev. x. 3.

μυκτηρίζω, *to sneer at; to mock*, Gal. vi. 7.

μυλικὸς, *of or belonging to a mill*, Luke, xvii. 2.

μύλινος, ὁ, *a millstone*, Rev. xviii. 21.

μύλος, ὁ, *a mill*, Matt. xxiv. 41; φωνὴ μύλου, *the sound of a mill*, Rev. xviii. 22; *a millstone*, Mrk. ix. 42. Matt. xviii. 6.

μυλὼν, ὁ, *a mill-house*, a var. lect. ad Matt. xxiv. 41.

μυριάς, ἡ, *ten thousand*, Acts, xix. 19; *an infinite number*, Luke, xii. 1. Hebr. xii. 22.

μυρίζω, *to anoint*, Mrk. xiv. 8.

μυρίος, *innumerable*, 1 Cor. iv. 15. xiv. 19; μύριοι, *ten thousand*, Matt. xviii. 24. (But this change of meaning according to change of accent is merely a fanciful refine-

ment of the grammarians. See Pape's Lex. in voc.)

μύρον, τό, *ointment*, Matt. xxvi. 7, 12. Luke, vii. 37 etc.

μυστήριον, τό, *a secret, a mystery*, Matt. xiii. 11. Coloss. i. 26. Rom. xi. 25; *the hidden meaning*, Rev. i. 20. xvii. 7; *the secret purpose*, 2 Thess. ii. 7.

μυωπάζω, *to be dim-sighted*, 2 Pet. i. 9.

μώλωψ, ὁ, *a wale; a wound, a stripe*, 1 Pet. ii. 24

μωμάομαι, *to blame*, 2 Cor. vi. 3. viii. 20.

μῶμος, ὁ, *mockery*; met., *a blemish*, 2 Pet. ii. 13.

μωραίνω, *to play the fool*; trans., *to make foolish*, 1 Cor. i. 20. Rom. i. 22; pass., *to become tasteless*, Matt. v. 13. Luke, xiv. 34.

μωρία, ἡ, *foolishness*, 1 Cor. i. 18, 21, 23 etc.

μωρολογία, ἡ, *foolish talking*, Ephes. v. 4.

μωρὸς, *foolish*, Matt. vii. 26. xxiii. 17; *impious*, Matt. v. 22.

N

Ναζαρὲτ, and **Ναζαρά**, ἡ, *Nazareth*, a town of lower Galilee, where the Saviour lived from his childhood until he made his public appearance, Mrk. i. 9. Luke, ii. 39. iv. 16. Matt. iv. 13.

Ναζαρηνὸς, ὁ, *a Nazarene*, a name applied to Jesus Christ, because he had lived at Nazareth, Mrk. i. 24. x. 47. xiv. 67. xvi. 6. Luke, iv. 34.

Ναζωραῖος, ὁ, *a Nazarene*, 'Ιησοῦς ὁ Ναζωραῖος, Acts, xxii. 8. Cf. Luke, xviii. 37. Joh. xix. 19. Acts, xxiv. 5. Matt. xxvi. 72.

ναί, an affirmative particle, *yea, verily, even so*, Matt. xi. 26. Luke, x. 21. Philem. 20. Rev. xiv. 13 etc.

ναὸς, ὁ, *a temple*, Matt. xxiii. 16, 17, 35. Joh. ii. 19 etc.

νάρδος, ἡ, *nard, oil of spikenard*, obtained from a fragrant East Indian plant, Joh. xii. 3. Mrk. xiv. 3.

ναυαγέω, *to suffer shipwreck*, 2 Cor. xi. 25. 1 Tim. i. 19.

ναύκληρος, ὁ, *a shipmaster*, Acts, xxvii. 11.

ναῦς, ἡ, *a ship*, Acts, xxvii. 41.

ναύτης, ὁ, *a sailor*, Acts, xxvii. 27, 30. Rev. xviii. 17.

νεανίας, ὁ, *a young man, a youth*, Acts, vii. 58. xx. 9.

νεανίσκος, ὁ, *a young man, a youth*, Matt. xix. 20, 22. Luke, vii. 14. Acts, ii. 17 etc.; *an attendant*, Acts, v. 10.

νεκρὸς, ὁ, *a corpse*, Rev. xvi. 3; *dead*, 2 Tim. iv. 1. Matt. viii. 22 etc.

νεκρόω, *to put to death, to kill; to mortify*, Coloss. iii. 5; *to render effete*, Rom. iv. 19. Hebr. xi. 12.

νέκρωσις, ἡ, *a dying*, 2 Cor. iv. 10; *deadness*, Rom. iv. 19.

νεομηνία, ἡ, *the new moon*, Coloss. ii. 16.

νέος, *young*, Tit. ii. 4; *new*, Matt. ix. 17. 1 Cor. v. 7. Coloss. iii. 10.

νεοσσὸς, ὁ, *a youngling*, Luke, ii. 24.

νεότης, ἡ, *youth*, Mrk. x. 20. Acts, xxvi. 4. 1 Tim. iv. 12.

νεόφυτος, *newly planted; a neophyte, a novice*, 1 Tim. iii. 6.

νεύω, *to nod;* with dat., *to beckon to, to make signs*, Joh. xiii. 24. Acts, xxiv. 10.

νεφέλη, ἡ, *a cloud*, Matt. xxiv. 30. Mrk. ix. 7. Luke, ix. 34 etc.

νέφος, τὸ, *a cloud;* met., *a multitude*, Hebr. xii. 1.

νεφρὸς, ὁ, *a kidney;* pl., *the secret thoughts*, Rev. ii. 23.

νεωκόρος, ὁ, Lat. *aedituus, the caretaker of a temple; a worshipper, a devotee*, Acts, xix. 35.

νεωτερικὸς, *peculiar to youth, youthful*, 2 Tim. ii. 22.

νεώτερος, compar. of νέος, *younger*, Joh. xxi. 18. Tit. ii. 6. 1 Tim. v. 1; *an attendant*, Acts, v. 6; *an inferior*, Luke, xxii. 26.

νὴ, a particle employed in affirmations and oaths, *by*, Lat. *per*, 1 Cor. xv. 31.

νήθω, *to spin*, Matt. vi. 28. Luke, xii. 27.

νηπιάζω, *to be a babe*, 1 Cor. xiv. 20.

νήπιος, ὁ, *a babe, a child*, Matt. xxi. 16. 1 Cor. xiii. 11; *a minor*, Gal. iv. 1; *a babe in knowledge*, Matt. xi. 25. Rom. ii. 20.

νησίον, τὸ, *a small island*, Acts, xxvii. 16.

νῆσος, ἡ, *an island*, Acts, xiii. 6. xxvii. 26 etc.

νηστεία, ἡ, *fasting*, Luke, ii. 37. Acts, xiv. 23; *the public fast* of the Jews, Acts, xxvii. 9; *want of food*, 2 Cor. vi. 5. xi. 27.

νηστεύω, *to fast*, Matt. iv. 2. vi. 16, 17, 18. Mrk. ii. 18 etc.

νῆστις, *without food, fasting*, Matt. xv. 32. Mrk. viii. 3.

νηφάλιος, *temperate*, 1 Tim. iii. 2, 11. Tit. ii. 2.

νήφω, *to be sober; to be circumspect*, 1 Pet. i. 13. iv. 7. v. 8. 1 Thess. v. 6, 8. 2 Tim. iv. 5. (RV uniformly *to be sober*.)

νικάω, *to conquer, to overcome*, Joh. xvi. 33. Luke, xi. 22; *to prevail*, Rev. v. 5; *to come off superior* in a suit or contest, Rom. iii. 4. Cf. Rev. xv. 2.

νίκη, ἡ, *victory*, 1 Joh. v. 4.

νῖκος, τὸ, a later form for νίκη, 1 Cor. xv. 54, 55, 57.

νιπτὴρ, ὁ, *a basin*, Joh. xiii. 5. (A NT form.)

νίπτω, *to wash*, 1 Tim. v. 10. Joh. xiii. 5, 8, 12, 14.

νοέω, *to understand*, Joh. xii. 40. Matt. xv. 17; *to reflect upon, to consider*, Matt. xxiv. 15. Mrk. xiii. 14.

νόημα, τὸ, *a thought*, 2 Cor. x. 5. Philipp. iv. 7; *the mind*, 2 Cor. iii. 14. iv. 4.

νόθος, *illegitimate; a bastard*, Hebr. xii. 8.

νομὴ, ἡ, *pasturage*, Joh. x. 9; met., *growth, increase*, νομὴν ἕξει, *shall spread*, 2 Tim. ii. 17.

νομίζω, *to think, to suppose,* Acts, vii. 25. viii. 20. xiv. 19; *νομίζεσθαι, to be customary,* Acts, xvi. 13. (Here Westcott reads οὗ ἐνομίζομεν προσευχὴν εἶναι, *where we supposed there was a place of prayer.*)

νομικὸς, *of* or *about the law,* Tit. iii. 9; as subst., *an interpreter* or *teacher of the law,* Matt. xxii. 35. Luke, x. 25. Cf. γραμματεύς.

νομίμως, *according to law, lawfully,* 1 Tim. i. 8. 2 Tim. ii. 5.

νόμισμα, τὸ, *money, coin,* Matt. xxii. 19.

νομοδιδάσκαλος, ὁ, *a teacher of the law,* Acts, v. 34. Luke, v. 17; applied also to those among Christians who went about as champions of the Mosaic law, 1 Tim. i. 7. (Confined to ecclesiastical writers.)

νομοθεσία, ἡ, *law-giving, legislation,* Rom. ix. 4.

νομοθετέω, *to give laws;* pass., *to be legislated for, to be furnished with laws;* νενομοθέτηται ἐπ᾽ αὐτῆς, *received the law upon the foundation of the priesthood,* Hebr. vii. 11; *to be enacted,* Hebr. viii. 6.

νομοθέτης, ὁ, *a lawgiver, a legislator,* James, iv. 12.

νόμος, ὁ, *a law,* Rom. iii. 27. ix. 31; *the Mosaic law,* Matt. v. 18. xii. 5. xxii. 36. Rom. ii. 17, 18; τὰ τοῦ νόμου, *the moral requirements of the law,* Rom. ii. 14; *the Old Testament Scriptures,* Joh. xii. 34. Acts, xxiv. 14.

νοσέω, *to be sick;* met., *to have depraved desires, to dote,* 1 Tim. vi. 4.

νόσημα, τὸ, *sickness, disease,* Joh. v. 4. (Omitted by Westcott.)

νόσος, ἡ, *disease,* Matt. iv. 23. viii. 17 etc.

νοσσία, ἡ, later form for νεοσσία, *a brood* of young birds, Luke, xiii. 34.

νοσσίον, τὸ, *a brood* of young birds, Matt. xxiii. 37.

νοσσὸς, ὁ, see νεοσσός.

νοσφίζω, *to remove;* mid., *to purloin,* Tit. ii. 10; *to withhold, to keep back,* Acts, v. 2, 3.

νότος, ὁ, *the south wind,* Luke, xii. 55. Acts, xxvii. 13; *the southern quarter of the heavens, the South,* Matt. xii. 42. Luke, xi. 31. xiii. 29.

νουθεσία, ἡ, *admonition,* Tit. iii. 10. 1 Cor. x. 11. Ephes. vi. 4.

νουθετέω, *to admonish,* Acts, xx. 31. 1 Cor. iv. 14 etc.

νουμηνία, ἡ, *the newmoon,* Coloss. ii. 16. (See νεομηνία.)

νουνεχῶς, adv., *wisely, discreetly,* Mrk. xii. 34.

νοῦς, ὁ, *mind, understanding,* 1 Cor. ii. 16. Rev. xvii. 9. Luke, xxiv. 45; *calculation,* Philipp. iv. 7; *opinion,* 1 Cor. i. 10; *concupiscence, desire,* Coloss. ii. 18.

νύμφη, ἡ, *a bride,* Joh. iii. 29. Rev. xviii. 23; *a daughter-in-law,* Matt. x. 35. Luke, xii. 53.

νυμφίος, ὁ, *a bridegroom,* Joh. ii. 9. iii. 29. Luke, v. 34.

νυμφὼν, ὁ, *the bride-chamber*, Mrk. ii. 19. Luke, v. 34; *the room in which the marriage ceremonies were held*, Matt. xxii. 10.

νῦν, and **νυνί**, adv. of time, *now*, Joh. iv. 18. ix. 21. (The reader is referred to his Greek Grammar.)

νύξ, ἡ, *night*, Joh. iii. 2. Matt. ii. 14. 1 Thess. v. 7; *death*, Joh. ix. 4.

νύσσω, *to pierce*, Joh. xix. 34.

νυστάζω, *to nod; to become drowsy*, Matt. xxv. 5; met., *to linger*, 2 Pet. ii. 3.

νυχθήμερον, τὸ, *a night and a day, the space of 24 hours*, 2 Cor. xi. 25. (Confined to the NT and very late writers.)

νωθρὸς, *sluggish, dull*, Hebr. v. 11. vi. 12.

νῶτος, ὁ, but in the plur. τὰ νῶτα, *the back*, Rom. xi. 10.

Ξ

ξενία, ἡ, *hospitality; a lodging-place, lodgings*, Acts, xxviii. 23.

ξενίζω, *to receive as a guest, to entertain*, Acts, x. 23. xxviii. 7; *to surprise, to astonish*, Acts, xvii. 20; pass., *to lodge*, Acts, x. 6, 18, 32. xxi. 16; *to be surprised*, 1 Pet. iv. 4, 12.

ξενοδοχέω, *to exercise hospitality*, 1 Tim. v. 10.

ξένος, ὁ, *a guest-friend; a foreigner, a stranger*, Matt. xxv. 35, 38, 43, 44. 3 Joh. 5; *an alien*, Ephes. ii. 12; *one who entertains guests, a host*, Rom. xvi. 23; as adj., *new, novel*, Acts, xvii. 18. Hebr. xiii. 9. 1 Pet. iv. 12.

ξέστης, ὁ, a vessel for measuring liquids, and holding about a pint, *a sextarius; a wooden vessel* or *cup*, Mrk. vii. 4.

ξηραίνω, *to dry up, to wither*, James, i. 11; pass., *to be withered*, Mrk. xi. 21. Matt. xiii. 6. xxi. 19; *to be dried up*, Mrk. v. 29. Rev. xvi. 12; *to be ripened, to be ripe*, Rev. xiv. 15; *to waste away, to pine away*, Mrk. ix. 18.

ξηρὸς, *dry*, Luke, xxiii. 31 ("If the good be treated so, what will be done to the wicked?" Thayer); ἡ ξηρὰ (sc. γῆ), *dry land, land*, Matt. xxiii. 15. Hebr. xi. 29; *withered, wasted*, Matt. xii. 10. Mrk. iii. 3. Luke, vi. 6, 8. Cf. Mrk. iii. 1.

ξύλινος, *wooden, made of wood*, 2 Tim. ii. 20. Rev. ix. 20.

ξύλον, τὸ, *wood*, 1 Cor. iii. 12. Rev. xviii. 12; *the stocks*, Acts, xvi. 24; *the cross*, Acts, v. 30. x. 39. xiii. 29; *a tree*, Luke, xxiii. 31; *a bludgeon, a staff*, Matt. xxvi. 47, 55. Luke, xxii. 52.

ξυράω, *to shave*, Acts, xxi. 24. 1 Cor. xi. 5, 6.

Ο

ὁ, ἡ, τὸ, originally a demonstrative pronoun, *he, she, it;* subsequently as a definitive article, *the*. (The reader is referred to his Greek Grammar.)

ὀγδοήκοντα, numer., *eighty*, Luke, ii. 37. xvi. 7.

ὄγδοος, numer., *the eighth*, Acts, vii. 8. Luke, i. 59.

ὄγκος, ὁ, *weight, encumbrance*, Hebr. xii. 1.

ὅδε, ἥδε, τόδε, a demonstrative pronoun, *this*, Luke, x. 39 etc. (The reader is referred to his Greek Grammar.)

ὁδεύω, *to journey*, Luke, x. 33.

ὁδηγέω, *to guide*, Matt. xv. 14. Luke, vi. 39. Rev. vii. 17 etc.

ὁδηγός, ὁ, *a guide*, Acts, i. 16. Matt. xv. 14. xxiii. 16, 24.

ὁδοιπορέω, *to journey*, Acts, x. 9. Cf. xxvi. 12.

ὁδοιπορία, ἡ, *a journey, a journeying*, Joh. iv. 6. 2 Cor. xi. 26.

ὁδοποιέω, *to construct a road; to journey*, Mrk. ii. 23. (Here Westcott reads ὁδὸν ποιεῖν.)

ὁδός, ἡ, *a way*, Matt. ii. 12. vii. 13, 14. Luke, x. 4 etc.; σαββάτου ὁδόν, *a sabbath day's journey*, Acts, i. 12; ὁδὸν ἐθνῶν, *a road that leads to the Gentiles*, Matt. x. 5 ; ὁδὸν ἁγίων, Hebr. ix. 8 (RV *the way into the holy place*); ἡ ὁδὸς, *the Christian religion*, Acts, ix. 2. xix. 9, 23. xxiv. 22.

ὁδούς, ὁ, *a tooth*, Matt. v. 38. Acts, vii. 54. Rev. ix. 8.

ὀδυνάω, *to cause pain;* pass., *to be tormented*, Luke, xvi. 24, 25 ; mid., *to feel pain, to sorrow*, Luke, ii. 48. Acts, xx. 38.

ὀδύνη, ἡ, *pain, sorrow*, Rom. ix. 2. 1 Tim. vi. 10.

ὀδυρμός, ὁ, *lamentation, mourning*, Matt. ii. 18. 2 Cor. vii. 7.

ὄζω, *to smell, to emit a smell*, Joh. xi. 39.

ὅθεν, adv., *whence*, Matt. xii. 44. Acts, xiv. 26 ; *from the place where*, Matt. xxv. 24, 26 ; *wherefore*, Acts, xxvi. 19. Matt. xiv. 7. Hebr. ii. 17. iii. 1 etc.; *whereby*, 1 Joh. ii. 18.

ὀθόνη, ἡ, *a linen cloth*, Acts, x. 11. xi. 5.

ὀθόνιον, τὸ, *a linen bandage*, Joh. xix. 40. xx. 5, 6, 7.

οἶδα, οἶσθα, (οἶδας), οἶδεν, etc., *to know*—a perfect strictly = *I have perceived*, from εἴδω.

οἰκειακὸς, see οἰκιακός.

οἰκεῖος, *belonging to the family, kindred*, 1 Tim. v. 8 (RV *his own household*); οἰκεῖοι τοῦ θεοῦ, *of the household of God*, Ephes. ii. 19 ; τοὺς οἰκείους τῆς πίστεως, *those that are well-disposed towards the faith*, Gal. vi. 10. (See Pape's Lex. in voc.)

οἰκετεία, ἡ, *servants, household*, Matt. xxiv. 45.

οἰκέτης, ὁ, *a domestic, a servant*, Luke, xvi. 13. Acts, x. 7. Rom. xiv. 4. 1 Pet. ii. 18.

οἰκέω, *to dwell*, 1 Tim. vi. 16. Rom. vii. 17, 20 etc.

οἴκημα, τὸ, *a habitation ; a prison*, Acts, xii. 7. (See Pape's Lex. in voc. οἴκημα, *fin.*)

οἰκητήριον, τὸ, *a dwelling place, a habitation*, Jude, 6 ; met., *the body*, 2 Cor. v. 2.

οἰκία, ἡ, *a house*, Matt. ii. 11. v. 15. Luke, xv. 8 etc.; *a household*, Matt. xii. 25. Joh. iv. 53; *goods, property*, Mrk. xii. 40. Luke, xx. 47. (See Shilleto ad Dem. Fals. Leg. § 279.)

οἰκιακὸς, *belonging to the household*, Matt. x. 25, 36. ("In opposition to οἰκοδεσπότης, Matt. x. 25," Pape in Lex.)

οἰκοδεσποτέω, *to be master of a house, to rule the household*, 1 Tim. v. 14.

οἰκοδεσπότης, ὁ, *the master of the house*, Matt. x. 25. xiii. 27. Luke, xiv. 21 etc.

οἰκοδομέω, *to build a house; to build*, Matt. vii. 24. Luke, xiv, 30 etc.; *to found*, Matt. xvi. 18; *to restore, to repair*, Matt. xxiii. 29. xxvi. 61. Luke, xi. 47; *to edify*, 1 Cor. viii. 1. xiv. 4; pass., *to be encouraged, to be emboldened*, 1 Cor. viii. 10.

οἰκοδομὴ, ἡ, *a building, a structure*, Matt. xxiv. 1. 1 Cor. iii. 9. Mrk. xiii. 1; *edification*, 1 Cor. xiv. 3. Rom. xiv. 19. xv. 2 etc.

οἰκοδομία, ἡ, *the act of building; advancement*, a var. lect. ad 1 Tim. i. 4.

οἰκοδόμος, ὁ, *a builder, an architect*, Acts, iv. 11.

οἰκονομέω, *to be a steward*, Luke, xvi. 2.

οἰκονομία, ἡ, *a stewardship*, Luke, xvi. 2, 3, 4; *a dispensation*, Ephes. i. 10. iii. 2, 9. 1 Tim. i. 4. Coloss. i. 25.

οἰκονόμος, ὁ, *a steward*, Luke, xii. 42. 1 Cor. iv. 2. Gal. iv. 2. 1 Pet. iv. 10 etc.; *a treasurer*, Rom. xvi. 23.

οἶκος, ὁ, *a house*, Luke, i. 23, 40, 56 etc.; κατ' οἴκους, *from house to house*, Acts, viii. 3. xx. 20; *race, lineage*, Luke, i. 27. ii. 4; *household*, Luke, x. 5. 1 Tim. iii. 4 ("οἰκία invariably means the *dwelling house*, or the *house* in the sense in which we say *House of Stuart, House of Brunswick*," Shilleto ad Dem. Fals. Leg. § 279.)

οἰκουμένη, ἡ, *the whole inhabited earth, the world*, Matt. xxiv. 14. Acts, xi. 28. Luke, xxi. 26; *the universe*, Hebr. ii. 5; *the Roman world*, Luke, ii. 1.

οἰκουργὸς, *occupied in household affairs, domestic*, Tit. ii. 5. (Found no where else.)

οἰκουρὸς, *domestic*, a var. lect. ad Tit. ii. 5.

οἰκτείρω, *to have compassion on*, Rom. ix. 15.

οἰκτιρμὸς, *compassion*, Coloss. iii. 12. Philipp. ii. 1; plur., *mercies*, Rom. xii. 1. Hebr. x. 28.

οἰκτίρμων, *compassionate, merciful*, Luke, vi. 36. James, vii. 11.

οἰνοπότης, ὁ, *a drinker of wine, a wine-bibber*, Matt. xi. 19. Luke, vii. 34.

οἶνος, ὁ, *wine*, Matt. ix. 17. Joh. ii. 3, 9, 10 etc.; οἶνος τοῦ θυμοῦ, *the wine of the wrath* of God, Rev. xiv. 10. xix. 15.

οἰνοφλυγία, ἡ, *drunkenness*, 1 Pet. iv. 3.

οἴο] GREEK-ENGLISH LEXICON [ὀλω

οἴομαι, *to think, to suppose*, Joh. xxi. 25. Philipp. i. 17. James, i. 7.

οἷος, *such as*, Matt. xxiv. 21. Mrk. ix. 3. xiii. 19 etc.; οἴῳ δήποτ' οὖν νοσήματι, *with whatsoever disease*, Joh. v. 4; οὐχ οἷον δὲ ὅτι ἐκπέπτωκεν ὁ λόγος τοῦ θεοῦ, *but not as though the word of God hath come to nought*, Rom. ix. 6.

ὀκνέω, *to be loath, to hesitate*, Acts, ix. 38.

ὀκνηρὸς, *slothful*, Matt. xxv. 26. Rom. xii. 11; οὐκ ὀκνηρόν μοί ἐστι, *I am not reluctant*, Philipp. iii. 1.

ὀκταήμερος, *on the eighth day*, Philipp. iii. 5. (A purely NT form.)

ὀκτὼ, numer., *eight*, Luke, ii. 21. Joh. xx. 26 etc.

ὀλέθριος, *destructive*, a var. lect. ad 2 Thess. i. 9.

ὄλεθρος, ὁ, *destruction*, 1 Thess. v. 3. 2 Thess. i. 9. 1 Tim. vi. 9. 1 Cor. v. 5.

ὀλιγοπιστία, ἡ, *littleness of faith*, Matt. xvii. 20. (An ecclesiastical form, but found nowhere else in the NT.]

ὀλιγόπιστος, *of little faith*, Matt. vi. 30. viii. 25 etc. (Found only in the NT.)

ὀλίγος, *little, few*, 1 Tim. v. 23. Acts, xiv. 28. Luke, xii. 48. Matt. ix. 37; ὀλίγον, *for a short while*, Mrk. vi. 31. Cf. James, iv. 14; *for little*, 1 Tim. iv. 8; ἐν ὀλίγῳ, *in few words, briefly*, Ephes. iii. 3; "ἐν ὀλίγῳ, *almost*, Acts, xxvi. 28, 29. (But the passage is rather to the effect that Agrippa says to Paul, "with a little trouble thou wouldest fain make me a Christian." The phrase contrasted with ἐν ὀλίγῳ is ἐν μεγάλῳ.) δι' ὀλίγων, *briefly*, 1 Pet. v. 12; ἐπ' ὀλίγα, *over a few things*, Matt. xxv. 21, 23.

ὀλιγόψυχος, *fainthearted*, 1 Thess. v. 14.

ὀλιγωρέω, *to make light of, to disregard*, Hebr. xii. 5.

ὀλίγως, adv., *scarcely*, 2 Pet. ii. 18.

ὀλοθρευτὴς, ὁ, *a destroyer*, 1 Cor. x. 10. (Found only in this passage.)

ὀλοθρεύω, *to destroy*, Hebr. xi. 28.

ὀλοκαύτωμα, τὸ, Lat. *holocaustum, a whole burnt offering*, Hebr. x. 6, 8. Mrk. xii. 33.

ὁλοκληρία, ἡ, *perfect soundness*, Acts, iii. 16.

ὁλόκληρος, *complete in all its parts; entire, sound*, 1 Thess. v. 23. James, i. 4.

ὀλολύζω, *to wail, to lament*, James, v. 1.

ὅλος, *whole*, Matt. xxii. 40. Joh. vii. 23. Acts, xi. 26.

ὁλοτελὴς, *complete in all respects*, 1 Thess. v. 23.

ὄλυνθος, ἡ, *an unripe fig*, Rev. vi. 13.

ὅλως, adv., *wholly, altogether*, 1 Cor. vi. 7; μὴ ὅλως, and οὐκ ὅλως, *not at all*, Matt. v. 34. 1 Cor. xv. 29.

ὄμβρος, ὁ, *a shower*, Luke, xii. 54.

ὁμείρομαι, a late form for ἱμείρομαι, with genit., *to strongly desire, to have a strong affection for*, 1 Thess. ii. 8.

ὁμιλέω, *to associate with; to converse with*, Acts, xx. 11. xxiv. 26. Luke, xxiv. 14.

ὁμιλία, ἡ, *companionship; communion*, 1 Cor. xv. 33.

ὅμιλος, ὁ, *a crowd, a multitude*, a var. lect. ad Rev. xviii. 17.

ὁμίχλη, ἡ, *a cloud, a mist*, 2 Pet. ii. 17.

ὄμμα, τὸ, *an eye*, Matt. xx. 34. Mrk. viii. 23.

ὄμνυμι, and ὀμνύω, *to swear*, James, v. 12. Matt. v. 34.

ὁμοθυμαδὸν, *with one accord*, Acts, i. 14. ii. 46. iv. 24 etc.

ὁμοιάζω, *to be like*, a var. lect. ad Matt. xxiii. 27.

ὁμοιοπαθὴς, *of like feelings*, Acts, xiv. 15. James, v. 17.

ὅμοιος, *like, similar*, Joh. ix. 9. Acts, xvii. 29. Jude, 7; *equal*, Rev. xiii. 4. xviii. 18.

ὁμοιότης, ἡ, *likeness*, Hebr. iv. 15. vii. 15.

ὁμοιόω, *to make like; to liken, to compare*, Matt. xi. 16. Mrk. iv. 30. Luke, vii. 31; pass., *to be likened to, to resemble*, Matt. vi. 8. vii. 24. xviii. 23.

ὁμοίωμα, τὸ, *likeness*, Rom. i. 23. vi. 5. viii. 3; *figure*, Rev. ix. 7.

ὁμοίως, adv., *in like manner, likewise*, Mrk. iv. 16. Joh. v. 19. Luke, iii. 11. x. 37.

ὁμοίωσις, ἡ, *likeness*, James, iii. 9.

ὁμολογέω, *to confess*, Joh. i. 20. 1 Joh. i. 9 etc.; *to promise*, Matt. xiv. 7. Acts, vii. 17.

ὁμολογία, ἡ, *confession*, 1 Tim. vi. 12, 13; *profession*, Hebr. iv. 14. x. 23.

ὁμολογουμένως, *confessedly, without controversy*, 1 Tim. iii. 16.

ὁμότεχνος, *of the same handicraft*, Acts, xviii. 3.

ὁμοῦ, adv., *together*, Acts, ii. 1. Joh. iv. 36. xx. 4.

ὁμόφρων, *of the same mind, like-minded*, 1 Pet. iii. 8.

ὅμως, *nevertheless, yet*, Gal. iii. 15; ὅμως μέντοι, *yet however*, Joh. xii. 42.

ὄναρ, τὸ, *a dream*, Matt. i. 20. ii. 12, 13, 19 etc. ("Used only in the nomin. and accus.," Pape's Lex. in voc.)

ὀνάριον, τὸ, *a little ass*, Joh. xii. 14.

ὀνειδίζω, *to upbraid, to reproach*, James, i. 5. Matt. v. 11. xi. 20; *to revile*, Mrk. xv. 32.

ὀνειδισμὸς, ὁ, *a reproach*, Rom. xv. 3. Hebr. xi. 26. xiii. 13.

ὄνειδος, τὸ, *reproach, disgrace*, Luke, i. 25.

ὀνικὸς, *for an ass*; μύλος ὀνικὸς, *a millstone*, Matt. xviii. 6. Mrk. ix. 42.

ὀνίνημι, *to profit, to help*; σου ὀναίμην, *may I have joy in thee*, Philem. 20.

ὄνομα, τὸ, *a name*, Philipp. ii. 10. Luke, i. 26, 27. ii. 25.

ὀνομάζω, *to name*, Luke, vi. 13, 14. 2 Tim. ii. 19. Rom. xv. 20.

ὄνος, ὁ and ἡ, *an ass*, Luke, xiii. 15. Matt. xxi. 7 etc.

ὄντως, adv., *truly, really*, Luke, xxiii. 47. Mrk. xi. 32.

ὄξος, τό, *vinegar, sour wine*, Joh. xix. 29. Luke, xxiii. 36.

ὀξύς, *sharp*, Rev. i. 16. xiv. 17; *swift, quick*, Rom. iii, 15.

ὀπή, ἡ, *a hole*, Hebr. xi. 38; *an opening, a fissure*, James, iii. 11.

ὄπισθεν, adv., *from behind; behind, after*, Matt. ix. 20. xv. 23. Luke, xxiii. 26 etc.

ὀπίσω, adv. *back*, Matt. xxiv. 18; *behind*, Luke, vii. 38; τὰ ὀπίσω, *the things that are behind*, Philipp. iii. 13; εἰς τὰ ὀπίσω ἀπέρχεσθαι, *to go backwards, to retreat*, Joh. xviii. 6; ἐστράφη εἰς τὰ ὀπίσω, *she turned back*, Joh. xx. 14. Cf. Mrk. xiii. 16. Luke, xvii. 31; βλέπειν εἰς τὰ ὀπίσω, *to look back*, Luke, ix. 62; as prepos. with genit., *after*; ὀπίσω τινὸς ἔρχεσθαι, *to follow any one*, Matt. xvi. 24. Luke, ix. 23; of time, *after*, Joh. i. 15, 27, 30. Matt. iii. 11.

ὁπλίζω. *to arm*; mid., *to furnish oneself with*, 1 Pet. iv. 1.

ὅπλον, τό, *an implement, an instrument*, Rom. vi. 13; in plur., *weapons, armour*, Rom. xiii. 12. 2 Cor. x. 4.

ὁποῖος, *of what sort*, 1 Cor. iii. 13; *what manner of*, James, i. 24. 1 Thess. i. 9; τοιοῦτος ὁποῖος, *such as*, Acts, xxvi. 29.

ὁπότε, *when*, Luke, vi. 3. [Westcott has ὅτε.]

ὅπου, adv., *where*, Matt. vi. 19, 20, 21; for ὅποι, *whither*, Joh. viii. 21. xiv. 4. Cf. Matt. viii. 19; *where*, i.e. *in which state*, Coloss. iii. 11. 1 Cor. iii. 3. 2 Pet. ii. 11. (RV in these two last passages *whereas*.)

ὀπτάνω, *to see;* mid., *to appear*, Acts, i. 3. ("ὀπτάνω = ὀπταίνω, NT." Pape's Lex.)

ὀπτασία, ἡ, *a vision*, 2 Cor. xii. 1. Acts, xxvi. 19. Luke, i. 22.

ὀπτός, *broiled*, Luke, xxiv. 42.

ὀπώρα, ἡ, *autumn; fruits*, Rev. xviii. 14.

ὅπως, *how, in what manner*, Matt. xxii. 15; *that, in order that*, Acts, ix. 2. (The reader is referred to his Greek Grammar.)

ὅραμα, τό, *that which is seen; a sight*, Acts, vii. 31; *a vision*, Acts, ix. 10. x. 3. xii. 9 etc.

ὅρασις, ἡ, *the act of seeing; appearance*, Rev. iv. 3; *a vision*, Rev. ix. 17. Acts, ii. 17.

ὁρατός, *visible*, Coloss. i. 16.

ὁράω, *to see*, Joh. viii. 57. xiv. 7, 9; *to perceive*, Acts, viii. 23. James, ii. 24; with εἰς τινα, *to look upon*, Joh. xix. 37; *to take heed, to beware*, Matt. viii. 4. xviii. 10; pass., *to appear*, Acts, xxvi. 16. Luke, i. 11. ix. 31.

ὀργὴ, ἡ, *anger, wrath*, Rom. ii. 5. Ephes. v. 6. Matt. iii. 7; *impulse*, Ephes. ii. 3.

ὀργίζω, *to provoke, to irritate;* pass., *to be angry, to be wroth*, Matt. v. 22. xviii. 34. Ephes. iv. 26 etc.

ὀργίλος, *prone to anger, irritable*, Tit. i. 7.

ὀργυιά, ἡ, *a fathom,* Acts, xxvii. 28.

ὀρέγω, *to stretch forth;* mid., *to desire,* 1 Tim. iii. 1. Hebr. xi. 16; *to indulge in,* 1 Tim. vi. 10.

ὀρεινός, *mountainous, hilly,* Luke, i. 39, 65. (Supply χώρα.)

ὄρεξις, ἡ, *desire, lust,* Rom. i. 27.

ὀρθοποδέω, *to walk in a straight course; to act uprightly,* Gal. ii. 14. (Not found elsewhere.)

ὀρθός, *straight,* Hebr. xii. 13; *upright, erect,* Acts, xiv. 10.

ὀρθοτομέω, *to cut straight;* met., *to handle aright, i.e. to teach correctly,* 2 Tim. ii. 15. (See Pape's Lexicon in voc. Found only in this passage and in ecclesiastical writers.)

ὀρθρίζω, *to rise early in the morning;* with πρός τινα, *to come early in the morning to a person,* Luke, xxi. 38. ("=ὀρθρεύω," Pape's Lex.)

ὀρθρινός, *early,* Luke, xxiv. 22.

ὄρθριος, *early,* a var. lect. ad Luke, xxiv. 22.

ὄρθρος, ὁ, *daybreak, dawn;* ὄρθρου βαθέως, *at early dawn,* Luke, xxiv. 1. (See βαθέως and βαθύς); ὄρθρου, *at dawn,* Joh. viii. 2; ὑπὸ τὸν ὄρθρον, *at the approach of dawn,* Acts, v. 21. (Cf. Lat. *sub lucem.*)

ὀρθῶς, adv., *rightly,* Luke, vii. 43. x. 28. xx. 21.

ὁρίζω, *to define; to determine,* Acts, xi. 29. xvii. 26; *to appoint,* Hebr. iv. 7. Acts, x. 42; ὡρισμένος, *determinate,* settled, Acts, ii. 23; κατὰ τὸ ὡρισμένον, *as hath been determined,* Luke, xxii. 22; τοῦ ὁρισθέντος υἱοῦ θεοῦ, *who was declared to be the son of God,* Rom. i. 4.

ὁρινὸς, see ὀρεινός.

ὅριον, τὸ, *a limit, a border;* in the NT always in the plural, Matt. ii. 16. iv. 13. viii. 34 etc.

ὁρκίζω, with accus. of person, *to administer an oath to;* with two accusatives, ὁρκίζω σε τὸν θεόν, *I adjure thee by God,* Mrk. v. 7. So also Acts, xix. 13. Cf. Matt. xxvi. 63.

ὅρκος, ὁ, *an oath,* Matt. xxvi. 72. Luke, i. 73 etc.; plur., *vows,* Matt. v. 33.

ὁρκωμοσία, ἡ, *the taking of an oath; an oath,* Hebr. vii. 20, 21, 28.

ὁρμάω, *to urge on;* intrans., *to rush,* Matt. viii. 32. Acts, vii. 57. xix. 29 etc.

ὁρμή, ἡ, *an impulse,* James, iii. 4; *a hostile movement, an onset,* Acts, xiv. 5.

ὅρμημα, τὸ, *an impulse, impetus,* Rev. xviii. 21.

ὄρνεον, τὸ, *a bird,* Rev. xviii. 2. xix. 17, 21.

ὄρνιξ, ὁ and **ἡ,** *a bird,* a var. lect. for ὄρνις ad Luke, xiii. 34. (Not found in the nominative.)

ὄρνις, ὁ and **ἡ,** *a bird; a hen,* Matt. xxiii. 37. Luke, xiii. 34.

ὁροθεσία, ἡ, *a fixing of limits;* plur., *bounds,* Acts, xvii. 26. (A purely ecclesiastical word.)

ὄρο]   *GREEK-ENGLISH LEXICON*   **[οὐδ**

ὄρος, τὸ, *a mountain*, Matt. v. 1, 14. viii. 1. xvii. 20.

ὀρύσσω, *to dig*, Matt. xxi. 33. xxv. 18. Mrk. xii. 1.

ὀρφανὸς, *deprived of parents; an orphan*, James, i. 27; *deserted, desolate*, Joh. xiv. 18.

ὀρχέομαι, *to dance*, Matt. xi. 17. xiv. 6. Luke, vii. 32.

ὅς, ἥ, ὅ, Lat. *qui, quae, quod, who, which*, Matt. i. 16. xxvii. 57 etc.; ὃς μὲν, ὃς δὲ, for ὁ μὲν, ὁ δὲ, *the one, the other*, Matt. xxi. 35. (The reader is referred to his Greek Grammar.)

ὁσάκις, *as often as*, 1 Cor. xi. 25. Rev. xi. 6.

ὅσιος, *pious, holy*, Tit. i. 8. Hebr. vii. 26. Acts, ii. 27; τὰ ὅσια, *the promised blessings*, Acts, xiii. 34.

ὁσιότης, ἡ, *holiness*, Luke, i. 75. Ephes. iv. 24.

ὁσίως, adv., *piously*, 1 Thess. ii. 10.

ὀσμὴ, ἡ, *smell, odour*, Joh. xii. 3. Ephes. v. 2. Philipp. iv. 18; *savour*, 2 Cor. ii. 14, 16.

ὅσος, *as much as*, Joh. vi. 11; ὅσοι, *as many as*, Matt. xiv. 36. Acts, iv. 6, 34; ἐφ' ὅσον, *inasmuch as*, Matt. xxv. 40, 45. Rom. xi. 13; ἐφ' ὅσον χρόνον, *as long as*, Rom. vii. 1. Cf. Matt. ix. 15. Mrk. ii. 19; μικρὸν ὅσον ὅσον, *for a very little while*, Hebr. x. 37; καθ' ὅσον, *by as much as*, Hebr. iii. 3; *inasmuch as*, Hebr. vii. 20. ix. 27; τοσούτῳ, ὅσῳ, *by so much, as*, Hebr. i. 4 etc.

ὀστέον, τὸ, *a bone*, Joh. xix. 36. Luke, xxiv. 39. Matt. xxiii. 27 etc.

ὅστις, ἥτις, ὅ τι, *whoever, whatever*, Matt. v. 39, 41; ἕως ὅτου, *until*, Luke, xiii. 8; *whilst*, Matt. v. 25.

ὀστράκινος, *of earthenware*, 2 Cor. iv. 7. 2 Tim. ii. 20.

ὄσφρησις, ἡ, *the sense of smelling*, 1 Cor. xii. 17.

ὀσφὺς, and ὀσφῦς, ἡ, *the hip, the loins*, Matt. iii. 4. Luke, xii. 35. Ephes. vi. 14 etc.

ὅταν, *whenever*, Matt. vi. 5; ὅτε, *when*, Joh. ix. 4. (The reader is referred to his Greek Grammar.)

ὅτι, *that*, Matt. ii. 16; *because*, Matt. ii. 18.

οὗ, adv., *where*, Matt. ii. 9; for οἷ, *whither*, Luke, x. i. xxiv. 28 etc.

οὐ, οὐκ, and οὐχ, a negative particle, *not, no*, Matt. v. 37. xii. 43. Joh. i. 20, 21.

οὐὰ, an interjection of derision, *aha!* Mrk. xv. 29.

οὐαὶ, an interjection of denunciation, *woe!* Matt. xi. 21. xviii. 7 etc.; ἡ οὐαὶ, as subst., *the woe*, Rev. ix. 12. xi. 14.

οὐδαμῶς, adv., *by no means*, Matt. ii. 6.

οὐδὲ, *neither, nor, not even, and not*. (The reader is referred to his Greek Grammar.)

οὐδεὶς, *no one*, Matt. vi. 24; οὐδὲν, *nothing*, Matt. v. 13. Joh. viii. 54.

οὐδέποτε, adv., *never at any time, never*, Matt. vii. 23. Luke, xv. 29; οὐδέποτε ἀνέ-

134

γνωτε; *did ye never read?* Matt. xxi. 16, 42.

οὐδέπω, adv., *not yet*, Joh. xx. 9; *never yet*, Joh. xix. 41.

οὐθείς, later and Macedonian Greek, for οὐδείς, 1 Cor. xiii. 2.

οὐκέτι, adv., *no longer*, Matt. xix. 6. Luke, xv. 19, 21 etc.

οὐκοῦν, *therefore;* but οὔκουν;= *nonne ergo?* Joh. xviii. 37, (See Hermann, *Vig.* n. 261.)

οὖν, conj., *therefore*, Matt. xviii. 4. Luke, iii. 9. (The reader is referred to his Greek Grammar.)

οὔπω, adv., *not yet*, Mrk. xiii. 7. Joh. ii. 4; οὔπω νοεῖτε; *do ye not yet perceive?* Matt. xvi. 9.

οὐρά, ἡ, *a tail*, Rev. ix. 10, 19. xii. 4.

οὐράνιος, *heavenly*, Matt. vi. 14, 26, 32. xv. 13.

οὐρανόθεν, adv., *from heaven*, Acts, xiv. 17. xxvi. 13.

οὐρανὸς, ὁ, and plur. οὐρανοί, *heaven, the heavens*, Matt. v. 34, 45. xix. 14. xxi. 25.

οὖς, ὠτὸς, τὸ, and plur. ὦτα, *the ear*, Matt. x. 27. xiii. 9. Acts, vii. 57.

οὐσία, ἡ, *substance, property*, Luke, xv. 12, 13.

οὔτε, conj., *neither;* οὔτε, οὔτε, *neither, nor*, Luke, xx. 35.

οὗτος, *this person, he*, always referring to the person last mentioned, 1 Joh. v. 21; καὶ ταῦτα, and καὶ τοῦτο, *and that too*, 1 Cor. vi. 6, 8; τοῦτο μὲν, τοῦτο δὲ, *partly, partly*, Hebr. x. 33; αὐτὸ τοῦτο, *this very thing*, 2 Cor. ii. 3; εἰς αὐτὸ τοῦτο, *for this very purpose*, Ephes. vi. 22. 2 Pet. i. 5.

οὕτω, and **οὕτως**, *thus, in this manner*, Matt. vi. 9; ὃς μὲν οὕτως, ὃς δὲ οὕτως, *one after this manner, another after that*, 1 Cor. vii. 7. (Here Westcott reads ὁ μὲν ... ὁ δέ).

ὀφειλέτης, ὁ, *a debtor*, Matt. xviii. 24. Rom. xv. 27; *a sinner*, Luke, xiii. 4.

ὀφειλὴ, ἡ, *a debt*, Matt. xviii. 32; plur., *dues*, Rom. xiii. 7.

ὀφείλημα, τὸ, *what is owed, a debt*, Rom. iv. 4; *sin, offence*, Matt. vi. 12.

ὀφείλω, *to owe*, Matt. xviii. 28. Luke, xvi. 5; *to be indebted*, Luke, xi. 4; τὸ ὀφειλόμενον, *the debt*, Matt. xviii. 30; *one ought*, Acts, xvii. 29. Rom. xv. 1.

ὄφελον, properly written ὤφελον, the 2nd aor. of ὀφείλω, but in late Greek appearing as a mere interjection=*would that* (see Hermann, *Vig.* n. 190); ὄφελον ψυχρὸς ἦς, *would that thou wast cold*, Rev. iii. 15; ὄφελον ἐβασιλεύσατε, *would that ye did reign*, 1 Cor. iv. 8; ὄφελον καὶ ἀποκόψονται, *would that they would even mutilate themselves*, Gal. v. 12. Cf. 2 Cor. xi. 1. (See Pape's Lex. in voc. ὀφείλω.)

ὄφελος, τὸ, *profit*, James, ii. 14, 16. 1 Cor. xv. 32.

ὀφθαλμοδουλεία, and **ὀφθαλμοδουλία, ἡ,** *eye-service*, Ephes. vi. 6. Coloss. iii. 22. (Found only in these two passages.)

ὀφθαλμὸς, ὁ, *an eye*, Matt. v. 29, 38. vi. 22, 23 etc.

ὄφις, ὁ, *a serpent*, Matt. vii. 10. x. 16; said of Satan, Rev. xii. 9. xx. 2.

ὀφρὺς, ἡ, *the eye-brow; the brow of a precipice*, Luke, iv. 29.

ὀχλέω, *to trouble, to vex;* pass., *to be vexed*, Acts, v. 16. Cf. Luke, vi. 18.

ὀχλοποιέω, *to collect a crowd*, Acts, xvii. 5. (Found nowhere else.)

ὄχλος, ὁ, *a crowd, a multitude*, Matt. iv. 25. v. 1; *the populace*, Joh. vii. 49; *disturbance, uproar*, Acts, xxiv. 18. Luke, xxii. 6.

ὀχύρωμα, τὸ, *a stronghold*, 2 Cor. x. 4.

ὀψάριον, τὸ, *a little fish*, Joh. vi. 9, 11 etc.

ὀψὲ, adv., *late*, Mrk. xi. 19. xiii. 35; ὀψὲ σαββάτων, *late on the sabbath*, Matt. xxviii. 1.

ὄψιμος, *latter*, James, v. 7.

ὄψιος, *late*, a var. lect. ad Mrk. xi. 11; ὀψία, as subst., *evening*, Matt. viii. 16. xiv. 15, 23. xx. 8 etc.

ὄψις, ἡ, *the sight; face, countenance*, Joh. xi. 44, Rev. i. 16; *appearance*, Joh. vii. 24.

ὀψώνιον, τὸ, *whatever is eaten with bread*, as fish etc.; *rations, wages*, Luke, iii. 14; ἰδίοις ὀψωνίοις, 1 Cor. ix. 7 (RV *at his own charges*); *recompense, wages*, Rom. vi. 23. 2 Cor. xi. 8.

Π

παγιδεύω, *to ensnare, to entrap*, Matt. xxii. 15. (A purely ecclesiastical word, and altogether unknown to the Greeks.)

παγὶς, ἡ, *a trap, a snare;* ὡς παγὶς, *as a snare*, Luke, xxi. 34. Cf. 1 Tim. vi. 9. Rom. xi. 9 2 Tim. ii. 26.

πάθημα, τὸ, *a suffering, an affliction*, Rom. viii. 18. 2 Cor. i. 5, 6, 7. Philipp. iii. 10; *passion*, Rom. vii. 5. Gal. v. 24; *an undergoing, an enduring*, Hebr. ii. 9.

παθητὸς, *destined to suffer*, Acts, xxvi. 23.

πάθος, τὸ, *passion*, Coloss. iii. 5; πάθη ἀτιμίας, *vile passions*, Rom. i. 26; ἐν πάθει ἐπιθυμίας, *in the passion of lust*, 1 Thess. iv. 5.

παιδαγωγὸς, ὁ, *a pedagogue, a tutor*, 1 Cor. iv. 15. Gal. iii. 24, 25.

παιδάριον, τὸ, *a little boy, a lad, a child*, Matt. xi. 16 (Westcott gives παιδίοις), Joh. vi. 9.

παιδεία, ἡ, *education, training*, Ephes. vi. 4; *instruction*, 2 Tim. iii. 16; *chastisement, chastising*, Hebr. xii. 5, 6, 8.

παιδευτὴς, ὁ, *an instructor*, Rom. ii. 20; *a chastiser*, Hebr. xii. 9.

παιδεύω, *to instruct, to admonish*, 2 Tim. ii. 25; *to chasten*, Hebr. xii. 7, 10; *to chastise*, Luke, xxiii. 16, 22; pass., *to be instructed, to be brought up*, Acts, vii. 22; *to be chastened*, 1 Cor. xi. 32. 2 Cor. vi. 9.

παιδόθεν, adv., *from childhood, from a child*, Mrk. ix. 21. (Here Westcott reads παιδιόθεν.)

παιδίον, τό, *a little boy, a young child*, Matt. ii. 8, 11, 13, 14, 20; παιδία, as an affectionate address, *children*, Joh. xxi. 5. 1 Joh. ii. 13, 18.

παιδίσκη, ἡ, *a damsel, a maidservant*, Matt. xxvi. 69. Mrk. xiv. 66, 69.

παίζω, *to play*, 1 Cor. x. 7.

παῖς, ὁ and ἡ, *a child, a boy or girl*, Matt. xvii. 18. Luke, ii. 43. viii. 51, 54; *a servant, a slave*, Matt. viii. 6, 8, 13. Luke, vii. 7. xii. 45. xv. 26.

παίω, *to strike, to smite*, Matt. xxvi. 68. Luke, xxii. 64; *to sting*, Rev. ix. 5.

πάλαι, adv., *long ago*, Matt. xi. 21. Luke, x. 13; *for some time past*, 2 Cor. xii. 19 (RV *all this time*); *in olden time*, Hebr. i. 1; ὁ πάλαι, *the former*, 2 Pet. i. 9.

παλαιὸς, *old, ancient*, Matt. ix. 16, 17. xiii. 52. Mrk. ii. 21, 22.

παλαιότης, ἡ, *oldness, obsoleteness*, Rom. vii. 6.

παλαιόω, *to make old; to abrogate*, Hebr. viii. 13; pass., *to grow old*, Luke, xii. 33. Hebr. i. 11. viii. 13.

πάλη, ἡ, *a wrestling*, Ephes. vi. 12.

παλιγγενεσία, and παλινγενεσία, ἡ, *new birth, regeneration*, Tit. iii. 5; *the restoration of the perfect state of things, the new age*, Matt. xix. 28 (here Pape renders it *the resurrection*).

πάλιν, adv., *back; again*, Matt. iv. 8. xx. 5. xxi. 36. Acts, xi. 10; εἰς τὸ πάλιν, *the second time*, 2 Cor. xiii. 2; *further, moreover*, Matt. v. 33. xiii. 45, 47. xix. 24. Luke, xiii. 20; *on the other hand*, Luke, vi. 43. 1 Cor. xii. 21.

παμπληθεὶ, adv., *all together*, Luke, xxiii. 18.

πάμπολυς, *very great*, Mrk. viii. 1 (here Westcott reads πάλιν πολλοῦ).

πανδοκίον, τό, and πανδοκεὺς, ὁ, see πανδοχεῖον, and πανδοχεύς.

πανδοχεῖον, τό, *an inn*, Luke, x. 34.

πανδοχεὺς, ὁ, *the innkeeper, the host*, Luke, x. 35.

πανήγυρις, ἡ, *a general festal assembly*, Hebr. xii. 23.

πανοικὶ, and πανοικεὶ, adv., *with all his house, with all his family*, Acts, xvi. 34.

πανοπλία, ἡ, *the whole armour*, Ephes. vi. 11, 13. Luke, xi. 22.

πανουργία, ἡ, *craftiness, cunning*, Luke, xx. 23. 2 Cor. iv. 2. xi. 3. Ephes. iv. 14; *false wisdom*, 1 Cor. iii. 19.

πανοῦργος, *crafty*, 2 Cor. xii. 16.

πανταχῇ, and πανταχῇ, adv., *everywhere*, Acts, xxi. 28 (where some read πανταχοῦ).

πανταχόθεν, adv., *from all sides, from every quarter*, a var. lect. ad Mrk. i. 45 (here Westcott reads πάντοθεν).

πανταχοῦ, adv., *everywhere*, Luke, ix. 6. Acts, xvii. 30 etc.

παντελὴς, *complete, perfect*; εἰς τὸ παντελὲς, as an adverb, *completely*, Hebr. vii. 25 (RV *to the uttermost)*; μὴ εἰς τὸ παντελὲς, *not at all,* Luke, xiii. 11.

πάντῃ, and **πάντη,** adv., *everywhere; in every way,* Acts, xxiv. 3.

πάντοθεν, adv., *from all sides, from every quarter,* Mrk. i. 45. Luke, xix. 43. Hebr. ix. 4.

παντοκράτωρ, ὁ, *the ruler of all, the Almighty,* Rev. i. 8. iv. 8. 2 Cor. vi. 18 etc.

πάντοτε, adv., *at all times, always,* Matt. xxvi. 11. Luke, xv. 31. xviii. 1 etc.

πάντως, adv., *altogether; assuredly, doubtless,* Luke, iv. 23. Acts, xxi. 22. xxviii. 4; οὐ πάντως, *not altogether, not at all, in no wise,* Rom. iii. 9. 1 Cor. v. 10.

παρά, prepos., with genit., accus., and dative; with genit., *from,* Gal. i. 12; παρὰ θεοῦ, *from God,* Joh. ix. 16, 33; with accus., *along side of,* Matt. iv. 18. Mrk. i. 16; *with the exception of,* 2 Cor. xi. 24; *contrary to,* Acts, xviii. 13. Rom. i. 26; with dat., *near, beside,* Joh. xix. 25. Luke, ix. 47; *with,* Acts, x. 6. 1 Pet. ii. 20. (The reader is referred to his Greek Grammar.)

παραβαίνω, *to transgress, to violate,* Matt. xv. 2, 3.

παραβάλλω, *to compare, to liken,* a var. lect. ad Mrk. iv. 30; of sailors, *to put in at,* Acts, xx. 15.

παράβασις, ἡ, *a transgression,* Rom. ii. 23. iv. 15. v. 14. Gal. iii. 19. 1 Tim. ii. 14.

παραβάτης, ὁ, *a transgressor,* Rom. ii. 25, 27. James, ii. 11. Gal. ii. 18.

παραβιάζομαι, *to constrain by entreaties,* Acts, xvi. 15. Luke, xxiv. 29. (Confined to the later writers.)

παραβολεύομαι, with ψυχῇ, *to expose himself to danger with regard to his life,* Philipp. ii. 30.

παραβολή, ἡ, *a comparison,* Mrk. iv. 30. xiii. 28. Matt. xxiv. 32; ἐν παραβολῇ, *in a figure,* Hebr. xi. 19; *a fictitious narrative with a heavenly meaning, a parable,* Matt. xiii. 3, 10, 13, 24, 33, 34; *a proverb,* Luke, iv. 23; *a precept,* Luke, xiv. 7; *an enigmatical saying,* Matt. xiii. 35. Mrk. vii. 17.

παραβουλεύομαι, *to consult amiss; to be reckless,* a var. lect. ad Philipp. ii. 30. ("= παραβολεύομαι, NT and late writers," Pape's Lex. in voc.)

παραγγελία, ἡ, *a charge, a command,* Acts, xvi. 24. 1 Tim. i. 5. 1 Thess. iv. 2.

παραγγέλλω, *to charge, to command,* Matt. x. 5. xv. 35. Luke, v. 14 etc.; παραγγελίᾳ παραγγέλλειν, *to charge strictly,* Acts, v. 28.

παραγίνομαι, *to be present, to come,* Matt. ii. 1. iii. 13. Luke, xix. 16. Joh. iii. 23; *to make one's public appearance,* Hebr. ix. 11. Matt. iii. 1; *to stand by one, to assist,* 2 Tim. iv. 16.

παράγω, *to lead past;* in the NT intrans., *to pass by,* Matt. xx. 30. Mrk. ii. 14. Joh. ix. 1; *to depart,* Matt. ix. 9, 27; *to pass away,* 1 Cor. vii. 31. 1 Joh. ii. 8, 17.

παραδειγματίζω, *to make a public example of, to put to open shame,* Hebr. vi. 6; also as a var. lect. ad Matt. i. 19.

παράδεισος, ὁ, a Persian word, *a large enclosure, a park; the heavenly Paradise,* Luke, xxiii. 43. 2 Cor. xii. 4. Rev. ii. 7.

παραδέχομαι, *to accept, to receive,* Mrk. iv. 20. Acts, xvi. 21. xxii. 18. 1 Tim. v. 19; *to acknowledge,* Hebr. xii. 6.

παραδιατριβή, ἡ, *a useless occupation,* a var. lect. ad 1 Tim. vi. 5 (here Westcott reads διαπαρατριβαί).

παραδίδωμι, *to deliver,* Matt. xi. 27. Luke, x. 22; *to give up,* Matt. xxvi. 45. Gal. ii. 20. Rom. i. 24; *to yield up,* Joh. xix. 30; *to commit, to commend,* Acts, xiv. 26. xv. 40; *to deliver up,* Rom. v. 25. Matt. iv. 12. xxvi. 15; *to deliver* verbally, Acts, vi. 14. 1 Cor. xi. 2. Jude, 3; *to permit, to allow,* Mrk. iv. 29.

παράδοξος, *uncommon, wonderful,* Luke, v. 26.

παράδοσις, ἡ, *a transmitting; what is transmitted, doctrine, precept,* 1 Cor. xi. 2. 2 Thess. ii. 15. iii. 6; *tradition,* Matt. xv. 2, 3, 6. Coloss. ii. 8.

παραζηλόω, *to provoke to rivalry,* Rom. x. 19. xi. 11, 14; *to provoke to anger,* 1 Cor. x. 22. (See Pape's Lexicon in voc.)

παραθαλάσσιος, *by the sea,* Matt. iv. 13.

παραθεωρέω, *to overlook, to neglect,* Acts, vi. 1.

παραθήκη, ἡ, *what is committed unto one,* 1 Tim. vi. 20. 2 Tim. i. 14; *a deposit,* 2 Tim. i. 12.

παραινέω, *to exhort, to admonish,* Acts, xxvii. 9, 22.

παραιτέομαι, *to offer excuses,* Luke, xiv. 18; *to excuse,* Luke, xiv. 19; *to deprecate,* Hebr. xii. 19. Acts, xxv. 11; *to refuse, to reject,* 1 Tim. v. 11. Tit. iii. 10. Hebr. xii. 25; *to avoid, to shun,* 1 Tim. iv. 7. 2 Tim. ii. 23.

παρακαθέζομαι, *to seat one's self,* Luke, x. 39.

παρακαθίζω, intrans., *to sit down,* a var. lect. ad Luke, x. 39.

παρακαλέω, *to call for, to summon,* Acts, xxviii. 20; *to exhort, to admonish,* Luke, iii. 18. Hebr. x. 25. Rom. xii. 8. 2 Tim. iv. 2; *to entreat, to beseech,* Matt. viii. 5, 31. xviii. 29, 32. Mrk. v. 23; *to console, to comfort,* 2 Cor. i. 4. ii. 7. vii. 6. Ephes. vi. 22; pass., *to be comforted,* 2 Cor. i. 6. vii. 7, 13. Acts, xx. 12. Matt. v. 4 etc.

παρακαλύπτω, *to hide, to conceal,* Luke, ix. 45.

παρακαταθήκη, ἡ, *a deposit,* a var. lect. ad 2 Tim. i. 12.

παράκειμαι, *to lie beside; to be present,* Rom. vii. 18, 21.

παράκλησις, ἡ, *supplication, entreaty*, 2 Cor. viii. 4; *exhortation*, Rom. xii. 8. Acts, xiii. 15. 1 Thess. ii. 3. 2 Cor. viii. 17; *consolation, comfort*, Luke, ii. 25. Acts, xv. 31. 2 Cor. i. 4, 7. Rom. xv. 5.

παράκλητος, ὁ, *an advocate, an intercessor*, 1 Joh. ii. 1; *the Comforter, the Paraclete*, Joh. xiv. 16, 26. xv. 26. xvi. 7.

παρακοή, ἡ, *a hearing amiss; disobedience*, Rom. v. 19. 2 Cor. x. 6. Hebr. ii. 2.

παρακολουθέω, *to investigate, to trace*, Luke, i. 3; *to follow, to conform to*, 1 Tim. iv. 6. 2 Tim. iii. 10.

παρακούω, *to hear amiss; to refuse to hear, to disregard*, Matt. xviii. 17. Mrk. v. 36.

παρακύπτω, *to stoop down and look into*, Luke, xxiv. 12. Joh. xx. 5, 11; *to look carefully into*, James, i. 25. 1 Pet. i. 12.

παραλαμβάνω, *to take to one's self, to take with one*, Matt. iv. 5, 8. xvii. 1. xxvi. 37. Luke, ix. 10, 28; *to receive, to accept*, Joh. i. 11; *to receive by transmission*, Coloss. iv. 17. Hebr. xii. 28; *to receive by instruction*, 1 Cor. xv. 1, 3. Gal. i. 9, 12. Philipp. iv. 9; pass., *to be taken away, to be carried off*, Matt. xxiv. 40, 41. Luke, xvii. 34, 35.

παραλέγομαι, *to sail past, to coast along*, Acts, xxvii. 8, 13. (See Pape's Lex. in voc.)

παράλιος, *by the sea, maritime*; ἡ παράλιος, sc. χώρα, *the sea coast*, Luke, vi. 17.

παραλλαγή, ἡ, *variation, change*, James, i. 17.

παραλογίζομαι, *to make a miscalculation; to delude, to deceive*, Coloss. ii. 4. James, i. 22.

παραλυτικὸς, *afflicted with paralysis, paralytic*, Matt. iv. 24. viii. 6. ix. 2, 6.

παραλύω, *to weaken, to enfeeble*; παραλελυμένος, *palsied*, Luke, v. 18. Acts, viii, 7. ix. 33; παραλελυμένα γόνατα, *feeble knees*, Hebr. xii. 12.

παραμένω, *to remain beside; to abide, to continue*, James, i. 25. Hebr. vii. 23. 1 Cor. xvi. 6. Philipp. i. 25.

παραμυθέομαι, *to speak to; to encourage, to console*, Joh. xi. 19, 31. 1 Thess. ii. 11. v. 14.

παραμυθία, ἡ, *consolation, comfort*, 1 Cor. xiv. 3.

παραμύθιον, τὸ, *consolation*, Philipp. ii. 1.

παρανομέω, *to act contrary to the law, to violate the law*, Acts, xxiii. 3.

παρανομία, ἡ, *transgression*, 2 Pet. ii. 16.

παραπικραίνω, *to provoke*, Hebr. iii. 16.

παραπικρασμὸς, ὁ, *provocation*, Hebr. iii. 8, 15. (This and the preceding word are confined to ecclesiastical writers.)

παραπίπτω, *to deviate from the right path; to fall away*, Hebr. vi. 6.

παραπλέω, *to sail past*, Acts, xx. 16.

παραπλήσιον, adv., *nigh to, almost*, Philipp. ii. 27.

παραπλησίως, adv., *similarly, in like manner*, Hebr. ii. 14.

παραπορεύομαι, *to pass by*, Matt. xxvii. 39. Mrk. xi. 20. xv. 29.

παράπτωμα, τὸ, *a trespass, a sin*, Matt. vi. 14. Mrk. xi. 25. Rom. iv. 25 etc.

παραρρέω, *to flow past;* pass., *to be carried past, to drift away*, Hebr. ii. 1.

παράσημος, *marked;* ἐν πλοίῳ παρασήμῳ Διοσκούροις, *in a ship marked with the figurehead of the Dioscuri*, Acts, xxviii. 11.

παρασκευάζω, *to prepare*, Acts, x. 10; pass., *to be prepared*, 2 Cor. ix. 2, 3; mid., *to prepare one's self, to get ready*, 1 Cor. xiv. 8.

παρασκευὴ, ἡ, *a making ready;* in the NT, *the day of preparation*, on which the Jews made preparation to celebrate a sabbath or a feast, Matt. xxvii. 62. Mrk. xv. 42. Luke, xxiii. 54. Joh. xix. 31.

παρατείνω, *to stretch out; to extend, to prolong*, Acts, xx. 7.

παρατηρέω, *to watch*, Luke, xx. 20. Mrk. iii. 2; mid., *to watch*, Luke. vi. 7. xiv. 1. Acts, ix. 24; *to keep scrupulously, to observe*, Gal. iv. 10.

παρατήρησις, ἡ, *observation*, Luke, xvii. 20. ("In such a manner that it can be watched with the eyes, i.e. in a visible manner,"Thayer.)

παρατίθημι, *to set before*, Mrk. vi. 41. viii. 6, 7. Luke, ix. 16. Acts, xvi. 34; *to lay before, to propound*, Matt. xiii. 24, 31; mid., *to set forth, to affirm*, Acts, xvii. 3; *to commit, to intrust*, Luke, xii. 48. 1 Tim. i. 18. 2 Tim. ii. 2; *to commend*, Luke, xxiii. 46. Acts, xiv. 23. xx. 32 etc.

παρατυγχάνω, *to meet with*, Acts, xvii. 17.

παραυτίκα, adv., *immediately;* ὁ, ἡ, τὸ παραυτίκα, *that which is at present* or *momentary;* τὸ γὰρ παραυτίκα ἐλαφρὸν τῆς θλίψεως, *for our momentary light affliction*, 2 Cor. iv. 17.

παραφέρω, *to lead aside, to carry away*, Jude, 12. Hebr. xiii. 9; *to remove*, Luke, xxii. 42. Mrk. xiv. 36.

παραφρονέω, *to be beside one's self*, 2 Cor. xi. 23.

παραφρονία, ἡ, *madness*, 2 Pet. ii. 16. (The word is found in no other author.)

παραχειμάζω, *to pass the winter at, to winter in*, Acts, xxvii. 12. xxviii. 11. 1 Cor. xvi. 6. Tit. iii. 12.

παραχειμασία, ἡ, *a wintering*, Acts, xxvii. 12.

παραχρῆμα, adv., *immediately, forthwith*, Matt. xxi. 19, 20. Luke, i. 64. iv. 39 etc.

πάρδαλις, ἡ, *a panther*, Rev. xiii. 2.

παρεδρεύω, *to wait upon, to attend to*, 1 Cor. ix. 13.

πάρειμι, *to be present*, Luke, xiii. 1. Joh. xi. 28 etc.; πρὸς τὸ παρὸν, *for the present*, Hebr. xii. 11; τὰ παρόντα, *what one has, one's property*, Hebr. xiii. 5.

πάρεισαγω, to bring in secretly, 2 Pet. ii. 1.

παρείσακτος, secretly brought in, Gal. ii. 4.

παρεισδύω, to enter secretly, to steal in, Jude, 4.

παρεισέρχομαι, to come in by stealth, to creep in privily, Gal. ii. 4; to enter in addition, to come in beside, Rom. v. 20.

παρεισφέρω, to contribute besides, 2 Pet. i. 5.

παρεκτὸς, prepos., with genit., with the exception of, except, Matt. v. 32. Acts, xxvi. 29; as adv., besides; χωρὶς τῶν παρεκτὸς, independent of those things that come upon me besides, 2 Cor. xi. 28.

παρεμβάλλω, to cast in by the side of; as a military term, to cast up; παρεμβαλοῦσιν οἱ ἐχθροί σου χάρακά σοι, thy enemies shall cast up an intrenchment against thee, Luke, xix. 43.

παρεμβολὴ, ἡ, an encampment, Hebr. xiii. 11, 13; an army, Hebr. xi. 34. Rev. xx. 9; a fortress, a castle, used as the barracks of the Roman garrison in Jerusalem, Acts, xxi. 34, 37. xxii. 24. xxiii. 10, 16, 32.

παρενοχλέω, to trouble, to disturb, Acts, xv. 19.

παρεπίδημος, residing in a foreign land; as subst., a stranger, a sojourner, Hebr. xi. 13. 1 Pet. i. 1. ii. 11.

παρέρχομαι, to pass by, Luke, xviii. 37. Mrk. vi. 48; ὁ παρεληλυθὼς χρόνος, time past, 1 Pet. iv. 3; to pass away, James, i. 10. Matt. xxiv. 35 etc.; to pass over, to neglect, Luke, xi. 42. xv. 29; to be removed, to be averted, Matt. xxvi. 39, 42. Mrk. xiv. 35; to come, Luke, xii. 37. xvii. 7.

πάρεσις, ἡ, a passing over, a remission, Rom. iii. 25. (See Pape's Lexicon in voc.)

παρέχω, to present, to offer, Luke, vi. 29; to shew, to give, Acts, xxii. 2. xxviii. 2. 1 Tim. vi. 17; to cause, to occasion, Luke, xi. 7. Gal. vi. 17. Matt. xxvi. 10; to shew, to exhibit, Tit. ii. 7; to render, to offer, Coloss. iv. 1. Luke, vii. 4.

παρηγορία, ἡ, consolation, comfort, Coloss. iv. 11.

παρθενία, ἡ, virginity, Luke, ii. 36.

παρθένος, ἡ, a virgin, Matt. i. 23. xxv. 1, 11 etc.; a marriageable daughter, 1 Cor. vii. 36; a man of pure life, Rev. xiv. 4.

παρίημι, to let pass; to omit, to neglect, Luke, xi. 42; to relax, to loosen; παρειμένος, relaxed, weakened, Hebr. xii. 12.

παρίστημι, and **παριστάνω**, to provide, Acts, xxiii. 24; to furnish one with, to give, Matt. xxvi. 53; to set before one, Acts, xxiii. 33; to present, Rom. vi. 13. xii. 1 etc; to shew, Acts, i. 3; to commend, 1 Cor. viii. 8; to prove, Acts, xxiv. 13; in the mid. perf. pluperf. and 2nd aor. it παρ] TO THE NEW TESTAMENT [πας

is intrans., *to stand by*, Acts, i. 10. ix. 39. xxvii. 23; *to stand before a person, to appear*, Acts, iv. 10. xxvii. 24. Luke, i. 19; *to aid, to assist*, Rom. xvi. 2. 2 Tim. iv. 17; *to be present, to have come*, Mrk. iv. 29.

πάροδος, ἡ, *a passing by*; ἐν παρόδῳ, *in passing by*, 1 Cor. xvi. 7.

παροικέω, *to dwell beside; to dwell as a stranger, to sojourn*, Luke, xxiv. 18; *to go as a stranger, to migrate*, Hebr. xi. 9.

παροικία, ἡ, *a dwelling in a strange land; a sojourning*, Acts, xiii. 17. 1 Pet. i. 17. (A very late word.)

πάροικος, *dwelling in a foreign land*; as subst., *a stranger, a sojourner*, Acts, vii. 6, 29. Ephes. ii. 19. 1 Pet. ii. 11.

παροιμία, ἡ, *a proverb*; τὸ τῆς παροιμίας, *according to the proverb*, 2 Pet. ii. 22; ἐν παροιμίαις λέγειν, *to speak in proverbs*, Joh. xvi. 25. Cf. Joh. x. 6. xvi. 29.

πάροινος, *given to wine, quarrelsome*, 1 Tim. iii. 3. Tit. i. 7.

παροίχομαι, *to go by*; παρῳχημένος, *past*, Acts, xiv. 16.

παρομοιάζω, *to be like*, Matt. xxiii. 27. (It is a purely ecclesiastical word.)

παρόμοιος, *like, similar*, Mrk. vii. 13.

παροξύνω, *to irritate, to provoke*, 1 Cor. xiii. 5. Acts, xvii. 16.

παροξυσμὸς, ὁ, *an incitement*; εἰς παροξυσμὸν ἀγάπης, Hebr. x. 24 (RV *to provoke unto love*); *strife, contention*, Acts, xv. 39.

παροργίζω, *to provoke*, Rom. x. 19. Ephes. vi. 4.

παροργισμὸς, ὁ, *exasperation, wrath*, Ephes. iv. 26. (It is a purely biblical form.)

παροτρύνω, *to incite, to stir up*, Acts, xiii. 50.

παρουσία, ἡ, *presence*, Philipp. ii. 12. 2 Cor. x. 10; *the arrival, the coming*, 1 Cor. xvi. 17. 2 Cor. vii. 6, 7; the future *Advent* of Christ, Matt. xxiv. 3, 37, 39. 2 Pet. i. 16. 1 Cor. xv. 23 etc.

παροψὶς, ἡ, *a side-dish, a dish of delicacies; a platter, a dish*, Matt. xxiii. 25, 26. (See Pape's Lexicon in voc.)

παρρησία, ἡ, *freedom of speech*, 2 Cor. iii. 12; παρρησίᾳ, ἐν παρρησίᾳ and μετὰ παρρησίας, adverbially, *boldly, freely, openly*, Joh. vii. 4, 13, 26. xi. 54. xvi. 25. Acts, ii. 29. iv. 29, 31; *boldness*, 1 Tim. iii. 13. Acts, iv. 13. Hebr. x. 19. Philem. 8.

παρρησιάζομαι, *to speak boldly*, Acts, ix. 27, 28. xiv. 3. xviii. 26; *to have boldness, to grow confident*, 1 Thess. ii. 2.

πᾶς, πᾶσα, πᾶν, *every*; "πᾶς has an *attributive* position, when it signifies *collectively*, *the whole*; as, τὸ πᾶν πλῆθος, *the whole multitude*; ὁ πᾶς ἀριθμὸς, *the sum total*; πᾶς stands before its substantive *without* the article in the sense of *every*; as, πᾶν δένδρον, *every tree*; with *numerals* ὁ πᾶς and οἱ πάντες signify *in all*; as, τριήρεσι ταῖς πάσαις τριάκοντα καὶ ἑκατὸν, *with a hundred and thirty triremes in all;* when πᾶς signifies *nothing but, wholly,* the substantive is *without* the article, as it is strictly *predicative;* as, φρουρεῖται ὑπὸ πάντων πολεμίων = πάντες, ὑφ' ὧν φρουρεῖται, πολέμιοί εἰσιν," Koch. οὐ πᾶς = *nullus,* 2 Pet. i. 20. Luke, i. 37. Mrk. xiii. 20. 1 Cor. i. 29. Ephes. v. 5. Rev. xxii. 3.

πάσχα, τό, indecl., *the paschal lamb,* which the Israelites were commanded to slay and eat on the fourteenth day of the month Nisan, the first month of their year, Luke, xxii. 7. Mrk. xiv. 12; *the paschal supper,* Matt. xxvi. 19; *the feast of the Passover,* extending from the fourteenth day of the month Nisan to the twentieth, Matt. xxvi. 2. Luke, ii. 41; *referred to Christ himself,* as being the true paschal lamb, 1 Cor. v. 7.

πάσχω, *to suffer,* Luke, xxii. 15. xxiv. 46; πάσχειν ὑπό τινος, *to suffer at their hands,* Matt. xvii. 12. 1 Thess. ii. 14. Mrk. v. 26.

πατάσσω, *to smite, to strike,* Luke, xxii. 49. Matt. xxvi. 51; *to afflict,* Rev. xi. 6.

πατέω, *to tread,* Rev. xiv. 20. xix. 15; *to tread upon,* Luke, x. 19; *to trample on,* Luke, xxi. 24. Rev. xi. 2.

πατήρ, ὁ, *a father,* Matt. ii. 22. iv. 21; *Our Heavenly Father,* Matt. v. 45, 48. vi. 14, 26; *a forefather,* Matt. iii. 9. xxiii. 30, 32; *source, author,* Joh. viii. 44.

πατραλῴας, and **πατραλοίας,** ὁ, *a parricide,* 1 Tim. i. 9.

πατριά, ἡ, *family,* Luke, ii. 4. Acts, iii. 25. Ephes. iii. 15.

πατριάρχης, ὁ, *a progenitor, a patriarch,* Acts, ii. 29. vii. 8, 9. Hebr. vii. 4.

πατρικὸς, *ancestral,* Gal. i. 14.

πατρὶς, ἡ, *a man's native country,* Joh. iv. 44. Matt. xiii. 54, 57; *a home,* Hebr. xi. 14.

πατροπαράδοτος, *handed down from one's ancestors,* 1 Pet. i. 18.

πατρῷος, *received from the fathers,* Acts, xxii. 3. xxiv. 14. xxviii. 17.

παύω, *to cause to cease, to restrain,* 1 Pet. iii. 10; mid., *to cease,* 1 Cor. xiii. 8. Luke, viii. 24. Acts, xx. 1; pass., *to get release, to cease,* 1 Pet. iv. 1.

παχύνω, *to make thick, to make fat;* pass., *to wax gross,* Matt. xiii. 15. Acts, xxviii. 27.

πέδη, ἡ, *a fetter,* Luke, viii. 29. Mrk. v. 4.

πεδινὸς, *level,* Luke, vi. 17.

πεζεύω, *to travel on foot, to go by land,* Acts, xx. 13.

πεζῇ, adv., *on foot, by land,* Matt. xiv. 13. Mrk. vi. 33.

πεζὸς, *on foot,* a var. lect. ad Matt. xiv. 13.

πειθαρχέω, *to be obedient, to obey,* Acts, v. 29, 32. xxvii. 21.

πειθὸς, and **πιθὸς**, *persuasive*, 1 Cor. ii. 4. (Not found elsewhere.)

Πειθώ, ἡ, *Persuasion*, a var. lect. ad 1 Cor. ii. 4. (Properly the name of a heathen goddess.)

πείθω, *to persuade*, Acts, xviii. 4. xix. 8; *to quiet, to tranquilize*, 1 Joh. iii. 19 (RV *to assure*); *to pacify*, Matt. xxviii. 14; *to gain over*, Acts, xii. 20; πέποιθα, *to be confident, to have confidence*, Philipp. i. 6. Rom. ii. 19. 2 Cor. ii. 3; *to trust*, Matt. xxvii. 43; pass., *to be persuaded*, Luke, xx. 6. Acts, xxi. 14; *to obey*, Acts, v. 36, 37; *to assent to*, Acts, v. 40.

πεινάω, *to be hungry, to hunger*, Matt. iv. 2. xii. 1, 3. Luke, vi. 21 etc.; *to be in want*, Philipp. iv. 12. 1 Cor. xi. 21; *to long for, to desire eagerly*, Matt. v. 6.

πεῖρα, ἡ, *a trial, an attempt*, Hebr. xi. 29, 36.

πειράζω, *to try, to attempt*, Acts, ix. 26. xvi. 7. xxiv. 6; *to make trial of, to test*, Joh. vi. 6. Rev. ii. 2; *to tempt*, Matt. iv. 1. 1 Cor. x. 13.

πειρασμὸς, ὁ, *a trial, a proving*, Gal. iv. 14. 1 Pet. iv. 12; *a temptation*, Luke, iv. 13. viii. 13. James, i. 12. 1 Cor. x. 13; *affliction*, Luke, xxii. 28. James, i. 2. 1 Pet. i. 6. (Almost exclusively confined to the NT.)

πειράω, and **πειράομαι**, *to make trial, to attempt*, Acts, xxvi. 21.

πεισμονὴ, ἡ, *conviction, confidence*, Gal. v. 8. (So translated in Pape's Lexicon. RV *persuasion*.)

πέλαγος, τὸ, *the sea*, Acts, xxvii. 5; but properly = *the high sea*; τὸ πέλαγος τῆς θαλάσσης, *the depth of the sea*, Matt. xviii. 6.

πελεκίζω, *to behead*, Rev. xx. 4.

πέμπτος, numer., *fifth*, Rev. vi. 9. ix. 1. xvi. 10. xxi. 20.

πέμπω, *to send*, Matt. xxii. 7. Luke, vii. 19. Joh. xiv. 26.

πένης, *poor*, 2 Cor. ix. 9.

πενθερά, ἡ, *a mother-in-law*, Matt. viii. 14. x. 35. Luke, iv. 38. xii. 53.

πενθερὸς, ὁ, *a father-in-law*, Joh. xviii. 13.

πενθέω, intrans., *to mourn*, Matt. v. 4. ix. 15. 1 Cor. v. 2; trans., with accus., *to mourn for, to lament over*, 2 Cor. xii. 21.

πένθος, τὸ, *mourning*, James, iv. 9. Rev. xviii. 7. xxi. 4.

πενιχρὸς, *poor*, Luke, xxi. 2.

πεντάκις, numer., *five times*, 2 Cor. xi. 24.

πεντακισχίλιοι, numer., *five thousand*, Matt. xiv. 21. xvi. 9. Luke, ix. 14.

πεντακόσιοι, numer., *five hundred*, Luke, vii. 41. 1 Cor. xv. 6.

πέντε, numer., *five*, Matt. xiv. 17, 19. xvi. 9 etc.

πεντεκαιδέκατος, numer., *the fifteenth*, Luke, iii. 1.

πεντήκοντα, numer., *fifty*, Luke, vii. 41. xvi. 6 etc.

πεντηκοστή, sc. ἡμέρα, *the fiftieth day after the Passover, Pentecost*, Acts, ii. 1. xx. 16. 1 Cor. xvi. 8. (See Pape's Lexicon in voc. πεντηκοστός.)

πεποίθησις, ἡ, *trust, confidence*, 2 Cor. i. 15. iii. 4. Ephes. iii. 12 etc. (A very late form.)

πέρ, "an enclitic particle, which gives to the word to which it refers, and which it usually follows, a strong emphasis; therefore appears to be merely a weakened πέρι, *very*," Pape. (In the NT appearing most frequently in the forms ὅσπερ, ὥσπερ, καίπερ, εἴπερ, καθάπερ, ἐπείπερ, ἐπειδήπερ etc.)

περαιτέρω, adv., *further, besides*, Acts, xix. 39.

πέραν, adv., *beyond; τὸ πέραν, the other side*, Matt. viii. 18, 28. Mrk. iv. 35; as prepos., πέραν τῆς θαλάσσης, *on the other side of the sea*, Joh. vi. 22, 25 etc.; τὸ πέραν τῆς θαλάσσης, *the other side of the sea*, Mrk. v. 1. Cf. Luke, viii. 22.

πέρας, τὸ, *extremity, bound, end*, Matt. xii. 42. Luke, xi. 31. Rom. x. 18; *termination*, Hebr. vi. 16.

περί, prepos., in the NT only with the genitive, *about, concerning*, and with the accusative, *about, touching* etc.; of time, *near, about*. (See Greek Grammar.)

περιάγω, *to lead about*, 1 Cor. ix. 5; intrans., *to go about*, Acts, xiii. 11. Matt. ix. 35. Mrk. vi. 6 etc.

περιαιρέω, *to take away*, Hebr. x. 11. 2 Cor. iii. 16. Acts, xxvii. 20, 40 (RV *casting off*.)

περιάπτω, *to bind around; to kindle*, Luke, xxii. 55.

περιαστράπτω, *to shine round about*, Acts, ix. 3. xxii. 6.

περιβάλλω, *to put around*, a var. lect. ad Luke, xix. 43 (see παρεμβάλλω); *to clothe* a person, Matt. xxv. 36, 38, 43; *to put on, to clothe* a person *with*, Luke, xxiii. 11. Joh. xix. 2. Rev. vii. 9, 13. x. 1 etc.; mid., *to put on*, Acts, xii. 8. Matt. vi. 31. Luke, xii. 27.

περιβλέπω, *to look around;* in the NT only in the mid., *to look round about*, Mrk. ix. 8. x. 23. Luke, vi. 10.

περιβόλαιον, τὸ, *a wrapper; a mantle*, Hebr. i. 12; *a covering*, 1 Cor. xi. 15.

περιδέω, *to bind round about*, Joh. xi. 44.

περιεργάζομαι, *to make one's self too busy, to be a busybody*, 2 Thess. iii. 11.

περίεργος, *over-officious; a busybody*, 1 Tim. v. 13; τὰ περίεργα, *curious arts, sorcery*, Acts, xix. 19.

περιέρχομαι, *to go about, to rove*, Acts, xix. 13. Hebr. xi. 37; περιέρχεσθαι τὰς οἰκίας, *to go about from house to house*, 1 Tim. v. 13; *to make a circuit*, Acts, xxviii. 13. (Not read by Westcott.)

περιέχω, *to contain*, Acts, xxiii. 25 (Westcott reads ἔχουσαν); *to take possession of, to seize*, Luke, v. 9; intrans., περιέχει ἐν γραφῇ, 1 Pet. ii. 6 (RV *it is contained in Scripture.* This latter usage is frequent in the Septuagint.)

περιζώννυμι, and περιζωννύω, *to gird round;* pass., *to be girded,* Luke, xii. 35; mid., *to gird one's self,* Luke, xii. 37. xvii. 8; met., τὴν ὀσφὺν, *to gird one's loins,* Ephes. vi. 14; with accus. of thing, *to gird on,* Rev. i. 13. xv. 6.

περίθεσις, ἡ, *a putting around, a wearing,* 1 Pet. iii. 3.

περιΐστημι, in the pres. imperf. fut. and 1 aor., *to place around;* in the perf., pluperf., 2 aor., and tenses of the mid., *to stand around,* Joh. xi. 42. Acts, xxv. 7; with accus. of thing, *to avoid, to shun,* 2 Tim. ii. 16. Tit. iii. 9.

περικάθαρμα, τὸ, *offscouring, refuse;* in plur., *the offscourings, the outcasts,* 1 Cor. iv. 13.

περικαθίζω, *to invest, to besiege;* intrans., *to sit around,* a var. lect. ad Luke, xxii. 55. (Westcott reads συνκαθισάντων).

περικαλύπτω, *to cover up, to cover over,* Hebr. ix. 4. Mrk. xiv. 65. Luke, xxii. 64 (RV *they blindfolded him*).

περίκειμαι, *to lie around, to be placed around,* Mrk. ix. 42. Luke, xvii. 2. Hebr. xii. 1 (RV *compassed about with so great a cloud of witnesses);* passively, *to be encompassed with,* Hebr. v. 2. Acts, xxviii. 20.

περικεφαλαία, ἡ, *a helmet,* 1 Thess. v. 8. Ephes. vi. 17.

περικρατὴς, *having full powers;* περικρατὴς γενέσθαι, with genit., *to get possession of,* Acts, xxvii. 16.

περικρύπτω, *to hide, to seclude,* Luke, i. 24.

περικυκλόω, *to encircle, to compass round about,* Luke, xix. 43.

περιλάμπω, *to shine round about,* Luke, ii. 9. Acts, xxvi. 13.

περιλείπω, *to leave remaining;* οἱ περιλειπόμενοι, *those who remain over, those who survive,* 1 Thess. iv. 15, 17.

περίλυπος, *very sorrowful,* Luke, xviii. 23. Mrk. vi. 26. xiv. 34. Matt. xxvi. 38.

περιμένω, *to wait for,* Acts, i. 4.

πέριξ, adv., *round about;* αἱ πέριξ πόλεις, *the cities round about, the circumjacent cities,* Acts, v. 16.

περιοικέω, *to dwell round about,* Luke, i. 65.

περίοικος, *dwelling around; a neighbour,* Luke, i. 58.

περιούσιος, *superabundant, rich; select, special;* λαὸς περιούσιος, Tit. ii. 14 (RV *a people for his own possession*).

περιοχὴ, ἡ, *a section, a passage* in a book, Acts, viii. 32.

περιπατέω, *to walk about,* Joh. vii. 1. 1 Pet. v. 8. Rev. xvi. 15; *to conduct one's self* in a certain manner, *to live,* Ephes. iv. 1. Coloss. i. 10. 1 Cor. iii. 3. Acts, xxi. 21 etc.; *to make due use of one's opportunities,* Joh. xii. 35.

περιπείρω, *to pierce through,* 1 Tim. vi. 10.

περιπίπτω, *to fall into,* James, i. 2; *to fall in with, to fall amongst,* Luke, x. 30; *to light upon,* Acts, xxvii. 41.

περιποιέω, *to cause to remain over;* mid., *to preserve,* Luke, xvii. 33; *to gain, to acquire,* 1 Tim. iii. 13; *to purchase,* Acts, xx. 28.

περιποίησις, ἡ, *a preservation, a saving,* Hebr. x. 39; *an obtaining,* 1 Thess. v. 9. 2 Thess. ii. 14; *a possession,* Ephes. i. 14. 1 Pet. ii. 9.

περιρραίνω, *to besprinkle,* Rev. xix. 13 (Westcott reads ῥεραντισμένον, and some editors βεβαμμένον. See ῥαντίζω).

περιρρήγνυμι, *to tear off,* Acts, xvi. 22.

περισπάω, *to draw around;* pass., *to be distracted, to be over-occupied,* Luke, x. 40.

περισσεία, ἡ, *abundance,* Rom. v. 17. 2 Cor. viii. 2; περισσείαν, abverbially, *over-abundantly, out of measure,* 2 Cor. x. 15 (Westcott reads εἰς περισσείαν); *residue, remains,* James, i. 21 (RV *overflowing*).

περίσσευμα, τὸ, *abundance,* 2 Cor. viii. 14. Matt. xii. 34. Luke, vi. 45; in the plur., *the remains, what remained over,* Mrk. viii. 8.

περισσεύω, *to remain over,* Joh. vi. 12, 13. Matt. xiv. 20. xv. 37; *to be over and above, to be a superfluity;* τὸ περισσεῦον, *their superfluity,* Mrk. xii. 44. Luke, xxi. 4; *to be in abundance, to abound,* Luke, xii. 15. 2 Cor. i. 5. ix. 12. Philipp. i. 26. Rom. v. 15 etc.; *to be rich,* 1 Cor. xiv. 12; *to increase,* Acts, xvi. 5; *to excel,* Matt. v. 20. 1 Cor. xv. 58. 2 Cor. iii. 9. viii. 7; trans., *to cause to abound,* 2 Cor. iv. 15. ix. 8. Ephes. i. 8. 1 Thess. iii. 12.

περισσὸς, *over and above, exceeding, more than* a certain number or quantity; τὸ περισσὸν τούτων, *what is more than this,* Matt. v. 37; ἐκ περισσοῦ, *with vehemence,* Mrk. xiv. 31 (Westcott reads ἐκπερισσῶς); ὑπὲρ ἐκ περισσοῦ, *exceedingly,* 1 Thess. iii. 10. v. 13. Ephes. iii. 20 (in these three passages Westcott reads ὑπερεκπερισσοῦ, as one word); περισσόν μοί ἐστιν, *it is superfluous for me,* 2 Cor. ix. 1; περισσὸν ἔχειν, *to have abundance,* Joh. x. 10; περισσότερόν τι, *anything more,* Luke, xii. 4; (but in 2 Cor. x. 8, *somewhat above measure*); περισσότερον αὐτῶν πάντων, *more abundantly than they all,* 1 Cor. xv. 10. Cf. Mrk. xii. 33; μᾶλλον περισσότερον, *much more abundantly,* Mrk. vii. 36; περισσότερον ἔτι κατάδηλὸν, *still more abundantly evident,* Hebr. vii. 15; περισσότερον προφήτου, *much more than a prophet,* Matt. xi. 9. Luke, vii. 26; περισσότερον κρίμα, *greater condemnation,* Mrk. xii. 40. Luke, xx. 47; τιμὴν περισσοτέραν, **greater**

honour, 1 Cor. xii. 23. Cf. 2 Cor. ii. 7; τί περισσὸν ποιεῖτε; *what do ye more than others?* Matt. v. 47; τὸ περισσὸν, *the superiority, the advantage*, Rom. iii. 1.

περισσοτέρως, adv., *more abundantly*, 2 Cor. i. 12. ii. 4. xi. 23. Philipp. i. 14; *more exceedingly*, Gal. i. 14. 1 Thess. ii. 17; *more earnestly*, Hebr. ii. 1. xiii. 19; *more vehemently*, Mrk. xv. 14 (here Westcott reads περισσῶς); περισσοτέρως μᾶλλον, *the more exceedingly*, 2 Cor. vii. 13.

περισσῶς, adv., *beyond measure, exceedingly*, Acts, xxvi. 11. Mrk. x. 26. Matt. xxvii. 23; *vehemently*, Mrk. xv. 14. (See περισσοτέρως.)

περιστερά, ἡ, *a dove*, Matt. iii. 16. x. 16. xxi. 12 etc.

περιτέμνω, *to circumcise*, Luke, i. 59. ii. 21. Joh. vii. 22. Acts, vii. 8; pass., *to be circumcised*, 1 Cor. vii. 18. Gal. ii. 3. v. 2, 3. vi. 12, 13. Coloss. ii. 11.

περιτίθημι, *to place around, to set about*, Matt. xxi. 33. Mrk. xii. 1; *to put on a person*, Matt. xxvii. 28. Mrk. xv. 17; *to place one thing on another*, Joh. xix. 29. Matt. xxvii. 48; *to bestow, to confer*, 1 Cor. xii. 23.

περιτομὴ, ἡ, *circumcision*, Acts, vii. 8. Rom. iv. 11. Gal. v. 11; = *the circumcised*, Rom. iii. 30. iv. 9. Gal. ii. 9. Ephes. ii. 11; *the removal of spiritual impurity*, Rom. ii. 29. Coloss. ii. 11.

περιτρέπω, *to turn about; to turn* a person *into a certain state*; σε εἰς μανίαν περιτρέπει, *is turning thee mad*, Acts, xxvi. 24.

περιτρέχω, *to run round about*, Mrk. vi. 55.

περιφέρω, *to carry about*, Mrk. vi. 55. 2 Cor. iv. 10; pass., *to be carried about*, Ephes. iv. 14.

περιφρονέω, *to consider carefully;* met., *to contemn, to despise*, Tit. ii. 15.

περίχωρος, *lying round about;* ἡ περίχωρος (sc. γῆ), *the region round about*, Matt. xiv. 35. Mrk. i. 28. Luke, iv. 14 etc.; met., *the inhabitants*, Matt. iii. 5.

περίψημα, τὸ, *what is rubbed off;* offscourings, *refuse*, 1 Cor. iv. 13. (A very late form.)

περπερεύομαι, *to boast, to vaunt one's self*, 1 Cor. xiii. 4. (See Pape's Lexicon in voc.)

πέρυσι, adv., *last year;* ἀπὸ πέρυσι, *a year ago*, 2 Cor. viii. 10. ix. 2.

"**πετάομαι**, *to fly*, a doubtful later Greek form for the earlier πέτομαι. See Lobeck ad Phryn. p. 581," Thayer; appears as a var. lect. ad Rev. iv. 7. viii. 13. xiv. 6. Westcctt reads πετόμενος in all such passages.

πετεινὸς, *flying, winged;* in the NT found only in the neuter plural, πετεινὰ and τὰ πετεινὰ, as subst., *winged animals, birds*, Matt. vi. 26. xiii. 4. Luke, xii. 24. Rom. i. 23 etc.

πέτομαι, *to fly*, Rev. iv. 7. viii. 13. xii. 14. xiv. 6. xix. 17. (See πετάομαι.)

πέτρα, ἡ, *a cliff, a rock*, Luke, vi. 48. Mrk. xv. 46. Matt. vii. 24. 1 Cor. x. 4; *rocky ground*, Luke, viii. 6, 13. (In Matt. xvi. 18 some have attached importance to the classical distinction between πέτρα, *a fixed, living rock*, and πέτρος, *a stone, a detached rock*; but this appears to be merely a fanciful refinement, and the interchange of words in Matt. xvi. 18 to be due to the *personal* reference in the first clause, and to the *material* reference in the second.)

πέτρος, ὁ, *a stone, a rock*, Matt. xvi. 18; also the name given by the Saviour to the apostle Peter, Joh. i. 42. Cf. Matt. x. 2. Acts, x. 5, 18, 32. xi. 13.

πετρώδης, *rocky, stony;* τὸ πετρῶδες, and τὰ πετρώδη, *stony ground*, Mrk. iv. 5, 16. Matt. xiii. 5, 20.

πήγανον, τὸ, *rue*, Luke, xi. 42.

πηγὴ, ἡ, *a fountain, a spring, a well*, James, iii. 11. Joh. iv. 6, 14. Rev. vii. 17. Mrk. v. 29 etc.

πήγνυμι, *to fasten; to pitch a tent*, Hebr. viii. 2.

πηδάλιον, τὸ, *a rudder*, James, iii. 4. Acts, xxvii. 40.

πηλίκος, *how great, how large*, Gal. vi. 11; *how distinguished*, Hebr. vii. 4.

πηλὸς, ὁ, *clay*, Rom. ix. 21. Joh. ix. 6, 11, 14.

πήρα, ἡ, *a wallet*, Matt. x. 10. Mrk. vi. 8 etc.

πῆχυς, ὁ, *a cubit*, Matt. vi. 27. Luke, xii. 25. Joh. xxi. 8. Rev. xxi. 17; "a measure of length equal to the distance from the joint of the elbow to the tip of the middle finger, i.e. about one foot and a half; but its precise length varied and is disputed," Thayer.

πιάζω, *to take hold of*, Acts, iii. 7; *to catch, to take*, Joh. xxi. 3, 10. Rev. xix. 20; *to seize, to apprehend*, Joh. vii. 30, 32, 44. viii. 20. x. 39. Acts, xii. 4 etc. (It is the Doric form for πιέζω.)

πιέζω, *to press hard; to press together*, Luke, vi. 38.

πιθανολογία, ἡ, *persuasive discourse; specious discourse*, Coloss. ii. 4 (RV *persuasiveness of speech*).

πικραίνω, *to make bitter*, Rev. viii. 11. x. 9, 10; pass. met., *to be embittered, to be exasperated*, Coloss. iii. 19.

πικρία, ἡ, *bitterness*, Acts, viii. 23. Hebr. xii. 15; *rancour, bitter hatred*, Ephes. iv. 31. Rom. iii. 14.

πικρὸς, *bitter*, James, iii. 11, 14.

πικρῶς, adv., *bitterly*, Matt. xxvi. 75. Luke, xxii. 62.

πίμπλημι, *to fill*, Matt. xxii. 10. xxvii. 48. Luke, v. 7. vi. 11 etc.; pass., *to be fulfilled, to be confirmed by the event*, Luke, xxi. 22; of time, *to be completed*, Luke, i. 23, 57. ii. 6, 21, 22.

πίμπρημι, and πιπράω, to burn; in the NT in the pass., to become swollen, to swell, Acts, xxviii. 6.

πινακίδιον, τὸ, a writing tablet, Luke, i. 63.

πίναξ, ὁ, a dish, a platter, Matt. xiv. 8, 11. Luke, xi. 39. Mrk. vi. 25, 28.

πίνω, to drink, Luke, xii. 19. Joh. iv. 7, 10. 1 Cor. xi. 25, 27, 28; met., to imbibe, to absorb, Hebr. vi. 7.

πιότης, ἡ, fatness, Rom. xi. 17.

πιπράσκω, to sell, Acts, ii. 45. iv. 34. Matt. xiii. 46. xviii. 25; πεπραμένος ὑπὸ τὴν ἁμαρτίαν, sold under sin, i.e. a slave to sin, Rom. vii. 14.

πίπτω, to fall, Matt. x. 29. xiii. 5, 8. xv. 14, 27. Acts, i. 26; to fail, to come to nought, 1 Cor. xiii. 8. Luke, xvi. 17.

πιστεύω, to place confidence in, to believe, Matt. viii. 13. Joh. iv. 50. Mrk. i. 15. [xvi. 13.] Luke, xxiv. 25; to trust, Rom. iv. 3, 17. Gal. iii. 6; to intrust a thing to a person, Luke, xvi. 11. Joh. ii. 24. Rom. iii. 2.

πιστικὸς, that can be relied on, faithful; genuine, unadulterated; νάρδου πιστικῆς, Mrk. xiv. 3 (RV of spikenard); νάρδου πιστικῆς, Joh. xii. 3 ("for nard was often adulterated," Thayer. Pape makes it a form distinct from πιστικὸς, faithful, and, deriving it from πίνω, translates it, potable, fluid, restricting its usage, in this sense, to the NT).

πίστις, ἡ, faith, belief, Hebr. xi. 1, 6. xii. 2. 1 Thess. i. 8. Coloss. ii. 5; persuasion, conviction, Rom. xiv. 22, 23; assurance, Acts, xvii. 31; faithfulness, honesty, Gal. v. 23.

πιστὸς, faithful, Matt. xxiv. 45. 1 Cor. i. 9; worthy belief, that can be relied on, 1 Tim. iii. 1. 2 Tim. ii. 2, 11; having Christian faith, a believer, Acts, x. 45. xvi. 1.

πιστόω, pass., to be assured of, 2 Tim. iii. 14.

πλανάω, to lead astray, to deceive, Matt. xxiv. 4, 5, 11, 24. Joh. vii. 12. 2 Tim. iii. 13; pass., to be led astray, Luke, xxi. 8. Joh. vii. 47 etc.; to err, Matt. xxii. 29. Mrk. xii. 24, 27.

πλάνη, ἡ, a wandering; error, Ephes. iv. 14. 1 Thess. ii. 3. James, v. 20; deceit, fraud, Matt. xxvii. 64.

πλανήτης, ὁ, a wanderer, wandering; ἀστέρες πλανῆται, wandering stars, Jude, 13.

πλάνος, wandering; met., misleading, 1 Tim. iv. 1; as subst., a deceiver, Matt.xxvii. 63. 2 Cor. vi. 8. 2 Joh. 7.

πλὰξ, ἡ, a broad, level surface; a tablet, 2 Cor. iii. 3.

πλάσμα, τὸ, that which has been formed, Rom. ix. 20.

πλάσσω, to mould, to form, Rom. ix. 20. 1 Tim. ii. 13.

πλαστὸς, moulded, formed; met., feigned, 2 Pet. ii. 3.

πλατεῖα, ἡ, (sc. ὁδὸς), a broad way, a street, Matt. vi. 5. xii. 19. Luke, x. 10. xiii. 26.

xiv. 21. Acts, v. 15 etc. (Properly fem. of πλατύς.)

πλάτος, τὸ, *breadth*, Ephes. iii. 18 ; τὸ πλάτος τῆς γῆς, *the whole extent of the earth*, Rev. xx. 9.

πλατύνω, *to make broad, to enlarge*, Matt. xxiii. 5. 2 Cor. vi. 11, 13.

πλατὺς, *broad, wide*, Matt. vii. 13.

πλέγμα, τὸ, *that which is plaited; braided hair*, 1 Tim. ii. 9. Cf. 1 Pet. iii. 3.

πλεῖστος, (superl. of πολὺς), *most*, Matt. xi. 20; *very great*, Mrk. iv. 1 ; ὁ πλεῖστος ὄχλος, *the greater part of the multitude*, Matt. xxi. 8 ; τὸ πλεῖστον, adverbially, *at the most*, 1 Cor. xiv. 27.

–λείων, (compar. of πολὺς), *more*, Matt. xxi. 36. Joh. xxi. 15. Luke, xxi. 3 ; *greater, more excellent*, Matt. vi. 25. xii. 41, 42. Luke, xi. 31, 32 ; ἐπὶ πλεῖον, *more widely, further*, Acts, iv. 17. 2 Tim. ii. 16. iii. 9 ; οἱ πλείονες, *the greater part, the majority*, Acts, xix. 32. xxvii. 12.

πλέκω, *to weave together, to plait*, Matt. xxvii. 29. Joh. xix. 2.

πλεονάζω, intrans., of persons, *to have a superfluity*, 2 Cor. viii. 15 ; of things, *to abound*, Rom. v. 20. vi. 1. 2 Cor. iv.15; *to be augmented, to increase*, 2 Thess. i. 3. Philipp. iv. 17. 2 Pet. i. 8 ; trans., *to cause to increase*, 1 Thess. iii. 12.

πλεονεκτέω, intrans., *to have a greater share, to have an advantage over;* trans., *to gain an advantage over, to overreach*, 2 Cor. vii. 2. xii. 17, 18. 1 Thess. iv. 6 ; pass., 2 Cor. ii. 11.

πλεονέκτης, *greedy of gain, covetous*, 1 Cor. v. 10, 11. vi. 10. Ephes. v. 5.

πλεονεξία, ἡ, *covetousness*, Luke, xii. 15. Rom. i. 29. Ephes. iv. 19. v. 3 etc. ; ὡς πλεονεξίαν, *as a matter of covetousness*, 2 Cor. ix. 5 ; plur., *covetings*, Mrk. vii. 22.

πλευρὰ, ἡ, *the side* of the body, Joh. xix. 34. xx. 20, 25, 27. Acts, xii. 7.

πλέω, *to sail*, Luke, viii. 23. Acts, xxi. 3. xxvii. 6, 24.

πληγὴ, ἡ, *a blow, a stripe*, Luke, x. 30. xii. 48. Acts, xvi. 23, 33. 2 Cor. vi. 5. xi. 23 ; *a wound;* ἡ πληγὴ τοῦ θανάτου, *the deadly wound*, Rev. xiii. 3, 12 ; τὴν πληγὴν τῆς μαχαίρας, *the sword-stroke*, Rev. xiii. 14 ; *an affliction, a plague*, Rev. ix. 18, 20. xi. 6 etc.

πλῆθος, τὸ, *a multitude, a great number*, Hebr. xi. 12. Luke, ii. 13. Joh. xxi. 6 ; with the article, *the assemblage*, Acts, xxiii. 7 etc.

πληθύνω, trans., *to increase, to multiply*, 2 Cor. ix. 10. Hebr. vi. 14 ; intrans., *to be increased, to multiply*, Acts, vi. 1 ; pass., *to be multiplied*, 1 Pet. i. 2. Matt. xxiv. 12. Acts, ix. 31. xii. 24.

πλήκτης, ὁ, *a bruiser, a quarrelsome person*, 1 Tim. iii. 3. Tit. i. 7.

πλήμμυρα, ἡ, *a flood*, Luke, vi. 48. ("It ought not to be written πλημμύρα, as the α is short," Pape's Lexicon.)

πλήν, adv., at the beginning of a sentence, *nevertheless, howbeit, however*, Matt. xi. 22, 24. xxvi. 39, 64 etc.; πλὴν ὅτι, *except that, save that*, Acts, xx. 23. Philipp. i. 18; as prepos., *except, but*, Mrk. xii. 32. Acts, viii. 1. xv. 28. xxvii. 22.

πλήρης, *full*, Joh. i. 14. Matt. xiv. 20. xv. 37; *complete, perfect*, 2 Joh. 8. Mrk. iv. 28.

πληροφορέω, *to carry through to the end, to accomplish*, Luke, i. 1; *to fulfil*, 2 Tim. iv. 5; pass., *to be fully convinced*, Rom. iv. 21. Coloss. iv. 12.

πληροφορία, ἡ, *fulness, abundance*, Hebr. vi. 11. x. 22; *full assurance*, Coloss. ii. 2. 1 Thess. i. 5. (Found only in the NT and ecclesiastical writers.)

πληρόω, *to fill completely*, Matt. xiii. 48. Joh. xii. 3. Acts, ii. 2; *to supply liberally*, Philipp. i. 11. iv. 18. Coloss. i. 9; *to complete*, as to number, Rev. vi. 11. Luke, xxi. 24; *to render perfect*, Joh. iii. 29. Philipp. ii. 2; *to fulfil*, Matt. i. 22. ii. 15, 17, 23. v. 17.

πλήρωμα, τὸ, *fulness*, Ephes. iii. 19. iv. 13. Coloss. ii. 9. Rom. xi. 12; *a filling up*; κοφίνων (or σπυρίδων) πληρώματα, *basketfuls*, Mrk. vi. 43. viii. 20; *a complement, a patch*, Matt. ix. 16. Mrk. ii. 21; *of time, completeness, fulness*, Gal. iv. 4; *abundance*, Joh. i. 16. Coloss. i. 19; *a fulfilling, a keeping*, Rom. xiii. 10; *inhabitants* (what fills the earth), 1 Cor. x. 26.

πλησίον, adv., *near*, Joh. iv. 5; ὁ πλησίον, *one's neighbour*, Matt. v. 43. xix. 19. xxii. 39. Luke, x. 36.

πλησμονὴ, ἡ, *satiety; gratification, indulgence*, Coloss. ii. 23.

πλήσσω, *to smite*, Rev. viii. 12.

πλοιάριον, τὸ, *a little vessel, a boat*, Mrk. iii. 9. Joh. vi. 22. xxi. 8.

πλοῖον, τὸ, *a vessel, a ship*, Matt. iv. 21, 22. Acts, xx. 13 etc.

πλόος, πλοῦς, ὁ, *a voyage*, Acts, xxi. 7. xxvii. 9, 10.

πλούσιος, *rich*, 2 Cor. viii. 9. Matt. xix. 23, 24. Luke, vi. 24 etc.

πλουσίως, adv., *richly*, Coloss. iii. 16. 1 Tim. vi. 17. Tit. iii. 6. 2 Pet. i. 11.

πλουτέω, *to be rich, to have abundance*, Luke, i. 53. 1 Tim. vi. 9; ἐπλούτησα, *I have been enriched*, Rev. xviii. 15. 1 Cor. iv. 8. 2 Cor. viii. 8.

πλουτίζω, *to make rich, to enrich*, 2 Cor. vi. 10. ix. 11 etc.

πλοῦτος, ὁ, *wealth, riches*, Ephes. iii. 8. Matt. xiii. 22. 1 Tim. vi. 17; *abundance, fulness*, Rom. xi. 33. 2 Cor. viii. 2. Ephes. i. 7; *a good, an advantage*, Hebr. xi. 26. Rom. xi. 12.

πλυ] GREEK-ENGLISH LEXICON [ποι

πλύνω, *to wash*, Luke, v. 2. Rev. vii. 14. xxii. 14.

πνεῦμα, τό, *wind*, Joh. iii. 8. Hebr. i. 7; *breath*, 2 Thess. ii. 8. Rev. xi. 11; *spirit*, Luke, xxiii. 46. Acts, vii. 59. Joh. iv. 24. vi. 63. James, ii. 26 etc.; *a disembodied spirit, a ghost*, Luke, xxiv. 37, 39. Acts, xxiii. 8, 9; *a human soul*, Rev. xxii. 6. 1 Cor. vii. 34. Hebr. xii. 23. James, ii. 26; with the article, τὸ πνεῦμα, τὸ ἅγιον πνεῦμα, τὸ πνεῦμα τὸ ἅγιον, *the Holy Ghost*, Matt. xxviii. 19. Joh. xx. 22. Acts, v. 3. viii. 19. x. 44. xiii. 2, 4. xv. 28. Hebr. iii. 7 etc. (See also πνευματικός, ψυχή, ψυχικός.)

πνευματικὸς, *pertaining to the spirit, spiritual;* τὰ πνευματικὰ, *spiritual gifts*, 1 Cor. xii. 1. xiv. 1; τὰ πνευματικὰ τῆς πονηρίας, *evil spirits*, Ephes. vi. 12; *spiritual*, as opposed to ψυχικὸς (*carnal, sensual*, 1 Cor. ii. 14. James, iii. 15. Jude, 19), 1 Cor. xv. 44, 46. Cf. Rom. vii. 14. xv. 27; "σῶμα πνευματικὸν, the body which is animated and controlled by the rational soul, opposed to σῶμα ψυχικὸν, 1 Cor. xv. 44," Thayer. Cf. 1 Pet. ii. 5; *divinely inspired*, Coloss. iii. 16. 1 Cor. xiv. 37.

πνευματικῶς, adv., *spiritually*, 1 Cor. ii. 14. Rev. xi. 8.

πνέω, ôf the wind, *to blow*, Matt. vii. 25, 27. Luke, xii. 55. Joh. iii. 8. vi. 18 etc.

πνίγω, *to choke*, Matt. xiii. 7 (Westcott reads ἀπέπνιξαν); *to seize by the throat*, Matt. xviii. 28; pass., *to be drowned*, Mrk. v. 13.

πνικτὸς, *strangled*, Acts, xv. 20, 29. xxi. 25.

πνοὴ, ἡ, *wind*, Acts, ii. 2; *breath*, Acts, xvii. 25.

ποδήρης, *reaching to the feet*, Rev. i. 13.

πόθεν, adv., *whence? from what place?* Matt. xv. 33. Luke, xiii. 25, 27 etc.; *from what source?* Matt. xiii. 54, 56. xxi. 25. Luke, xx. 7 etc.; *by what means?* Joh. i. 48. Mrk. viii. 4; *how?* Luke, i. 43. Mrk. xii. 37. Joh. iv. 11.

ποία, ἡ, *grass*, James, iv. 14 ("but there ποία is more correctly taken as the fem. of ποῖος, *of what sort?*" Thayer).

ποιέω, *to make*, Joh. ii. 15. Matt. xvii. 4 etc.; *to create*, Acts, iv. 24. Matt. xix. 4; *to establish*, Hebr. viii. 9; *to cause*, Matt. v. 32. Joh. xi. 37; *to gain, to acquire*, Luke, xix. 18; *to get, to procure*, Luke, xii. 33; *to appoint*, Mrk. iii. 14; *to commit*, Matt. xiii. 41. xxvii. 23. 1 Joh. iii. 8; *to practise, to adhere to*, Joh. iii. 21. Rom. iii. 12; *to observe, to keep*, Matt. v. 19. vii. 21, 24, 26 etc.; *to celebrate, to keep*, as a feast, Matt. xxvi. 18. Hebr. xi. 28; *to spend*, as time, James, iv. 13. Matt. xx. 12. Acts, xv. 33; *to produce, to bring forth*,

Matt. iii. 8, 10. vii. 17, 18, 19; δῆλον ποιεῖν, *to make manifest, to betray*, Matt. xxvi. 73; ἐκδίκησιν ποιεῖν, *to avenge*, Luke, xviii. 7, 8; ἔκθετον ποιεῖν, *to expose, as infants*, Acts, vii. 19; ἐνέδραν ποιεῖν, *to lie in wait*, Acts, xxv. 3; ἐξουσίαν ποιεῖν, *to exercise authority*, Rev. xiii. 12; ἔξω ποιεῖν, *to cause to depart, to put forth*, Acts, v. 34; κρίσιν ποιεῖν, *to act as judge*, Joh. v. 27; λύτρωσιν ποιεῖν, *to procure deliverance*, Luke, i. 68; μονὴν ποιεῖσθαι, *to dwell*, Joh. xiv. 23; πόλεμον ποιεῖν, *to make war, to fight*, Rev. xi. 7; συμβούλιον ποιεῖν, *to consult*, Mrk. iii. 6 (but here Westcott reads ἐδίδουν); φανερὸν ποιεῖν, *to make known*, Matt. xii. 16; ἀναβολὴν μηδεμίαν ποιεῖσθαι, *to make no delay*, Acts, xxv. 17; συστροφὴν ποιεῖσθαι, *to band together*, Acts, xxiii. 12; δεήσεις ποιεῖσθαι, *to offer prayers*, Luke, v. 33; ἐκβολὴν ποιεῖσθαι, *to throw the cargo overboard*, Acts, xxvii. 18; οὐδενὸς λόγου ποιεῖσθαι, *to make of no account, to set no value on*, Acts, xx. 24; μνείαν ποιεῖσθαι, *to make mention of*, Rom. i. 9; μνήμην ποιεῖσθαι, *to remember*, 2 Pet. i. 15; πρόνοιαν ποιεῖσθαι, *to provide for*, Rom. xiii. 14; σπουδὴν ποιεῖσθαι, *to act diligently*, Jude, 3.

ποίημα, τὸ, *that which has been made; a work*, Rom. i. 20; *workmanship*, Ephes. ii. 10.

ποίησις, ἡ, *a performance, a doing*, James, i. 25.

ποιητής, ὁ, *a poet*, Acts, xvii. 28; *a performer, a doer*, Rom. ii. 13. James, i. 22, 23. iv. 11.

ποικίλος, *of divers sorts, various*, Matt. iv. 24. Luke, iv. 40; *manifold*, 1 Pet. i. 6. iv. 10.

ποιμαίνω, *to keep sheep*, Luke, xvii. 7; *to feed*, Joh. xxi. 16. Acts, xx. 28. 1 Cor. ix. 7. Jude, 12; *to rule, to govern*, Rev. ii. 27. xii. 5. xix. 15.

ποιμήν, ὁ, *a shepherd*, Matt. ix. 36. xxv. 32. xxvi. 31. Joh. x. 2, 12 etc.; *a pastor*, Ephes. iv. 11. 1 Pet. ii. 25.

ποίμνη, ἡ, *a flock*, Matt. xxvi. 31. Luke, ii. 8. Joh. x. 16.

ποίμνιον, τὸ, *a flock*, Luke, xii. 32. 1 Pet. v. 2, 3.

ποῖος, interrog. pronoun, *of what sort*, Luke, xxiv. 19. Matt. xxi. 23. xxii. 36.

πολεμέω, *to carry on war, to fight*, Rev. ii. 16. xii. 7. xix. 11; *to wrangle, to quarrel*, James, iv. 2.

πόλεμος, ὁ, *war*, Matt. xxiv. 6. Luke, xiv. 31 etc.; *battle*, Hebr. xi. 34. Rev. ix. 9. xvi. 14; *strife, quarrel*, James, iv. 1.

πόλις, ἡ, *a city*, Matt. ii. 23. Mrk. i. 45. Luke, iv. 29 etc.; *the inhabitants* of a city, Matt. viii. 34. x. 15. Acts, xiv. 21; with the article, = *Jerusalem*, Matt. xxi. 18. xxviii. 11; *an abode, a home*, Hebr. xi. 16. xiii. 14.

πολιτάρχης, ὁ, *a ruler of a city*, Acts, xvii. 6, 8. (Confined to the NT and late Inscriptions.)

πολιτεία, ἡ, *the commonwealth*, Ephes. ii. 11; *the rights of a citizen, citizenship*, Acts, xxii. 28.

πολίτευμα, τὸ, *the administration of civil affairs; a commonwealth*, Philipp. iii. 20.

πολιτεύω, *to live as a citizen*, Acts, xxiii. 1. Philipp. i. 27.

πολίτης, ὁ, *a citizen*, Acts, xxi. 39. Luke, xv. 15; *a fellow-citizen*, Hebr. viii. 11. Luke, xix. 14.

πολλάκις, adv., *oftentimes, frequently*, Matt. xvii. 15. Joh. xviii. 2 etc.

πολλαπλασίων, *many times as much, much more*, Matt. xix. 29. Luke, xviii. 39.

πολυεύσπλαγχνος, *very merciful*, a var. lect. ad James, v. 11. (Here Westcott reads πολύσπλαγχνος. The other form is not recognized in Pape's Lexicon.)

πολυλογία, ἡ, *much speaking*, Matt. vi. 7.

πολυμερῶς, adv., *in many parts*, Hebr. i. 1. (The word is not recognized in Pape's Lexicon, and Westcott omits it.)

πολυποίκιλος, *much variegated; manifold*, Ephes. iii. 10.

πολὺς, *much*, Joh. xii. 24. xv. 5, 8; *great*, Mrk. v. 24. Acts, xi. 21; *abundant, plenteous*, Matt. ix. 37. Luke, x. 2; *of time, long*, Joh. v. 6. Matt. xxv. 19; ἐπὶ πολὺ, *for a long time*, Acts, xxviii. 6; μετ' οὐ πολὺ, *not long after*, Acts, xxvii. 14; πολὺ, adverbially, *much*, Rom. iii. 2. Luke, vii. 47; πολλοῦ, *at a great price*, Matt. xxvi. 9; πολλοὶ, *many*, Luke, x. 24. 1 Cor. i. 26; οἱ πολλοὶ, *the greater part, most of them, the majority*, Matt. xxiv. 12. 1 Cor. x. 33; τὰ πολλὰ, *for the most part*, Rom. xv. 22.

πολύσπλαγχνος, *very merciful*, James, v. 11. (Confined to the NT and ecclesiastical writers.)

πολυτελὴς, *very costly*, Mrk. xiv. 3. 1 Tim. ii. 9; *of great value*, 1 Pet. iii. 4.

πολύτιμος, *of great price, very precious*, Matt. xiii. 46. Joh. xii. 3. 1 Pet. i. 7.

πολυτρόπως, adv., *in divers manners*, Hebr. i. 1.

πόμα, τὸ, the un-Attic form for πῶμα, *a drink*, 1 Cor. x. 4.

πονηρία, ἡ, *wickedness, iniquity*, Ephes. vi. 12. Luke, xi. 39 etc.; plur., *iniquities*, Acts, iii. 26. Mrk. vii. 22.

πονηρὸς, *wicked*, Matt. xiii. 49. 1 Cor. v. 13 etc.; *evil*, Ephes. v. 16. vi. 13. Matt. xii. 45; *diseased*, Matt. vi. 43; *grudging*, Matt. xx. 15; *grievous*, Rev. xvi. 2; ὁ πονηρὸς, *the evil one*, Matt. v. 37. xiii. 19, 38; τὸ πονηρὸν, *that which is wicked, wickedness, evil*, Luke, vi. 45. Rom. xii. 9. Matt. vi. 13. 1 Thess. v. 22. 2 Thess. iii. 3. Cf. Acts, xxviii. 21.

πόνος, ὁ, *labour; anxiousness*, Coloss. iv. 13; *pain*, Rev. xvi. 10.

πορεία, ἡ, *a journey*, Luke, xiii. 22; *a pursuit*, James, i. 11.

πορεύομαι, *to go*, Luke, xxii. 33. Acts, xxiii. 23 etc.; *to depart*, Matt. xix. 15. Acts, xvi. 36 etc.; *to depart from life, to die*, Luke, xxii. 22; πορεύεσθαι ὀπίσω τινὸς, *to follow one, to become his adherent*, Luke, xxi. 8; *to pursue a course of life, to walk*, 1 Pet. iv. 3. 2 Pet. ii. 10. Jude, 16, 18.

πορθέω, *to lay waste; to destroy*, Gal. i. 13, 23. Acts, ix. 21.

πορισμὸς, ὁ, *a source of gain*, 1 Tim. vi. 5, 6.

πορνεία, ἡ, *fornication*, Matt. xv. 19. Acts, xv. 20, 29. 1 Cor. vi. 18; met., *idolatry*, Rev. ii. 21. xiv. 8. xvii. 2, 4.

πορνεύω, *to commit fornication*, 1 Cor. vi. 18. x. 8; met., *to practise idolatry*, Rev. xvii. 2. xviii. 3, 9.

πόρνη, ἡ, *a harlot*, Luke, xv. 30. James, ii. 25 etc.; met., *an idolatress*, Rev. xvii. 1, 5. xix. 2.

πόρνος, ὁ, *a male prostitute*; and, generally, *a fornicator*, 1 Cor. v. 9, 11. Ephes. v. 5. 1 Tim. i. 10. Hebr. xii. 16 etc.

πόρρω, adv., *at a distance, a great way off*, Luke, xiv. 32; *far*, Matt. xv. 8. Mrk. vii. 6; πορρώτερον, *further*, Luke, xxiv. 28. (Here other texts give πορρωτέρω.)

πόρρωθεν, adv., *from afar*, Luke, xvii. 12. Hebr. xi. 13.

πορφύρα, ἡ, *a purple garment*, Mrk. xv. 17, 20. Luke, xvi. 19 etc.

πορφύρεος, πορφυροῦς, *of purple, dyed of a purple colour*, Joh. xix. 2, 5; πορφυροῦν, sc. ἔνδυμα, *a purple garment*, Rev. xvii. 4. xviii. 16.

πορφυρόπωλις, ἡ, *a female seller of purple*, Acts, xvi. 14.

ποσάκις, adv., *how often*, Matt. xviii. 21. xxiii. 37. Luke, xiii. 34.

πόσις, ἡ, *drink*, Joh. vi. 55. Coloss. ii. 16; *drinking*, Rom. xiv. 17.

πόσος, *how great*, Matt. vi. 23. 2 Cor. vii. 11; πόσος χρόνος; *how long a time?* Mrk. ix. 21; πόσον; *how much?* Luke, xvi. 5, 7; πόσῳ; *by how much?* Matt. xii. 12; πόσῳ μᾶλλον; *by how much more?* Matt. vii. 11. x. 25; πόσοι; *how many?* Matt. xv. 34. Luke, xv. 17; πόσα, *how great things*, Matt. xxvii. 13. Mrk. xv. 4.

ποταμὸς, ὁ, *a river*, Matt. iii. 6. 2 Cor. xi. 26. Acts, xvi. 13 etc.; *a flood*, Matt. vii. 25, 27. Rev. xii. 15, 16 etc.; plur. met., *streams*, Joh. vii. 38.

ποταμοφόρητος, *carried away by the stream*, Rev. xii. 15. (Found only in this place, and in Hesychius.)

ποταπὸς, a later form for ποδαπὸς, *of what country?* In the NT *of what sort?* Matt. viii. 27. Luke, i. 29. vii. 39. 2 Pet. iii. 11. Mrk. xiii. 1.

πότε, an interrogative particle, *when? at what time?* Matt. xxv. 37, 38, 39. Luke, xxi.

7. Joh. vi. 25; ἕως πότε; *how long?* Matt. xvii. 17. Luke, ix. 41. Joh. x. 24; and, according to late Greek usage, in indirect questions, for ὁπότε, Mrk. xiii. 33, 35.

ποτὲ, an enclitic particle, referring either to the past, or to the future, *once, aforetime, formerly*, Rom. vii. 9. xi. 30. Gal. i. 13, 23. Joh. ix. 13; ἤδη ποτε, *now at length*, Rom. i. 10. Philipp. iv. 10; after negatives, as in οὐδείς ποτε, *ever*, Ephes. v. 29. 2 Pet. i. 10; similarly, τίς ποτε, *who at any time?* 1 Cor. ix. 7. Hebr. i. 5, 13; ὁποῖοί τινες, *of whatever sort*, Gal. ii. 6.

πότερος, *whether of the two*; πότερον ... ἢ, *whether ... or*, Joh. vii. 17.

ποτήριον, τό, *a cup*, Matt. xxiii. 25, 26. xxvi. 27. 1 Cor. xi. 25; *a person's lot, or dispensation*, Matt. xxvi. 39. Joh. xviii. 11. Mrk. xiv. 36. Luke, xxii. 42 etc.

ποτίζω, with accus., *to give drink to*, Matt. xxv. 35, 37, 42. Luke, xiii. 15 etc.; γάλα ὑμᾶς ἐπότισα, οὐ βρῶμα, 1 Cor. iii. 2 (RV *I fed you with milk, not with meat); to irrigate, to water*, 1 Cor. iii. 6, 8; ἓν πνεῦμα ἐποτίσθημεν, *were made to drink of one spirit*, i.e. *were imbued with one spirit*, 1 Cor. xii. 13.

πότος, ὁ, *a drinking, a carousing*, 1 Pet. iv. 3.

ποῦ, an interrogative particle, *where? in what place?* Matt. ii. 2. xxvi. 17 etc.; in indirect questions, Joh. xi. 57. Matt. ii. 4.

πού, an enclitic particle, *somewhere*, Hebr. ii. 6. iv. 4; with numerals, *about, nearly*, Rom. iv. 19.

πούς, *a foot*, Matt. iv. 6. xxii. 13. Luke, i. 79 etc.

πρᾶγμα, τό, *a deed*, James, iii. 16; *a matter*, Rom. xvi. 2. Luke, i. 1. Acts, v. 4; *a thing*, Hebr. x. 1. xi. 1; *a case, a lawsuit*, 1 Cor. vi. 1.

πραγματεία, and **πραγματία**, ἡ, *an affair, a pursuit*, 2 Tim. ii. 4.

πραγματεύομαι, *to carry on business, to trade*, Luke, xix. 13.

πραιτώριον, τό, Lat. *praetorium, the general's tent; the palace* in which the governor of a province resided, Matt. xxvii. 27. Mrk. xv. 16. Acts, xxiii. 35; *the emperor's palace* at Rome, Philipp. i. 13 (more probably, *praetorian guard*).

πράκτωρ, ὁ, *an exactor of penalties;* and, generally, *the officer* of a magistrate's court, Luke, xii. 58.

πρᾶξις, ἡ, *an act, a transaction*, the title of the "Acts of the Apostles"; *a deed, conduct, behaviour*, Acts, xix. 18. Matt. xvi. 27. Rom. viii. 13: *office, occupation*, Rom. xii. 4.

πρᾶος, and **πραΰς**, *mild, gentle*, and, of animals, *tame: gentle*, Matt. v. 5 (here AV and RV render it *meek;* but the words never did, at any time, or in any passage of any author signify *meek*. Further, the virtue of *meekness* is already commended in the first Beatitude—"*the poor*, i.e. *the lowly in spirit.*" Add that, the Beatitudes are admittedly ranged in an *ascending* order, so that a higher place is given to *gentleness* than to *meekness*, as being a much rarer virtue. Moreover, πραότης, and πραΰτης, = *gentleness*, 1 Cor. iv. 21, though here also AV and RV render it *meekness*. See Pape's Lexicon in voc. πραότης). For πρᾶος, and πραΰς, see also Matt. xi. 29. xxi. 5. 1 Pet. iii. 4.

πραότης (or **πραΰτης**), ἡ, Gal. v. 23. vi. 1. Ephes. iv. 2. 2 Cor. x. 1. Coloss. iii. 12. 2 Tim. ii. 25. Tit. iii. 2. James, i. 21.

πρασιά, ἡ, *a garden-bed;* "in the NT, metaphorically, *a division*, Mrk. vi. 40," Pape in Lex.; "ἀνέπεσον πρασιαί πρασιαί (a Hebraism), *they reclined in ranks* or *divisions*, Mrk. vi. 40," Thayer.

πράσσω, *to practise*, Acts, xix. 19; *to attend to*, 1 Thess. iv. 11; *to do, to perform*, 1 Cor. ix. 17. Acts, xix. 36. xxvi. 26. Rom. ix. 11; *to observe, to keep*, Rom. ii. 25; *to commit, to perpetrate*, 1 Cor. v. 2. 2 Cor. xii. 21. Rom. i. 32; *to exact*, as tribute, Luke, iii. 13. xix. 23; intrans., *to act*, Acts, xvii. 7; *to be in a certain state, to fare*, Acts, xv. 29. Ephes. vi. 21.

πραϋπάθεια, and **πραϋπαθία**, ἡ, 1 Tim. vi. 11, "*mildness*," Pape in Lex.

πραΰς, and **πραΰτης**, see **πρᾶος**.

πρέπω, *to be conspicuous;* πρέπειν τινί, *to befit a person* or *thing*, Hebr. vii. 26. Tit. ii. 1. 1 Tim. ii. 10; impers., πρέπει, or πρέπον ἐστίν, *it is fitting, it befitteth*, Ephes. v. 3. Matt. iii. 15. Hebr. ii. 10.

πρεσβεία, ἡ, *an embassy*, Luke, xiv. 32. xix. 14.

πρεσβεύω, *to be an ambassador*, Ephes. vi. 20. 2 Cor. v. 20.

πρεσβυτέριον, τό, *an assembly of the elders*, i.e. the Jewish Sanhedrin, Luke, xxii. 66. Acts, xxii. 5; the *council* of the Christian Church, 1 Tim. iv. 14.

πρεσβύτερος, where two are mentioned, the *elder*, Luke, xv. 25; *an elder*, 1 Tim. v. 1; οἱ πρεσβύτεροι, *the elders*, Hebr. xi. 2. Matt. xv. 2. Mrk. vii. 3, 5; *the members of the Jewish Sanhedrin*, Luke, ix. 22. Acts, xxv. 15. Matt. xxi. 23. xxvi. 3; *the members of the heavenly Sanhedrin*, Rev. iv. 4, 10. v. 8 etc.

πρεσβύτης, ὁ, *an aged man*, Luke, i. 18. Tit. ii. 2. Philem. 9.

πρεσβῦτις, ἡ, *an aged woman*, Tit. ii. 3.

πρηνὴς, *headlong*, Acts, i. 18.

πρίζω, *to saw in two, to saw asunder*, Hebr. xi. 37.

πρίν, adv., *before*, Mrk. xiv. 72 etc. (The reader is referred to his Greek Grammar.)

πρό, prepos. with genit., *before*, Acts, xii. 14. Matt. viii. 29 etc. (The reader is referred to his Greek Grammar.)

προάγω, trans., *to bring out, to bring forth*, Acts. xvi. 30. xvii. 5. xxv. 26; intrans., *to go before*, Matt. xiv. 22. 1 Tim. v. 24. Luke xviii. 39. Mrk. vi. 45; in a bad sense, *to proceed, to go forward*, 2 Joh. 9 ("to transgress the limits of true doctrine," Thayer.)

προαιρέομαι, *to prefer; to purpose*, 2 Cor. ix. 7.

προαιτιάομαι, *to bring a charge against previously*, Rom. iii. 9. (Not found in any other author, or in any other passage of the NT.)

προακούω, *to hear of before*, Coloss. i. 5.

προαμαρτάνω, *to sin before* (i.e. before being a Christian), 2 Cor. xii. 21. xiii. 2.

προαύλιον, τό, *a forecourt, a porch*, Mrk. xiv. 68. (Cf. Matt. xxvi. 71.)

προβαίνω, *to go forwards*, Matt. iv. 21. Mrk. i. 19 ; προβεβηκὼς ἐν ταῖς ἡμέραις, *advanced in years*, Luke, i. 7, 18. ii. 36.

προβάλλω, *to throw forward ; to put forth*, as leaves, Luke, xxi. 30 ; *to put forward*, Acts, xix. 33.

προβατικὸς, *pertaining to sheep;* ἡ προβατικὴ, sc. πύλη, *the sheep-gate*, Joh. v. 2.

προβάτιον, τὸ, *a lamb*, Joh. xxi. 16.

πρόβατον, τὸ, *a sheep*, Matt. vii. 15. x. 16. Luke, xv. 4, 6 etc.

προβιβάζω, *to urge forward, to induce*, Matt. xiv. 8.

προβλέπομαι, *to provide*, Hebr. xi. 40.

προγίνομαι, *to happen before;* προγεγονότα ἁμαρτήματα, *sins previously committed*, Rom. iii. 25.

προγινώσκω, *to know beforehand, to foreknow*, 1 Pet. i. 20. 2 Pet. iii. 17. Rom. viii. 29. xi. 2. Acts, xxvi. 5.

πρόγνωσις, ἡ, *foreknowledge, pre-arrangement*, 1 Pet. i. 2. Acts, ii. 23.

πρόγονος, ὁ, *an ancestor*, 2 Tim. i. 3 ; *a progenitor, a parent*, 1 Tim. v. 4.

προγράφω, *to write before*, Rom. xv. 4. Ephes. iii. 3 ; *to set forth* or *designate beforehand*, Jude, 4 ; *to depict* or *portray openly*, Gal. iii. 1.

πρόδηλος, *plainly manifest*, Hebr. vii. 14. 1 Tim. v. 24, 25.

προδίδωμι, *to give before, to give first*, Rom. xi. 35.

προδότης, ὁ, *a betrayer, a traitor*, Luke, vi. 16. Acts, vii. 32. 2 Tim. iii. 4.

πρόδρομος, *running before;* as substantive, *a forerunner*, Hebr. vi. 20.

προεῖδον, 2 aor. of προοράω, *to foresee*, Acts, ii. 31. Gal. iii. 8.

προεῖπα (and **ον**), *to say* or *mention before*, Rom. ix. 29. 2 Cor. vii. 3. Acts, i. 16. 2 Pet. iii. 2 etc.; *to tell beforehand*, Mrk. xiii. 23. Matt. xxiv. 25. 2 Cor. xiii. 2. Gal. v. 21.

προελπίζω, *to hope before*, Ephes. i. 12.

προ] *TO THE NEW TESTAMENT* [προ

προενάρχομαι, *to make a beginning previously*, 2 Cor. viii. 6; *to be the first to make a beginning*, 2 Cor. viii. 10. (Not found in any other author.)

προεπαγγέλλω, *to announce beforehand; to promise before*, Rom. i. 2. 2 Cor. ix. 5.

προέρχομαι, *to go before, to go in advance*, 2 Cor. ix. 5; *to go forward*, Mrk. xiv. 35. Acts, xii. 10; *to go before, to precede*, Luke, i. 17. xxii. 47; *to outstrip*, Mrk. vi. 33.

προετοιμάζω, *to prepare beforehand*, Rom. ix. 23. Ephes. ii. 10.

προευαγγελίζομαι, *to preach the gospel beforehand*, Gal. iii. 8.

προέχομαι, *to surpass, to have an advantage*, Rom. iii. 9.

προηγέομαι, with accus., *to prefer*, Rom. xii. 10 [lit. *to go before deferentially*].

πρόθεσις, ή, *a setting forth; οἱ ἄρτοι τῆς προθέσεως*, and ή πρόθεσις τῶν ἄρτων, *the shewbread*, Matt. xii. 4. Mrk. ii. 26. Luke, vi. 4. Heb. ix. 2; *a purpose*, Acts, xi. 23. xxvii. 13. Rom. viii. 28. ix. 11. Ephes. i. 11. iii. 11 etc.

προθεσμία, ή, sc. ήμέρα, *the day pre-determined*, Gal. iv. 2. (Properly, it is an Attic law-term.)

προθυμία, ή, *readiness*, Acts, xvii. 11. 2 Cor. viii. 11, 19. ix. 2.

πρόθυμος, *ready, willing*, Matt. xxvi. 41. Mrk. xiv. 38; τὸ πρόθυμον = ή προθυμία, Rom. i. 15.

προθύμως, adv., *willingly*, 1 Pet. v. 2.

πρόϊμος, see πρώϊμος.

προΐστημι, trans., *to set over;* intrans., *to be over, to rule, to superintend*, 1 Tim. iii. 4, 12. v. 17. 1 Thess. v. 12. Rom. xii. 8; προΐστασθαι, *to care for, to give attention to*, Tit. iii. 8, 14 (RV *to maintain good works*).

προκαλέομαι, *to challenge, to provoke*, Gal. v. 26.

προκαταγγέλλω, *to foretell, to predict*, Acts, iii. 18. vii. 52; *to promise*, var. lect. ad 2 Cor. ix. 5.

προκαταρτίζω, *to prepare beforehand*, 2 Cor. ix. 5.

πρόκειμαι, *to be placed before one, to be set forth*, Jude, 7; *to be offered, to be set before one*, Hebr. vi. 18. xii. 1, 2; *to be present*, 2 Cor. viii. 12.

προκηρύσσω, *to announce beforehand*, Acts, xiii. 24.

προκοπή, ή, *progress, advancement*, Philipp. i. 12, 25. 1 Tim. iv. 15.

προκόπτω, *to go forward; to advance*, Rom. xiii. 12; *to make progress, to increase*, Luke, ii. 52. Gal. i. 14. 2 Tim. ii. 16. iii. 9, 13.

πρόκριμα, τὸ, *prejudgment, prejudice*, 1 Tim. v. 21. (A very late form.)

προκυρόω, *to ratify beforehand*, Gal. iii. 17. (Confined to the NT and eccles. writers.)

προλαμβάνω, *to take before*, 1 Cor. xi. 21; *to anticipate*; προέλαβε μυρίσαι, *hath anointed beforehand*, Mrk. xiv.

161

8; pass., *to be surprised, to be overtaken*, Gal. vi. 1.

προλέγω, *to forewarn, to say or tell beforehand*, 2 Cor. xiii. 2. Gal. v. 21.

προμαρτύρομαι, *to testify beforehand*, 1 Pet. i. 11.

προμελετάω, *to meditate beforehand*, Luke, xxi. 14.

προμεριμνάω, *to be anxious beforehand*, Mrk. xiii. 11.

προνοέω, *to provide beforehand*, 2 Cor. viii. 21; *to provide for*, 1 Tim. v. 8; προνοεῖσθαι, *to take thought for*, Rom. xii. 17.

πρόνοια, ἡ, *forethought, provident care*, Acts, xxiv. 3; πρόνοιαν ποιεῖσθαί τινος, *to make provision for*, Rom. xiii. 14.

προοράω, *to see previously*, Acts, xxi. 29; προορᾶσθαι, *to keep before one's eyes, to be ever mindful of*, Acts, ii. 25.

προορίζω, *to predetermine*, 1 Cor. ii. 7. Acts, iv. 28; *to appoint beforehand, to foreordain*, Rom. viii. 29. Ephes. i. 5, 11.

προπάσχω, *to suffer before*, 1 Thess. ii. 2.

προπάτωρ, ὁ, *a forefather*, Rom. iv. 1.

προπέμπω, *to send before; to send on his way, to escort*, Acts, xx. 38. xxi. 5. 1 Cor. xvi. 6, 11. Rom. xv. 24; *to set a person forward, to equip him for his journey*, Acts, xv. 3. Tit. iii. 13. 2 Cor. i. 16. 3 Joh. 6.

προπετὴς, *precipitate, rash*, Acts, xix. 36. 2 Tim. iii. 4 (RV *headstrong*).

προπορεύομαι, with genit., *to go before one*, Acts, vii. 40. Luke, i. 76.

πρὸς, prepos., with genitive, dative, and accusative. In the NT it is seldom used with the genitive (*on the side of*); somewhat more frequently with the dative (*near*); but often appears with the accusative (*to, towards* etc.). (The reader is referred to his Greek Grammar.)

προσάββατον, τὸ, *the day before the sabbath*, Mrk. xv. 42.

προσαγορεύω, *to address; to name, to style*, Hebr. v. 10.

προσάγω, trans., *to lead to, to bring*, 1 Pet. iii. 18. Luke, ix. 41. Matt. xviii. 24 etc.; *to bring before the court, to summon*, Acts, xii. 6; intrans., *to approach*, Acts, xxvii. 27.

προσαγωγὴ, ἡ, *approach, access*, Rom. v. 2, Ephes. ii. 18. iii. 12. ("=*access*, especially in later writings, as the NT," Pape's Lex. in voc.)

προσαιτέω, *to ask alms, to beg*, Joh. ix. 8, var. lect. ad Luke, xviii. 35.

προσαίτης, ὁ, *a beggar*, Mrk. ix. 46. Joh. ix. 8.

προσαναβαίνω, *to go up higher*, Luke, xiv. 10.

προσαναλίσκω, *to expend besides*, a var. lect. ad Luke, viii. 43. (Cf. Luke, x. 35.)

προσαναπληρόω, *to fill up, to supply*, 2 Cor. ix. 12. xi. 9.

προσανατίθεμαι, with dat. of person, *to confer with, to consult,* Gal. i. 16; *to communicate, to impart,* Gal. ii. 6.

προσανέχω, *to rise up towards, to approach,* a doubtful var. lect. ad Acts, xxvii. 27. (Westcott reads προσάγειν. See Pape's Lexicon in voc. προσανέχω.)

προσαπειλέω, *to add threats, to threaten besides,* Acts, iv. 21.

προσδαπανάω, *to spend besides,* Luke, x. 35.

προσδέομαι, *to need in addition,* Acts, xvii. 25.

προσδέχομαι, *to give access to, to receive,* Luke, xv. 2. Rom. xvi. 2. Philipp. ii. 29; *to accept,* Hebr. x. 34. xi. 35; *to look for, to expect,* Luke, ii. 25, 38. xii. 36.

προσδοκάω, *to expect,* Matt. xxiv. 50. Luke, xii. 46. Acts, iii. 5 etc.

προσδοκία, ἡ, *expectation,* Acts, xii. 11. Luke, xxi. 26.

προσεάω, *to permit one to approach,* Acts, xxvii. 7. (RV *suffer further.* It is a ἅπαξ λεγόμενον, being found nowhere else.)

προσεγγίζω, *to approach nigh to,* a var. lect. ad Mrk. ii. 4. (Westcott reads προσενέγκαι.)

προσεδρεύω, *to sit near; assiduously to attend to,* 1 Cor. ix. 13. (Westcott παρεδρεύω.)

προσεργάζομαι, *to gain besides by trading,* Luke, xix. 16.

προσέρχομαι, *to come to,* Matt. iv. 3, 11. Luke, xiii. 31; *to draw near to,* Hebr. iv. 16. x. 1, 22; *to assent to,* 1 Tim. vi. 3.

προσευχή, ἡ, *a prayer* addressed to God, Matt. xxi. 22. Luke, xxii. 45. Acts, iii. 1 etc.; *a place set apart for prayer,* Acts, xvi. 13, 16.

προσεύχομαι, *to pray, to offer prayers,* Matt. vi. 5, 7, 9. xiv. 23 etc. (Everywhere of prayers offered to God.)

προσέχω, *to give heed to, to pay attention to,* Acts, viii. 6, 10, 11. xvi. 14. xx. 28 etc.; *to take care,* Matt. vi. 1; with ἀπὸ, *to beware of,* Matt. vii. 15. Luke, xii. 1; *to addict oneself to,* 1 Tim. iii. 8.

προσηλόω, *to nail to,* Coloss. ii. 14.

προσήλυτος, *a new comer, a stranger;* "in the language of the NT, a convert from paganism to Judaism; therefore our *proselyte,*" Pape in Lex. See Matt. xxiii. 15. Acts, ii. 10. vi. 5. xiii. 43. Some have divided them into two classes, (1) *proselytes of righteousness,* who accepted the whole of the Mosaic law, including circumcision, and (2) *proselytes of the gate,* who accepted only the seven precepts of Noah,—against idolatry, blasphemy, homicide, unchastity, rebellion against God, theft, and the use of flesh with the blood, but remained uncircumcised. (It is an adjective, and not a substantive, as some have made it.)

πρόσκαιρος, *continuing only for a time, temporary*, Matt. xiii. 21. Mrk. iv. 17. 2 Cor. iv. 18. Hebr. xi. 25.

προσκαλέομαι, *to call to oneself, to summon*, Matt. x. 1. xv. 10, 32. Acts, ii. 39. xvi. 10; *to call* to an office, *to appoint*, Acts, xiii. 2. (The form προσκαλέω does not appear in the NT.)

προσκαρτερέω, *to persevere, to continue steadfastly in*, Acts, i. 14. ii. 42. vi. 4. Rom. xii. 12. Coloss. iv. 2; *to adhere to* a person, *to attend upon*, Acts, viii. 13. x. 7; *to give constant attention to*, Rom. xiii. 6; with ἐν, *to continue in*, Acts, ii. 46; *to be in attendance on, to wait on*, Mrk. iii. 9.

προσκαρτέρησις, ἡ, *perseverance*, Ephes. vi. 18. ("A late form," Pape in Lex. "Nowhere else," Thayer.)

προσκεφάλαιον, τὸ, *a pillow, a cushion*, Mrk. iv. 38.

προσκληρόω, *to allot*, Acts, xvii. 4.

πρόσκλησις, ἡ, *an invitation*, a var. lect. ad 1 Tim. v. 21. (Westcott reads κατὰ πρόσκλισιν.)

προσκλίνω, *to cause to lean against*; pass., *to incline towards a person*, Acts, v. 36.

πρόσκλισις, ἡ, *inclination* to one party rather than to the other, 1 Tim. v. 21 (RV *partiality*. See πρόσκλησις;

προσκολλάω, *to glue to*; pass., *to give oneself to, to cleave to*, Ephes. v. 31.

πρόσκομμα, τὸ, *a stumblingblock*, 1 Cor. viii. 9. Rom. xiv. 13; *a stumbling*; λίθος προσκόμματος, *a stone of stumbling*, Rom. ix. 32, 33. 1 Pet. ii. 8; *an offence* against the conscience; ἐσθίων διὰ προσκόμματος, *eating with offence*, Rom. xiv. 20.

προσκοπή, ἡ, *an occasion of stumbling*, 2 Cor. vi. 3. ("= πρόσκομμα, *an offence*," Pape in Lex.)

προσκόπτω, *to stumble against; to stumble*, Rom. ix. 32. xiv. 21. Joh. xi. 9, 10; τὸν πόδα πρὸς λίθον προσκόπτειν, *to dash the foot against a stone*, Matt. iv. 6. Luke, iv. 11.

προσκυλίω, *to roll to*, Matt. xxvii. 60. Mrk. xv. 46.

προσκυνέω, *to do reverence to, to worship*, Matt. ii. 2, 8. xiv. 33. xv. 25. 1 Cor. xiv. 25. Joh. iv. 23 etc.

προσκυνητής, ὁ, *a worshipper*, Joh. iv. 23.

προσλαλέω, *to speak to*, Acts, xiii. 43. xxviii. 20.

προσλαμβάνομαι, *to take as an associate*, Acts, xvii. 5. xviii. 26; *to receive* with kindness or hospitality, Acts, xxviii. 2. Rom. xv. 7. Philem. 17; *to take*, as food, Acts, xxvii. 33, 36; *to accept*, Rom. xiv. 3. xv. 7. (The active form is not used in the NT.)

πρόσλημψις, ἡ, *a receiving*, Rom. xi. 15. (Westcott reads πρόσλημψις.)

προσμένω, *to tarry*, Acts, xviii. 18. 1 Tim. i. 3; *to continue in, to persevere in*, Acts, xiii.

43. 1 Tim. v. 5; *to cleave to*, Acts, xi. 23.

προσορμίζω, *to moor a ship*; pass., *to come to anchor*, Mrk. vi. 53.

προσοφείλω, *to owe besides*, Philem. 19.

προσοχθίζω, *to be displeased with*, Hebr. iii. 10.

προσπαίω, *to beat against*, a var. lect. ad Matt. vii. 25. (Westcott reads προσέπεσαν.)

πρόσπεινος, *very hungry*, Acts, x. 10. ("Not found elsewhere," Thayer.)

προσπήγνυμι, *to fasten to* the cross; *to crucify*, Acts, ii. 23.

προσπίπτω, *to fall down before*, Mrk. iii. 11. v. 33. Luke, viii. 28, 47. Acts, xvi. 29 etc.; *to beat against*, Matt. vii. 25. See προσπαίω.

προσποιοῦμαι, *to pretend*, *to affect*, Luke, xxiv. 28.

προσπορεύομαι, *to approach*, Mrk. x. 35.

προσρήγνυμι, intrans., *to break against, to dash against*, Luke, vi. 48, 49.

προστάσσω, *to prescribe*, *to command*, Matt. i. 24. viii. 4. Luke, v. 14 etc.; pass., *to be appointed*, Acts, x. 33. xvii. 26.

προστάτις, ἡ, *a female guardian; a protector*, Rom. xvi. 2 (RV *a succourer*).

προστίθημι, *to add to*, Matt. vi. 27. Luke, xii. 25; pass., *to be added*, Acts, ii. 41. v. 14. xi. 24. Matt. vi. 33; προσετέθη πρὸς πατέρας αὐτοῦ, *was gathered to his fathers*, Acts, xiii. 36.

προστρέχω, *to run to*, Mrk. ix. 15. Acts, viii. 30.

προσφάγιον, τὸ, =ὄψον, *anything eaten with bread as a relish*; and, generally, *victuals, food*, Joh. xxi. 5. See ὀψάριον.

πρόσφατος, *new*, Hebr. x. 20.

προσφάτως, adv., *lately, recently*, Acts, xviii. 2.

προσφέρω, *to bring to*, Matt. iv. 24. viii. 16. ix. 2, 32 etc.; *to offer*, Matt. ii. 11. Acts, vii. 42. viii. 18. Hebr. xi. 4; pass. with dative, *to conduct oneself, to deal with*, Hebr. xii. 7.

προσφιλής, *pleasing, acceptable*, Philipp. iv. 8 (RV *lovely*. See Pape's Lexicon in voc.)

προσφορά, ἡ, *an offering, a sacrifice*, Acts, xxi. 26. xxiv. 17. Hebr. x. 5, 8, 10, 14, 18; ἡ προσφορὰ τῶν ἐθνῶν, Rom. xv. 16 ("the sacrifice which I offer in turning the Gentiles to God," Thayer).

προσφωνέω, *to call to, to address*, Luke, xiii. 12. Matt. xi. 16. Acts, xxii. 2; *to summon*, Luke, vi. 13.

πρόσχυσις, ἡ, *a sprinkling*, Hebr. xi. 28. (It is confined to the NT and very late writers.)

προσψαύω, *to touch*, Luke, xi. 46.

προσωπολημπτέω, and **προσωπολημπτέω**, *to have respect of persons*, James, ii. 9.

προσωπολήπτης, and **προσωπολήμπτης**, ὁ, *a respecter of persons*, Acts, x. 34. (This and the preceding word are very unclassical forms.)

προσωποληψία, and **προσωπο-ληψία**, ἡ, *respect of persons*, Rom. ii. 11. Ephes. vi. 9. Coloss. iii. 25. James, ii. 1. (Confined to the NT and ecclesiastical writers.)

πρόσωπον, τὸ, *the face, the countenance*, Matt. vi. 16, 17. xvii. 2, 6; πρόσωπον πρὸς πρόσωπον, *face to face*, i.e. *clearly*, 1 Cor. xiii. 12; *appearance*, Matt. xvi. 3. Luke, xii. 56; *the person* of any one, Matt. xxii. 16. Mrk. xii. 14. Luke, xx. 21; εἰς πρόσωπόν τινος, *in the presence of*, 2 Cor. viii. 24.

προτάσσω, *to assign beforehand*, Acts, xvii. 26. (Westcott reads προστεταγμένους.)

προτείνω, *to extend, to stretch out* for the purpose of scourging, Acts, xxii. 25 ("For it appears from vs. 25 that he had already been bound," Thayer).

πρότερος, *former, prior;* πρότερον, *before, in time past*, Joh. vii. 50; τὸ πρότερον, *previously, before*, Joh. vi. 62; *the first time*, Gal. iv. 13; αἱ πρότερον ἡμέραι, *the former days*, Hebr. x. 32.

προτίθημι, *to set before, to expose to public view;* mid., *to purpose, to determine*, Ephes. i. 9. Rom. i. 13; *to set forth*, Rom. iii. 25.

προτρέπω, *to urge forwards;* mid., *to exhort, to encourage*, Acts, xviii. 27.

προτρέχω, *to run before, to outrun*, Luke, xix. 4. Joh. xx. 4.

προϋπάρχω, *to be before, to be previously*, Luke, xxiii. 12. Acts, viii. 9.

πρόφασις, ἡ, *a pretext*, 1 Thess. ii. 5 (RV *a cloke of covetousness); an excuse*, Joh. xv. 22; *a pretence*, Acts, xxvii. 30. Luke, xx. 47. Philipp. i. 18.

προφέρω, *to bring forth*, Luke, vi. 45.

προφητεία, ἡ, *prophecy*, Matt. xiii. 14. 2 Pet. i. 20, 21. Rom. xii. 6. 1 Cor. xii. 10. xiii. 8 etc. [= "*prediction*" and "*teaching*."]

προφητεύω, *to predict, to prophesy*, Matt. xi. 13. xv. 7. Acts, ii. 17, 18. Luke, i. 67 etc.

προφήτης, ὁ, *a prophet*, Matt. i. 22. Luke, xvi. 29 etc.

προφητικὸς, *proceeding from a prophet, prophetic*, Rom. xvi. 26. 2 Pet. i. 19.

προφῆτις, ἡ, *a prophetess*, Luke, ii. 36. Rev. ii. 20.

προφθάνω, *to anticipate*, Matt. xvii. 25.

προχειρίζομαι, *to appoint*, Acts, xxii. 14. xxvi. 16; pass., *to be appointed*, Acts, iii. 20.

προχειροτονέω, *to fore-appoint, to choose previously*, Acts, x. 41.

πρύμνα, ἡ, *the stern* of a ship, Mrk. iv. 38. Acts, xxvii. 29, 41.

πρωΐ, adv., *early*, Joh. xviii. 23. Acts, xxviii. 23 etc.

πρωΐα, see πρώϊος.

πρώϊμος, and **πρόϊμος**, *early*, James, v. 7.

πρωϊνὸς, *of the morning*, Rev. ii. 28. xxii. 16.

[πρω] TO THE NEW TESTAMENT [πυγ

πρώϊος, *early;* ἡ πρωΐα, sc. ὥρα, *morning,* Matt. xxvii. 1. Joh. xxi. 4.

πρῷρα, ἡ, *the prow* of a vessel, Acts, xxvii. 30, 41.

πρωτεύω, *to have the pre-eminence,* Coloss. i. 18.

πρωτοκαθεδρία, ἡ, *a sitting in the first seat, the chief seat,* Matt. xxiii. 6. Mrk. xii. 39. Luke, xi. 43. xx. 46.

πρωτοκλισία, ἡ, *the chief place at table,* Matt. xxiii. 6. See also the other passages cited under πρωτοκαθεδρία.

πρῶτος, *first;* τὸ πρῶτον, *at first.* (The reader is referred to his Greek Grammar.)

πρωτοστάτης, ὁ, *a chief, a leader,* Acts, xxiv. 5.

πρωτοτόκια, τὰ, *right of primogeniture, birthright,* Hebr. xii. 16. (But see Pape's Lexicon on πρωτοτοκεῖα and πρωτοτοκία, the first of which he renders *the right of primogeniture,* and the second *the first bringing forth.*)

πρωτοτόκος, *bearing for the first time,* and **πρωτότοκος**, *first born;* see these forms discussed under κτίσις.

πρώτως, adv., *first,* Acts, xi. 26.

πταίω, *to stumble; to err, to sin,* James, ii. 10. iii. 2. Rom. xi. 11. 2 Pet. i. 10.

πτέρνα, ἡ, *the heel* of the foot; τὴν πτέρναν ἐπαίρειν ἐπί τινα, *to lift up the heel against one,* Joh. xiii. 18.

πτερύγιον, τὸ, *a little wing;* any pointed extremity, *the top* or *pinnacle* of a building, *an aisle,* Matt. iv. 5. Luke, iv. 9.

πτέρυξ, ἡ, *a wing* of a bird, Matt. xxiii. 37. Luke, xiii. 34. Rev. xii. 14 etc.

πτηνὸς, *winged;* τὰ πτηνὰ, *birds,* 1 Cor. xv. 39.

πτοέω, *to scare;* pass., *to be terrified,* Luke, xxi. 9. xxiv. 37.

πτόησις, ἡ, *terror;* φοβεῖσθαι πτόησιν, *to be frightened with terror,* 1 Pet. iii. 6.

πτύον, τὸ, *a winnowing-shovel, a fan,* Matt. iii. 12. Luke, iii. 17.

πτύρω, *to frighten;* pass., *to be frightened,* Philipp. i. 28.

πτύσμα, τὸ, *spittle,* Joh. ix. 6.

πτύσσω, *to fold up, to close,* Luke, iv. 20.

πτύω, *to spit,* Joh. ix. 6. Mrk. vii. 33. viii. 23.

πτῶμα, τὸ, *that which has fallen; a corpse,* Matt. xiv. 12. Mrk. vi. 29. xv. 45; *a carcase,* Matt. xxiv. 28. Rev. xi. 8, 9.

πτῶσις, ἡ, *a falling, a fall,* Matt. vii. 27. Luke, ii. 34.

πτωχεία, ἡ, *beggary; poverty,* 2 Cor. viii. 9. Rev. ii. 9; ἡ κατὰ βάθους πτωχεία αὐτῶν, *their deep poverty,* 2 Cor. viii. 2.

πτωχεύω, *to beg; to become poor,* 2 Cor. viii. 9.

πτωχὸς, ὁ, *a beggar,* Luke, xvi. 20, 22; as adjective, *poor,* James, ii. 5. Luke, vi. 20. xiv. 13, 21 etc.; *lowly,* Matt. v. 3; *beggarly, sorry,* Gal. iv. 9.

πυγμὴ, ἡ, *the fist;* πυγμῇ νίπτεσθαι τὰς χεῖρας, Mrk. vii. 3 ("*to wash the hands with the fist,* i.e. so that one hand is rubbed with the clenched fist of the other," Thayer. RV *diligently*).

Πύθων, ὁ, *Python*, the name of the Pythian serpent that guarded the oracle at Delphi, and was slain by Apollo; πνεῦμα πύθωνα, *a divining spirit, a spirit of divination,* Acts, xvi. 16.

πυκνὸς, *dense; frequent,* 1 Tim. v. 23; πυκνὰ, as adverb, *often, frequently,* Luke, v. 33; πυκνότερον, *more frequently,* Acts, xxiv. 26.

πυκτεύω, *to box; to fight,* 1 Cor. ix. 26.

πύλη, ἡ, *a gate, entrance,* Luke, vii. 12. Acts, ix. 24. xvi. 13.

πυλὼν, ὁ, *a gate,* Luke, xvi. 20. Acts, x. 17. xiv. 13. Rev. xxi. 12, 13 etc.; *a porch,* Matt. xxvi. 71. Acts, xii. 13.

πυνθάνομαι, *to ask, to enquire,* Acts, iv. 7. xxi. 33. Joh. iv. 52 etc.; *to ascertain,* Acts, xxiii. 34.

πῦρ, τὸ, *fire,* Matt. iii. 10. vii. 19 etc.; *the fire of hell,* τὸ πῦρ, Matt. v. 22. xviii. 8, 9. xxv. 41. Rev. xix. 20 etc.; φλὸξ πυρὸς, *a fiery flame,* Acts, vii. 30. Hebr. i. 7. Rev. i. 14.

πυρὰ, ἡ, *a fire, a pile of burning fuel,* Acts, xxviii. 2, 3.

πύργος, ὁ, *a tower,* Luke, xiii. 4. xiv. 28. Matt. xxi. 33.

πυρέσσω, *to be ill of a fever,* Matt. viii. 14. Mrk. i. 30.

πυρετὸς, ὁ, *a fever,* Matt. viii. 15. Luke, iv. 38, 39. Joh. iv. 52 etc.

πύρινος, *of fire,* Rev. ix. 17.

πυρόω, *to set on fire, to kindle,* in the NT used only in the passive, *to be on fire,* 2 Pet. iii. 12; *to be fiery,* Ephes. vi. 16; *to burn, to be incensed,* 2 Cor. xi. 29; *to be inflamed with lust,* 1 Cor. vii. 9; *to be melted, to be refined,* Rev. i. 15. iii. 18.

πυρράζω, *to be fiery red,* Matt. xvi. 2. ("Confined to the NT and late writers," Pape in Lex.)

πυρρὸς, *red,* Rev. vi. 4. xii. 3.

πύρωσις, ἡ, *a burning,* Rev. xviii. 9, 18; *a fiery trial,* 1 Pet. iv. 12.

πωλέω, *to sell,* Matt. xiii. 44. xix. 21. xxi. 12 etc.

πῶλος, ὁ, *an ass's colt,* Matt. xxi. 2, 5, 7. Joh. xii. 15. Luke, xix. 30, 33, 35.

πώποτε, adv., *ever at any time,* Joh. i. 18. v. 37. viii. 33 etc.

πωρόω, *to harden,* Joh. xii. 40; pass., *to grow hard, to be hardened,* 2 Cor. iii. 14. Rom. xi. 7. Mrk. vi. 52. viii. 17.

πώρωσις, ἡ, *hardening* (of mind or heart), Mrk. iii. 5. Rom. xi. 25.

πῶς, adv., *how? in what way?* Luke, i. 24. x. 26. Also πως, enclitic, *in some way, in any way.* (See Greek Grammar.)

P

ῥαββὶ, and **ῥαββεὶ,** indecl., *Rabbi, a title of respect, a teacher,* Joh. iii. 26. Matt. xxvi. 25, 49. Mrk. ix. 5. xi. 21 etc.

ῥαββονὶ, and **ῥαββουνεὶ,** indecl., *Rabboni, master, teacher,* Joh. xx. 16. Mrk. x. 51.

ῥαβδίζω, to beat with rods, Acts, xvi. 22. 2 Cor. xi. 25.

ῥάβδος, ἡ, a rod, Hebr. iv. 4. 1 Cor. iv. 21; a walking-stick, a staff, Matt. x. 10. Luke, ix. 3. Hebr. xi. 21; ἐν ῥάβδῳ σιδηρᾷ, with a rod of iron, Rev. ii. 27 ("indicates the severest, most rigorous rule," Thayer); a sceptre, Hebr. i. 8.

ῥαβδοῦχος, ὁ, a lictor, Acts, xvi. 35, 36.

ῥᾳδιούργημα, τὸ, a careless action; villany, Acts, xviii. 14.

ῥᾳδιουργία, ἡ, levity in acting; wickedness, Acts, xiii. 10.

ῥακὰ, and ῥαχὰ, indecl., a senseless fellow, Matt. v. 22.

ῥάκος, τὸ, a torn garment; and, generally, cloth, Mrk. ii. 21. Matt. ix. 16.

ῥαντίζω, to sprinkle, Hebr. ix. 13, 21; met., to purify; ῥεραντισμένος τὰς καρδίας, purified as to our hearts, Hebr. x. 22.

ῥαντισμὸς, ὁ, a sprinkling; αἵματι ῥαντισμοῦ, the blood of sprinkling, Hebr. xii. 24 ("appointed for sprinkling," Thayer); εἰς ῥαντισμὸν αἵματος Ἰησοῦ Χριστοῦ, 1 Pet. i. 2 ("that they may be purified from the guilt of their sins by the blood of Christ," Thayer).

ῥαπίζω, to smite with a rod; and, generally, to smite, Matt. v. 39. xxvi. 67.

ῥάπισμα, τὸ, a blow with a rod; a slap with the hand, Mrk. xiv. 65. Joh. xviii. 22. xix. 3.

ῥαφὶς, ἡ, a needle, Matt. xix. 24. Mrk. x. 25.

ῥέδη, ἡ, Lat. rheda, a chariot, Rev. xviii. 13.

Ῥεμφὰν, or Ῥομφὰ, indecl., Remphan, a Coptic name of the pagan deity Saturn, Acts, vii. 43.

ῥέω, to flow, Joh. vii. 38.

ῥῆγμα, τὸ, a fracture; a fall, a ruin, Luke, vi. 49.

ῥήγνυμι, to rend, to burst, Luke, v. 37. Mrk. ii. 22. Matt. ix. 17; to tear in pieces, to rend, Matt. vii. 6; to cast down, Mrk. ix. 18. Luke, ix. 42; to utter a loud voice, Gal. iv. 27.

ῥῆμα, τὸ, a word, Hebr. xii. 19. 2 Cor. xii. 4; a saying, Luke, ii. 50. ix. 45. xviii. 34 etc.; a promise, Hebr. vi. 5; a command, Luke, v. 5; a thing, Luke, ii. 15. Acts, x. 37.

ῥήτωρ, ὁ, an orator, Acts, xxiv. 1.

ῥητῶς, adv., expressly, 1 Tim. iv. 1.

ῥίζα, ἡ, a root, Matt. iii. 10. Luke, iii. 9; ῥίζα πικρίας, a root of bitterness, Hebr. xii. 15 ("of a person disposed to apostatize, and to induce others to commit the same offence," Thayer); a cause, a source, 1 Tim. vi. 10; a descendant, Rom. xv. 12. Rev. v. 5. xxii. 16.

ῥιζόω, to cause to strike root; pass., to be firmly rooted, Ephes. iii. 17. Coloss. ii. 7.

ῥιπὴ, ἡ, a rapid movement; ἐν ῥιπῇ ὀφθαλμοῦ, in the twinkling of an eye, 1 Cor. xv. 52

(See Pape's Lexicon in voc. ῥιπή.)

ῥιπίζομαι, *to be tossed to and fro*, James, i. 6.

ῥιπτέω, and **ῥίπτω**, *to cast*, Luke, iv. 35. xvii. 2; *to throw out*, Acts, xxvii. 19, 29; *to cast down*, Matt. xxvii. 5; *to throw off*, Acts, xxii. 23; *to deposit*, Matt. xv. 30; pass., *to be scattered*, Matt. ix. 36 ("*to be prostrated*," Thayer).

ῥοιζηδὸν, adv., *with a loud noise*, 2 Pet. iii. 10.

ῥομφαία, ἡ, *a large sword*; and, generally, *a sword*, Rev. i. 16. ii. 12. vi. 8; met., *anguish*, Luke, ii. 35.

ῥύμη, ἡ, *a street, a lane*, Matt. vi. 2. Luke, xiv. 21. Acts, ix. 11. xii. 10.

ῥύομαι, *to deliver*, Matt. vi. 13. xxvii. 43. 2 Pet. ii. 7; ὁ ῥυόμενος, *the deliverer*, Rom. xi. 26; pass., *to be delivered*, Rom. xv. 31. Luke, i. 74.

ῥυπαίνω, *to make foul*; pass., *to be made filthy*, Rev. xxii. 11.

ῥυπαρεύομαι = ῥυπαίνομαι, a var. lect. ad Rev. xxii. 11.

ῥυπαρία, ἡ, *filthiness*, James, i. 21.

ῥυπαρὸς, *dirty, mean*, James, ii. 2; *filthy*, Rev. xxii. 11.

ῥύπος, ὁ, *filth*, 1 Pet. iii. 21.

ῥύσις, ἡ, *a flowing, an issue*, Mrk. v. 25. Luke, viii. 43.

ῥυτὶς, ἡ, *a wrinkle*, Ephes. v. 27.

Ῥωμαϊστὶ, adv., *in Latin*, Joh. xix. 20.

ῥώννυμι, *to strengthen*; hence the imperatives ἔρρωσο, *farewell*, and ἔρρωσθε, *fare ye well*, as a formula in closing a letter, Acts, xv. 29.

Σ

σαβαχθανὶ, and **σαβαχθανεὶ**, *thou hast forsaken me*, Matt. xxvii. 46. Mrk. xv. 34.

σαβαὼθ, a Hebrew plural, *hosts, armies*, Rom. ix. 29. James, v. 4.

σαββατισμὸς, ὁ, *a day of rest*, Hebr. iv. 9.

σάββατον, τὸ, (and in plural) the Jewish *sabbath*, Matt. xii. 2, 5, 8 etc.; ὁδὸς σαββάτου, *a sabbath day's journey*, Acts, i. 12 ("according to the Talmud, the distance is two thousand cubits, according to Epiphanius, six stadia," Thayer); *a week*, Mrk. xvi. 9. Luke, xviii. 12. 1 Cor. xvi. 2.

σαγήνη, ἡ, *a drag net*, Matt. xiii. 47.

Σαδδουκαῖος, ὁ, *a Sadducee*, one belonging to the sect of the *Sadducees*, who derived their name from *Zadok*, who was high priest in the time of David, Matt. xxii. 23. Mrk. xii. 18. Acts, xxiii. 8.

σαίνω, *to fawn upon, to flatter*; pass., *to be disturbed, to be troubled*, 1 Thess. iii. 3.

σάκκος, ὁ, a sort of dark, coarse cloth, made of the hair of animals, *sackcloth*, Rev. vi. 12. xi. 3. Matt. xi. 21. Luke, x. 13.

σαλεύω, *to agitate, to shake*, Matt. xi. 7. Luke, vii. 24;

σαλ] TO THE NEW TESTAMENT [σεα

to cause to totter, to shake, Matt. xxiv. 29. Luke, vi. 48. xxi. 26. Hebr. xii. 26 ; τὰ μὴ σαλευόμενα, *things that are not shaken*, Hebr. xii. 27 ; *to shake together*, Luke, vi. 38 ; *to cast down, to overthrow*, Acts, ii. 25 ; *to disturb*, 2 Thess. ii. 2 ; *to stir up, to excite*, Acts, xvii. 13.

σάλος, ὁ, *the tossing of the waves*, Luke, xxi. 25.

σάλπιγξ, ἡ, *a trumpet*, Matt. xxiv. 31. 1 Cor. xiv. 8. xv. 52. Hebr. xii. 19 etc.

σαλπίζω, *to sound with a trumpet*, Rev. viii. 6, 7, 8 etc.

σαλπιστὴς, ὁ, a later form for σαλπιγκτὴς, *a trumpeter*, Rev. xviii. 22.

Σαμαρείτης, and Σαμαρίτης, ὁ, *a Samaritan*, Luke, x. 33 etc.

Σαμαρεῖτις, and Σαμαρῖτις, ἡ, *a Samaritan woman*, Joh. iv. 9.

σανδάλιον, τὸ, *a sandal*, Mrk. vi. 9. Acts, xii. 8.

σανὶς, ἡ, *a plank*, Acts, xxvii. 44.

σαπρὸς, *rotten ; bad, worthless*, Matt. vii. 17, 18. xii. 33. xiii. 48. Luke, vi. 43 etc.

σάπφειρος, ἡ, *a precious stone, the sapphire*, Rev. xxi. 19.

σαργάνη, ἡ, *a basket*, 2 Cor. xi. 33.

σάρδινος, ὁ, = σάρδιον, a var. lect. ad Rev. iv. 3.

σάρδιον, τὸ, *a precious stone, the cornelian*, Rev. iv. 3. xxi. 20.

σαρδιόνυξ, ὁ, = σαρδόνυξ, a var. lect. ad Rev. xxi. 20.

σαρδόνυξ, ὁ, *a prec.ous stone, exhibiting the red colours of the cornelian and the white of the onyx in alternate layers, the sardonyx*, Rev. xxi. 20. (See Pape's Lexicon in voc.)

σαρκικὸς, *of the flesh, carnal*, 1 Cor. iii. 1, 3. (In the first passage Westcott reads σαρκίνοις.) 1 Pet. ii. 11 ; *belonging to the flesh, human*, 2 Cor. i. 12. x. 4 ; *pertaining to the body, worldly*, Rom. xv. 27. 1 Cor. ix. 11.

σάρκινος, *pertaining to the flesh, fleshly*, 2 Cor. iii. 3 ; *carnal*, Rom. vii. 14. 1 Cor. iii. 1 ; *earthly*, Hebr. vii. 16.

σὰρξ, ἡ, *flesh*, 1 Cor. xv. 39. Luke, xxiv. 39. Joh. vi. 52, 53 ; *the body*, Gal. iv. 13, 14. Jude, 8. Acts, ii. 31 ; *the animal nature*, Rom. vii. 18. 1 Joh. ii. 16. 2 Pet. ii. 18 ; *a living creature*, 1 Pet. i. 24. Luke, iii. 6. Matt. xxiv. 22 ; *impure desire, carnality*, Rom. vii. 5.

σαρόω, a later form for σαίρω, *to sweep*, Luke, xi. 25. xv. 8. Matt. xii. 44.

σάτον, τὸ, *a dry measure, about a peck and a half*, Matt. xiii. 33. Luke, xiii. 21.

σβέννυμι, *to extinguish, to quench*, Matt. xii. 20. Ephes. vi. 16. Hebr. xi. 34 ; *to suppress, to stifle*, 1 Thess. v. 19 ; pass., *to be extinguished, to go out*, Matt. xxv. 8.

σεαυτοῦ, a reflexive pronoun of the 2d person ; σεαυτοῦ, *of thyself*, Joh. viii. 13 ; σεαυτῷ *to thyself*, Acts, xvi. 28; σεαυτὸν, *thyself*, Joh. viii. 53.

σεβάζομαι, *to worship*, Rom. i. 25.

σέβασμα, *τὸ, an object of worship*, 2 Thess. ii. 4. Acts, xvii. 23. (A late form.)

σεβαστὸς, *revered;* ὁ σεβαστὸς, Lat. *Augustus*, the title of the Roman Emperors, Acts, xv. 21, 25; *Augustan*, i.e. taking its name from the Emperor, a title of honour given to certain legions, or cohorts; σπεῖρα σεβαστὴ, *the Augustan band*, Acts, xxvii. 1.

σέβομαι, *to revere, to worship*, Matt. xv. 9. Acts, xviii. 13. xix. 27; σεβόμενοι, *devout*, a term applied to certain proselytes, Acts, xiii. 43; and to certain Greek converts, Acts, xvii. 4; and to certain pious women, Acts, xiii. 50. Cf. Acts, xvii. 17.

σειρὰ, ἡ, *a chain*, 2 Pet. ii. 4. (Here Westcott reads σειροῖς. See σειρός.)

σειρὸς, ὁ, and **σιρὸς,** *a pit;* σειροῖς ζόφου, *to pits of darkness*, 2 Pet. ii. 4. (Here the usual reading was σειραῖς. See the preceding word.)

σεισμὸς, ὁ, *an earthquake*, Luke, xxi. 11. Acts, xvi. 26. Matt. xxvii. 54 etc.; *a commotion*, Matt. viii. 24 (RV *a tempest*).

σείω, *to shake*, Hebr. xii. 26. Rev. vi. 13. Matt. xxvii. 51; σεισθῆναι ἀπὸ φόβον, *to quake for fear*, Matt. xxviii. 4; ἐσείσθη, *was agitated*, Matt. xxi. 10.

σελήνη, ἡ, *the moon*, Matt. xxiv. 29. Luke, xxi. 25. Acts, ii. 20 etc.

σεληνιάζομαι, *to be epileptic*, Matt. iv. 24. xvii. 15.

σεμίδαλις, ἡ, *the finest wheaten flour*, Rev. xviii. 13. (See Pape's Lex. in voc.)

σεμνὸς, *august, venerable, honourable*, 1 Tim. iii. 8, 11. Tit. ii. 2. Philipp. iv. 8.

σεμνότης, ἡ, *gravity*, 1 Tim. ii. 2. iii. 4. Tit. ii. 7.

σημαίνω, *to give a sign, to indicate*, Joh. xii. 33. xviii. 32. xxi. 19; *to make known*, Acts, xi. 28. Rev. i. 1.

σημεῖον, τὸ, *a mark, a token*, 2 Cor. xii. 12; *a sign*, Mrk. xiii. 4. Luke, xxi. 7, 25. Matt. xxiv. 30 etc.; *a portent*, Acts, ii. 19. Rev. xii. 1, 3. xv. 1. Mrk. xiii. 22; *a miracle*, Acts, iv. 16, 22. xiv. 3. xv. 12.

σημειοῦμαι, *to mark, to note*, 2 Thess. iii. 14.

σήμερον, adv., *to-day, this day*, Matt. vi. 11. Luke, iv. 21. xix. 5. xxiii. 43 etc.; ἡ σήμερον ἡμέρα, *this very day*, Acts, xx. 26.

σήπω, *to make corrupt;* pass., *to become corrupt;* 2d perf., *to be corrupt;* ὁ πλοῦτος ὑμῶν σέσηπεν, James, v. 2 (RV *your riches are corrupted*).

σηρικὸς, *pertaining to the Seres;* τὸ σηρικὸν, *silken garments*, Rev. xviii. 12. (Here Westcott reads σιρικοῦ.)

σὴς, ὁ, *a moth*, Matt. vi. 19. Luke, xii. 33.

σητόβρωτος, *moth-eaten*, James, v. 2. (A very late form.)

σθενόω, *to strengthen*, 1 Pet. v. 10.

σιαγών, ἡ, *the jaw, the cheek*, Matt. v. 39. Luke, vi. 29.

σιγάω, *to be silent, to keep one's peace*, Luke, ix. 36. xviii. 39. Acts, xii. 17 etc.; pass., *to be kept in silence, to be concealed*, Rom. xvi. 25.

σιγὴ, ἡ, *silence*, Acts, xxi. 40. Rev. viii. 1.

σιδήρεος, *of iron*, Acts, xii. 10. Rev. ii. 27. xii. 5. xix. 15.

σίδηρος, ὁ, *iron*, Rev. xviii. 12.

σικάριος, ὁ, *an assassin, a cut-throat*, Acts, xxi. 38 [a Latin word].

σίκερα, τὸ, *intoxicating drink*, Luke, i. 15.

Σίλας, ὁ, *Silas*, a Roman citizen, the companion and associate of S. Paul in preaching the gospel, Acts, xvi. 19, 25, 37 etc.

σιμικίνθιον, τὸ, *an apron*, Acts, xix. 12. (Pape in Lex. says it is a false reading for σημικίνθιον, which latter he translates a *pocket-handkerchief*. See σουδάριον.)

σίναπι, τὸ, *mustard*, Matt. xiii. 31. xvii. 20. Luke, xiii. 19 etc.

σινδών, ἡ, *fine linen*, Matt. xxvii. 59. Luke, xxiii. 53. Mrk. xiv. 51, 52. xv. 46. ("The word is either of Egyptian origin, or to be derived from Σινδὸς = 'Ινδὸς," Pape in Lex.)

σινιάζω, *to sift*, Luke, xxii. 31.

σιτευτὸς, *fattened, fatted*, Luke, xv. 23, 27, 30.

σιτίον, τὸ, *corn, grain*, Acts, vii. 12.

σιτιστὸς, *fattened; τὰ σιτιστὰ, fatlings*, Matt. xxii. 4.

σιτομέτρον, τὸ, *a measured portion of food*, Luke, xii. 42.

σῖτος, ὁ, *wheat, corn*, Matt. iii. 12. xiii. 25, 29, 30. Luke, iii. 17.

σιωπάω, *to be silent, to hold one's peace*, Matt. xx. 31. xxvi. 63. Luke, xix. 40 etc.

σκανδαλίζω, *to cause offence*, Joh. vi. 61; *to cause to stumble*, Matt. xvii. 27; *to cause to sin*, Matt. v. 29, 30. xviii. 6, 8. 1 Cor. viii. 13 etc.; pass., *to be offended*, Matt. xi. 6. xiii. 21. xxvi. 33. (Confined to the NT and ecclesiastical writers.)

σκάνδαλον, τὸ, *a stumbling block*, 1 Cor. i. 23. Rom. xiv. 13. Gal. v. 11. (It is a purely biblical form for σκανδάληθρον.)

σκάπτω, *to dig*, Luke, vi. 48. xiii. 8. xvi. 3.

σκάφη, ἡ, *a hollow vessel; a boat*, Acts, xxvii. 16, 30, 32.

σκέλος, τὸ, *the leg*, Joh. xix. 31, 32, 33.

σκέπασμα, τὸ, *a covering; clothing*, 1 Tim. vi. 8.

σκευὴ, ἡ, *furniture; the tackling* of a ship, Acts, xxvii. 19. (See σκεῦος.)

σκεῦος, τὸ, *a vessel*, Mrk. xi. 16. Joh. xix. 29. 2 Cor. iv. 7. Acts, ix. 15; *the tackling* of a ship, Acts, xxvii. 17; *household furniture, goods*, Matt. xii. 29. Mrk. iii. 27. Luke, xvii. 31.

σκηνή, ή, *a tent; a tabernacle*, Matt. xvii. 4. Hebr. viii. 2. Acts, vii. 43; *an abode, a habitation*, Luke, xvi. 9. Rev. xiii. 6.

σκηνοπηγία, ή, *the feast of tabernacles*, Joh. vii. 2. This the Jews observed, partly in remembrance of their dwelling in tents while passing through the wilderness, and partly in gratitude for the ingathering of the harvest and the vintage; hence called also "the feast of ingathering." It was observed yearly for seven days, beginning with the 15th of the month Tisri; and the Jews were accustomed to construct booths of the branches of trees in the courts of their dwellings, or in the streets and squares, and to adorn them with flowers and fruits.

σκηνοποιός, ό, *a tentmaker*, Acts, xviii. 3. (Found only in Julius Pollux and the NT.)

σκῆνος, τό, *a tabernacle*, 2 Cor. v. 1, 4.

σκηνόω, *to pitch a tent* or *tabernacle; to dwell in a tent* or *tabernacle;* and, generally, *to dwell; ἐν ἡμῖν, amongst us,* Joh. i. 14. Rev. xii. 12. xiii. 6; μετ' αὐτῶν, *with them*, Rev. xxi. 3; σκηνώσει ἐπ' αὐτούς, *shall spread his tabernacle over them*, i.e. shall keep them in perfect security, Rev. vii. 15.

σκήνωμα, τό, = σκῆνος; *a habitation*, Acts, vii. 46; *a tabernacle*, i.e. the human body, 2 Pet. i. 13, 14.

σκιά, ή, *a shadow*, Mrk. iv. 32. Acts, v. 15; *darkness*, Matt. iv. 16. Similarly σκιὰ θανάτου, *the shadow of death = the thickest darkness*, Luke, i. 79; *a mere adumbration*, Coloss. ii. 17. Hebr. viii. 5. x. 1.

σκιρτάω, *to leap*, Luke, i. 41, 44. vi. 23.

σκληροκαρδία, ή, *hardness of heart*, Matt. xix. 8. Mrk. x. 5. xvi. 14. (It is a purely biblical form.)

σκληρός, *hard*, Matt. xxv. 24. Joh. vi. 60. Jude, 15. Acts, xxvi. 14; *violent*, James, iii. 4.

σκληρότης, ή, *hardness*, Rom. ii. 5.

σκληροτράχηλος, *stiffnecked, obstinate*, Acts, vii. 51. (It is a purely biblical form.)

σκληρύνω, *to harden*, Rom. ix. 18. Hebr. iii. 8, 15. iv. 7; pass., *to be hardened*, Acts, xix. 9. Hebr. iii. 13.

σκολιός, *crooked*, Luke, iii. 5; met., *perverse, wicked*, Acts, ii. 40. Philipp. ii. 15; *harsh, unjust*, 1 Pet. ii. 18.

σκόλοψ, ό, *a stake; a thorn*, 2 Cor. xii. 7. (See Pape's Lexicon in voc.)

σκοπέω, *to look at, to consider*, 2 Cor. iv. 18. Philipp. ii. 4; *to note, to mark*, Rom. xvi. 17. Philipp. iii. 17; *to look to, to take heed to*, Gal. vi. 1.

σκοπός, ό, *the mark* or *goal*, Philipp. iii. 14.

σκορπίζω, *to scatter*, Matt. xii. 30. Luke, xi. 23. Joh. x. 12.

xvi. 32; met., *to scatter abroad*, i.e. *to distribute liberally*, 2 Cor. ix. 9.

σκορπίος, ὁ, *a scorpion*, Luke, x. 19. xi. 12. Rev. ix. 3, 5, 10.

σκοτεινὸς, *full of darkness*, Matt. vi. 23. Luke, xi. 34; *dark*, Luke, xi. 36.

σκοτία, ἡ, *darkness*, Joh. vi. 17. xx. 1; *spiritual darkness*, Matt. iv. 16. Joh. i. 5. viii. 12. xii. 35, 46 etc.; *privacy, secrecy*, Matt. x. 27. Luke, xii. 3.

σκοτίζω, *to darken*; pass., *to be darkened*, Matt. xxiv. 29. Mrk. xiii. 24. Rev. viii. 12.

σκότος, ὁ, *darkness*, a var. lect. ad Hebr. xii. 18.

σκότος, τὸ, *darkness*, Matt. xxvii. 45. Mrk. xv. 33. Luke, xxiii. 44. Acts, ii. 20; met., *a dark place*, Matt. viii. 12. xxii. 13. xxv. 30; *spiritual darkness*, Joh. iii. 19. Acts, xxvi. 18. Coloss. i. 13. 2 Cor. iv. 14; met., *persons enslaved to sin*, Ephes. v. 8.

σκοτόω, *to darken*; pass., *to be darkened*, Rev. ix. 2. xvi. 10. Ephes. iv. 18.

σκύβαλον, τὸ, *refuse; dung*, Philipp. iii. 8.

σκυθρωπὸς, *of a sad countenance*, Matt. vi. 16; *with sad face*, Luke, xxiv. 17.

σκύλλω, *to skin, to flay;* met., *to vex, to trouble*, Mrk. v. 35. Luke, viii. 49. Matt. ix. 36 (RV *distressed*); mid., *to trouble one's self*, Luke, vii. 6.

σκῦλον, τὸ, *a skin stripped off from a slaughtered animal*; plur., *the spoils taken from an enemy*, Luke, xi. 22.

σκωληκόβρωτος, *eaten by worms*, Acts, xii. 23.

σκώληξ, ὁ, *a worm*, Mrk. ix. 48. (In vss. 44, 46, where older editions give the word, it is omitted by Westcott.)

σμαράγδινος, *of the colour of an emerald*, Rev. iv. 3.

σμάραγδος, ὁ, and ἡ, *the emerald*, Rev. xxi. 19.

σμύρνα, ἡ, *myrrh*, Matt. ii. 11. Joh. xix. 39.

σμυρνίζω, *to mingle with myrrh*, Mrk. xv. 23.

σορὸς, ἡ, *a funeral urn; a bier*, Luke, vii. 14.

σὸς, *thy, thine*, Matt. vii. 3, 22 etc.; οἱ σοὶ, *thy disciples*, Luke, v. 33; οἱ σοὶ, *thy relatives*, Mrk. v. 19; τὸ σὸν, *what is thine*, Matt. xx. 14; τὰ σὰ, *thy goods*, Luke, vi. 30.

σουδάριον, τὸ, *a napkin*, Acts, xix. 12. Joh. xi. 44. xx. 7. Luke, xix. 20. (See σημικίνθιον.) A Latin word.

σοφία, ἡ, *wisdom*, Luke, xi. 49. Rom. xi. 33 etc.

σοφίζω, *to make wise*, 2 Tim. iii. 15; pass., *to be cunningly devised*, 2 Pet. i. 16.

σοφὸς, *wise*, Rom. xvi. 19. Ephes. v. 15. 1 Cor. i. 25 etc.

σπαράσσω, *to tear, to convulse*, Mrk. i. 26. Luke, ix. 39.

σπαργανόω, *to wrap in swaddling clothes*, Luke, ii. 7, 12.

σπαταλάω, *to live luxuriously*, James, v. 5. 1 Tim. v. 6. (It is a late form.)

σπάω, *to draw*, Mrk. xiv. 47. Acts, xvi. 27.

σπεῖρα, ἡ, *a band* of soldiers, Matt. xxvii. 27. Acts, x. 1. Joh. xviii. 3, 12 etc.

σπείρω, *to sow*, Matt. vi. 26. xiii. 3. Gal. vi. 7, 8. 1 Cor. ix. 11.

σπεκουλάτωρ, ὁ, Lat. *speculator*, *a spy, a scout;* "under the Emperors an attendant and member of the bodyguard, employed as messenger, and executioner," Thayer; *an attendant*, Mrk. vi. 27. (It is an utterly un-Greek word, and is omitted in Pape's Lexicon.)

σπένδω, *to make a libation;* "in the NT σπένδεσθαι, *to be offered as a libation*, is figuratively used of one whose blood is poured out in a violent death for the cause of God, Philipp. ii. 17. 2 Tim. iv. 6," Thayer.

σπέρμα, τό, *seed*, Matt. xiii. 24, 27, 37. 1 Cor. xv. 38; *children, offspring*, Luke, xx. 28. Rom. ix. 7; *a residue*, Rom. ix. 29.

σπερμολόγος, *picking up seeds;* as subst., *a babbler*, Acts, xvii. 18.

σπεύδω, *to hasten, to make haste*, Luke, ii. 16. xix. 5, 6. Acts, xx. 16. xxii. 18; *to desire earnestly*, 2 Pet. iii. 12.

σπήλαιον, τό, *a cave, a den*, Hebr. xi. 38. Mrk. xi. 17. Matt. xxi. 17 etc.

σπιλάς, ἡ, *a rock in the sea, a reef*, Jude, 12 (RV *hidden rocks*).

σπίλος, ἡ, "= σπιλάς, *a rock;* the accentuation σπῖλος is false, for the ι is short," Pape in Lex.; met., *a moral blemish, a spot*, Ephes. v. 27. 2 Pet. ii. 13.

σπιλόω, *to defile*, James, iii. 6. Jude, 23.

σπλαγχνίζομαι, *to be moved with compassion*, Luke, x. 33. xv. 20. Matt. xx. 34. Mrk. i. 41 etc.

σπλάγχνον, τό, plur., σπλάγχνα, *bowels*, Acts, i. 18. Coloss. iii. 12; *tender mercies*, Philipp. i. 8. 2 Cor. vii. 15. Luke, i. 78.

σπόγγος, ὁ, *a sponge*, Matt. xxvii. 48. Mrk. xv. 36. Joh. xix. 29.

σποδός, ἡ, *ashes*, Matt. xi. 21. Luke, x. 13.

σπορά, ἡ, *a sowing; seed*, 1 Pet. i. 23.

σπόριμος, *to be sown;* τὰ σπόριμα, *the cornfields*, Matt. xii. 1. Luke, vi. 1. Mrk. ii. 23.

σπόρος, ὁ, *a sowing; seed*, Mrk. iv. 26. Luke, viii. 5, 11. 2 Cor. ix. 10.

σπουδάζω, *to give diligence, to endeavour*, 2 Tim. iv. 9, 21. Tit. iii. 12. Ephes. iv. 3. 1 Thess. ii. 17 etc.; *to be eager, to be anxious*, Gal. ii. 10.

σπουδαῖος, *diligent, earnest*, 2 Cor. viii. 17, 22.

σπουδαίως, adv., *diligently*, 2 Tim. i. 17. Tit. iii. 13; *earnestly*, Luke, vii. 4.

σπουδὴ, ἡ, *haste*, Mrk. vi. 25. Luke, i. 39; *earnestness, diligence*, Rom. xii. 11. 2 Cor. vii. 11, 12. viii. 7, 8, 16; πᾶσαν σπουδὴν ποιεῖσθαι, *to give all diligence*, Jude, 3.

σπυρὶς, ἡ, *a basket*, Matt. xv. 37. Mrk. viii. 8, 20. Acts, ix. 25. (In all these passages Westcott reads σφυρίς.)

στάδιον, τὸ, plur. τὰ στάδια, and οἱ στάδιοι, *a stadium*, a measure of length, one eighth of a Roman mile, or 606¾ English feet, Matt. xiv. 24. Luke, xxiv. 13. Joh. vi. 19. xi. 18 etc.; (RV *a furlong*); *a racecourse, a race*, 1 Cor. ix. 24.

στάμνος, ὁ and ἡ, *an earthenware vessel, a jar*, Hebr. ix. 4.

στασιαστὴς, ὁ, a late form for στασιώτης, *the author of an insurrection*, Mrk. xv. 7.

στάσις, ἡ, *a standing*; ἔτι ἔχειν στάσιν, *to be yet standing*, Hebr. ix. 8; *an insurrection*, Mrk. xv. 7. Luke, xxiii. 19, 25. Acts, xxiv. 5; *a riot*, Acts, xix. 40; *strife, dissension*, Acts, xv. 2. xxiii. 7, 10.

στατὴρ, ὁ, *a stater*, a silver coin, equal to 4 Attic dracamae, or to the Jewish shekel, and somewhat less than 3 shillings, Matt. xvii. 27.

σταυρὸς, ὁ, *the cross*, Matt. xxvii. 32, 40, 42 etc.; *the crucifixion*, 1 Cor. i. 17. Ephes. ii. 16; τὸν σταυρὸν αἴρειν, λαμβάνειν, βαστάζειν, *to bear with patience persecutions, troubles and distresses*, Matt. x. 38. xvi. 24. Luke, ix. 23. xiv. 27 etc.

σταυρόω, *to crucify*, Matt. xx. 19. xxiii. 34. xxvii. 35. Mrk. xv. 24. Luke, xxiii. 33. Joh. xix. 18; *to mortify, to deaden*, Gal. v. 24; pass., *to become dead to*, Gal. vi. 14.

σταφυλὴ, ἡ, *a cluster of grapes; grapes*, Matt. vii. 16. Luke, vi. 44. Rev. xiv. 18.

στάχυς, ὁ, *an ear of corn*, Matt. xii. 1. Luke, vi. 1. Mrk. ii. 23. iv. 28.

στέγη, ἡ, *the roof*, Luke, vii. 6. Matt. viii. 8. Mrk. ii. 4.

στέγω, *to bear, to endure*, 1 Cor. ix. 12. xiii. 7 [or *to cover up, excuse*]; *to forbear*, 1 Thess. iii. 1, 5.

στεῖρος, =στέρρος, *barren*, Luke, i. 7, 36. xxiii. 29. Gal. iv. 27.

στέλλω, *to place*; mid., *to withdraw oneself*, 2 Thess. iii. 6; with μὴ, *to avoid*, 2 Cor. viii. 20.

στέμμα, τὸ, *a garland*, Acts, xiv. 13.

στεναγμὸς, ὁ, *a groaning*, Acts, vii. 34. Rom. viii. 26.

στενάζω, *to groan*, 2 Cor. v. 2, 4. Rom. viii. 23. Hebr. xiii. 17; *to sigh*, Mrk. vii. 34; *to complain, to murmur*, James, v. 9.

στενὸς, *narrow*, Luke, xiii. 24. Matt. vii. 13, 14.

στενοχωρέω, *to be narrow*; pass., *to be straitened*, 2 Cor. iv. 8. vi. 12.

στενοχωρία, ἡ, *a narrow space*, met., *embarrassment, distress*, Rom. ii. 9. viii. 35. 2 Cor.

στε]   *GREEK-ENGLISH LEXICON*   **[στρ**

vi. 4. xii. 10. (See Pape's Lexicon in voc.)

στερεὸς, *solid, firm*, Hebr. v. 12, 14. 2 Tim. ii. 19; *steadfast*, 1 Pet. v. 9.

στερεόω, *to make strong*, Acts, iii. 7, 16; pass., *to be straightened*, Acts, xvi. 5.

στερέωμα, τὸ, *a foundation; firmness, steadfastness*, Coloss. ii. 5.

στέφανος, ὁ, *a crown*, Matt. xxvii. 29. Joh. xix. 2, 5. 2 Tim. iv. 8. James, i. 12.

στεφανόω, *to crown*, 2 Tim. ii. 5. Hebr. ii. 7.

στῆθος, τὸ, *the breast*, Luke, xviii. 13. xxiii. 48. Joh. xiii. 25. xxi. 20.

στήκω, a barbarous form for ἕστηκα, *to stand*, Mrk. iii. 31; *to stand fast, to persevere*, 2 Thess. ii. 15. Philipp. iv. 1; *to stand erect*, i.e. not to fall into sin, Rom. xiv. 4. (It is omitted in Pape's Lexicon.)

στηριγμὸς, ὁ, *steadfastness*, 2 Pet. iii. 17.

στηρίζω, *to fix, to place firmly*, Luke, xvi. 26; στηρίζειν τὸ πρόσωπον, *to set one's face steadfastly*, Luke, ix. 51; *to confirm*, Luke, xxii. 32. Rom. i. 11. xvi. 25 etc.

στιβὰς, ἡ, *branches of trees*, Mrk. xi. 8.

στίγμα, τὸ, *a mark, a brand*, Gal. vi. 17. ("The marks are the traces left by the perils, hardships, imprisonments, and scourgings endured for the cause of Christ," Thayer.)

στιγμὴ, ἡ, *a point or momenn of time*, Luke, iv. 5.

στίλβω, *to shine, to glisten*, Mrk. ix. 3.

στοὰ, ἡ, *a portico or porch*, Joh v. 2. x. 23. Acts, iii. 11. v. 12.

στοιχεῖον, τὸ, *an element or first principle*, Hebr. v. 12. Coloss. ii. 8, 20. Gal. iv. 3, 9; *the heavenly bodies*, 2 Pet. iii. 10, 12.

στοιχέω, *to stand in order; to follow*, Rom. iv. 12; *to walk, to direct one's life*, Gal. v. 25. vi. 16. Philipp. iii. 16. Acts, xxi. 24.

στολὴ, ἡ, *a robe, a garment*, Mrk. xii. 38. xvi. 5. Luke, xv. 22. xx. 46 etc.

στόμα, τὸ, *the mouth*, Joh. xix. 29. Acts, xi. 8. Matt. xvii. 27 etc.; στόμα πρὸς στόμα, *face to face*, 2 Joh. 12. 3 Joh. 14; στόμα μαχαίρας, *the edge of the sword*, Luke, xxi. 24. Hebr. xi. 34.

στόμαχος, ὁ, *the stomach*, 1 Tim. v. 23.

στρατεία, ἡ, *a military expedition; warfare*, 2 Cor. x. 4. 1 Tim. i. 18.

στράτευμα, τὸ, *an army*, Matt. xxii. 7. Rev. ix. 16. xix. 14; *a band of soldiers*, Acts, xxiii. 10, 27; *soldiers*, Luke, xxiii. 11,

στρατεύομαι, *to be a soldier, to serve as a soldier*, Luke, iii. 14. 1 Cor. ix. 7. 2 Tim. ii. 4; *to carry on war*, 1 Pet. ii. 11. James, iv. 1. 2 Cor. x. 3. 1 Tim. i. 18.

στρατηγὸς, ὁ, *a general;* in the NT *a governor, a provincial* *magistrate*, Acts, xvi. 20, 22, 35, 38 ; ὁ στρατηγὸς τοῦ ἱεροῦ, *the captain of the temple*, Acts, iv. 1. v. 24. Luke, xxii. 52 etc.

στρατιά, ἡ, *an army;* οὐράνιος στρατιά, *the heavenly host*, i.e. angels, Luke, ii. 13; ἡ στρατιὰ τοῦ οὐρανοῦ = *the stars*, Acts, vii. 42.

στρατιώτης, ὁ, *a soldier*, Matt. viii. 9. Joh. xix. 2. Luke, xxiii. 36. 2 Tim. ii. 3 etc.

στρατολογέω, *to enlist soldiers ;* ὁ στρατολογήσας, *the person who enlisted him*, 2 Tim. ii. 4.

στρατοπεδάρχης, ὁ, *the commander of the praetorian cohorts, the prefect of the praetorian guard*, a var. lect. ad Acts, xxviii. 16.

στρατόπεδον, τὸ, *a camp; an army*, Luke, xxi. 20.

στρεβλόω, *to put to the rack, to torture;* met., *to twist, to pervert*, 2 Pet. iii. 16.

στρέφω, *to turn*, Matt. v. 39. Rev. xi. 6. Acts, vii. 42 ; pass., *to turn about*, Matt. xvi. 23. Luke, vii. 9; *to be converted*, Matt. xviii. 3. Joh. xii. 40 ; *to turn back*, Acts, vii. 39. Cf. Joh. xx. 14.

στρηνιάω, *to be wanton, to live luxuriously*, Rev. xviii. 7, 9.

στρῆνος, τὸ, *luxury, wantonness*, Rev. xviii. 3.

στρουθίον, τὸ, *a sparrow*, Matt. x. 29, 31. Luke, xii. 6, 7.

στρώννυμι, and **στρωννύω**, *to strew*, and **to spread**, Mrk. xi. 8. Matt. xxi. 8; στρῶσον σαυτῷ, *make thy own bed*, Acts, ix. 34 ; pass., *to be spread with couches*, Matt. xiv. 15. Luke, xxii. 12.

στυγητὸς, *hateful*, Tit. iii. 3.

στυγνάζω, *to be gloomy, to be sorrowful*, Mrk. x. 22 ; *of the sky, to be overcast*, Matt. xvi. 3 (Westcott brackets this verse).

στῦλος, ὁ, *a pillar*, Rev. iii. 12. x. 1. Gal. ii. 9 ; *a prop, a support*, 1 Tim. iii. 15.

σύ, pronoun of the 2nd person, *thou*, Matt. ii. 6. (The reader is referred to his Greek Grammar.)

συγγένεια, ἡ, *relationship, kinship; kindred, relatives*, Luke, i. 61. Acts, vii. 3, 14.

συγγενὴς, *related to, akin to*, Joh. xviii. 26. Acts, x. 24. Rom. xvi. 7, 11, 21 etc.; *of the same race, a fellow-countryman*, Rom. ix. 3.

συγγενὶς, ἡ, *a kinswoman*, Luke, i. 36. (A late form.)

συγγνώμη, ἡ, *pardon;* κατὰ συγγνώμην, *by way of permission*, i.e. *Christi veniâ*, 1 Cor. vii. 6.

συγκάθημαι, *to sit together*, Mrk. xiv. 54. Acts, xxvi. 30.

συγκαθίζω, *to cause to sit with*, Ephes. ii. 6 ; intrans., *to sit down together*, Luke, xxii. 55.

συγκακοπαθέω, *to suffer hardships with*, 2 Tim. i. 8. ii. 3. (Only in late writers.)

συγκακουχέομαι, *to suffer ill-treatment in company with*, Hebr. xi. 25. (Found no where else.)

συγκαλέω, to call together, to assemble, Luke, xv. 6. xxiii. 13. Mrk. xv. 16 etc.

συγκαλύπτω, to conceal, to cover up, Luke, xii. 2.

συγκάμπτω, to bend together; to bow down, Rom. xi. 10.

συγκαταβαίνω, to go down with, Acts, xxv. 5.

συγκατάθεσις, ἡ, agreement, 2 Cor. vi. 16.

συγκατατίθημι, to deposit a vote with; συγκατατίθεμαι, to agree with, Luke, xxiii. 51.

συγκαταψηφίζω, to vote along with; pass., to be elected, Acts, i. 26. (A late and unusual form.)

συγκεράννυμι, to mingle together, to blend, 1 Cor. xii. 24; pass., to be united, Hebr. iv. 2 (RV because they were not united by faith with those that heard).

συγκινέω, to excite, to stir up, Acts, vi. 12.

συγκλείω, to enclose, Luke, v. 6; with εἰς or ὑπὸ, to include in or under, Rom. xi. 32. Gal. iii. 22, 23.

συγκληρονόμος, a fellow-heir, a joint-heir, Rom. viii. 17; a fellow-participant, Ephes. iii. 6. Hebr. xi. 9. 1 Pet. iii. 7. (Confined to the NT.)

συγκοινωνέω, with dative of object, to have fellowship with, Ephes. v. 11. Rev. xviii. 4. Philipp. iv. 14.

συγκοινωνός, partaking with others; as subst., a joint partaker, Rom. xi. 17. 1 Cor. ix. 23. Philipp. i. 7. Rev. i. 9. (Confined to the NT.)

συγκομίζω, to help in carrying; to help to bury, Acts, viii. 2. (See Pape's Lex. in voc. fin.)

συγκρίνω, to join together, to combine; πνευματικοῖς πνευματικὰ, combining spiritual things with spiritual things, 1 Cor. ii. 13; to compare, 2 Cor. x. 12.

συγκύπτω, to bend together; to be bent double; ἦν συγκύπτουσα, Luke, xiii. 11 (RV she was bowed together).

συγκυρία, ἡ, chance, accident; κατὰ συγκυρίαν, by chance, Luke, x. 31. ("An unusual form for συγκύρησις," Pape in Lex.)

συγχαίρω, to rejoice with, Luke, i. 58. xv. 6, 9. Philipp. ii. 17, 18; to sympathise with, 1 Cor. xii. 26.

συγχέω, to mingle together; to confound, Acts, ii. 6. ix. 22; to stir up, Acts, xxi. 27; to throw into confusion, Acts, xix. 32. xxi. 31.

συγχράομαι, to associate with, to have dealings with, Joh. iv. 9.

σύγχυσις, ἡ, disturbance, confusion, Acts, xix. 29.

συζάω, to live with, 2 Tim. ii. 11. Rom. vi. 8; to live together, 2 Cor. vii. 3.

συζεύγνυμι, to yoke together; to join together, to unite in marriage, Matt. xix. 6. Mrk. x. 9.

συζητέω, to discuss, to debate, Mrk. i. 27. ix. 10, 14, 16; to argue, to dispute, Acts, vi. 9. Mrk. viii. 11. xii. 28.

συζήτησις, ἡ, *disputation, discussion*, Acts, xxviii. 29 (Westcott omits this verse).

συζητητής, ὁ, *a disputer*, 1 Cor. i. 20.

σύζυγος, *yoked together; a yokefellow, a fellow labourer*, Philipp. iv. 3. (But here many take it as a *proper name*.)

συζωοποιέω, *to make alive together with*, Ephes. ii. 5. Coloss. ii. 13. (Confined to the NT.)

συκάμινος, ἡ, *the sycamine*, Luke, xvii. 6. ("A tree having the form and foliage of the mulberry, but fruit resembling that of the fig-tree," Thayer.)

συκῆ, ἡ, *the fig-tree*, Matt. xxi. 19, 20, 21. xxiv. 32. Luke, xiii. 6, 7 etc.

συκομορέα, ἡ, and συκομορία, ἡ, ("=συκόμορος," Pape in Lex.), Luke, xix. 4. (Thayer renders it *the sycamore tree*.)

σῦκον, τό, *a fig*, Matt. vii. 16. Mrk. xi. 13 etc.

συκοφαντέω, *to accuse wrongfully; wrongfully to exact money from any one*, Luke, iii. 14. xix. 8.

συλαγωγέω, with accus. of person, *to make spoil of*, Coloss. ii. 8.

συλάω *to rob, to despoil*, 2 Cor. xi. 8.

συλλαλέω, *to talk with*, Mrk. ix. 4. Luke, ix. 30 etc.; *to speak with one another*, Luke, iv. 36.

συλλαμβάνω, *to seize, to take a person prisoner*, Joh. xviii. 12. Luke, xxii. 54. Matt. xxvi. 55; *to catch*, Luke, v. 9; of a woman, *to conceive*, Luke, i. 24, 31. ii. 21; met. of lust, James, i. 15; mid., *to make a prisoner of*, Acts, xxvi. 21; with dat. of person, *to assist, to help*, Luke, v. 7. Philipp. iv. 3.

συλλέγω, *to gather, to collect*, Matt. vii. 16. xiii. 28, 29, 30, 41. Luke, vi. 44.

συλλογίζομαι, *to reason with oneself*, Luke, xx. 5.

συλλυπέω, *to grieve at the same time*; pass., *to be grieved*, Mrk. iii. 5.

συμβαίνω, *to befall, to happen*, Mrk. x. 32. Acts, xx. 19. 1 Cor. x. 11. Luke, xxiv. 14.

συμβάλλω, *to dispute with*, Acts, xvii. 18; *to confer with one another, to deliberate*, Acts, iv. 15; *to consider, to ponder*, Luke, ii. 19; *to meet*, Acts, xx. 14; with εἰς πόλεμον, *to encounter in war*, Luke, xiv. 31; mid., *to contribute to, to help*, Acts, xviii. 27.

συμβασιλεύω, *to reign together*, 1 Cor. iv. 8. 2 Tim. ii. 12.

συμβιβάζω, *to bring together, to conclude, to infer*, Acts, xvi. 10; *to prove*, Acts, ix. 22; *to instruct*, 1 Cor. ii. 16. Acts, xix. 32 (RV *they brought out*); pass., *to be knit together*, Ephes. iv. 16. Coloss. ii. 2, 19.

συμβουλεύω, *to advise, to give counsel to*, Joh. xviii. 14. Rev. iii. 18; mid., *to consult, to deliberate*, Matt. xxvi. 4. Acts, ix. 23.

συμβούλιον, τὸ, *counsel*, Matt. xii. 14. xxii. 15. Mrk. iii. 6 etc.; *a council*, Acts, xxv. 12.

σύμβουλος, ὁ, *a counsellor, an adviser*, Rom. xi. 34.

συμμαθητής, ὁ, *a fellow-disciple*, Joh. xi. 16.

συμμαρτυρέω, *to bear witness with*, Rom. ii. 15. viii. 16. ix. 1.

συμμερίζομαι, *to have a portion with, to share with*, 1 Cor. ix. 13.

συμμέτοχος, *having a share with;* as subst., *a fellow-partaker*, Ephes. iii. 6. v. 7.

συμμιμητής, ὁ, *an imitator with others* of a person, Philipp. iii. 17. (Not found elsewhere.)

συμμορφίζω, *to make like;* pass., *to be conformed unto*, Philipp. iii. 10. (Not found elsewhere.)

σύμμορφος, *conformed unto*, Rom. viii. 29. Philipp. iii. 21.

συμμορφόω = συμμορφίζω, a var. lect. ad Philipp. iii. 10. (See Pape's Lex. in voc.)

συμπαθέω, *to sympathise with, to have compassion on*, Hebr. iv. 15. x. 34.

συμπαθής, *compassionate*, 1 Pet. iii. 8.

συμπαραγίνομαι, *to come together*, Luke, xxiii. 48.

συμπαρακαλέω, *to exhort with others;* pass., *to be comforted with* another, Rom. i. 12.

συμπαραλαμβάνω, *to take with one*, Acts, xii. 25. xv. 37, 38. Gal. ii. 1.

συμπαραμένω, *to abide with*, Philipp. i. 25.

συμπάρειμι, *to be present with one*, Acts, xxv. 24.

συμπάσχω, *to suffer with*, 1 Cor. xii. 26. Rom. viii. 17.

συμπέμπω, *to send with*, 2 Cor. viii. 18, 22.

συμπεριλαμβάνω, *to embrace*, Acts, xx. 10.

συμπίνω, *to drink with*, Acts, x. 41.

συμπίπτω, *to fall in, to collapse*, Luke, vi. 49.

συμπληρόω, *to fill up;* pass., *to become full*, Luke, viii. 23; of time, *to be completed, to be fully come*, Luke, ix. 51. Acts, ii. 1.

συμπνίγω, *to choke utterly*, Matt. xiii. 22. Mrk. iv. 7, 19. Luke, viii. 14; *to crowd upon*, Luke, viii. 42.

συμπολίτης, ὁ, *a fellow-citizen*, Ephes. ii. 19.

συμπορεύομαι, *to go with one*, Luke, vii. 11. xiv. 25; *to journey along with*, Luke, xxiv. 15; *to come together, to assemble*, Mrk. x. 1.

συμπόσιον, τὸ, *a drinking party;* plur., συμπόσια συμπόσια, (a Hebraism), *in companies*, Mrk. vi. 39. See πρασιά.

συμπρεσβύτερος, ὁ, *a fellow-elder*, 1 Pet. v. 1.

συμφέρω, *to bring together*, Acts, xix. 19; intrans., *to be expedient, to be profitable*, 1 Cor. vi. 12. x. 23. 2 Cor. viii. 10; συμφέρει, *it is profitable, it is expedient*, Matt. v. 29, 30. Joh. xi. 50. xvi. 7 etc.; τὸ συμφέρον, *what is profitable*,

Acts, xx. 20. 1 Cor. xii. 7 etc.

σύμφημι, *to consent*, Rom. vii. 16.

σύμφορος, *suitable, fit;* τὸ σύμφορον, *advantage, profit*, 1 Cor. vii. 35. x. 33.

συμφυλέτης, ὁ, *of the same tribe, a fellow-countryman*, 1 Thess. ii. 14. (Confined to the NT and ecclesiastical writers.)

σύμφυτος, *congenital;* met., *united with*, Rom. vi. 5.

συμφύω, *to let grow together;* pass., *to grow together with*, Luke, viii. 7.

συμφωνέω, *to be in accord, to harmonise; to agree together,* περὶ, *about*, Matt. xviii. 19; *to be in harmony with, to agree*, Luke, v. 36 etc.

συμφώνησις, ἡ, *concord, agreement*, 2 Cor. vi. 15.

συμφωνία, ἡ, *music*, Luke, xv. 25.

σύμφωνος, *harmonious, agreeing;* τὸ σύμφωνον, *agreement;* ἐκ συμφώνου, *by mutual consent*, 1 Cor. vii. 5.

συμψηφίζω, *to compute, to reckon up*, Acts, xix. 19.

σύμψυχος, *of the same mind*, Philipp. ii. 2.

σύν, prepos. governing the dative, *with, together with*, Matt. xxvi. 35 etc. (The reader is referred to his Greek Grammar.)

συνάγω, *to gather together, to gather*, Matt. ii. 4. Luke, xv. 13. Joh. vi. 12. xv. 6; *to bring together, to collect*, Joh. xi. 52; pass., *to be gathered together*, Acts, iv. 27, 31. xi. 26.

συναγωγὴ, ἡ, *a synagogue*, Luke, xii. 11. Acts, ix. 2. xiii. 43.

συναγωνίζομαι, *to strive together with a person in something, to co-operate with*, Rom. xv. 30. Cf. Rom. viii. 26, 27.

συναθλέω, *to co-operate with*, Philipp. iv. 3; *to strive for*, Philipp. i. 27.

συναθροίζω, *to gather together, to assemble*, Acts, xix. 25; pass., *to be gathered together*, Acts, xii. 12.

συναίρω, *to raise along with;* συναίρειν λόγον, *to settle accounts*, Matt. xviii. 23, 24. xxv. 19.

συναιχμάλωτος, *a fellow-prisoner*, Rom. xvi. 7. Coloss. iv. 10. Philem. 23.

συνακολουθέω, *to follow together with, to accompany*, Mrk. v. 37. xiv. 51. Luke, xxiii. 49.

συναλίζω, *to bring together;* pass., *to be assembled together with*, Acts, i. 4 ("where αὐτοῖς is to be supplied," Thayer. Others connect with ἅλς, and render *eating with*).

συναλλάσσω, *to change something with another;* met., *to unite, to reconcile*, Acts, vii. 26.

συναναβαίνω, *to come up with*, Mrk. xv. 41. Acts, xiii. 31.

συνανάκειμαι, *to sit at meat with*, Matt. ix. 10. xiv. 9. Luke, vii. 49. xiv. 10, 15 etc.

συναναμίγνυμι, *to mix up together;* pass., *to associate with*, 1 Cor. v. 9, 11. 2 Thess. iii. 14.

συναναπαύομαι, to find rest in company with, Rom. xv. 32.

συναντάω, with dat. of person, to meet, Luke, ix. 37. xxii. 10. Acts, x. 25 ; to happen to, to befall, Acts, xx. 22.

συνάντησις, ή, a meeting, Matt. viii. 34. (Here Westcott reads εἰς ὑπάντησιν τῷ Ἰησοῦ.)

συναντιλαμβάνομαι, with dat., to help, Luke, x. 40. Rom. viii. 26.

συναπάγω, to lead away along with ; pass., to be led astray, 2 Pet. iii. 17. Gal. ii. 13 ; to be conformed to, to condescend to, Rom. xii. 16.

συναποθνήσκω, to die with a person, Mrk. xiv. 31 ; to die together, 2 Cor. vii. 3 ; to die after the manner of another, 2 Tim. ii. 11 (" to meet death as Christ did, for the cause of God," Thayer).

συναπόλλυμι, to destroy together; mid., to perish along with, Hebr. xi. 31.

συναποστέλλω, to send with, 2 Cor. xii. 18.

συναρμολογέω, to fit together ; pass., to be framed together, Ephes. ii. 21. iv. 16. (It is a purely NT form. "συναρμολογέω=συναρμόζω, NT," Pape in Lex.)

συναρπάζω, to seize by force, Acts, vi. 12. xix. 29. Luke, viii. 29 ; pass., to be violently seized, Acts, xxvii. 15.

συναυξάνω, to cause to increase together ; pass., to grow together, Matt. xiii. 30.

σύνδεσμος, ὁ, a bond, Coloss. iii. 14. Ephes. iv. 3. Acts, viii. 23 ; a ligature, a band, Coloss. ii. 19.

συνδέω, to bind together ; pass., to be fellow-prisoners; ὡς συνδεδεμένοι, as being bound with them, Hebr. xiii. 3.

συνδοξάζω, to glorify together ; pass., to be glorified with a person, Rom. viii. 17.

σύνδουλος, ὁ, a fellow-servant, Matt. xviii. 28, 29, 31, 33 etc. ; a fellow-worker, Coloss. i. 7. iv. 7.

συνδρομή, ή, a concourse, Acts, xxi. 30.

συνεγείρω, to raise up with another, Ephes. ii. 6. Coloss. ii. 12. iii. 1.

συνέδριον, τό, an assembly ; in the NT especially used of the Jewish Sanhedrin, which consisted of 71 persons, Matt. xxvi. 59.

συνείδησις, ή, consciousness, Hebr. x. 2 ; the moral instinct, the conscience, Rom. ii. 15. ix. 1. xiii. 5. 1 Pet. iii. 21 etc.

συνεῖδον, to perceive, to understand ; συνιδών, when he had considered, Acts, xii. 12 ; σύνοιδα, to be conscious of, 1 Cor. iv. 4 ; to be privy to a matter, Acts, v. 2.

σύνειμι, to be with, Acts, xxii. 11. Luke, ix. 18.

σύνειμι, to go with ; to come together, Luke, viii. 4.

συνεισέρχομαι, to enter into along with, Joh. vi. 22. xviii. 15.

συνέκδημος, going abroad with ; as subst., a fellow-traveller, Acts, xix. 29. 2 Cor. viii. 19.

συνεκλεκτὸς, *elected together with*, 1 Pet. v. 13. (A purely NT form.)

συνελαύνω, *to drive together*; met., *to urge*, a var. lect. ad Acts, vii. 26.

συνεπιμαρτυρέω, *to bear witness with*, Hebr. ii. 4.

συνεπιτίθεμαι, *to join in charging a person*, Acts, xxiv. 9.

συνέπομαι, *to follow with, to accompany*, Acts, xx. 4.

συνεργέω, *to work together with, to help in the work*, 1 Cor. xvi. 16. 2 Cor. vi. 1. Mrk. xvi. 20; *to co-operate*, Rom. viii. 28. James, ii. 22.

συνεργὸς, *working with*; as subst., *a fellow-worker*, Rom. xvi. 3, 9, 21. 2 Cor. i. 24. Philipp. ii. 25 etc.

συνέρχομαι, *to come together, to assemble*, Mrk. iii. 20. xiv. 53; *to accompany*, Luke, xxiii. 55. Acts, x. 23; *to associate with*, Acts, i. 21.

συνεσθίω, *to eat with*, Luke, xv. 2. Acts, x. 41. xi. 3 etc.

σύνεσις, ἡ, *understanding*, Luke, ii. 47. Coloss. i. 9. ii. 2.

συνετὸς, *intelligent, prudent*, Matt. xi. 25. Luke, x. 21. 1 Cor. i. 19. Acts, xiii. 7.

συνευδοκέω, *to consent unto, to approve of*, Acts, viii. 1. xxii. 20. Luke, xi. 48. Rom. i. 32; with infin., *to agree, to consent*, 1 Cor. vii. 12.

συνευωχέομαι, *to feast sumptuously with, to banquet*, 2 Pet. ii. 13. Jude, 12.

συνεφίστημι, 2 aor. συνεπέστην, *to rise up together*. Acts, xvi. 22.

συνέχω, *to hold together; to close, to stop*, Acts, vii. 57; *to keep in, to confine*, Luke, xix. 43; *to hold in custody*, Luke, xxii. 63; *to press upon*, Luke, viii. 45; *to impel, to constrain*, 2 Cor. v. 14; pass., *to be compelled, to be urged*, Acts, xviii. 5; *to be afflicted with*, Matt. iv. 24. Luke, iv. 38; *to be hard pressed*, Luke, xii. 50. Philipp. i. 23.

συνζ, see συς.

συνήδομαι, *to rejoice with; to take delight in*, Rom. vii. 22.

συνήθεια, ἡ, *custom*, Joh. xviii. 39. 1 Cor. xi. 16.

συνηλικιώτης, ὁ, *of the same age*, Gal. i. 14.

συνθάπτω, *to bury together with*; pass., *to be buried with*, Rom. vi. 4. Coloss. ii. 12.

συνθλάω, *to break in pieces, to shatter*, Luke, xx. 18. Matt. xxi. 44.

συνθλίβω, *to press on all sides, to crowd upon*, Mrk. v. 24, 31.

συνθρύπτω, *to crush, to break*, Acts, xxi. 13.

συνίημι, *to understand*, Matt. xiii. 23, 51. Luke, ii. 50. xviii. 34; (morally), Rom. iii. 11.

συνίστημι, *to place together; to commend*, 2 Cor. iii. 1. vi. 4. x. 12, 18; *to show*, Rom. v. 8. Gal. ii. 18. 2 Cor. vii. 11; in the 2nd aor. perf. and pluperf., intransitive, *to stand with*, Luke, ix. 32; *to consist, to be compacted*, 2 Pet. iii. 5. Coloss. i. 17.

συνοδεύω, to travel with, Acts, ix. 7.

συνοδία, ἡ, a company of travellers, a company, Luke, ii. 44.

συνοικέω, to dwell together, 1 Pet. iii. 7.

συνοικοδομέω, to build up together, Ephes. ii. 22.

συνομιλέω, to associate with; to talk with, Acts, x. 27. (Confined to the NT and late writers.)

συνομορέω, to be contiguous to, Acts, xviii. 7.

συνοχή, ἡ, a narrowing, a strait; met., anguish, distress, 2 Cor. ii. 4. Luke, xxi. 25.

συντάσσω, to arrange together; to appoint, Matt. xxi. 6. xxvi. 19. xxvii. 10.

συντέλεια, ἡ, the completion, the end, Matt. xiii. 39, 40. Hebr. ix. 26.

συντελέω, to complete, to finish, Luke, iv. 2, 13. Acts, xxi. 27; to accomplish, Rom. ix. 28; to conclude, to make, Hebr. viii. 8; pass., to be accomplished, to come to pass, Mrk. xiii. 4; to be finished, to be consumed, Joh. ii. 3.

συντέμνω, to cut short, Rom. ix. 28.

συντηρέω, to preserve, Matt. ix. 17. Mrk. vi. 20 (RV kept him safe); to keep in mind, to remember, Luke, ii. 19.

συντίθημι, to put together; mid., to agree together, to determine, Acts, xxiii. 20; to bargain, to covenant, Luke, xxii. 5.

συντόμως, adv., concisely; briefly, in few words, Acts, xxiv. 4.

συντρέχω, of a multitude of people, to run together, Acts, iii. 11. Mrk. vi. 33; to run with others, 1 Pet. iv. 4.

συντρίβω, to break, Matt. xii. 20. Mrk. xiv. 3. Joh. xix. 36; to break in pieces, Rev. ii. 27. Mrk. v. 4; to bruise, Luke, ix. 39. Rom. xvi. 20; pass., to be broken in heart, Luke, iv. 18 (RV bruised). [Westcott omits the clause.]

σύντριμμα, τὸ, a fracture; met., ruin, destruction, Rom. iii. 16. (Confined to the NT and late writers.)

σύντροφος, brought up with; as subst., a foster-brother, Acts, xiii. 1.

συντυγχάνω, to meet with, to get to, Luke, viii. 19.

συνυποκρίνομαι, to dissemble along with, Gal. ii. 13.

συνυπουργέω, to help together, 2 Cor. i. 11.

συνωδίνω, to be in travail together, Rom. viii. 22.

συνωμοσία, ἡ, a conspiracy, Acts, xxiii. 13.

Συροφοίνισσα, and **Συροφοινίκισσα**, ἡ, a Syrophenician woman, Mrk. vii. 26.

Σύρτις, ἡ, quicksand, esp. two on the coast of N. Africa, Acts, xxvii. 17.

σύρω, to drag, Joh. xxi. 8. Acts, xiv. 19. xvii. 6 etc.

συσπαράσσω, to convulse at the same time, Luke, ix. 42. Mrk. ix. 20. (Confined to the NT and late writers.)

σύσσημον, τὸ, a sign agreed upon, Mrk. xiv. 44. (A late form.)

σύσσωμος, *of the same body; as* subst., *a fellow-member,* Ephes. iii. 6. (Confined to the NT.)

συστασιωτὴς, ὁ, *a companion in insurrection,* a var. lect. ad Mrk. xv. 7. (Westcott reads στασιαστῶν.)

συστατικὸς, *commendatory;* ἐπιστολαὶ συστατικαί, *letters of recommendation,* 2 Cor. iii. 1.

συσταυρόω, *to crucify with another,* Matt. xxvii. 44. Joh. xix. 32. Mrk. xv. 32; met., ὁ παλαιὸς ἡμῶν ἄνθρωπος συνεσταυρώθη, sc. τῷ Χριστῷ, Rom. vi. 6 ("the death of Christ upon the cross has wrought the extinction of our former corruption," Thayer); Χριστῷ συνεσταύρωμαι, Gal. ii. 19 ("by the death of Christ upon the cross I have become utterly dead to my former habits of feeling and action," Thayer).

συστέλλω, *to contract; to wrap round, to enshroud,* Acts, v. 6; pass., *to be shortened,* 1 Cor. vii. 29.

συστενάζω, *to groan together,* Rom. viii. 22. (See συνωδίνω.)

συστοιχέω, *to stand in the same row;* met., *to answer to, to correspond to,* Gal. iv. 25.

συστρατιώτης, ὁ, *a fellow-soldier,* Philipp. ii. 25. Philem. 2.

συστρέφω, *to roll together, to gather,* Acts, xxviii. 3; pass., *to be gathered together, to assemble,* Matt. xvii. 22.

συστροφὴ, ἡ, *a conspiracy,* Acts, xxiii. 12; *a riotous assembly,* Acts, xix. 40.

συσχηματίζω, *to conform;* mid., *to conform one's self,* Rom. xii. 2 (RV *be ye transformed*); 1 Pet. i. 14.

σφαγὴ, ἡ, *slaughter;* πρόβατα σφαγῆς, *sheep destined for slaughter,* Rom. viii. 36; ἡμέρα σφαγῆς, *a day of destruction,* James, v. 5 [or, *day of feasting*].

σφάγιον, τὸ, *a victim,* Acts, vii. 42.

σφάζω, *to slaughter, to slay,* 1 Joh. iii. 12. Rev. v. 6, 9, 12. vi. 4, 9 etc.; κεφαλὴ ἐσφαγμένη εἰς θάνατον, *mortally wounded,* Rev. xiii. 3 (RV *smitten unto death*).

σφόδρα, adv., *exceedingly, greatly,* Luke, xviii. 23. Matt. ii. 10. xvii. 6, 23 etc.

σφοδρῶς, adv., *exceedingly,* Acts, xxvii. 18.

σφραγίζω, *to seal,* Matt. xxvii. 66. Rev. vii. 3. xx. 3; *to keep silence about,* Rev. x. 4; *to confirm, to prove,* Joh. iii. 33. vi. 27; mid., *to assure,* Rom. xv. 28. 2 Cor. i. 22; pass., *to be marked by God as his,* Ephes. i. 13. iv. 30.

σφραγὶς, ἡ, *a seal,* Rev. v. 1. vi. 1, 3, 5, 7, 9, 12 etc.; *a signet-ring,* Rev. vii. 2; *the impression* or *mark* made by a seal, Rev. ix. 4. 2 Tim. ii. 19; *a token,* Rom. iv. 11. 1 Cor. ix. 2.

σφυδρὸν, τὸ, *the ancle,* Acts, iii. 7. (The word is not recognized in Pape's Lex.)

σφυρὶς, ἡ, and **σπυρὶς**, *a basket,* Matt. xvi. 10. Mrk. viii. 8. (See σπυρίς.)

σφυρὸν, τὸ, *the ancle*, a var. lect. ad Acts, iii. 7.

σχεδὸν, adv., *nearly, almost*, Acts, xiii. 44. xix. 26. Hebr. ix. 22.

σχῆμα, τὸ, *the fashion*, 1 Cor. vii. 31; *appearance*, Philipp. ii. 7.

σχίζω, *to split; to rend*, Luke, v. 36. xxiii. 45. Matt. xxvii. 51. Mrk. i. 10; pass., *to be split up into opposite parties, to be divided*, Acts, xiv. 4. xxiii. 7.

σχίσμα, τὸ, *a rent*, Matt. ix. 16. Mrk. ii. 21; *a division, a dissension*, 1 Cor. i. 10. xi. 18. xii. 25. Joh. vii. 43 etc.

σχοινίον, τὸ, *a rope*, Joh. ii. 15. Acts, xxvii. 32.

σχολάζω, *to have leisure*, 1 Cor. vii. 5; *to be unoccupied, to be empty*, Matt. xii. 44.

σχολὴ, ἡ, *a school*, Acts, xix. 9.

σώζω, *to save*, Matt. viii. 25. Luke, viii. 50; *to restore to health, to heal*, Matt. ix. 22. Mrk. v. 34. x. 52; *to save from eternal death*, Rom. v. 9. James, v. 20; τοὺς σωζομένους, *those in the way of salvation*, Acts, ii. 47. Cf. 1 Cor. i. 18. 2 Cor. ii. 15.

σῶμα, τὸ, *the body*, Luke, xi. 34. xii. 23 etc.; *a dead body, a corpse*, Matt. xiv. 12 (here Westcott reads πτῶμα), xxvii. 58. Luke, xxiii. 55; τὸ σῶμα τῆς σαρκὸς, *his physical body*, Coloss. i. 22; τὸ σῶμα τοῦ θανάτου, *the body given over to death*, Rom. vii. 24. Cf. Rom. viii. 23. Coloss. ii. 11.

Rom. vi. 6; *a slave*, Rev. xviii. 13; *a society of men united into one body, the church*, Rom. xii. 5. 1 Cor. xii. 13. Ephes. iv. 16. Coloss. i. 18; *the thing itself, the reality*, as distinguished from the shadow, Coloss. ii. 17.

σωματικὸς, *bodily*, Luke, iii. 22. 1 Tim. iv. 8.

σωματικῶς, adv., *bodily*, Coloss. ii. 9.

σωρεύω, *to heap up*, Rom. xii. 20; pass., met., *to be laden with*, 2 Tim. iii. 6.

σωτὴρ, ὁ, *a saviour;* and (1) applied to God the Father, Luke, i. 47. 1 Tim. i. 1. Tit. i. 3. Jude, 25 etc.; (2) to Christ, Philipp. iii. 20. ("The title is confined—with the exception of the writings of S. Luke—to the later writings of the NT," Westcott.)

σωτηρία, ἡ, *deliverance, preservation, salvation*, Acts, vii. 25. xxvii. 34. Joh. iv. 22. Acts, iv. 12 etc.

σωτήριος, *imparting salvation*, Tit. ii. 11; τὸ σωτήριον = ἡ σωτηρία, Luke, ii. 30. iii. 6. Acts, xxviii. 28. Ephes. vi. 17.

σωφρονέω, *to be of sound mind; to be soberminded*, Tit. ii. 6. 1 Pet. iv. 7; *to be in one's right mind*, Mrk. v. 15. Luke, viii. 35. 2 Cor. v. 13; *to think of one's self soberly*, Rom. xii. 3.

σωφρονίζω, *to bring to a sound mind; to admonish*, Tit. ii. 4.

σωφρονισμὸς, ὁ, *self-control; sobermindedness*, 2 Tim. i. 7 [more probably, *discipline*.]

σωφρόνως, adv., *with sound mind; soberly*, Tit. ii. 12.

σωφροσύνη, ἡ, *soundness of mind, sanity*, Acts, xxvi. 25; *sobriety*, 1 Tim. ii. 9, 15.

σώφρων, *sane; under self-control, soberminded*, 1 Tim. iii. 2. Tit. i. 8. ii. 2, 5.

T

ταβέρναι, αἱ, Lat. *tabernae*, *taverns*, τρεῖς ταβέρναι (Acts, xxviii. 15), *The Three Taverns*, the name of an inn or halting-place on the Appian Way, between Rome and the Appii Forum, about 10 Roman miles from the latter place and 33 from Rome.

τάγμα, τὸ, *settled-order*, 1 Cor. xv. 23.

τακτὸς, *arranged, fixed, set*, Acts, xii. 21.

ταλαιπωρέω, *to endure hardships, to be afflicted*, James, iv. 9.

ταλαιπωρία, ἡ, *hardship, misery*, James, v. 1. Rom. iii. 16.

ταλαίπωρος, *afflicted, wretched*, Rom. vii. 24. Rev. iii. 17.

ταλαντιαῖος, *of the weight of a talent*, Rev. xvi. 21.

τάλαντον, τὸ, the name of a *weight*, varying at different places and different times; *a sum of money* weighing a talent, but varying in the different states; the *Attic Talent* was equal to 60 Attic minae, or 6000 drachmae, and, according to Pape, worth £206 5s.; "but in the NT probably the *Syrian Talent* is referred to, which was equal to about 237 dollars, Matt. xviii. 24. xxv. 15, 16, 20, 22, 24, 25, 28," Thayer.

ταλιθά, or **ταλειθά**, indecl., *a damsel*, Mrk. v. 41 [a Chaldee word].

ταμιεῖον, and **ταμεῖον**, τὸ, a *store-chamber*, Luke, xii. 24; *a chamber, a secret room*, Matt. vi. 6. xxiv. 26. Luke, xii. 3 (RV in all three passages *inner chamber*).

τάξις, ἡ, *arrangement; order*, Luke, i. 8. Coloss. ii. 5; κατὰ τάξιν, *in order*, 1 Cor. xiv. 40; *the position*, or *rank* a person holds, Hebr. v. 6, 10. vi. 20. vii. 11, 17.

ταπεινὸς, *low; of low degree*, James, i. 9; *lowly in mind*, 2 Cor. vii. 6. Matt. xi. 29. Rom. xii. 16; *humble*, James, iv. 6. 1 Pet. v. 5.

ταπεινοφροσύνη, ἡ, *lowliness of mind, humility*, Acts, xx. 19. Ephes. iv. 2. Philipp. ii. 3 etc. (Not found in classical authors.)

ταπεινόφρων, *humble-minded*, 1 Pet. iii. 8. (A late form.)

ταπεινόω, *to make low;* ταπεινόω ἐμαυτὸν, *to humble myself*, 2 Cor. xi. 7. Philipp. ii. 8. iv. 12; pass., *to be humbled*, James, iv. 10.

ταπείνωσις, ἡ, *lowliness, low estate*, Luke, i. 48. Philipp. iii. 21; *humiliation*, Acts, viii. 33. James, i. 10.

ταράσσω, *to agitate, to trouble*, Joh. v. 4; *to disquiet, to* *trouble*, Acts, xv. 24. xvii. 8, 13. Gal. v. 10 etc.; pass., *to be troubled*, Matt. ii. 3. xiv. 26. Joh. xii. 27. Luke, i. 12.

ταραχή, ἡ, *disturbance*, Joh. v. 4; plur., *troubles*, a var. lect. ad Mrk. xiii. 8.

τάραχος, ὁ, *commotion*, Acts, xii. 18; *disturbance*, Acts, xix. 23.

Ταρσεύς, *of Tarsus*, Acts, ix. 11. xxi. 39.

ταρταρόω, *to cast down to Tartarus*, or *Gehenna*, 2 Pet. ii. 4. (A purely NT form.)

τάσσω, *to appoint, to order*, Acts, xv. 2.; pass., *to be appointed, to be ordained*, Rom. xiii. 1. Acts, xiii. 48 (unless it is to be taken in a middle sense], xxii. 10; *to be set*, Matt. viii. 9. Luke, vii. 8; mid., *to appoint*, Matt. xxviii. 17. Acts, xxviii. 23.

ταῦρος, ὁ, *a bull, an ox*, Hebr. ix. 13. x. 4. Matt. xxii. 4. Acts, xiv. 13.

ταφή, ἡ, *a burial*, Matt. xxvii. 7.

τάφος, ὁ, *a grave, a sepulchre*, Matt. xxiii. 27, 29. xxvii. 61, 64, 66. Rom. iii. 13 etc.

τάχα, adv., *quickly*, Matt. xxviii. 7, 8. But Westcott reads ταχὺ in both places; *perhaps, peradventure*, Rom. v. 7. Philem. 15.

ταχέως, adv., *quickly, soon*, 2 Thess. ii. 2. Luke, xiv. 21. xvi. 6 etc.; *hastily*, 1 Tim. v. 22.

ταχινὸς, *swift, quick,* 2 Pet. i. 14. ii. 1.

τάχιον, and **τάχειον,** adv., *more quickly, more swiftly,* Joh. xiii. 27. xx. 4. Hebr. xiii. 19, 23.

τάχιστα, superlative adverb, *very quickly;* ὡς τάχιστα, *as soon as possible,* Acts, xvii. 15.

τάχος, τὸ, *speed, quickness;* ἐν τάχει, *quickly, soon,* Luke, xviii. 8. Acts, xii. 7. xxii. 18 etc.

ταχὺ, adv., *quickly, speedily,* Matt. v. 25. xxviii. 7. Joh. xi. 29 etc.

ταχὺς, *quick, swift,* James, i. 19.

τὲ, *a copulative enclitic particle, and;* τὲ .. καὶ, *both ... and.* (The reader is referred to his Greek Grammar.)

τεῖχος, τὸ, *a wall*, Acts, ix. 25. 2 Cor. xi. 33. Hebr. xi. 30.

τεκμήριον, τὸ, *a sign; an indubitable evidence, a proof,* Acts, i. 3.

τεκνίον, τὸ, a diminutive of τέκνον, *a little child;* in the NT used as a term of kindly address by teachers to their disciples, and always in the plural, *little children,* Joh. xiii. 33. 1 Joh. ii. 1, 12, 28. iii. 18. iv. 4. (Found only in the NT and the Anthology.)

τεκνογονέω, *to beget children,* 1 Tim. v. 14 (RV *bear children*).

τεκνογονία, ἡ, *the begetting of children,* 1 Tim. ii. 15 (RV *childbearing*).

τέκνον, τὸ, *a child,* Mrk. xiii. 12. Luke, i. 7; as a term of affection to converts, Philem. 10. 2 Tim. i. 2. 3 Joh. 4;

τέκνα, *the children of a city*, i.e. *its inhabitants*, Matt. xxiii. 37. Luke, xiii. 34. Gal. iv. 25; κατάρας τέκνα, *children exposed to the curse of God*, 2 Pet. ii. 14. Cf. Ephes. ii. 3.

τεκνοτροφέω, *to bring up children*, 1 Tim. v. 10.

τέκτων, ὁ, *a worker in wood, a carpenter*, Matt. xiii. 55. Mrk. vi. 3.

τέλειος, *complete, perfect*, James, i. 4, 25. 1 Joh. iv. 18. 1 Cor. xiii. 10; *full-grown, adult*, Hebr. v. 14; εἰς ἄνδρα τέλειον, Ephes. iv. 13 ("until we rise to the same level of knowledge which we ascribe to a full-grown man," Thayer); οἱ τέλειοι, *the perfect*, 1 Cor. ii. 6 ("i.e. the more intelligent to apprehend divine things," Thayer). Cf. Matt. v. 48. James, iii. 2. Coloss. iv. 12.

τελειότης, ἡ, *completeness, perfectness*, Coloss. iii. 14; *perfection*, Hebr. vi. 1.

τελειόω, *to accomplish, to fulfil*, Joh. iv. 34. v. 36. xix. 28. Acts, xx. 24; *to make perfect*, Hebr. ii. 10. vii. 19; pass., *to be perfected*, Luke, xiii. 32. 1 Joh. ii. 5. iv. 12, 17, 18. Philip. iii. 12.

τελείως, adv., *completely, perfectly*, 1 Pet. i. 13.

τελείωσις, ἡ, *a fulfilment*, Luke, i. 45; *completion, finality*, Hebr. vii. 11.

τελειωτής, ὁ, *the perfecter*, Hebr. xii. 2. ("The word occurs nowhere else," Thayer.)

τελεσφορέω, *to bring* anything *to perfection*, Luke, viii. 14.

τελευτάω, *to come to an end, to die*, Matt. ii. 19. ix. 18. xxii. 25. Luke, vii. 2; θανάτῳ τελευτάτω, Matt. xv. 4 ("*let him surely die*," Thayer).

τελευτή, ἡ, *the end, death*, Matt. ii. 15.

τελέω, *to finish, to end*, Matt. vii. 28. xi. 1. xix. 1; οὐ μὴ τελέσητε τὰς πόλεις, *ye shall not have gone through the cities*, Matt. x. 23; *to pay*, Matt. xvii. 24. Rom. xiii. 6; pass., *to be finished*, Joh. xix. 30. Rev. xv. 1. xx. 3, 5, 7.

τέλος, τὸ, *the end*, Luke, i. 33. Hebr. iii. 6. vii. 3; εἰς τέλος, *unto the end*, Joh. xiii. 1; *continually*, Luke, xviii. 5; *completely, to the uttermost*, 1 Thess. ii. 16; τέλος ἔχειν, *to be finished, to be fulfilled*, Luke, xxii. 37; τὸ δὲ τέλος, *and finally*, 1 Pet. iii. 8; *a tax, a toll*, Matt. xvii. 25. Rom. xiii. 7.

τελώνης, ὁ, *a farmer of taxes;* also, and commonly, *a collector of taxes, a publican*, Matt. v. 46. ix. 10. xxi. 31. Luke, iii. 12.

τελώνιον, τὸ, *the toll-house, the collector's office*, Matt. ix. 9. Luke, v. 27. Mrk. ii. 14.

τέρας, τὸ, *a portent, a wonder*, Acts, ii. 19, 43. Joh. iv. 48. ("In the NT it is found only in the plural, and joined with σημεῖα," Thayer.)

τεσσαράκοντα, numer., *forty*, Matt. iv. 2. Joh. ii. 20.

τεσσαρακονταετὴς, *forty years old*, Acts, vii. 23.

τέσσαρες, and τέσσερες, numer., *four*, Matt. xxiv. 31. Luke, ii. 37. Joh. xi. 17 etc.

τεσσαρεσκαιδέκατος, numer., *the fourteenth*, Acts, xxvii. 27, 33.

τεταρταῖος, numer., *four days ago; τεταρταῖός ἐστιν, he hath been dead four days*, Joh. xi. 39.

τέταρτος, numer., *the fourth*, Matt. xiv. 25. Mrk. vi. 48. Acts, x. 30 etc.

τετράγωνος, *four-square, quadrangular*, Rev. xxi. 16.

τετράδιον, and τετραδεῖον, τὸ, *a guard consisting of four soldiers, a quaternion*, Acts, xii. 4. (Confined to the NT and very late writers.)

τετρακισχίλιοι, numer., *four thousand*, Matt. xv. 38. xvi. 10. Acts, xxi. 38.

τετρακόσιοι, numer., *four hundred*, Acts, v. 36. vii. 6. xiii. 20 etc.

τετράμηνος, *of four months; ἔτι τετράμηνός ἐστιν*, sc. χρόνος, *there is still a space of four months*, Joh. iv. 35.

τετραπλόος, *four-fold*, Luke, xix. 8.

τετράπους, *four-footed*, Acts, x. 12. xi. 6. Rom. i. 23.

τετραρχέω, *to be a tetrarch*, Luke, iii. 1.

τετράρχης, ὁ, *a tetrarch, i.e. the ruler of the fourth part of any region*, Matt. xiv. 1. Luke, iii. 19. ix. 7. Acts, xiii. 1.

τεφρόω, *to reduce to ashes*, 2 Pet. ii. 6.

τέχνη, ἡ, *an art; a trade, a handicraft*, Acts, xvii. 29. xviii. 3. Rev. xviii. 22.

τεχνίτης, ὁ, *an artificer, a craftsman*, Acts, xix. 24, 38. Rev. xviii. 22; *an architect*, Hebr. xi. 10.

τήκω, trans., *to melt;* pass., *to be melted*, 2 Pet. iii. 12.

τηλαυγῶς, adv., *clearly, distinctly*, Mrk. viii. 25.

τηλικοῦτος, *of so great a size*, James, iii. 4; met., *so great*, Hebr. ii. 3. 2 Cor. i. 10. Rev. xvi. 18.

τηρέω, *to guard*, Matt. xxvii. 54. Acts, xvi. 23. xxv. 4, 21; *to keep*, 1 Tim. v. 22. James, i. 27. Joh. xvii. 15; *to maintain, to hold firmly*, 2 Tim. iv. 7. Ephes. iv. 3. Rev. xiv. 12; *to observe, to keep*, Acts, xv. 5. James, ii. 10. Joh. ix. 16. Matt. xix. 17; *to reserve*, 2 Pet. ii. 9. iii. 7. Acts, xxv. 21; pass., *to be kept, to be preserved*, 1 Thess. v. 23. Jude, 1.

τήρησις, ἡ, *a keeping, an observing*, 1 Cor. vii. 19; met., *prison*, Acts, iv. 3. v. 18.

τίθημι, *to place, to lay*, 1 Cor. iii. 10. Rom. ix. 33 etc.; *to serve up*, Joh. ii. 10; *to lay aside, to put off*, Joh. xiii. 4; *to lay down*, Luke, xix. 21, 22; *to assign*, Matt. xxiv. 51; *to make*, Rom. iv. 17; *τιθέναι τὰ γόνατα, to kneel down*, Luke, xxii. 41. Acts, vii. 60. xx. 36 etc.; mid., *to cause to be put*, Acts, v. 25. xii. 4; *to put, to set*, Acts, i. 7. 1 Cor. xii. 18; *to place*, i.e. *to entrust to*, 2 Cor. v. 19; *to appoint*, Acts, xx. 28. 1 Thess. v. 9. 1 Tim.

i. 13; τίθεσθαι ἐν τῇ καρδίᾳ, to lay up in their hearts, Luke, i. 66; also, to determine on, to purpose, Acts, v. 4. xix. 21; so τίθεσθαι εἰς καρδίας, to settle, to determine, Luke, xxi. 14 [Westcott reads θέτε]; τίθεσθαι εἰς τὰ ὦτα, to listen attentively to, Luke, ix. 44.

τίκτω, to bring forth, to bear, Matt. i. 21, 23, 25. Luke, ii. 7 etc.; met., to cause, to bring forth, James, i. 15.

τίλλω, to pluck, Matt. xii. 1. Luke, vi. 1. Mrk. ii. 23.

τιμάω, to honour, Matt. xv. 8. xix. 19. Joh. v. 23 etc.; mid., to fix the value of, to price, Matt. xxvii. 9.

τιμή, ἡ, honour, Rom. ix. 21, 1 Pet. iii. 7. Hebr. v. 4; the price, Matt. xxvii. 6, 9. Acts, v. 2: τιμῆς, at a price, 1 Cor. vi. 20. vii. 23; value, Coloss. ii. 23; preciousness, 1 Pet. ii. 7.

τίμιος, valuable, precious, Rev. xvii. 4. xviii. 12, 16. 1 Cor. iii. 12; held in honour, esteemed, Hebr. xiii. 4. Acts, v. 34.

τιμιότης, ἡ, costliness, Rev. xviii. 19.

τιμωρέω, with accus., to take vengeance on, to punish, Acts, xxii. 5. xxvi. 11.

τιμωρία, ἡ, vengeance, punishment, Hebr. x. 29.

τίνω, to pay as a penalty; to suffer, 2 Thess. i. 9.

τίς, τί, interrogative pronoun, quis? quid? and τὶς, τὶ, indefinite pronoun, a certain person, some one. (The reader is referred to his Greek Grammar.)

τίτλος, ὁ, Lat. titulus, an inscription, giving the accusation under which the condemned person suffered, Joh. xix. 19, 20.

τοιγαροῦν, a strengthened form of the enclitic particle τοί, wherefore, Hebr. xii. 1. 1 Thess. iv. 8.

τοίνυν, therefore, Luke, xx. 25. (Here it stands at the beginning of the sentence, which is contrary to established custom.)

τοιόσδε, a demonstrative pronoun, answering to the interrogative ποῖος, such a one, such, 2 Pet. i. 17.

τοιοῦτος, a strengthened demonstrative pronoun, such; ὁ τοιοῦτος, such as the above-mentioned. (The reader is referred to his Greek Grammar.)

τοῖχος, ὁ, a wall, Acts, xxiii. 3.

τόκος, ὁ, interest on money, Luke, xix. 23. Matt. xxv. 27.

τολμάω, to dare, Luke, xx. 40. Matt. xxii. 56; to endure, Rom. v. 7. 1 Cor. vi. 1; to be bold, 2 Cor. x. 2. xi. 21.

τολμηρότερον, adverbially, more boldly, Rom. xv. 15. (Here Westcott reads τολμηροτέρως.)

τολμητής, ὁ, an audacious man, 2 Pet. ii. 10.

τομώτερος, comparative of τομὸς, sharper, Hebr. iv. 12.

τόξον, τὸ, a bow, Rev. vi. 2.

τοπάζιον, τὸ, "*the topaz, a transparent gold-gleaming precious stone, to be distinguished from the opaque, green topaz of Pliny,*" Pape in Lex., Rev. xxi. 20.

τόπος, ὁ, *a place*, Matt. xxiv. 15. Luke, vi. 17. Joh. xiv. 3; *passage* (in a book), Luke, iv. 17; *an opportunity*, Acts, xxv. 16. Hebr. xii. 17.

τοσοῦτος, *so great*, Matt. viii. 10; of time, *so long*, Joh. xiv. 9; in the plural, *so many*, Matt. xv. 33. Joh. vi. 9.

τότε, adv. of time, *then, at that time*, Matt. ii. 17. xi. 20; ἀπὸ τότε, *from that time*, Matt. iv. 17. xvi. 21.

τράγος, ὁ, *a he-goat, a goat*, Hebr. ix. 12. x. 4.

τράπεζα, ἡ, *a table*, Matt. xv. 27. Hebr. ix. 2; τράπεζα Κυρίου, *the table of the Lord*, 1 Cor. x. 21; met., *food*, Acts, xvi. 34; *the counter of a money-changer*, Matt. xxi. 12. Mrk. xi. 15. Joh. ii. 15; *a bank*, Luke, xix. 23.

τραπεζίτης, and **τραπεζείτης**, ὁ, *a money-changer, a banker*, Matt. xxv. 27.

τραῦμα, τὸ, *a wound*, Luke, x. 34.

τραυματίζω, *to wound*, Luke, xx. 12. Acts, xix. 16.

τραχηλίζω, *to bend back the neck;* met., *to lay bare, to make manifest*, Hebr. iv. 13.

τράχηλος, ὁ, *the neck*, Acts, xv. 10. Luke, xvii. 2 etc.; τὸν ἑαυτῶν τράχηλον ὑπέθηκαν, *laid down their own necks*, i.e. exposed themselves to imminent peril, Rom. xvi. 4.

τραχύς, *rough*, Luke, iii. 5; *rocky*, Acts, xxvii. 29.

τρεῖς, numer., *three*, Matt. xii. 40. Mrk. viii. 2 etc.

τρέμω, *to tremble*, Mrk. v. 33. Luke, viii. 47; *to be afraid, to fear*, 2 Pet. ii. 10.

τρέφω, *to nourish, to feed*, Matt. vi. 26. xxv. 37; *to bring up*, Luke, iv. 16; *to give suck*, Luke, xxiii. 29.

τρέχω, *to run*, Joh. xx. 2, 4. Mrk. v. 6; *to exert oneself*, Gal. ii. 2. v. 7; *to make progress*, 2 Thess. iii. 1.

τρῆμα, τὸ, *a perforation; the eye* of a needle, Matt. xix. 24. Luke, xviii. 25.

τριάκοντα, numer., *thirty*, Mrk. iv. 8. Luke, iii. 23 etc.

τριακόσιοι, numer., *three hundred*, Joh. xii. 5. Mrk. xiv. 5.

τρίβολος, ὁ, *a thistle*, Matt. vii. 16. Hebr. vi. 8.

τρίβος, ἡ, also ὁ, *a trodden road, a path*, Matt. iii. 3. Mrk. i. 3. Luke, iii. 4.

τριετία, ἡ, *a space of three years*, Acts, xx. 31.

τρίζω, *to make a shrill noise;* met., τρίζειν τοὺς ὀδόντας, *to grind the teeth*, Mrk. ix. 18.

τρίμηνος, *of three months;* τρίμηνον, *the space of three months*, Hebr. xi. 23.

τρὶς, adv., *thrice*, Matt. xxvi. 34, 75 etc.; ἐπὶ τρὶς, *three times*, Acts, x. 16. xi. 10.

τρίστεγος, *having three stories;* τὸ τρίστεγον, *the third story*, Acts, xx. 9.

τρισχίλιοι, numer., *three thousand*, Acts, ii. 41.

τρίτος, numer., *the third*, Acts, ii. 15. Luke, xxiv. 21; τὸ τρίτον, *the third part*, Rev. viii. 7, 8, 9, 10, 11, 12; also τὸ τρίτον, *the third time*, Mrk. xiv. 41. Joh. xxi. 17; also τρίτον, *a third time*, Luke, xxiii. 22; τοῦτο ἤδη τρίτον ἐφανερώθη Ἰησοῦς, *this is now the third time that Jesus was manifested*, Joh. xxi. 14. Cf. 2 Cor. xii. 14. xiii. 1; τρίτον, *thirdly*, 1 Cor. xii. 28; ἐκ τρίτου, *a third time*, Matt. xxvi. 44.

τρίχινος, *made of hair*, Rev. vi. 12.

τρόμος, ὁ, *a trembling*, 2 Cor. vii. 15. Ephes. vi. 5 etc.

τροπή, ἡ, *a turning*, James, i. 17.

τρόπος, ὁ, *manner, way*; ὃν τρόπον, *in the same manner as*, Matt. xxiii. 37. Acts, i. 11. vii. 28. 2 Tim. iii. 8; τὸν ὅμοιον τρόπον τούτοις, *in like manner as these*, Jude, 7; καθ' ὃν τρόπον, *even as*, Acts, xv. 11. xxvii. 25; κατὰ πάντα τρόπον, *in every way*, Rom. iii. 2; so also παντὶ τρόπῳ, Philipp. i. 18; κατὰ μηδένα τρόπον, *in no wise*, 2 Thess. ii. 3; *disposition, character*, Hebr. xiii. 5.

τροποφορέω, with accus. of person, *to bear with the manners of*, Acts, xiii. 18. (See Pape's Lexicon in voc.)

τροφή, ἡ, *food, nourishment*, Matt. iii. 4. vi. 25. Luke, xii. 23. Joh. iv. 8 etc.; met., *doctrine*, Hebr. v. 12, 14.

τροφὸς, ἡ, *a nurse*, 1 Thess. ii. 7.

τροφοφορέω, *to bear with as a nurse*, a var. lect. ad Acts, xiii. 18.

τροχιά, ἡ, *the track of a wheel; a path*, Hebr. xii. 13.

τροχὸς, ὁ, *a wheel*, James, iii. 6. (But perhaps, τὸν τρόχον, *the course*.)

τρύβλιον, τὸ, *a dish*, Matt. xxvi. 23. Mrk. xiv. 20. ("It is no diminutive, and therefore not to be accentuated τρυβλίον," Pape in Lex.)

τρυγάω, *to gather in the vintage*, Rev. xiv. 18, 19. Luke, vi. 44.

τρυγὼν, ἡ, *a turtle dove*, Luke, ii. 24.

τρυμαλιὰ, ἡ, *the eye* of a needle, Mrk. x. 25.

τρύπημα, τὸ, *the eye* of a needle, Matt. xix. 24. (Here Westcott reads διὰ τρήματος.)

τρυφάω, *to live luxuriously*, James, v. 5.

τρυφὴ, ἡ, *luxury*, Luke, vii. 25. 2 Pet. ii. 13.

τρώγω, *to eat*, Matt. xxiv. 38. Joh. vi. 54, 56, 58. xiii. 18.

τυγχάνω, *to strike, to hit the mark; to attain, to obtain*, Luke, xx. 35. Acts, xxiv. 2. xxvi. 22. 2 Tim. ii. 10 etc.; *to happen;* εἰ τύχοι, *it may be, perchance*, 1 Cor. xiv. 10. xv. 37; οὐ τυχὼν, *no common, no ordinary*, person or thing, Acts, xix. 11. xxviii. 2; τυχὸν, adverbially, *perhaps*, 1 Cor. xvi. 6.

τυμπανίζω, *to beat the timbrel;* pass., *to be tortured,* Hebr. xi. 35.

τυπικῶς, adv., *figuratively; by way of example,* 1 Cor. x. 11.

τύπος, ὁ, *a mark, a print,* Joh. xx. 25; *a figure, an image,* Acts, vii. 43; *a form,* Rom. vi. 17. Acts, xxiii. 25; *an example,* 2 Thess. iii. 9. Tit. ii. 7; *a warning,* 1 Cor. x. 6; *a pattern,* Hebr. viii. 5. Acts, vii. 44; *a type,* Rom. v. 14.

τύπτω, *to smite,* Luke, xviii. 13. xxiii. 48; *to disquiet,* 1 Cor. viii. 12; *to punish,* Acts, xxiii. 3.

τυρβάζω, *to trouble, to disturb;* pass., *to be troubled* in mind, *to be disquieted,* Luke, x. 41. (Here Westcott reads θορυβάζῃ.)

τυφλὸς, *blind,* Matt. ix. 27, 28. xi. 5 etc.

τυφλάω, *to make blind;* met., *to darken the moral perception, to darken,* 2 Cor. iv. 4. Joh. xii. 40. 1 Joh. ii. 11.

τυφόω, *to puff up with pride;* pass., *to be puffed up with pride,* 1 Tim. iii. 6. vi. 4. 2 Tim. iii. 4.

τύφω, *to cause a smoke;* pass., *to smoke,* Matt. xii. 20.

τυφωνικὸς, *tempestuous,* Acts, xxvii. 14.

Υ

ὑακίνθινος, *of hyacinth, of the colour of hyacinth,* Rev. ix. 17.

ὑάκινθος, ὁ, also ἡ, *the hyacinth, the name of a flower;* "ἡ ὑάκινθος, a precious stone, of the colour of the flower,—perhaps our *sapphire,*" Pape in Lexicon, Rev. xxi. 20.

ὑάλινος, *of glass, glassy,* Rev. iv. 6. xv. 2.

ὕαλος, ὁ, *glass,* Rev. xxi. 18, 21.

ὑβρίζω, *to insult, to maltreat,* Matt. xxii. 6. Luke, xviii. 32. Acts, xiv. 5.

ὕβρις, ἡ, *insolence; an injury,* 2 Cor. xii. 10; *damage,* Acts, xxvii. 10, 21.

ὑβριστὴς, *insolent, injurious,* Rom. i. 30. 1 Tim. i. 13.

ὑγιαίνω, *to be in sound health,* Luke, v. 31. vii. 10. xv. 27; "the phrase ὑγιαίνειν ἐν τῇ πίστει is used of one whose Christian opinions are free from any admixture of error, Tit. i. 13," Thayer; cf. Tit. ii. 2. 1 Tim. i. 10. 2 Tim. iv. 3; so λόγοι ὑγιαίνοντες, *sound words,* 1 Tim. vi. 3. 2 Tim. i. 13.

ὑγιὴς, *sound* in health, Joh. v. 11, 15; *sound* in doctrine, Tit. ii. 8.

ὑγρὸς, *moist;* of trees, *full of sap, green,* Luke, xxiii. 31.

ὑδρία, ἡ, *a water-pot,* Joh. ii. 6. iv. 28.

ὑδροποτέω, *to drink water,* 1 Tim. v. 23.

ὑδρωπικὸς, *afflicted with dropsy,* Luke, xiv. 2.

ὕδωρ, τὸ, *water,* Joh. iv. 7. v. 3. Matt. iii. 16 etc.; plur. τὰ ὕδατα, *the waves,* Matt. xiv. 28, 29; πολλὰ ὕδατα, *many springs* or *fountains,* Joh. iii. 23.

ὑετός, ὁ, *rain*, Acts, xiv. 17. xxviii. 2.

υἱοθεσία, ἡ, *adoption*, Rom. ix. 4. Gal. iv. 5. Ephes. i. 5; υἱοθεσίαν ἀπεκδεχόμενοι, Rom. viii. 23 ("*waiting for adoption*, i.e. the consummate condition of the sons of God, which will render it evident that they are the sons of God," Thayer. It is a purely NT form).

υἱός, ὁ, *a son*, Matt. i. 21, 25. vii. 9 etc.; ὁ υἱὸς τοῦ ἀνθρώπου, a term frequently used by Christ of himself, Matt. viii. 20. ix. 6 etc.; ὁ υἱὸς τοῦ θεοῦ, a title of the Messiah, Matt. xxvi. 63. Joh. i. 34, 50 etc.

ὕλη, ἡ, *wood*, James, iii. 5.

ὑμέτερος, possessive pronoun, *your*, Joh. viii. 17. Acts, xxvii. 34.

ὑμνέω, *to sing*, Matt. xxvi. 30. Mrk. xiv. 26.

ὕμνος, ὁ, *a hymn*, Ephes. v. 19. Coloss. iii. 16.

ὑπάγω, *to lead under;* in the NT always intrans., *to go away, to depart*, Joh. viii. 21. xiv. 5, 28. Matt. xxvi. 24.

ὑπακοή, ἡ, *a hearkening to; obedience*, Rom. v. 19. vi. 16. xvi. 19. (It is a purely NT word. Pape in Lex. assigns it only *one* meaning, viz., *obedience*.)

ὑπακούω, *to hearken; to answer the knock* at the door, Acts, xii. 13; *to obey*, Philipp. ii. 12. Acts, vi. 7.

ὕπανδρος, *subject to a husband, married*, Rom. vii. 2.

ὑπαντάω, *to meet*, Matt. viii. 28. Joh. xi. 20, 30; *to encounter in arms*, Luke, xiv. 31.

ὑπάντησις, ἡ, *a meeting;* εἰς ὑπάντησιν αὐτῷ, *to meet him*, Joh. xii. 13. Matt. viii. 34.

ὕπαρξις, ἡ, *goods, possessions*, Acts, ii. 45. Hebr. x. 34.

ὑπάρχω, *to begin; to be*, Philipp. ii. 6. Acts, xix. 40. xxvii. 12; ὑπάρχει μοι, *I possess*, Acts, iii. 6. iv. 36; τὰ ὑπάρχοντα, *their substance, their property*, Luke, viii. 3. xii. 15. Matt. xix. 21.

ὑπείκω, *to yield, to submit*, Hebr. xiii. 17.

ὑπεναντίος, *opposite to; contrary to*, Coloss. ii. 14; ὁ ὑπ., *the adversary*, Hebr. x. 27.

ὑπέρ, prepos., with genitive, *for, on behalf of*, Matt. v. 44 etc.; with accusative, *beyond, above*, Philipp. ii. 9; as adv., *more*, ὕπερ ἐγὼ, 2 Cor. xi. 23. (The reader is referred to his Greek Grammar.)

ὑπεραίρω, *to raise above;* mid., *to exalt oneself above measure*, 2 Cor. xii. 7; with ἐπί τινα, *to exalt himself against*, 2 Thess. ii. 4.

ὑπέρακμος, *beyond the prime of life*, 1 Cor. vii. 36. (It is a purely NT form.)

ὑπεράνω, adv., *above*, Ephes. i. 21. iv. 10. Hebr. ix. 5.

ὑπεραυξάνω, *to increase beyond measure*, 2 Thess. i. 3.

ὑπερβαίνω, *to go beyond;* met., *to overreach, to defraud*, 1 Thess. iv. 6.

ὑπερβαλλόντως, adv., *above measure*, 2 Cor. xi. 23.

ὑπερβάλλω, *to show beyond; to surpass;* ὑπερβάλλων, as adjective, *excelling, preeminent*, 2 Cor. iii. 10. ix. 14. Ephes. i. 19. ii. 7; ἡ ὑπερβάλλουσα τῆς γνώσεως ἀγάπη τοῦ Χριστοῦ, Ephes. iii. 19 (RV *the love of Christ which passeth knowledge*).

ὑπερβολή, ἡ, *the crossing* of a river or mountain; *excellence, preeminence*, 2 Cor. iv. 7. xii. 7; καθ' ὑπερβολήν, *exceedingly*, Rom. vii. 13. 2 Cor. i. 8 etc.; καθ' ὑπερβολὴν εἰς ὑπερβολήν, 2 Cor. iv. 17 (RV *more and more exceedingly*).

ὑπερεῖδον, *to overlook, to take no notice of*, Acts, xvii. 30.

ὑπερέκεινα, adv., *beyond*, 2 Cor. x. 16. (It is a very late form.)

ὑπερεκπερισσοῦ, adv., *superabundantly, exceedingly*, 1 Thess. 5. 13. Ephes. iii. 20. (Only in the NT.)

ὑπερεκπερισσῶς, adv., *beyond measure*, a var. lect. ad 1 Thess. v. 13. (This form is not recognized in Pape's Lexicon.)

ὑπερεκτείνω, *to stretch out overmuch*, 2 Cor. x. 14.

ὑπερεκχύνω, and ὑπερεκχύννω, *to pour out above measure;* pass., *to overflow, to run over*, Luke, vi. 38.

ὑπερεντυγχάνω, *to intercede for*, Rom. viii. 26. (A purely NT form.)

ὑπερέχω, *to hold over;* intrans., *to be superior, to be supreme*, 1 Pet. ii. 13; ἐξουσίαι ὑπερέχουσαι, *higher powers*, Rom. xiii. 1; τὸ ὑπερέχον, as a substantive, *the surpassing value, the excellency*, Philipp. iii. 8; with genitive, *to be superior to*, Philipp. ii. 3; with accusative, *to surpass*, Philipp. iv. 7.

ὑπερηφανία, ἡ, *haughtiness, pride*, Mrk. vii. 22.

ὑπερήφανος, *haughty*, Rom. i. 30. Luke, i. 51. James, iv. 6. 1 Pet. v. 5.

ὑπερλίαν, adv., *preeminently;* τῶν ὑπερλίαν ἀποστόλων, 2 Cor. xi. 5. xii. 11 ("*the most eminent apostles*," Thayer).

ὑπερνικάω, *to be more than a conqueror*, Rom. viii. 37. (Confined to the NT and ecclesiastical writers.)

ὑπέρογκος, *overswollen; immoderate;* λαλεῖν ὑπέρογκα, Jude, 16 (RV *to speak great swelling words;* cf. 2 Pet. ii. 18.

ὑπεροχή, ἡ, *superiority, excellence*, 1 Cor. ii. 1; *high position*, 1 Tim. ii. 2.

ὑπερπερισσεύω, *to abound exceedingly*, Rom. v. 20; depon. mid., *to overflow*, 2 Cor. vii. 4. (See Pape's Lexicon in voc.)

ὑπερπερισσῶς, adv., *beyond measure*, Mrk. vii. 37.

ὑπερπλεονάζω, *to be exceedingly abundant*, 1 Tim. i. 14.

ὑπερυψόω, *to exalt preeminently*, Philipp. ii. 9. (Confined to ecclesiastical writers.)

ὑπερφρονέω, *to have high thoughts*, Rom. xii. 3.

ὑπερῷον, τὸ, *an upper chamber*, Acts, i. 13. ix. 37, 39. xx. 8.

ὑπέχω, *to hold under;* met., ὑπέχειν δίκην, *to suffer punishment*, Jude, 7.

ὑπήκοος, *obedient*, Philipp. ii. 8. 2 Cor. ii. 9. Acts, vii. 39.

ὑπηρετέω, *to serve*, Acts, xiii. 36; *to minister to*, Acts, xx. 34. xxiv. 23.

ὑπηρέτης, ὁ, *a servant, an attendant, an officer*, Joh. xviii. 36. Matt. xxvi. 58. Acts, v. 22, 26 etc.; *an assistant, a minister*, Acts, xxvi. 16. 1 Cor. iv. 1. Luke, i. 2.

ὕπνος, ὁ, *sleep*, Matt. i. 24. Joh. xi. 13 etc.

ὑπὸ, prepos., with genit., *by*, Matt. i. 22; with accus., *under*, Matt. v. 15; with dative, *beneath.* (The reader is referred to his Greek Grammar.)

ὑποβάλλω, *to cast under; to instigate, to suborn*, Acts, vi. 11.

ὑπογραμμὸς, ὁ, *a writing-copy; an example*, 1 Pet. ii. 21.

ὑπόδειγμα, τὸ, *a copy*, Hebr. viii. 5. ix. 23; *an example*, Joh. xiii. 15. James, v. 10. 2 Pet. ii. 6.

ὑποδείκνυμι, *to warn*, Matt. iii. 7. Luke, iii. 7; *to shew*, Luke, vi. 47. xii. 5. Acts, ix. 16. xx. 35.

ὑποδέχομαι, *to receive* as a guest, Luke, x. 38. xix. 6. Acts, xvii. 7. James, ii. 25.

ὑποδέω, *to bind under;* mid., *to put on, to bind on*, Acts, xii. 8; *to shoe*, Ephes. vi. 15; pass., *to be shod*, Mrk. vi. 9.

ὑπόδημα, τὸ, *a sandal*, Matt. iii. 11. x. 10. Luke, iii. 16 etc.

ὑπόδικος, *guilty;* ὑπόδικος τῷ θεῷ, *under the sentence of God*, Rom. iii. 19.

ὑποζύγιος, *under the yoke;* τὸ ὑποζύγιον, *a beast of burden, an ass*, Matt. xxi. 5. 2 Pet. ii. 16.

ὑποζώννυμι, *to under-gird* a ship, Acts, xxvii. 17. ("To bind a ship together with girths or cables, to enable it to survive the force of waves and tempest," Thayer.)

ὑποκάτω, adv., *underneath*, Mrk. vi. 11. vii. 28 etc.

ὑποκρίνομαι, *to play a part* on the stage; met., *to give oneself out to be, to pretend to be*, Luke, xx. 20.

ὑπόκρισις, ἡ, *pretence, hypocrisy*, Matt. xxiii. 28. Mrk. xii. 15. Luke, xii. 1.

ὑποκριτὴς, ὁ, *a play-actor; a pretender, a hypocrite*, Matt. vi. 2, 5, 16. Luke, vi. 42 etc.

ὑπολαμβάνω, *to receive, to carry away*, Acts, i. 9; *to receive hospitably, to welcome*, 3 Joh. 8; *to take up a discourse, to answer*, Luke, x. 30; *to suppose*, Acts, ii. 15. Luke, vii. 43.

ὑπόλειμμα, and **ὑπόλιμμα**, τὸ, *a remnant*, Rom. ix. 27.

ὑπολείπω, *to leave behind;* pass., *to be left behind, to be left remaining*, Rom. xi. 3.

ὑπολήνιον, τὸ, *a pit underneath the press to receive the juice of the grapes, a wine press* or *vat*, Mrk. xii. 1.

ὑπολιμπάνω, a late form of ὑπολείπω, to leave behind, 1 Pet. ii. 21.

ὑπομένω, to remain behind, Luke, ii. 43. Acts, xvii. 14; to persevere, to endure, Matt. x. 22. xxiv. 13. 2 Tim. ii. 12; to be patient, Rom. xii. 12; to bear a thing patiently, 1 Pet. ii. 20; to hold out, Hebr. xii. 7.

ὑπομιμνήσκω, to remind a person, Joh. xiv. 26. 2 Tim. ii. 14. Tit. iii. 1; pass., to recollect, Luke, xxii. 61.

ὑπόμνησις, ἡ, a reminding; ἐν ὑπομνήσει, by putting you in remembrance, 2 Pet. i. 13. iii. 1; a remembrance, 2 Tim. i. 5.

ὑπομονή, ἡ, steadfastness, patience, Luke, viii. 15. xxi. 19. Rom. v. 3. viii. 25 etc.; the patient waiting for, 2 Thess. iii. 5; a patient enduring, 2 Cor. i. 6.

ὑπονοέω, to surmise, to suppose, Acts, xiii. 25. xxv. 18. xxvii. 27.

ὑπόνοια, ἡ, a surmising, 1 Tim. vi. 4.

ὑποπιάζω, Doric form of ὑποπιέζω, to depress or keep under a little, 1 Cor. ix. 27 (see Pape's Lexicon in voc. Westcott reads ὑπωπιάζω here, which see).

ὑποπλέω, to sail close by, Acts, xxvii. 4, 7.

ὑποπνέω, to blow gently, Acts, xxvii. 13.

ὑποπόδιον, τό, a footstool, Matt. v. 35. (cf. xxii. 44.) Acts, ii. 35 etc.

ὑπόστασις, ἡ, actual nature, substance, Hebr. i. 3; confidence, 2 Cor. ix. 4. xi. 17. Hebr. iii. 14. xi. 1 (but in this last passage the word is open to doubt).

ὑποστέλλω, to draw down; to draw back, Gal. ii. 12; mid., to shrink back, Hebr. x. 38. Acts, xx. 27; with accus. of thing, to withhold, Acts, xx. 20.

ὑποστολή, ἡ, timidity, a shrinking back; ἡμεῖς οὐκ ἐσμὲν ὑποστολῆς, Hebr. x. 39 (RV we are not of them that shrink back into perdition).

ὑποστρέφω, intrans., to turn back, Luke, ii. 20. iv. 1 etc.

ὑποστρώννυμι, to strew, to spread, Luke, xix. 36.

ὑποταγή, ἡ, obedience, 2 Cor. ix. 13; subjection, 1 Tim. ii. 11. iii. 4. Gal. ii. 5.

ὑποτάσσω, to place beneath; to subject, to put in subjection, 1 Cor. xv. 27. Philipp. iii. 21. Hebr. ii. 5 etc.; pass., to be subject, to submit, Rom. viii. 7. xiii. 5. 1 Cor. xiv. 34.

ὑποτίθημι, to place under; to lay down, to imperil, Rom. xvi. 4; mid., with dat. of person and accus. of thing, to suggest, 1 Tim. iv. 6.

ὑποτρέχω, to run under, Acts, xxvii. 16.

ὑποτύπωσις, ἡ, pattern, example, 1 Tim. i. 16. 2 Tim. i. 13.

ὑποφέρω, to bear patiently, to endure, 1 Cor. x. 13. 2 Tim. iii. 11. 1 Pet. ii. 19.

ὑποχωρέω, to retire, to withdraw, Luke, v. 16. ix. 10.

ὑπωπιάζω, *to distress, to wear one out*, Luke, xviii. 5. (It is also given by some editors in 1 Cor. ix. 27. But see ὑποπιάζω.)

ὗς, ὁ and ἡ, *a swine*, 2 Pet. ii. 22.

ὕσσωπος, ἡ, *hyssop*, a plant, a bunch of which was used by the Jews in their ritual sprinklings, Hebr. ix. 19. Joh. xix. 29.

ὑστερέω, *to be behindhand, to come short of* a thing, Hebr. iv. 1. xii. 15; *to be deficient, to lack*, Matt. xix. 20; with οὐδέν or μηδέν, *to be inferior to another in nothing*, 2 Cor. xi. 5. xii. 11; *to be wanting*, Mrk. x. 21. Joh. ii. 3; with genitive of thing, *to be in want of*, Luke, xxii. 35; pass., *to suffer want*, 2 Cor. xi. 9. Luke, xv. 14. Hebr. xi. 37; *to come short of*, Rom. iii. 23. 1 Cor. i. 7; *to be in a worse position*, 1 Cor. viii. 8.

ὑστέρημα, τό, *deficiency; want, poverty*, Luke, xxi. 4. 2 Cor. viii. 14. ix. 12. xi. 9; *what is lacking*, Coloss. i. 24. Philipp. ii. 30. 1 Cor. xvi. 17.

ὑστέρησις, ἡ, *want, poverty*, Mrk. xii. 44; καθ' ὑστέρησιν, *on account of want*, Philipp. iv. 11.

ὕστερος, *later, subsequent*, 1 Tim. iv. 1; ὁ ὕστερος, *the second*, Matt. xxi. 31; ὕστερον, as adverb, *afterwards*, Matt. iv. 2. xxi. 29, 32, 37.

ὑφαίνω, *to weave*, a var. lect. ad Luke, xii. 27.

ὑφαντός, *woven*, Joh. xix. 23.

ὑψηλὸς, *high, lofty*, Matt. iv. 8. xvii. 1 etc.; ἐν ὑψηλοῖς, *on high*, Hebr. i. 3; ὑψηλότερος, *more exalted*, Hebr. vii. 26. Cf. Luke, xvi. 15; ὑψηλὰ φρονεῖν, *to be highminded*, Rom. xi. 20. xii. 16. 1 Tim. vi. 17. (Here Westcott's text gives ὑψηλοφρονεῖν.)

ὑψηλοφρονέω, *to be highminded*, Rom. xi. 20. (Here Westcott's text gives μὴ ὑψηλὰ φρόνει, but in 1 Tim. vi. 17 ὑψηλοφρονεῖν.)

ὕψιστος, superlative of the adverb ὕψι, *highest, most high*, Matt. xxi. 9. Luke, ii. 14 etc.; ὁ θεὸς ὁ ὕψιστος, *the most High God*, Mrk. v. 7. Acts, xvi. 17 etc.; and simply ὁ ὕψιστος, *the most High*, Acts, vii. 48; and without the article, ὕψιστος, Luke, i. 32, 35, 76. vi. 35.

ὕψος, τό, *height*, Ephes. iii. 18. Rev. xxi. 16; εἰς ὕψος, *on high*, Ephes. iv. 8; ἐξ ὕψους, *from on high*, Luke, i. 78. xxiv. 49; *high station*, James, i. 9.

ὑψόω, *to lift up*, Joh. iii. 14. viii. 28; *to exalt*, Matt. xi. 23. xxiii. 12. Luke, i. 52.

ὕψωμα, τό, *height*, Rom. viii. 39; *a barrier, a bulwark*, 2 Cor. x. 5.

Φ

φάγος, ὁ, *a glutton*, Matt. xi. 19. Luke, vii. 34.

φαιλόνης, ὁ, and **φαινόλης**, Lat. *paenula*, *a thick travelling cloak*, 2 Tim. iv. 13. (Westcott reads φελόνης, while Pape recognizes φαινόλης only.)

φαίνω, *to make visible;* pass., *to shine, to appear,* Matt. xxiv. 27; in the NT also φαίνω often appears for φαίνομαι, Joh. i. 5. v. 35. 2 Pet. i. 19. Rev. viii. 12.

φανερὸς, *manifest, evident,* Gal. v. 19. Rom. i. 19. Acts. iv. 16. vii. 13; εἰς φανερὸν ἐλθεῖν, *to come to light,* Luke, viii. 17; ἐν τῷ φανερῷ, *openly,* a var. lect. ad Matt. vi. 4; *visibly, outwardly,* Rom. ii. 28.

φανερόω, *to make manifest or visible,* Joh. ii. 11. Mrk. iv. 22 etc.; *to make known,* Coloss. iv. 4. Tit. i. 3.

φανερῶς, *manifestly, clearly,* Acts, x. 3; *openly,* Mrk. i. 45.

φανέρωσις, ἡ, *manifestation,* 1 Cor. xii. 7. 2 Cor. iv. 2 ("a late, and especially ecclesiastical form," Pape in Lex.)

φανὸς, ὁ, *a light, a lantern,* Joh. xviii. 3.

φαντάζω, *to make visible;* pass., *to be made visible;* τὸ φανταζόμενον, *the appearance, the sight,* Hebr. xii. 21.

φαντασία, ἡ, *showy display, pomp,* Acts, xxv. 23.

φάντασμα, τὸ, *a spectral appearance, an apparition,* Matt. xiv. 26. Mrk. vi. 49.

φάραγξ, ἡ, *a ravine,* Luke, iii. 5.

Φαρισαῖος, ὁ, *a Pharisee,* a member of the sect of the Pharisees.

φαρμακεία, and **φαρμακία**, ἡ, *the practice of magical arts, sorcery,* Gal. v. 20. Rev. xviii. 23.

φαρμακεὺς, ὁ, *a sorcerer,* a var. lect. ad Rev. xxi. 8.

φάρμακον, τὸ, *a drug;* plur., *sorceries,* Rev. ix. 21.

φαρμακὸς, as subst., *a sorcerer,* Rev. xxi. 8. xxii. 15.

φάσις, ἡ, *information, report,* Acts, xxi. 31.

φάσκω, *to allege, to affirm,* Acts, xxiv. 9. xxv. 19; *to profess,* Rom. i. 22.

φάτνη, ἡ, *a manger,* Luke, ii. 7, 12, 16. xiii. 15.

φαῦλος, *evil, bad,* Tit. ii. 8. James, iii. 16. Joh. iii. 20. v. 29.

φέγγος, τὸ, *light,* Matt. xxiv. 29. Mrk. xiii. 24.

φείδομαι, *to spare,* Rom. viii. 32. xi. 21. 2 Cor. i. 23; *to forbear,* 2 Cor. xii. 6.

φειδομένως, adv., *sparingly,* 2 Cor. ix. 6.

φελόνης, see φαιλόνης.

φέρω, *to carry, to bear,* Luke, xxiii. 26. Mrk. ii. 3; *to endure,* Rom. ix. 22. Hebr. xii. 20; *to bring forth, to produce,* Joh. xii. 24. xv. 2; of a gate or road, *to lead;* Acts, xii. 10; pass., *to be brought in, to be offered,* 1 Pet. i. 13; *to be introduced, to be mentioned,* Hebr. ix. 16; *to be moved or influenced,* 2 Pet. i. 21; *to be borne along,* Acts, xxvii. 15, 17; mid., *to press forward,* Hebr. vi. 1.

φεύγω, *to flee away*, Matt. viii. 33. xxvi. 56. Acts, xxvii. 30; *to shun* or *avoid*, 1 Cor. vi. 18. 1 Tim. vi. 11. 2 Tim. ii. 22; *to escape*, Hebr. xi. 34.

φήμη, ἡ, *report*, *fame*, Matt. ix. 26. Luke, iv. 14.

φημί, *to say*, *to declare*, Luke, xxii. 58. Acts, viii. 36 etc.; *to allege*, *to affirm*, Rom. iii. 8.

φημίζω, *to spread abroad* as a report, a var. lect. ad Matt. xxviii. 15. (Westcott reads διεφημίσθη.)

φθάνω, *to anticipate*; ἡμεῖς οὐ μὴ φθάσωμεν τοὺς κοιμηθέντας, *we shall not get the start of those who have fallen asleep*, 1 Thess. iv. 15; ἔφθασεν ἐπ' αὐτοὺς ἡ ὀργή, *God's wrath came upon them unexpectedly*, 1 Thess. ii. 16; ἔφθασεν ἐφ' ὑμᾶς ἡ βασιλεία τοῦ θεοῦ, *the kingdom of God has come upon you sooner than you expected*, Matt. xii. 28. Luke, xi. 20; *to attain unto*, Rom. ix. 31. Philipp. iii. 16; *to reach*, 2 Cor. x. 14.

φθαρτός, *perishable, corruptible*, 1 Pet. i. 18. Rom. i. 23. 1 Cor. ix. 25 etc.

φθέγγομαι, *to speak, to utter*, Acts, iv. 18. 2 Pet. ii. 16, 18.

φθείρω, *to corrupt, to destroy*, 1 Cor. iii. 17. xv. 33; pass., *to be destroyed, to perish*, Jude, 10; *to become corrupt*, Ephes. iv. 22.

φθινοπωρινός, *autumnal; withered, worthless*, Jude, 12.

φθόγγος, ὁ, *a sound*, 1 Cor. xiv. 7. Rom. x. 18.

φθονέω, *to envy*, Gal. v. 26.

φθόνος, ὁ, *envy*, Matt. xxvii. 18. Mrk. xv. 10. Rom. i. 29; πρὸς φθόνον ἐπιποθεῖ τὸ πνεῦμα ὃ κατῴκισεν ἐν ἡμῖν, James, iv. 5 ("doth the Holy Spirit which took up its abode within us long *enviously*," Thayer).

φθορά, ἡ, *corruption*, Rom. viii. 21. 2 Pet. i. 4. 1 Cor. xv. 42: met., *what is perishable*, 1 Cor. xv. 50; *loss of salvation*, Gal. vi. 8.

φιάλη, ἡ, *a cup, a bowl*, Rev. v. 8. xv. 7 etc.

φιλάγαθος, *loving goodness*, Tit. i. 8.

φιλαδελφία, ἡ, *brotherly love*, Rom. xii. 10. 1 Thess. iv. 9. 1 Pet. i. 22 etc.

φιλάδελφος, *loving as brethren*, 1 Pet. iii. 8.

φίλανδρος, *loving their husbands*, Tit. ii. 4.

φιλανθρωπία, ἡ, *benevolence, kindness*, Acts, xxviii. 2. Tit. iii. 4.

φιλανθρώπως, adv., *humanely, kindly*, Acts. xxvii. 3.

φιλαργυρία, ἡ, *love of money, covetousness*, 1 Tim. vi. 10.

φιλάργυρος, *fond of money, covetous*, Luke, xvi. 14. 2 Tim. iii. 2.

φίλαυτος, *loving himself, selfish*, 2 Tim. iii. 2.

φιλέω, *to love*, Joh. v. 20. Matt. x. 37; *to kiss*, Matt. xxvi. 48. Luke, xxii. 47. Mrk. xiv. 44; *to set a great value on*, Joh. xii. 25.

φιλήδονος, *loving pleasure*, 2 Tim. iii. 4.

φίλημα, τό, *a kiss*, Luke, vii. 45. xxii. 48. Rom. xvi. 16 etc.

φιλία, ἡ, *friendship*, James, iv. 4.

φιλόθεος, *loving God*, 2 Tim. iii. 4.

φιλονεικία, ἡ, *love of strife; a dispute*, Luke, xxii. 24.

φιλόνεικος, *fond of strife, contentious*, 1 Cor. xi. 16.

φιλοξενία, ἡ, *love towards guests; hospitality*, Rom. xii. 13. Hebr. xiii. 2.

φιλόξενος, *loving towards guests; hospitable*, 1 Tim. iii. 2. Tit. i. 8. 1 Pet. iv. 9.

φιλοπρωτεύω, *to be emulatious of preeminence*, 3 Joh. 9.

φίλος, *friendly;* as subst., *a friend*, Luke, vii. 6. xi. 5, 6, 8; τοὺς ἀναγκαίους φίλους, Acts, x. 24 (RV *his near friends*); *an associate*, Matt. xi. 19. Luke, vii. 34; ἡ φίλη, *a female friend*, Luke, xv. 9.

φιλοσοφία, ἡ, *the love of wisdom, philosophy*, Coloss. ii. 8.

φιλόσοφος, ὁ, *a philosopher*, Acts, xvii. 18.

φιλόστοργος, *affectionate*, Rom. xii. 10.

φιλότεκνος, *loving their children*, Tit. ii. 4.

φιλοτιμέομαι, *to be emulatious of honour; to strive earnestly, to make it one's aim*, 2 Cor. v. 9. Rom. xv. 20. 1 Thess. iv. 11.

φιλοφρόνως, adv., *kindly, courteously*, Acts, xxviii. 7.

φιλόφρων, *friendly*, a var. lect. ad 1 Pet. iii. 8.

φιμόω, *to muzzle*, 1 Cor. ix. 9. 1 Tim. v. 18; met., *to put to silence*, Matt. xxii. 34; pass., *to be silent, to be speechless*, Mrk. i. 25. Matt. xxii. 12; of the winds, *to be hushed*, Mrk. iv. 39.

φλογίζω, *to set on fire*, James, iii. 6.

φλόξ, ἡ, *a flame*, Luke, xvi. 24.

φλυαρέω, *to talk folly;* with accus., *to prate against*, 3 Joh. 10.

φλύαρος, *indulging in foolish jests; babbling, tattling*, 1 Tim. v. 13.

φοβερὸς, *formidable; fearful*, Hebr. x. 27, 31. xii. 21.

φοβέω, *to terrify, to frighten;* pass., *to fear*, Matt. x. 31. xxv. 25. Mrk. v. 33, 36 etc.; also with accus. of object, *to fear*, Matt. x. 26. xiv. 5. xxi. 26, 46 etc.; with ἀπό, Matt. x. 28; followed by μή, *to fear lest*, Acts, xxiii. 10. Hebr. iv. 1; *revere*, espec. in phrase used of proselytes, οἱ φοβούμενοι τὸν Θεόν, Acts, xiii. 16, 26.

φόβητρον, τό, *that which causes fright;* οἱ *terror*, Luke, xxi. 11.

φόβος, ὁ, *fear*, Joh. vii. 13. xix. 38. Hebr. ii. 15. Rev. xviii. 10, 15; *due respect, reverence*, Rom. xiii. 7. 1 Pet. ii. 18. iii. 2

φοίνιξ, ὁ, *a palm-tree*, Joh. xii. 13; φοίνικες, *palm-branches*, Rev. vii. 9; also as a proper name, *Phoenix*, a city and haven of Crete, Acts, xxvii. 12.

φονεύς, ὁ, *a murderer*, Matt. xxii. 7. Acts, iii. 14. vii. 52. xxviii. 4. 1 Pet. iv. 15 etc.

φονεύω, *to slay, to kill*, Matt. xxiii. 31, 35; *to commit murder*, Matt. v. 21. xix. 18. Rom. xiii. 9 etc.

φόνος, ὁ, *slaughter, murder*, Mrk. xv. 7. Luke, xxiii. 19, 25. Acts, ix. 1; φόνοι, *murders*, Matt. xv. 19. Mrk. vii. 21. Gal. v. 21.

φορέω, of clothing etc., *to wear*, James, ii. 3. Matt. xi. 8. Joh. xix. 5; of weapons, *to carry*, Rom. xiii. 4.

φόρον, τὸ, Lat. *forum*, *the forum*, Acts, xxviii. 15.

φόρος, ὁ, *an annual tax levied upon lands, houses, and persons, tribute*; φόρον, or φόρους διδόναι Καίσαρι, Luke, xx. 22. xxiii. 2. Cf. Rom. xiii. 6, 7.

φορτίζω, *to place a burden upon, to load*; φορτίζειν τινὰ φορτίον, *to load one with a burden*, Luke, xi. 46; πεφορτισμένους, *heavy laden*, Matt. xi. 28.

φορτίον, τὸ, *the lading* or *cargo* of a ship, Acts, xxvii. 10; *a load, a burden*, Luke, xi. 46. Matt. xi. 30. Gal. vi. 5.

φόρτος, ὁ, *the lading*, a var. lect. ad Acts, xxvii. 10.

φραγέλλιον, τὸ, *a scourge*, Joh. ii. 15. (Lat. *flagellum*.)

φραγελλόω, *to scourge*, Matt. xxvii. 26. Mrk. xv. 15 ("NT and ecclesiastical writers.")

φραγμός, ὁ, *a fence, a hedge*, Matt. xxi. 33. Mrk. xii. 1. Luke, xiv. 23; met., *a separating fence, a partition*, Ephes. ii. 14.

φράζω, *to set forth plainly; to explain*, Matt. xv. 15.

φράσσω, *to fence in, to shut, to close*, Hebr. xi. 33; *to put to silence*, Rom. iii. 19. 2 Cor. xi. 10.

φρέαρ, τὸ, *a well*, Joh. iv. 11, 12. Luke, xiv. 5; τὸ φρέαρ τῆς ἀβύσσου, *the pit of the abyss*, Rev. ix. 1, 2.

φρεναπατάω, *to deceive*, Gal. vi. 3.

φρεναπάτης, ὁ, *a deceiver*, Tit. i. 10. ("Several times in ecclesiastical writers," Thayer.)

φρήν, ἡ, *the mind*, 1 Cor. xiv. 20.

φρίσσω, *to be rough, to stand erect*, as the bristles of a boar; met., *to shudder*, James, ii. 19.

φρονέω, *to think*, 1 Cor. xiii. 11. Rom. xii. 3. Acts, xxviii. 22; *to have thought for*, Philipp. iv. 10; φρονεῖν τὸ αὐτὸ, *to be of the same mind*, 2 Cor. xiii. 11. Philipp. ii. 2. Rom. xii. 16; *to have a mind towards, to seek after*, Matt. xvi. 23. Rom. viii. 5. Philipp. iii. 19; *to regard* (ἡμέραν), Rom. xiv. 6.

φρόνημα, τὸ, *thought, mind*, Rom. viii. 6, 7, 27.

φρόνησις, ἡ, *understanding, wisdom*, Luke, i. 17. Ephes. i. 8.

φρόνιμος, *prudent, wise*, Matt. vii. 24. x. 16. xxiv. 45. Rom. xi. 25. 2 Cor. xi. 19 etc.

φρονίμως, adv., *prudently, wisely*, Luke, xvi. 8.

φροντίζω, *to be careful, to be anxious*, Tit. iii. 8.

φρουρέω, *to guard*, 2 Cor. xi. 32; *to keep*, Philipp. iv. 7; pass., *to be kept under guard*, Gal. iii. 23; *to be guarded*, 1 Pet. i. 5.

φρυάσσω, *to act tumultuously, to rage*, Acts, iv. 25. (This form is found only in the LXX. and NT; the Deponent form, φρυάσσομαι, *to stamp, to snort*, as unruly horses, is Classical.)

φρύγανον, τὸ, *fuel, firewood*, Acts, xxviii. 3.

φυγή, ἡ, *flight*, Matt. xxiv. 20.

φυλακή, ἡ, *a guard, a watch*; φυλάσσειν φυλακὰς, *to keep watch*, Luke, ii. 8; *persons keeping watch, a guard*, Acts, xii. 10; *prison*, Matt. xiv. 10. xxv. 36, 39; *imprisonment*, 2 Cor. vi. 5. 1 Pet. iii. 19. Hebr. xi. 36; *a watch or division of the night*, which the Jews, after their subjection to the Romans, divided into *four* periods of *three* hours each, called the *first, second, third, fourth watch* of the night, Matt. xxiv. 43. Luke, xii. 38. Mrk. vi. 48.

φυλακίζω, *to imprison*, Acts, xxii. 19.

φυλακτήριον, τὸ, *a preservative, an amulet, a phylactery*, Matt. xxiii. 5 (with the Jews a strip of parchment on which texts were written).

φύλαξ, ὁ, *a guard, a keeper*, Acts, v. 23. xii. 6, 19.

φυλάσσω, *to keep watch*, Luke, ii. 8; *to protect, to guard*, Joh. xvii. 12. 2 Thess. iii. 3. 2 Pet. ii. 5; mid., *to guard oneself against, to beware*, Luke, xii. 15. 2 Pet. iii. 17.

φυλή, *a tribe*, Matt. xix. 28. Luke, ii. 36; *a nation, a race*, Matt. xxiv. 30. Rev. i. 7. v. 9. vii. 9 etc.

φύλλον, τὸ, *a leaf*, Matt. xxi. 19. xxiv. 32 etc.

φύραμα, τὸ, *any substance that is mixed with water and kneaded; a mass, a lump*, Rom. ix. 21. xi. 16. 1 Cor. v. 16. Gal. v. 9.

φυσικὸς, *natural*, Rom. i. 26, 27; *subject to animal appetites*, 2 Pet. ii. 12.

φυσικῶς, adv., *naturally*, Jude, 10.

φυσιόω, in the NT as equivalent to φυσιάω, *to inflate, to puff up* with pride, 1 Cor. viii. 1; pass., *to be puffed up*, 1 Cor. iv. 6, 19. v. 2. xiii. 4.

φύσις, ἡ, *nature*, Rom. xi. 21, 24. Ephes. ii. 3; *use, custom*, 1 Cor. xi. 14.

φυσίωσις, ἡ, *a puffing up, pride*, 2 Cor. xii. 20 (RV *swellings*. Confined to the NT and ecclesiastical writers).

φυτεία, ἡ, *a plant*, Matt. xv. 13.

φυτεύω, *to plant*, Matt. xv. 13. xxi. 33. 1 Cor. iii. 6, 8.

φύω, *to produce*; pass., *to grow*, Luke, viii. 6, 8; *to shoot forth, to spring up*, Hebr. xii. 15.

φωλεὸς, ὁ, *a den, a lair*, Matt. viii. 20. Luke, ix. 58.

φωνέω, *to cry out*, Luke, viii. 8. xvi. 24. xxiii. 46; *to call to, to invoke*, Matt. xxvii. 47; of the cock, *to crow*, Matt.

[φων]   TO THE NEW TESTAMENT   [χαν

xxvi. 34, 74, 75; *to call, to entitle,* Joh. xiii. 13; *to invite,* Luke, xiv. 12; *send for,* Luke, xvi. 2. Joh. xii. 17.

φωνή, ἡ, *a sound,* Matt. xxiv. 31. Joh. iii. 8; *a voice,* Matt. iii. 17. xvii. 5. xxvii. 46, 50; *a language,* 1 Cor. xiv. 10.

φῶς, τὸ, *light,* Matt. xvii. 2. 2 Cor. iv. 6; *a candle, a light* (in plur.), Acts, xvi. 29; (of stars etc.), James, i. 17; *a fire,* Luke, xxii. 56. Mrk. xiv. 54.

φωστήρ, ὁ, *a cause of light, a luminary,* Philipp. ii. 15; *radiance,* Rev. xxi. 11.

φωσφόρος, ὁ, *the morning star,* 2 Pet. i. 19.

φωτεινὸς, *bright,* Matt. xvii. 5; *full of light,* Luke, xi. 34, 36. Matt. vi. 22.

φωτίζω, *to illuminate,* Luke, xi. 36. Rev. xviii. 1; *to enlighten,* Joh. i. 9. Ephes. i. 18. iii. 9.

φωτισμὸς, ὁ, *enlightening, light,* 2 Cor. iv. 4, 6.

X

χαίρω, *to rejoice, to be glad,* Luke, xv. 5. Matt. v. 12. xviii. 13. Mrk. xiv. 11 etc.; χαίρειν ἀπό τινος, *to derive joy from,* 2 Cor. ii. 3; imperat., χαῖρε, and χαίρετε, *hail!* Matt. xxvi. 49. xxviii. 9; λέγω χαίρειν, *to greet,* 2 Joh. 10, 11; χαίρειν, as an epistolary formula, *greeting,* Acts, xv. 23. xxiii. 26. James, i. 1.

χάλαζα, ἡ, *hail,* Rev. viii. 7. xi. 19. xvi. 21.

χαλάω, *to slacken, to relax; to let down, to lower,* Acts, ix. 25. xxvii. 17, 30. Mrk. ii. 4. Luke, v. 4.

χαλεπὸς, *difficult, hard,* 2 Tim. iii. 1 (RV *grievous*); *fierce,* Matt. viii. 28.

χαλιναγωγέω, *to bridle, to restrain,* James, i. 26. iii. 2.

χαλινὸς, ὁ, *a bridle,* James, iii. 3. Rev. xiv. 20.

χάλκεος, *brazen, of brass,* Rev. ix. 20.

χαλκεὺς, ὁ, *a coppersmith,* 2 Tim. iv. 14.

χαλκηδὼν, ὁ, *the chalcedony,* Rev. xxi. 19.

χαλκίον, τὸ, *a brazen vessel,* Mrk. vii. 4.

χαλκολίβανον, τὸ,—more correctly χαλκολίβανος, ἡ, a word of doubtful meaning, found only in Rev. i. 15 and ii. 18; Vulg. *aurichalum* or *orichalcum,* in the RV *burnished brass.* "The sense of the passages in Rev. compel us to understand *some metal, like gold if not more precious,* a metal compounded of gold and silver; and this interpretation is confirmed by the gloss. of Suidas," Thayer. (The word is omitted in Pape's Lexicon.)

χαλκὸς, ὁ, *brass,* Rev. xviii. 12. 1 Cor. xiii. 1; *money,* Mrk. vi. 8. xii. 41. Matt. x. 9.

χαμαί, adv., *on the ground,* Joh. ix. 6. xviii. 6.

Χαναναῖος, *Canaanitish* (i.e. Phœnician), Matt. xv. 22.

χαρά, ἡ, *joy, gladness*, Luke, i. 14. xv. 7, 10. Joh. xv. 11. Acts, viii. 8.

χάραγμα, τό, *a stamp, a mark*, Rev. xiii. 16, 17. xvi. 2. xix. 20 etc.; *graven work, image*, Acts, xvii. 29.

χαρακτήρ, ὁ, *an exact expression, an exact reproduction*, Hebr. i. 3. (See Pape's Lexicon in voc.)

χάραξ, ὁ, *a stake, a palisade; an entrenchment* (RV *bank*), Luke, xix. 43.

χαρίζομαι, *to be kind to*, Gal. iii. 18; *to gratify; to bestow*, Luke, vii. 21. Acts, xxv. 11; *to forgive*, 2 Cor. ii. 7, 10. xii. 13; *to give up a person who is still on his trial to the demands of his adversaries*, Acts, xxv. 11, 16.

χάριν, the accus. of χάρις, but used absolutely as a preposition with the genitive, *for the sake of, on account of*; τούτου χάριν, *on this account*, Ephes. iii. 1, 14; οὗ χάριν, *for which reason*, Luke, vii. 47; everywhere in the NT, except in 1 Joh. iii. 12, χάριν is placed *after* the genitive, as usually in Classical Greek.

χάρις, ἡ, *pleasantness, charm; graciousness*, Luke, iv. 22. Coloss. iv. 6; *that spiritual condition which God has bestowed, as a perfectly free gift, on those that are His, to enable them to do his will and to keep his commandments, which free gift*, or χάρισμα, Ernest Naville has well defined as "The power of a holy life," i.e. the implanted power to lead such a life; so we have τὴν χάριν ταύτην ἐν ᾗ ἑστήκαμεν, Rom. v. 2. ἐνδυναμοῦ ἐν τῇ χάριτι τῇ ἐν Χριστῷ Ἰησοῦ, 2 Tim. ii. 1. Cf. 1 Pet. v. 12. 2 Pet. iii. 18; in this sense also it is used by the Apostles at the close of their Epistles, Rom. xvi. 20. 1 Cor. xvi. 23. 2 Cor. xiii. 13. Gal. vi. 18. Ephes. vi. 24 etc.; *thanks* (cf. "saying grace"), Luke, xvii. 9. 1 Tim. i. 12. 2 Tim. i. 3; *recompense, reward*, Luke, vi. 32, 33, 34. Cf. Matt. v. 46; *favour* (in plur.), Acts, xxiv. 27; so of *alms*, 2 Cor. viii. 19.

χάρισμα, τό, *that which is bestowed as a free gift*, Rom. v. 15, 16; *a gift* (of a spiritual kind), Rom. xii. 6. 1 Cor. xii. 9, 28, 30 etc.

χαριτόω, with accus. of person, *to freely bestow upon, bless*, Ephes. i. 6; pass., κεχαριτωμένη, *full of grace*, Luke, i. 28 (RV, in margin, *endued with grace*); so εἰλκωμένος, *full of sores*, Luke, xvi. 20.

χάρτης, ὁ, *paper*, 2 Joh. 12. (See Pape's Lexicon in voc.)

χάσμα, τό, *a chasm, a gulf*, Luke, xvi. 26.

χεῖλος, τό, *the lip; the mouth*, Matt. xv. 8. Mrk. vii. 6. Rom. iii. 13. 1 Cor. xiv. 21; χεῖλος τῆς θαλάσσης, *the sea-shore*, Hebr. xi. 12.

χειμάζω, *to afflict with a storm*; pass., *to be tempest-tossed*, Acts, xxvii. 18.

χείμαρρος, ὁ, *a winter-flowing stream, a brook*, Joh. xviii. 1.

χειμών, ὁ, *tempest*, Acts, xxvii. 20; *winter*, Joh. x. 22; χειμῶνος, *in the winter*, Matt. xxiv. 20. Mrk. xiii. 18.

χείρ, ἡ, *the hand*, Matt. iii. 12. iv. 6 etc.; χείρ Κυρίου, *the help of the Lord*, Acts, xi. 21.

χειραγωγέω, *to lead by the hand*, Acts, ix. 8. xxii. 11.

χειραγωγός, *leading by the hand;* as subst., *a guide*, Acts, xiii. 11.

χειρόγραφον, τό, *what is written with the hand, handwriting; a bond*, Coloss. ii. 14.

χειροποίητος, *done* or *made with hands*, Mrk. xiv. 58. Acts, vii. 48. xvii. 24. Hebr. ix. 11, 24. Ephes. ii. 11.

χειροτονέω, *to elect, to appoint*, Acts, xiv. 23. 2 Cor. viii. 19.

χείρων, compar. form, *worse*, Matt. ix. 16. xii. 45.

Χερουβίμ and **Χερουβείν**, τά, *Cherubim* and *Cherubin*, Hebr. ix. 5.

χήρα, ἡ, (widowed and so) *a widow*, Mrk. xii. 40, 42. Luke, xviii. 3, 5. 1 Cor. vii. 8. 1 Tim. v. 3, 4, 5; figuratively, Rev. xviii. 7.

χθές, see ἐχθές.

χιλίαρχος, ὁ, *an officer over a thousand;* perhaps *a military tribune* (commanding a cohort), Joh. xviii. 12. Acts, xxii. 24. xxiii. 10; generally *a chief captain*, Mrk. vi. 21. Rev. vi. 15.

χιλιάς, ἡ, *a thousand*, plur., Luke, xiv. 31. Acts, iv. 4. Rev. v. 11 etc.

χίλιοι, *a thousand*, 2 Pet. iii. 8. Rev. xi. 3.

χιτών, ὁ, *a garment*, Mrk. xiv. 63; espec. *an under garment, a tunic*, opp. to ἱμάτιον, Matt. v. 40. Luke, vi. 29. Acts, ix. 39.

χιών, ἡ, *snow*, Matt. xxviii. 3. Mrk. ix. 3. Rev. i. 14.

χλαμύς, ἡ, *a cloak* (AV *robe*) worn by generals, kings, emperors, Matt. xxvii. 28, 31.

χλευάζω, *to mock, to jeer*, Acts, xvii. 32. (Cf. διαχλευάζω.)

χλιαρός, *lukewarm*, Rev. iii. 16.

χλωρός, *green*, Mrk. vi. 39. Rev. viii. 7; *pale*, Rev. vi. 8.

χοϊκός, *made of earth, earthy*, 1 Cor. xv. 47, 48, 49.

χοῖνιξ, ἡ, *a measure* (holding less than a quart), Rev. vi. 6.

χοῖρος, ὁ, *a swine*, Matt. vii. 6. Mrk. v. 11, 12, 13. Luke, xv. 15 etc.

χολάω, *to be angry*, Joh. vii. 23. (Classical form is χολοῦμαι.)

χολή, ἡ, *gall*, Matt. xxvii. 34. Acts, viii. 23.

χορηγέω, *to equip, to furnish sumptuously* (strictly of one who pays the expense of providing a chorus), 2 Cor. ix. 10. 1 Pet. iv. 11.

χορός, ὁ, *a dance, dancing*, Luke, xv. 25.

χορτάζω, *to pasture, to feed, to fatten*, pass., Luke, xv. 16.

xvi. 21. Rev. xix. 21; opp. to πεινάω, Philipp. iv. 12. Matt. v. 6.

χόρτασμα, τὸ, *fodder, food*, Acts, vii. 11.

χόρτος, ὁ, *grass*, Matt. vi. 30. Luke, xii. 28. Joh. vi. 10. James, i. 10; applied to green blade of corn, Matt. xiii. 26; *hay*, 1 Cor. iii. 12.

χοῦς, ὁ, *an earth-heap; dust*, Mrk. vi. 11. Rev. xviii. 19.

χράομαι, *to use*, Acts, xxvii. 17. 1 Cor. vii. 31. ix. 12, 15; *to deal with* (of persons), Acts, xxvii. 3 (RV *treat*).

χρεία, ἡ, *need, necessity*, Hebr. vii. 11. Matt. vi. 8. Mrk. xi. 3. Joh. xiii. 29; τὰ πρὸς τὴν χρείαν (or τὰς χρείας), the *necessaries* for the journey, 1 Thess. iv. 12 etc. ; *want*, Philipp. ii. 25. iv. 19; *business*, Acts, vi. 3.

χρεοφειλέτης and **χρεωφειλέτης**, ὁ, *a debtor*, Luke, vii. 41. xvi. 5.

χρή, *it is necessary;* with inf. *should, ought*, James, iii. 10.

χρῄζω, *to be in want of*, Luke, xi. 8. xii. 30. 2 Cor. iii. 1 etc.

χρῆμα, τὸ, (lit. what is needful, so) *money*, Acts, iv. 37; in plur., *money, possessions, riches*, Mrk. x. 23. Luke, xviii. 24. Acts, viii. 18, 20.

χρηματίζω, *to answer* or *speak as an oracle*, Hebr. xii. 25; in pass., *to be warned, advised* (as by an oracle), Luke, ii. 26. Matt. ii. 12, 22; *to get a name* (strictly from some business), Acts, xi. 26. Rom. vii. 3.

χρηματισμὸς, ὁ, *an oracle*, Rom. xi. 4.

χρήσιμος, *useful, serviceable*, 2 Tim. ii. 14.

χρῆσις, ἡ, *use*, Rom. i. 26.

χρηστεύομαι, *to be kind*, 1 Cor. xiii. 4.

χρηστολογία, ἡ, *plausibility, fair speech*, Rom. xvi. 18.

χρηστὸς, *useful, good*, 1 Cor. xv. 33; *mild, kind*, 1 Pet. ii. 3; *easy* (AV), of Christ's yoke, Matt. xi. 30; (of wine) *mellow*, Luke, v. 39.

χρηστότης, ἡ, *goodness*, Rom. iii. 12; *kindness*, Rom. ii. 4. xi. 2. 2 Cor. vi. 6. Gal. v. 22.

χρῖσμα, τὸ, *an unction*, 1 Joh. ii. 20, 27.

Χριστιανὸς, ὁ, *a Christian*, Acts, xi. 26. xxvi. 28. 1 Pet. iv. 16.

Χριστὸς, ὁ, *the anointed one, the Messias* or *Christ;* 'Ιησοῦς ὁ λεγόμενος Χριστὸς, Matt. xxvii. 22 etc. (The name is used to denote the *office* of Jesus.)

χρίω, *to anoint*, Luke, iv. 18. Hebr. i. 9. Acts, iv. 27. x. 38. 2 Cor. i. 21.

χρονίζω, *to linger, to tarry*, Matt. xxv. 5. Luke, i. 21. xii. 45.

χρόνος, ὁ, *time*, Hebr. xi. 32. Rev. x. 6. Acts, vii. 17. 1 Pet. iv. 3; διὰ τὸν χρόνον, *because of the* (long) *time*, Hebr. v. 12; ἐπὶ χρόνον, *for a time*, Luke, xviii. 4. Acts, xviii. 20 etc.; ἱκανῷ χρόνῳ, *for a long time*, Luke, viii. 27. Acts, viii. 11; χρόνον, *for*

χρονοτριβέω, *to spend time*, Acts, xx. 16.

χρύσεος, *of gold, overlaid with gold*, 2 Tim. ii. 20. Hebr. ix. 4. Rev. i. 12, 20 etc.

χρυσίον, τὸ, *gold*, Rev. iii. 18. xxi. 18, 21 ; *objects made of gold*, 1 Tim. ii. 9. 1 Pet. iii. 3. Rev. xvii. 4.

χρυσοδακτύλιος, *with a gold ring*, James, ii. 2.

χρυσόλιθος, ὁ, *chrysolite, a topaz*, Rev. xxi. 20.

χρυσόπρασος, ὁ, *a chrysoprasus* (coloured like a leek, πράσον), Rev. xxi. 20.

χρυσὸς, ὁ, *gold*, Matt. ii. 11. Rev. ix. 7 ; *gold coin*, Matt. x. 9 ; *a gold image*, Acts, xvii. 29 ; *objects made of gold*, Matt. xxiii. 16.

χρυσόω, *to deck with gold*, Rev. xvii. 4. xviii. 16.

χρὼς, ὁ, *the skin*, Acts, xix. 12.

χωλὸς, *lame*, Matt. xi. 5. Luke, vii. 22 ; τὸ χωλὸν, Hebr. xii. 13 ; *halt*, Matt. xviii. 8. Mrk. ix. 45.

χώρα, ἡ, *a tract, a region*, Joh. xi. 54 ; *a province, country*, Mrk. v. 10. vi. 55. Luke, iii. 1. Acts, x. 39 ; *land* (as opp. to sea), Acts, xxvii. 27 ; *ground*, Luke, xii. 16. xxi. 21. Joh. iv. 35. James, v. 4.

χωρέω, *to go away, to pass*, Matt. xv. 17 ; *to turn oneself*, 2 Pet. iii. 9 ; *to advance, to make progress*, Joh. viii. 37 ; *to have room for*, Mrk. ii. 2 ; *to hold* (of measures), Joh. ii. 6 ; (of a thought or word) *a while*, Acts, xix. 22. 1 Cor. xvi. 7. Acts, xiv. 3.

χωρίζω, *to separate*, Matt. xix. 6. Mrk. x. 9. Rom. viii. 35, 39 ; in mid. and pass., *to be divorced*, 1 Cor. vii. 11, 15 ; *go away*, Philem. 15. Acts, i. 4. xviii. 1.

χωρίον, τὸ, *a place* (as a field, garden, etc.), Matt. xxvi. 36 (of Gethsemane), Joh. iv. 5. Acts, i. 18 ; *an estate*, Acts, xxviii. 7.

χωρὶς, *apart*, Joh. xx. 7 ; (as prep.) *apart from, outside of*, Joh. xv. 5. Ephes. ii. 12. Philem. 14 ; *besides*, Matt. xiv. 21. 2 Cor. xi. 28.

χῶρος, ὁ, *the north-west wind*, Acts, xxvii. 12.

Ψ

ψάλλω, *to strike* a musical instrument ; *to sing hymns*, James, v. 13. Ephes. v. 19. Rom. xv. 9. 1 Cor. xiv. 15.

ψαλμὸς, ὁ, *a psalm*, Ephes. v. 19. Coloss. iii. 16 ; plur., *the Psalms*, Luke, xxiv. 44 (cf. Luke, xx. 42. Acts, i. 20).

ψευδάδελφος, ὁ, *a false brother*, 2 Cor. xi. 26. Gal. ii. 4.

ψευδαπόστολος, ὁ, *a false apostle*, 2 Cor. xi. 13.

ψευδὴς, *false, lying*, Rev. ii. 2. Acts, vi. 13 ; subst., *a liar*, Rev. xxi. 8.

ψευδοδιδάσκαλος, ὁ, *a false teacher*, 2 Pet. ii. 1.

ψευδολόγος, *speaking lies*, 1 Tim. iv. 2.

ψεύδομαι, *to lie*, Hebr. vi. 18. 1 Joh. i. 6. 1 Tim. ii. 7 ; *to deceive*, Acts, v. 3.

ψευ] *GREEK-ENGLISH LEXICON* [ω

ψευδομάρτυρ or **ψευδόμαρτυς**, ὁ, *a false witness*, 1 Cor. xv. 15.

ψευδομαρτυρέω, *to bear false witness*, Matt. xix. 18. Mrk. xiv. 56 etc.

ψευδομαρτυρία, ἡ, *false witness*, Matt. xv. 19. xxvi. 59.

ψευδοπροφήτης, ὁ, *a false prophet*, Matt. vii. 15. Luke, vi. 26. Acts. xiii. 6. 2 Pet. ii. 1. 1 Joh. iv. 1 etc. (In classical Greek ψευδόμαντις.)

ψεῦδος, τὸ, *falsehood, a lie*, Joh. viii. 44. Ephes. iv. 25 ; τέρατα ψεύδους, *marvels to deceive*, 2 Thess. ii. 9.

ψευδόχριστος, ὁ, *a false Christ*, Matt. xxiv. 24. Mrk. xiii. 22.

ψευδώνυμος, *falsely called*, 1 Tim. vi. 20.

ψεῦσμα, τὸ, *a lie*, Rom. iii. 7.

ψεύστης, ὁ, *a liar*, Joh. viii. 44, 55. 1 Joh. i. 10. Tit. i. 12. Rom. iii. 4.

ψηλαφάω, *to handle, to feel*, Luke, xxiv. 39. 1 Joh. i. 1 ; *feel for, grope for*, Hebr. xii. 18. Acts, xvii. 27.

ψηφίζω, *to calculate*, Luke, xiv. 28. Rev. xiii. 18.

ψῆφος, ἡ, *a pebble*, Rev. ii. 17 ; *a vote*, Acts, xxvi. 10.

ψιθυρισμὸς, ὁ, *a whispering* (against character), 2 Cor. xii. 20.

ψιθυριστὴς, ὁ, *a whisperer* (against character), Rom. i. 30.

ψιχίον, τὸ, *a crumb, a morsel*, Matt. xv. 27. Luke, xvi. 21.

ψυχὴ, ἡ, *animal life, the breath*, Rev. viii. 9. Acts, xx. 10. 1 Thess. v. 23. Hebr. iv. 12 ; *the earthly life* and *the blessed or eternal life*, set side by side, Matt. x. 39. Luke, ix. 24. xvii. 23 ; *a living thing*, Rev. xvi. 3 ; in plur., *souls* (cf. *capita*), i.e. *persons*, Acts, ii. 41. 1 Pet. iii. 20 ; ψυχαὶ ἀνθρώπων, *souls* or *lives of men* (of slaves), Rev. xviii. 13. Luke, xii. 19 (where a man addresses his own soul); *the soul* (including the emotions, affections, and intellect), Luke, i. 46. Acts, xiv. 2, 22. Hebr. vi. 19. 2 Pet. ii. 8, 14 ; *the soul* (as equivalent to the spirit), 3 Joh. 2. Hebr. xiii. 17. 1 Pet. ii. 11. James, i. 21 ; (as contrasted with σῶμα), Matt. x. 28. Acts, ii. 27. Rev. vi. 9.

ψυχικὸς, *natural* (lit. with animal nature), 1 Cor. xv. 44 ; *sensuous, sensual*, 1 Cor. ii. 14. James, iii. 15. Jude, 19.

ψύχος or **ψῦχος**, τὸ, *cold*, Joh. xviii. 18. Acts, xxviii. 2. 2 Cor. xi. 27.

ψυχρὸς, *cold* ; neut., *cold water*, Matt. x. 42 ; met., Rev. iii. 15.

ψύχω, *to cool* ; pass., *to grow cold*, Matt. xxiv. 12.

ψωμίζω, *to feed by morsels*; gen., *to feed*, Rom. xii. 20 ; *give in small portions*, 1 Cor. xiii. 3.

ψωμίον, τὸ, *a morsel (sop)*, Joh. xiii. 26, 30.

ψώχω, *to rub*, Luke, vi. 1.

Ω

Ω, *omega*, the last letter of the Greek alphabet, so τὸ Ω = τὸ τέλος, *the End* or *the Last*;

applied to Christ, Rev. i. 8. xxi. 6. xxii. 13.

ὦ, *O*, in exclamations, Matt. xv. 28; as a marked reproof, James, ii. 20. Luke, xxiv. 25; in simple addresses, Acts, i. 1. xviii. 14. Rom. ii. 3 etc.

ὧδε, *thus, this being so*, 1 Cor. iv. 2; *here, hither, in this place*, Matt. viii. 29. xii. 6. Joh. vi. 9; (*in this city*), Acts, ix. 14; (*in one place and in another place*), Hebr. vii. 8; ὧδε ἢ ὧδε, *here or there*, Matt. xxiv. 23; *in this thing*, Rev. xiii. 10, 18. xiv. 12. xvii. 9.

ᾠδή, ἡ, *a song*, Rev. xv. 3; plur., Ephes. v. 19. Coloss. iii. 16.

ὠδίν, ἡ, *birth-pang*, 1 Thess. v. 3; generally, *pangs, anguish*, Acts, ii. 24. Matt. xxiv. 8.

ὠδίνω, *to travail*, Gal. iv. 19, 27. Rev. xii. 2.

ὦμος, ὁ, *the shoulder*, Matt. xxiii. 4. Luke, xv. 5.

ὠνέομαι, *to buy*, Acts, vii. 16.

ᾠόν, τό, *an egg*, Luke, xi. 12.

ὥρα, ἡ, *a season*, πρὸς ὥραν, *for a season*, Joh. v. 35. 2 Cor. vii. 8; *a day*, Matt. xiv. 15; in phrases, ἤδη ὥρας πολλῆς γενομένης, Mrk. vi. 35; ὀψίας ...οὔσης τῆς ὥρας, Mrk. xi. 11; *an hour*, Joh. xi. 9. xix. 14; metaph., *one's hour* (i.e. time of death or of some crisis), Joh. xii. 27. xvii. 1.

ὡραῖος, *blooming, beautiful*, Acts, iii. 2, 10. Rom. x. 15.

ὠρύομαι, *to roar*, 1 Pet. v. 8.

ὡς, (1) (of time) *when, since*, Luke, i. 23, 41, 44. Acts, i. 10. v. 24; *while* (in sense of *in place where*), ὡς λέγει, *where he says*, Luke, xx. 37; with ἄν, *whensoever*, Rom. xv. 24. 1 Cor. xi. 34. Philipp. ii. 23. (2) As a final particle, *to, in order to* (with inf.), Luke, ix. 52. Acts, xx. 24; ὡς ἔπος εἰπεῖν, *so to say*. (3) In comparisons, *as, just as, like, as it were*, 1 Cor. iii. 15. iv. 1. 2 Cor. xiii. 2. Rev. i. 15. iv. 6; *as though, as if*, Rom. iii. 7. Acts, iii. 12. Hebr. xi. 27. Gal. iii. 16; almost equivalent to ὅτι after words of saying, explaining, Luke, viii. 47. xxiv. 35. (4) With numbers, *about*, Mrk. v. 13. viii. 9. Joh. i. 39. iv. 6. Rev. viii. 1. (5) *how*, ὡς ὡραῖοι, Rom. x. 15; ὡς τάχιστα, *as quickly as possible*, Acts, xvii. 15.

ὡσαννά, *hosanna* (lit. save us, or *save them*), Matt. xxi. 9, 15. Mrk. xi. 9. Joh. xii. 13.

ὡσαύτως, *likewise*, Matt. xx. 5. Mrk. xiv. 31. Rom. viii. 26. Tit. ii. 3, 6.

ὡσεί, *as, as though*, Matt. iii. 16. Rom. vi. 13. Hebr. i. 12; *about* (of numbers), Luke, iii. 23. Acts, ii. 41; (of space) ὡσεὶ λίθου βολήν, *about a stone's cast*, Luke, xxii. 41.

Ὡσηέ, ὁ, *Hosea*, the prophet, Rom. ix. 25.

ὥσπερ, *as*, ὥσπερ γέγραπται, 1 Cor. x. 7; *like to, even as*, Matt. xviii. 17. Acts, ii. 2; followed often by οὕτως or οὕτως καί, Luke, xvii. 24. 1 Cor. xi. 12. xv. 22. Gal. iv. 29.

ὡσπερεί, *as it were*, 1 Cor. xv. 8.

ὥστε, *so that* (with indic.), Joh. iii. 16. Gal. ii. 3; *therefore, and so* (with indic.), Mrk. ii. 28. 1 Cor. iii. 7. Gal. iii. 9, 24 etc.; *so that* (with inf.), with or without some such word as οὕτως, τοσοῦτος preceding, Matt. xv. 33. Acts, xiv. 1. 1 Pet. i. 21 etc.; *so as to* (of design), Matt. xxiv. 24. Luke, xx. 20.

ὠτάριον, τό, *the ear*, Mrk. xiv 47. Joh. xviii. 10.

ὠτίον, τό, *the ear*, Matt. xxvi. 51. Luke, xxii. 51.

ὠφέλεια, ἡ, *profit*, Rom. iii. 1. Jude, 16.

ὠφελέω, *to profit*, Rom. ii. 25. Mrk. viii. 36. Joh. vi. 63; pass., *to be profited*, Matt. xv. 5. 1 Cor. xiii. 3 etc.

ὠφέλιμος, *profitable*, Tit. iii. 8. 2 Tim. iii. 16.